Dick Meshe

On the front cover: Artillery Model Luger in 9mm Parabellum caliber with 8-inch barrel. Courtesy of Val Forgett, Navy Arms Company, Ridgefield, New Jersey.

On the back cover, from top: Colt Government Model in 45 ACP; S & W 9mm Double Action Automatic; Llama blue-engraved 380 Automatic.

PISTOL
GUIDE

PISTOL
GUIDE

George C. Nonte, Jr.

Stoeger Publishing Company

Published by the Stoeger Publishing Company
55 Ruta Court, South Hackensack, N.J. 07606

Library of Congress Catalog Card No.: 79-66958

ISBN: 0-88317-095-7

Manufactured in the United States of America

Distributed to the book trade by Follett Publishing Company and to the sporting goods trade by Stoeger Industries. In Canada, distributed to the book trade and to the sporting goods trade by Stoeger Trading Company, 2020R 32nd Avenue, Northeast, Calgary, Alberta T2E 6T4

Contents

About the Author

The book you hold in your hand is unique in several respects, not the least of which is that it is one of the last two books written by the late George C. Nonte, Jr.: the *Pistol Guide* and *Revolver Guide*, both published by Stoeger. It is not easy to think of the world of gun books without this distinguished author, who managed to produce several new and unusual books each year and to sandwich his writing among a myriad of consulting activities in the fields of arms and ammunition.

George C. Nonte, Jr., was born in Monticello, Illinois, on February 9, 1926. He entered the United States Army during World War Two and served for twenty years, retiring as a Major in the Ordnance Corps in 1964. His military career included service in the United States, Europe and the Middle East.

George was the author of several thousand magazine articles that appeared in the major firearms and outdoor magazines. His book credits include *Cartridge Conversions, Firearms Encyclopedia, Pistolsmithing, Guide to Muzzle Loading,* and *Modern Handloading.* For Stoeger, he wrote *Pistol & Revolver Guide, Gunsight Guide, To Stop a Thief: The Complete Guide to House, Apartment and Property Protection,* and *Black Powder Guide.* His last works, the twin *Pistol Guide* and *Revolver Guide,* are separate revisions of his highly popular *Pistol & Revolver Guide,* which itself went through three editions in eight years and a multitude of reprintings.

George died at work in his office on June 30, 1978. Death came swiftly, as George would have wanted.

These are the bare bones of George Nonte's biographical data. However, no abbreviated biographical entry can capture the man. I prefer to remember him as he was during our last meeting: alive, lusty, vibrant and excited about his twin book projects for Stoeger. George was an essentially modest human being who considered all human beings absurd, including himself. We met in a New York restaurant famous for its hearty food. After he had ordered a drink and lit up a smoke, he settled back to talk about his plans for the books, sketching them and fleshing them out with details from his encyclopedic memory and experience.

As he talked, I reflected that he was essentially an anachronism in modern garb. His frame and visage called for leather and buckles, a claymore at his belt and a pair of dragoon pistols in his jackboots. The board should have been bare and brown, washed by the slops from heavy pewter tankards and worn smooth by muscular sword hands. The light should have been from flickering flambeaux. There would have been a huge fire over which a dripping roast slowly turned on a spit. Rabelais and Villon should have been our tablemates.

Every book should have a dedication, and this one, his book, is fittingly for George, who unfortunately had to leave early.

—ROBERT F. SCOTT

Introduction

Looking over the many shelves of my library at the spines of a couple of thousand books there, I find nearly a score of titles devoted to handguns in general, to "pistols and revolvers," or to narrower facets of the handgun game. Almost all of them offer at least substantial coverage of autoloading pistols, and some of them deal with nothing else. One might wonder, then, why on earth anyone would undertake to write yet another book devoted almost exclusively to autoloading handguns (aside, of course, from the fact that authors like myself make a living from writing), with so many titles already in existence. At one time I'd have wondered, too, even when the crop was smaller than it is today, except for the fact that literally thousands of readers and correspondents have written over the past few years for information not found in those older books. They have even written asking for information I didn't put in some of my own handgun books.

Today, though, we live in a time in which guns are undergoing rapid change—change in technology, change in thinking, change in design, even change in the law that governs all we do. Books written only a couple of years back can easily be deficient in some areas by now, just by virtue of changes that take place so rapidly and plentifully. This book is written in part to include material that couldn't be put in books of earlier days—material that either didn't exist in usable form or was excluded by considerations of size and economy. But that is only part of the reason—

new shooting games have sprung up, accompanied by new techniques and guns, ammunition, accessories, and equipment to pursue them. New designs and models, even new manufacturers have risen. These things aren't covered in other books, at least not to the degree desired by all those people who write to have questions answered. Then, there is the simple fact that the *modern* autoloading pistol has not been the subject of a major book in many long years. The auto is the handgun of the future, if not in the form we know it now, then in some other form that nevertheless enables the pistolero to fire a large number of shots very quickly by simply pulling the trigger, without any other actions. The revolver, the "frontier sixshooter" or the more recent double-action sixgun, is a permanent and prominent part of the lore and legend of our country, and is still the most common handgun to be found the nation over—but the auto is coming up on it from behind. The auto, especially in the more recent and sophisticated designs you'll read about in the following pages, is becoming more and more popular among enthusiasts and tyros alike. A couple of decades back no self-respecting law enforcement agency would even consider adopting an auto for service use—yet, today, we find dozens of agencies armed with Colt or S&W autos and perhaps others we don't know about. Discounting the plethora of cheap (in both price and quality) foreign guns that swarmed into this country under dozens of names in the 1920s and 1930s, more *good* autoloading pistols are being offered today than at any time in shooting history. A whole new generation of sophisticated designs has sprung up since World War II, combining methods, materials and features not even thought of in the 1940s.

All of these factors make it appropriate that there be another book on autoloaders, whether by this author or someone else who has worked with handguns all his life. On the other hand, far be it from me to claim that this volume is all-inclusive and that it will teach all and answer all—in fact, we know it won't. But it is my sincere hope that the following pages, the result of some months of considerable labor, and the culmination of the experiences of many people will add to the knowledge of the reader.

If this book is laid down after the last page has been digested and you have the feeling that you have learned more about autoloading pistols and all the subjects that surround them, then, well, I'll feel satisfaction in having contributed a small share to our store of gunning literature and will be pleased with the results of my efforts.

—GEORGE C. NONTE, JR.
Major ORDC, U.S. Retired
Peoria, Illinois

Chapter One
Autoloading Pistol History

Man's hunger for a fast-firing handgun is as old as the firearm itself. The first almost-practical multiple-shot pistols were those with more than one barrel. They date back to the earliest form of flintlock and perhaps even earlier to the wheellock, but you can't add much fire power by stacking on more barrels without making the gun too heavy and bulky for practicality. There were also attempts at "Roman candle" guns, more technically called "superposed-load" guns, in which several additional charges of powder and ball were placed on top of the first, depending upon blow-by or ignition passages through them to ignite successive charges. The charge uppermost in the barrel would be ignited first, and hopefully each beneath it would ignite in succession by the flame of the preceding powder charge, theoretically producing a burst of several shots with a single action of the firing mechanism.

If and when they functioned as intended, such guns fired at a rate exceeding that of some machine guns. But they simply weren't practical since they took far too long to load and were far too uncertain in action. There were also attempts to use a movable lock, firing the top charge first, then moving it rearward to fire the next and more in succession.

However, as long as guns were loaded from the muzzle, it simply wasn't possible to develop an autoloading mechanism of any sort, much less one that could be handled with one hand.

The coming of the metallic cartridge in the 1850s provided lots of hope, but the cartridge revolver was so much better than what had been available before, that most efforts were aimed at improving it and making a buck from it, rather than exploring the possibilities of autoloading systems.

By the 1870s, the single-action revolver had reached more or less definitive form, and the revolver cartridge had become what we know it as today. Early attempts at autoloading pistol designs utilizing the rimmed, straight-case, lead-bullet, black-powder revolver cartridge were not successful for several reasons. The large case rims interfered with feeding and stowage; the lead bullet also introduced feeding problems. But probably more important the copious, solid particulate fouling of black powder (56 percent of its bulk remains behind as ash after combustion)

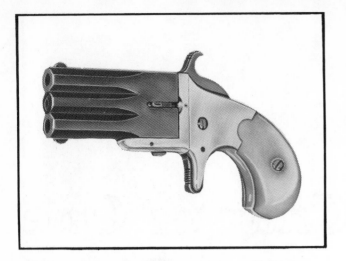

Early multi-hot handguns had a barrel for each shot. This modern two-shot pistol has two barrels that rotate about a central pin. The cartridge in each chamber is fired by the same hammer after the barrels are manually rotated.

would quickly clog any small closely fitted autoloading mechanism. Actually, practical autoloading pistols waited upon ammunition improvements and, in the late 1880s and early 1890s along came the rimless cartridge case, the metal-jacketed bullet and smokeless powder. The rimless or semi-rimmed brass case and metal-jacketed bullet made possible a cartridge that would feed smoothly through an autoloading mechanism. The smokeless powder not only eliminated the propellant-residue problem, but its much greater energy content made it possible to make do with much smaller amounts of propellant. This greatly reduced the size of the cartridge, permitting a much more compact mechanism.

With these developments, literally dozens of designers worked feverishly on autoloading pistol mechanisms during the 1890s. Several were marginally successful, notably the Borchardt, Mannlicher, and the incredibly complex Mauser of 1896 which

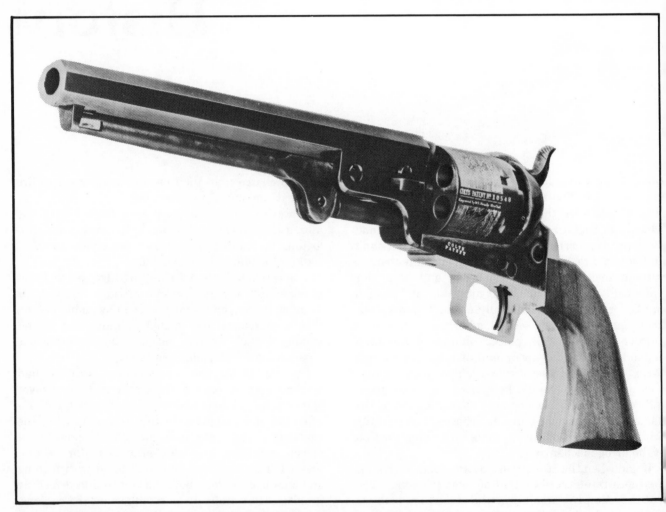

In muzzle loaders, the only practical multiple-shot firearms were those using revolving barrels or cylinders. Sam Colt offered a wide variety of revolvers, typified by this Navy model in 36 caliber.

subsequently remained in production for roughly four decades. While the Mannlicher dropped by the wayside by World War I, the Borchardt went on to become the famous Luger/Parabellum after being redesigned by George Luger.

During this same decade, American Mormon arms genius John M. Browning—already with a most impressive string of weapon successes behind him—devoted his talents to autoloading pistol design. Almost simultaneously, he produced the parallel-ruler locked-breech mobile-barrel 38-caliber auto introduced by Colt in 1900 and manufactured in various forms until 1927; also, what was to become by far the most successful of all the early autoloaders, his blowback pocket-size 32-caliber pistol introduced by Fabrique Nationale. Patents for this small gun were applied for in 1897 and granted in early 1899; FN began manufacture of it immediately as the Model

All cartridges for autoloading pistols usually have several features in common: a rimless or semi-rimmed case, a deep extractor groove and a hardcoated bullet.

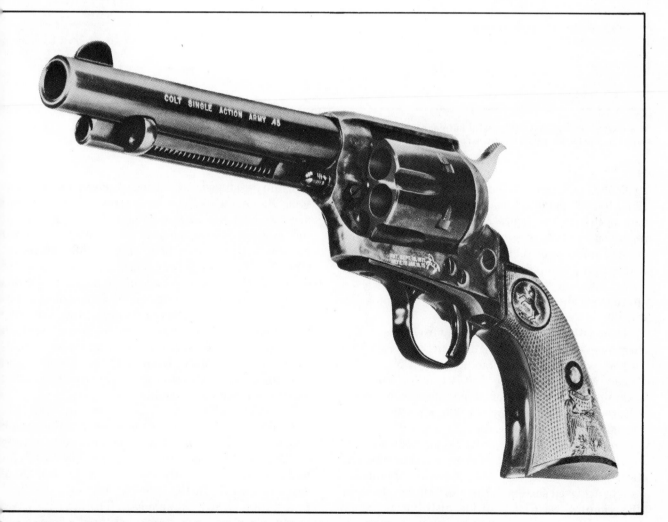

By the 1870s, single-action revolvers had reached their full development. Without a doubt, the all-time favorite was the Colt Single Action Army.

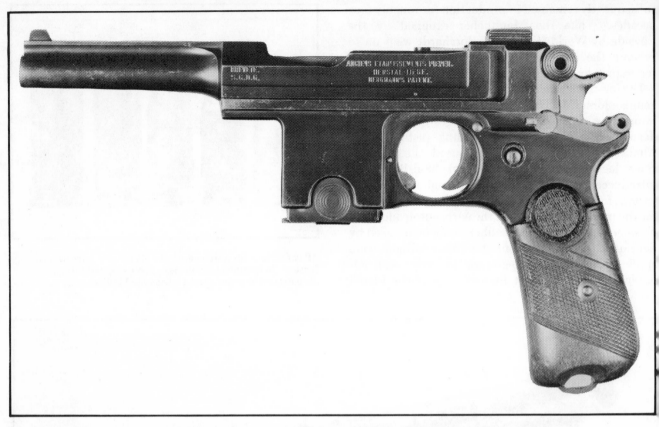

The Bayard was an early successful autoloader but it would be prohibitively expensive to produce today. Complex planes and precision-fit make the design a machinist's nightmare.

1900 and its commercial success was astounding. By 1904, 100,000 units had been manufactured and sold, and by 1909, the figure had reached 500,000. It remained in production only ten years, during which 724,450 units were sold. While many other designs entered production during this same period, some of them with far longer lives, none of them even approached the ten-year record of the Browning/FN M1900.

Never satisfied, working basically from this model, Browning developed the M1903 in 32 (later 380) caliber, which was manufactured by Colt as the Pocket Model, producing 710,224 units from the beginning until termination of manufacture in 1946.

European designers were not idle, with the Mauser M1896 success already assured, and the Parabellum (improved from the Borchardt) having been adopted by the German Navy in 1904 after initial commercial successes beginning in 1900. Several Mannlicher designs achieved success during the first decade of the 20th century, seeing worldwide distribution; Spain developed the Campo-Giro which was to become the Astra M400 later; Austria developed its Steyr-Hahn;

Belgium produced the various Bayard pistols, and some Bergmann designs saw success. By the second decade of the new century, the autoloading pistol and the cartridge type developed concurrently with it had become firmly entrenched, and literally scores of manufacturers were producing a wide variety of designs for both military and commercial use. Nations arming for World War I demanded tremendous quantities of new auto pistols, and during the war, they were produced in unprecedented numbers. Spanish firms alone produced uncounted hundreds of thousands of small autoloaders for the French, and virtually all of the scores of successful designs existing by 1914 were employed militarily.

By 1911, when the U.S. Army adopted the Browning/Colt 45 Auto, virtually every nation which had not already adopted an autoloader was eagerly seeking one. The advantages of the autoloader for military use were clearly seen, and if by then there was any need for further proving the type, the 1914–1918 period clearly eliminated it. The incredibly bad conditions of trench warfare constituted a field test of the utmost severity.

The end of that war found autoloading pistols firmly established in both military and civilian usages, and the various types had reached reasonably definitive form. With the single exception of the Astra, big-bore military/police types were of locked-breech construction, employing the recoil impulse and a mobile barrel to cycle the action; most housed the cartridge magazine inside the grip or butt, and the majority enclosed the barrel in a recoiling slide. Calibers of this type pistol ranged generally from 9mm to 45, though limited use was made of the 7.65mm Parabellum cartridge which was essentially the 9mm necked down to 30 caliber. All employed rimless cartridge cases of generally cylindrical but very slightly tapered shape, loaded with smokeless powder and fully metal-jacketed bullets. Performance ranged generally from muzzle velocities of slightly over 800 fps up to about 1200 fps.

Pistols intended generally for civilian use were smaller and lighter, quite similar in appearance, recoil-operated, but generally of blowback or unlocked-breech construction with a fixed barrel enclosed by a recoiling slide. Such guns were generally chambered for the 32 ACP (7.65mm Browning) cartridge, though a minor percentage of the same designs were chambered for the larger 380 ACP (9mm Browning Short) cartridge. Such guns generally weighed in the vicinity of one and one-half pounds or less, compared to the roughly two and one-half pounds of the military/police types. Though these civilian pistols were generally considered to be of pocket size, the appellation can be correctly applied only if one is thinking in terms of an overcoat pocket. A second size of civilian pistol had also developed, almost invariably chambered for the very small, 25 ACP cartridge developed from the original Browning design of the type. Such guns were truly of pocket size, weighed substantially less than one pound, but were mechanically essentially the same as the larger civilian guns.

It is particularly interesting to note that most of the features of the civilian guns had been developed by Browning and that the majority of such guns, regardless of place of manufacture, were little more than slightly modified Browning copies.

During the 1920s, there were many attempts at developing newer and better pistol designs, most of them in the civilian field. However, little of note achieved commercial success until late in the decade when the Carl Walther Firm introduced the first pocket pistols featuring double-action first-shot capability. Aside from the rather complex double-action lockwork and superb workmanship, the Walther

One of the most famous autoloaders of all time, the luger or P08 as developed from the earlier Borchardt design.

True pocket-sized autoloaders, such as this Sterling 22 caliber Model 302, are currently offered by many firms. Most are found in either 22 or 25ACP caliber and usually weigh less than a pound.

PP/PPK pistols offered no features that had not already been developed in other models. In the 1930s, similar double-action pistols were developed by both Sauer & Sohn and Mauser-Werke, and all three of these manufacturers produced hundreds of thousands of the new types during World War II. Though perhaps slow in achieving wide initial success, the double-action feature has become highly desirable in the past two or three decades. It is unusual today for a new pocket-pistol design to appear without double-action. At least ten makers produce the type today.

In the middle 1930s, Walther also developed the first successful, double-action military pistol finally adopted by the German military establishment as the

Colt's Government Model is produced by several companies and is offered in slightly different styles. All are based on the M1911, which is still used by U.S. military forces as well as those of other nations.

Several prewar designs were commercial successes in Europe. Probably the two most popular were the Walther PP or PPk and the Mauser HSc. The HSc shown here was produced in the mid-1930s.

Walther's Model PPK was produced in 22 rimfire, 32ACP and 380ACP calibers. It was a popular sidearm throughout Europe before World War II and it enjoyed even greater popularity with the German officer corps during the war. The PPK is known for its excellent fit and finish as well as its compact efficiency.

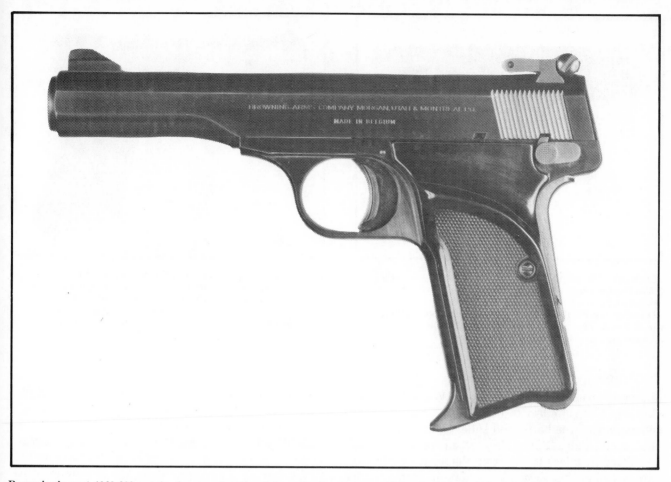

Browning's post-1968 380 autoloader was developed from basic patents used in the M1900. Although referred to as a "pocket pistol," the current Browning would require unusually large pockets for carrying or concealing.

P38 in the year 1938. The P38 deviated from the tubular barrel-enclosing slide of so many other military autoloaders and also featured an unusual locking block and rearward placement of recoil springs. In fact, the Walther P38 contained the most significant developments in the military-pistol field since the early acceptance of the type. It was the only full-sized, double-action military pistol manufactured and widely used during World War II.

Following World War II, autoloading pistol designs remained more or less stagnant. In both the military and civilian field, tremendous quantities of wartime guns were available and their presence limited sales potential of new guns to the point that several of the more popular civilian models were discontinued.

Military pistol development also lagged for the same reasons, except in the U.S.S.R. and the U.S. In the U.S.S.R., the Stechkin machine pistol and Makarov belt pistol were developed, mainly by relatively minor modifications to the basic Walther PP design.

Both guns represented a down-sizing of the military pistol and a reduction in power of its cartridge. In the U.S., the early 1950s produced the Smith & Wesson M39, a locked-breech 9mm pistol borrowing heavily from both Browning and Walther, but with a very simple and reliable double-action system. The M39 also featured an aluminum-alloy frame and unusual compactness. Light-alloy frames had been pioneered in Germany just before and during World War II and were first adopted here in the Colt Commander of 1949.

Further military pistol developments were few until the German firm of Heckler & Koch produced its P9S design built primarily from stamped, sheet-metal parts welded together with stamped, cast, and machined spacers. Both frame and slide of this design were constructed in this fashion, producing substantial cost savings in large-scale production and a very substantial material savings at any level. The P9S also featured a new locking system developed for

The Smith & Wesson M39 hit the U.S. market in the early 1950s. It uses a very simple and reliable double-action system and includes features borrowed from both Browning and Walther. Along with the Colt Commander, the M39 was one of the earliest pistols available in this country to use a lightweight alloy frame.

Heckler & Koch produces the P9S for both military and civilian markets. Its design permits large-scale production by cost-saving methods. The pistol uses a roller-locked recoil system developed late during World War II and incorporates double-action capability and extremely simple field stripping.

automatic weapons late in World War II by the German Vorgrimmler. It employed hardened-steel rollers locking the barrel and slide together, the rollers being wedged into the locked position, and permitted to unlock by precisely shaped cam surfaces and a mobile bolt-head. This system permitted a locked breech to be combined with a fixed barrel, with the obvious advantage of improved accuracy over a movable barrel. The P9S also featured a manual cocking and decocking lever, apparently based upon the success of a manual cocking lever employed in the prewar Sauer M38.

Simultaneously with the P9, H&K also developed the HK-4 pocket pistol from the earlier Mauser HSc. The HK-4 also features sheet-metal slide construction but combined with an investment-cast light-alloy frame. A most interesting feature of the HK-4 is its multiple-caliber capability. By substituting barrel, recoil spring and in some instances the magazine, it may be readily converted among any of the four calibers, 22 LR, 25 ACP, 32 ACP, and 380 ACP. Switching barrels and magazines to change calibers was not unknown, but utilizing the same slide and switching it from rimfire to centerfire (by means of a rotating, firing-pin locating plate) was a thoroughly new development. The HK-4 was the first gun to be offered as a multiple-caliber set with all changeover parts.

Both the P9S and the HK-4 feature sophisticated double-action lockwork with cocking and chamber indicators and operating methods deviating from the traditional.

To bring us up to date, the most recent development in military/police pistols is the SIG P220 design manufactured by Sauer & Sohn in Germany as the SIG/Sauer. It is also sold under the Browning Arms name, manufactured specifically for Browning, but otherwise unchanged. Just introduced, this pistol features a combination of investment-cast light-alloy frame and welded sheet-metal slide. It is of cam-operated, locked-breech construction with a tubular slide. It possesses a double-action first-shot capability and is fitted with a decocking lever which allows safe manual lowering of the hammer. The P220 is most unconventional in that it eliminates the traditional, manual safety entirely. Instead, it employs a fully automatic internal firing-pin safety actuated by the trigger. The firing pin is blocked in its rearward position at all times except when the trigger is deliberately held fully rearward to drop the hammer. As a practical matter, this makes the double-action autoloader fully as safe from inadvertent discharge as the modern double-action revolver.

To date, all successful autoloading pistols continue to be operated by the recoil impulse. Over the years, various gas-operated designs have been proposed, but none has ever achieved production status. It is significant to note at this time that a gas-operated design—which originated in Sweden quite some years ago—is now being refined in this country for production in

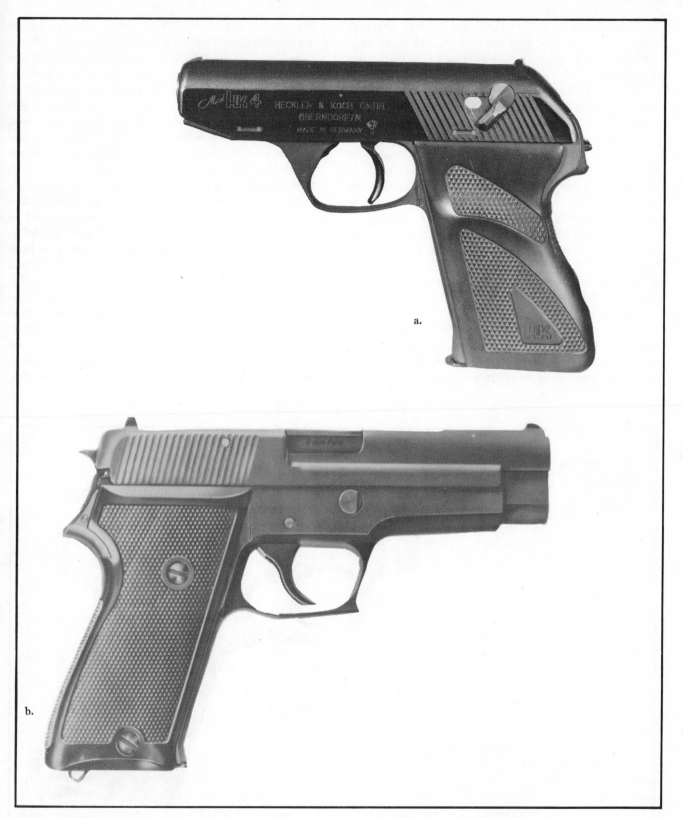

a. Heckler & Koch manufactures a wide variety of military arms, but also offers some remarkable products for the civilian market. The HK4 shown above has the unique feature of interchangeable calibers. By changing only the barrel, recoil spring and magazine, the caliber can be changed.   b. The Hawes Sig-Sauer P220 has an automatic firing pin lock that ensures complete safety, even if the weapon is dropped.

the near future by Wildey Firearms. To date, this gun exists only in single, prototype form, and there may well be many changes before it achieves intended production.

As a practical matter, ammunition for locked-breech pistols has been generally limited in performance by the inability of the guns to withstand chamber pressures of much more than 33–35,000 CUP. This isn't to say those designs, or at least some of them, won't stand much higher pressures occasionally, but for continuous use and long life, they have generally been limited to those levels, with some, such as the 45 caliber Colt/Browning M1911, limited to levels of around 20,000 CUP. These limitations are not imposed so much by mechanical design as by weight and size. With parts of greater dimensions, the same basic designs could be made to withstand substantially greater pressures—however, the resulting gun would be clumsy and heavy.

As a result of all this, Harry Sanford produced the massive rotating-bolt, locked-breech, recoil-operated Auto-Mag pistol in the mid 1960s. This gun was designed specifically to operate at working chamber pressures in the 50–55,000 CUP range. This permitted it a much higher level of ballistic performance, driving 44 caliber 180-grain bullets at velocities of 2000 fps or greater. In that it allowed a higher level of ballistic performance, the Auto-Mag pistol was a substantial success. On the other hand, because of its great weight and size, it was not practical for most handgun uses. As a result, the gun enjoyed a relatively short life, and is now passing from the scene, production having terminated after less than 10,000 units.

Materials in autoloading pistols have naturally improved over the years. In the 1950s, it had become obvious that stainless steels existed which could be employed in handgun construction. These materials had been used in some military small arms as far back as the 1930s, and in the mid 1960s, Smith & Wesson introduced the first all-stainless-steel revolver. This gun achieved tremendous popularity, and the same firm followed with a wide variety of stainless-steel revolvers. Though the mechanical properties of practical stainless steels are actually inferior to some common steels used in autoloading pistol construction, many shooters are quite willing to pay this price,

The Wildey Firearms Co. is ready to produce the first gas-operated autoloading pistol. It is based on a design which originated in Sweden some years ago. Technical problems have delayed its introduction.

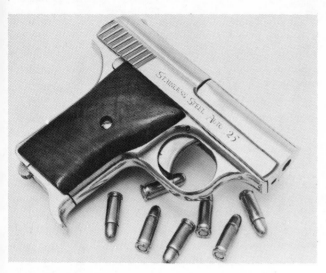

A new generation of handguns is now being built of stainless steel.

and a greater dollar price as well, for the ease of maintenance and freedom from corrosion which stainless steel offers. As a result, a number of small pocket-size stainless-steel autoloading pistols have been introduced in recent years. Aside from the use of this material, these guns offer no significant design advances. In fact, some such guns are available in either ordinary or stainless steel, but are mechanically quite identical. Also significant is the fact that the OMC Company is currently manufacturing a more or less exact copy of the Colt GM manufactured from stainless steel.

As a consequence of the tremendous interest in stainless, we expect to see it used much more widely in new designs that come along. In fact, we are advised that the Wildey gas-operated pistol will be made only of stainless steel when it enters production.

Chapter Two
Uses

How useful is the autoloading pistol? For what different purposes may it be used and how efficiently will it perform in those different roles?

As a practical matter, the autoloader may be used for any shooting purpose that might be met by any other handgun. That is an oversimplification, of course, but it will hold true for the average pistolero who makes general use of his guns for plinking, modest target shooting, small- or medium-game hunting, and has self- or home-defense forever in the back of his mind.

For general use, the auto gives away only one point to the revolver; that is ammunition versatility. A revolver will function correctly with virtually any cartridge loading that will push the bullet out of the barrel, is not longer than the cylinder, and does not exceed the gun's maximum allowable chamber pressure limits. Size, shape, weight, and type of bullet has no effect on the revolver's ability to function reliably. The auto, on the other hand, requires its cartridges to be loaded with bullets that fall within fairly narrow limits of size, weight and shape, and loaded to veloci-

ties that will produce a recoil impulse that falls within the functional design parameters of the particular gun. Aside from that, the auto will handle any shooting chore you might have in mind, using either factory or handloaded ammunition.

Plinking is probably the most common handgun use, and I know of no firearm that is more a joy for this purpose than the typical 22 rimfire autoloader, almost invariably chambered for the Long Rifle cartridge. Most such guns will function reliably with standard-velocity cartridges which may often be obtained at discount stores under brand names at extremely low prices. Yet, they function equally well and with equal accuracy using the more expensive high-velocity solid and hollow-point loads. At the present time, you can get a superb 22 plinking auto for as little as $100 in the form of the Ruger "Standard Model." From there, the price goes up almost as high as you can stand, with the low-end S&W and High Standard models selling for roughly twice as much. Of course, any of the more costly target autos, including those of foreign manufacture for 500 bucks

Ruger's "Standard Model" is the lowest-priced, high-quality plinking pistol (autoloader) available on today's U.S. market. It offers extreme reliability, reasonable accuracy and excellent durability for less than $100.

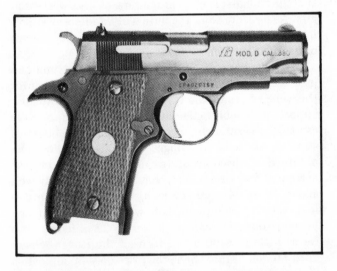

Plinking pistols in calibers other than 22 rimfire pose no problem for the handloader. Guns such as the Llama 380, Sterling 380 or Star 380 can be more rewarding to shoot than the smaller calibers if the cost of ammo is not a factor.

or so, serve equally well for plinking if one cares t invest that much money. Frankly, I can't see an point in using the high-priced guns for ordinary fu shooting. Their sophistication and pin-point accurac simply isn't needed.

Plinking need not be limited to 22 pistols. In fact, good many pistoleros who enjoy a plinking session two every weekend may not even own a 22. In day when military-surplus ammunition was less costly, a manner of big-bore pistols were widely used for plin ing. Today the cost of ammunition has somewh restricted plinking with such guns, but this presen no problem at all to the handloader. The fellow wh reloads his own empties can shoot even a 9mm or 4 auto for scarcely more per shot than he can fee factory loads to a 22.

As fond as I am of the 22 autos, I must admit that have probably fired a good many more plinkir rounds with the big-bores, using low-cost handloac assembled in my spare time. Probably the on

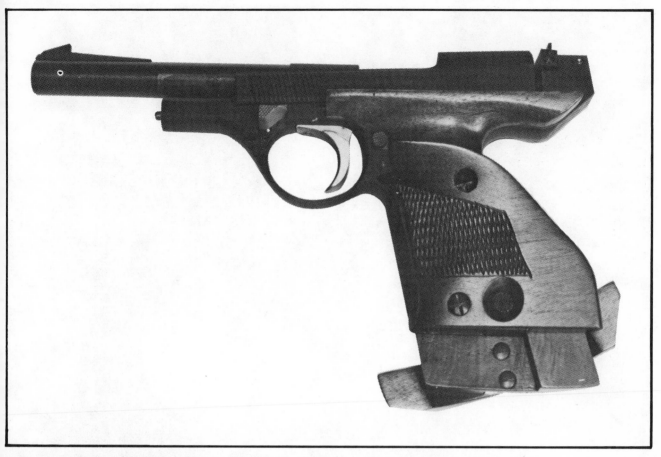

Rimfire autoloaders span a huge price range. Top-quality competition pistols such as the Unique D.E.S. 69 Standard Match Automatic Pistol demand premium prices expressed in hundreds of dollars. This gun is a 22 Long Rifle with a 5-shot magazine and a 5.9 inch barrel.

measurable disadvantage of the big-bore auto for plinking is the fact that it tosses all of its empty cases well clear of the shooter. This presents no particular problem on a clean formal range where the brass can easily be seen and recovered, but in a typical plinking environment, it's easy to lose a goodly percentage of the fired cases in grass, leaves and brush. Or if you're shooting from a boat—as is common in many parts of the country—most of the brass will be lost in the water, and that plays hell with loading costs. Even the smaller centerfire pistols, such as the 25s, the 32s and 380s, can produce a lot of plinking fun. Some of them aren't noted for fine accuracy, but, then, neither are the smaller and cheaper revolvers of comparable caliber.

Yes, as far as I'm concerned, the auto is fully as useful for plinking as any other type of gun, and it's also great for teaching youngsters to shoot.

Serious target shooting is a field virtually dominated by the autoloader. Aside from the special competitions such as Police Matches and Handgun Metallic Silhouette Matches, autoloaders have almost completely displaced revolvers in serious competition over the past few decades. It began in the 1930s when the Colt Match Target Woodsman demonstrated its superiority over the revolver for 22 rimfire matches where rapidity of fire was required. With the coming of even better autos by other makers after World War II, revolvers went down for the count in 22 matches. Thus, the auto is not only quite good for 22 competition, it is better than anything else in any matches where shots are fired fairly rapidly. No effort need be expended in recocking after each shot as with the revolver, and a very light and precise trigger pull is available.

In centerfire matches, the same changeover from the revolver took place some years later. By the early 1960s, techniques had been developed by which centerfire autoloaders could be produced (by manufacture and modification) to equal or exceed the accuracy and reliability of target revolvers. Once this was achieved, the auto's superiority in speed of fire

Favorite small game for handgunners is probably squirrel since most shots are at moderate ranges and the target is not moving rapidly. A few brave souls pride themselves on their ability to hit running rabbits consistently, but they are in the minority.

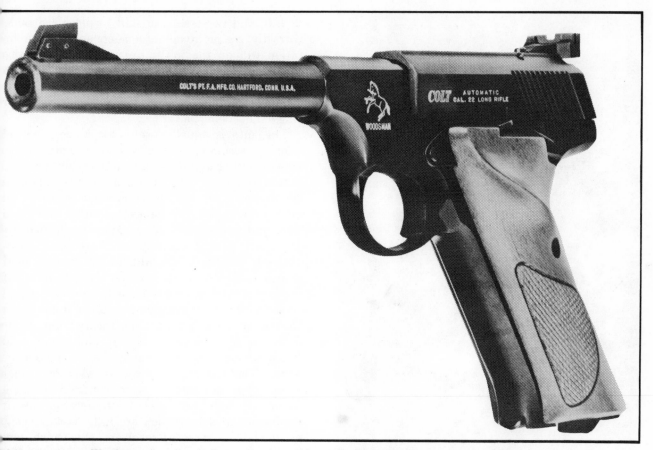

olt's most recent Woodsman is quite similar to its sire of the 1930's. The Colt design was partially
esponsible for the shooter acceptance of autoloading designs over the revolvers. Rapid fire with accuracy
as far easier to learn with the auto and even shooters who were hard-headed traditionalists had to
dmit it was time for a change.

ng the death knell of the sixgun. Today, a properly
ned target auto in 32, 38 or 45 caliber will exceed
e accuracy of a comparable revolver. Add to this its
her advantages, and it's easy to see why a properly
osen auto is the best selection for serious target
rk in matches which will allow it.

While it's true that the large percentage of people
ying handguns aren't the least bit concerned with
nting, most of those outside urban areas at least
ink casually of it. In the past couple of decades,
nting with handguns has blossomed tremendously,
d ardent pistoleros have taken all species of North
nerican game with various short guns. If one thinks
terms of only small game (rabbits, squirrels, grouse,
rkeys, etc.), then the typical 22 rimfire autoloader
th high-velocity ammunition is a superb hunting
oice. It offers top accuracy, easier control and
eater rapidity of fire (if you consider that an advan-
ge in the field). For fast follow-up shots on scam-
ring squirrels or bounding bunnies, it is superior to
e sixgun.

Moving up to larger game, conventional autos of
9mm, 38 and 45 caliber are quite adequate for
medium-sized animals of the deer and black bear
class. Of course, that comment assumes proper selection of ammunition and a high degree of stalking and
marksmanship skill. I think it is unfortunate that too
many pistoleros think only in terms of the heavy
magnum revolver cartridges for hunting. In this
respect, autos do suffer some disadvantage; with the
exception of the apparently defunct Auto-Mag and
the as-yet-to-be-produced Wildey magnum auto,
none of the standard auto cartridges approach the
smashing power of the sixgun magnums. However,
this scribe has killed—and has observed the killing—
many head of game in Europe, the Near East, Africa,
Canada, and the U.S. with conventional autos. I've
seen everything from 75-pound Texas whitetail up
through 500-pound, Russian boars (with mulies and
black bear in between) killed cleanly with conventional autos from 9mm to 45 caliber. Most of those
animals wouldn't have been a bit more dead or died

The author poses with a badger taken by a long shot from his custom Auto-Mag. Game much larger than the badger has fallen to the big autoloader, but smaller targets help to keep the hand and eye sharp for serious business.

more quickly had they been struck with a 44 magnum bullet from a sixgun.

As in any other type of hunting, bullet placement is far more important than power level, and if one has the marksmanship and stalking skill to take a deer cleanly with a 44 magnum, he could kill it just as well with a less powerful 45 or 38 Super Auto. Lee Jurras and I once drove from St. Louis to northern New Mexico, and on the way we took both game and predators in almost every state—all species that were lawful—with 9mm, 38 Super and 45 Autos. We finished the trip by each taking a fine pronghorn antelope, but we switched to the magnum-like Auto-Mag pistols for that one species simply because of the long ranges involved; my pronghorn went down at about 80 yards, and Jurras killed his at over 200 yards. But, if one limits his hunting shots to 50 yards

or less, and possesses the skill to place the bullet correctly, conventional autoloaders and their ammunition will do the job quite nicely. At the longer ranges, especially for varmint shooting, the flatter trajectories—rather than greater power—of the sixgun magnums are better, with the long-barreled single shots being better yet.

The auto is equally useful for home and self defense, assuming the gun and ammunition are chosen with care. It is unfortunate but true that untold thousands of defense autos are chosen for small size. When the choice is made on that basis, autos seldom perform well except under ideal conditions and in the hands of an expert marksman. And an expert most likely wouldn't have made such a choice in the first place. Much is often made of the fact that a double-action revolver is quite safe against accidental discharge when loaded, and that it may be brought into action simply by grabbing it and pulling the trigger. Those who tout this theory point out that autos are less safe when loaded, and require additional actions and movements to be placed into action. That was true at one time when only single-action type autoloaders were generally available. Today, though, we have a proliferation of fine double-action autos which are fully as safe against accidental discharge as revolvers and which, when left in the proper condition, are brought safely into action by simply grabbing them and pulling the trigger.

Once we recognize that certain modern autos are as safe and as quick for the first shot as a revolver, then we note that the autoloader is superior to the revolver in controllability, rapidity of fire and sustained fire.

So, in the case of defensive handguns, we don't say that all autos are equally useful, but the modern DA types (which are available in calibers from 22 up through 45) are damned fine weapons. Your neighbor who brags about his 38 Special sixgun over your 9mm DA auto is simply happily ignorant of the true usefulness and versatility of your gun for home defense.

Thirty years ago you'd have had to search far and wide in this country to find any major law enforcement agency or department equipping its officers with autoloading pistols. The exalted authorities charged with selecting sidearms for both uniformed and undercover use had been so misled by old tales of "auto unreliability" and by equally unfounded tales of revolver performance that they simply wouldn't think of allowing anything but a 38 sixgun. Since the mid 1960s though, the auto's true worth as a police sidearm has been reluctantly recognized in many circles. It is, in fact, superior to the revolver

ne of the many types of game that can be obtained using a 44 Auto-Mag pistol.

The Beretta Brigadier, a big-bore autoloader, was designed for police use.

handling, rapidity of fire, ease and speed of reloading and sustained fire. As a result, more and more major departments and agencies are either adopting or authorizing big-bore autoloaders in either SA or DA form every year. Those who once doubted or denied the usefulness of the auto for urban combat are slowly being forced to eat their words.

Once we force ourselves to look objectively at modern autoloading pistols, we can only conclude that for all but very narrow and specialized purposes they possess all the versatility and usefulness that the shooter might desire. In fact, although they generally lack the ability to handle pip-squeak loads or smashing magnum cartridges, they are in most other areas actually superior to the revolver.

Chapter Three
"Gentlemen, Choose Your Weapons"

Take a look in the latest edition of the SHOOTER'S BIBLE or similar books of handguns and you'll see literally dozens of different makes and models, both domestic and foreign, ranging from diminutive 22 and 25 designs weighing only a few ounces, up through all manner of 32, 380, 9mm, 38, and 45 models in both single-action and double-action persuasion. A quick shuffle through the pages might well make it seem as if choosing the best gun would be virtually an impossible task. Actually, it isn't nearly as hard as it might seem to make an intelligent selection of a gun suited to one's particular circumstances.

The first step in any wise selection is to determine what you *need* or *want;* and the two are not necessarily synonymous. If you're a cop or other professional gun-carrier, then you'll have fairly specific *needs* and it will be necessary to select the gun that fits them best. On the other hand, if you only want a gun, there are quite a few selections that will suit you.

As we've already said, probably the most versatile of all the autoloaders is the ubiquitous 22 LR pistol of ordinary belt size. It's probably the best for plinking,

great for hunting small game, makes a lovely vehicle for introducing others to the joys of handgunning, will serve nicely for some phases of competition, and it really isn't all that bad as a defensive weapon when loaded with high-velocity hollow-point ammunition. Added to that, its ammunition is the most economical of all, recoil/blast/flash are negligible, and the service life seems to be virtually unlimited. Consequently, I would say that if you do not already own other handguns and if you are not already experienced, your first gun should be a good 22 LR auto with a four or six inch barrel.

At the moment, three domestic manufacturers offer two or more models each in this category. Least sophisticated and costly of the lot is the Ruger Standard Model costing as little as $100. When we say that it is not particularly sophisticated, we mean that it does not possess features such as an adjustable trigger, automatic slide stop, compensator, ribbed barrel, etc., and it is not what we might call "finely finished," with brightly polished surfaces and careful internal handfitting. Yet, it is a thoroughly durable and reliable gun offering superb accuracy. For only a few

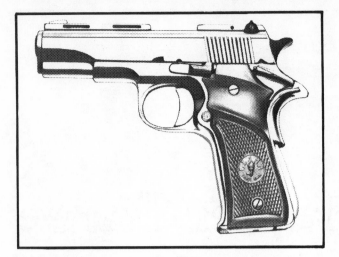

The Llama 380 caliber small-frame automatic pistol is a compact handgun.

The Sterling Arms Model 400 Mark III 380 cal. double-action pistol.

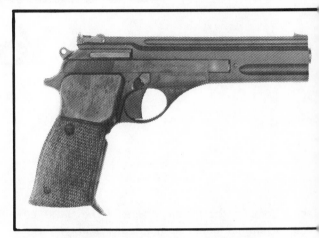

A 22 long Rifle pistol, such as the Beretta Model 76 pictured above, is probably best for plinking. The 22 LR is a good gun for beginning handgunners.

dollars more, one may have the Ruger MKI model which is essentially the same with the addition of a heavier and/or longer barrel and micrometer-adjustable target-type sights. For a limited investment, I simply can't think of a better bargain than either of the two Rugers.

To step above this level, we come to the S&W M41 and the High Standard Supermatic series. Both, in their several variations, are priced in the $200+ range, and are intended primarily as target guns. As such, they are fitted with finely adjustable target sights, adjustable triggers, slide stops, nicely checkered wood grips, long barrels and provisions for weights and compensators, and are generally quite nicely finished and fitted so that they are a delight to look upon as well as to shoot. The two makers use vastly different designs and appearances are also quite different. The basic M41 is supplied with a standard compensator, while the High Standard is not. The High Standard offers a quick and easy interchange of various barrel weights and lengths, and while such changes are easily made on the M41, the options are fewer. I don't think one could go wrong with either make, though I personally am somewhat partial to the Smith & Wesson.

Beyond this, there are several highly sophisticated and very costly European Target 22 Autos. Considering that the least of them costs around $375 with prices ranging upward to nearly twice that much, they must be viewed only as tools for the most discriminating competitive shooter who can afford (or is at least willing) to invest the cost of three or four domestic guns in a single specialized piece. As a practical matter, we can't recommend them to the ordinary shooter unless he's on the sort of ego trip which

justifies spending the price of a good used automobil just so he can brag that he owns one of the world' finest 22 target autos.

No matter how much you study catalogs, it boil down to the simple fact that you can have a fin utilitarian gun in the form of the Ruger at aroun $100, or the more sophisticated S&W or High Stan dard at only twice that much. The Ruger will serve fo everything but highest-level competition, while eithe of the others is quite capable of performing all othe functions and then carrying you through the U.S National Championships if you are marksma enough.

Of course, as you look through the catalog page you'll see a wide variety of smaller 22 autos. They range from the tiny palm-size Bauer with less tha two inches of barrel up to the Walther PP/PPKS an

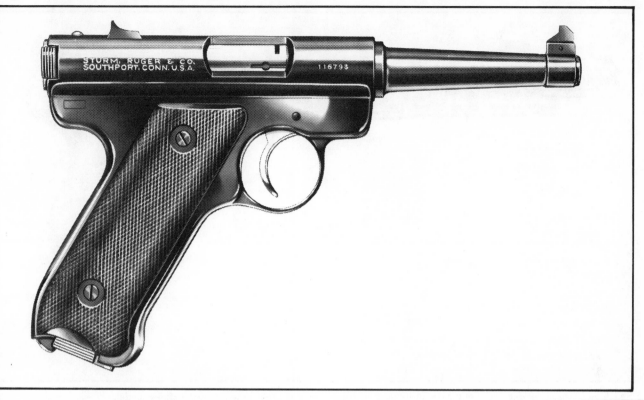

Ruger's Standard Model Auto pistol is a 22 long rifle.

The Mark I, a 22 long rifle made by Ruger, is available as a Target pistol or a Bull Barrel Target pistol.

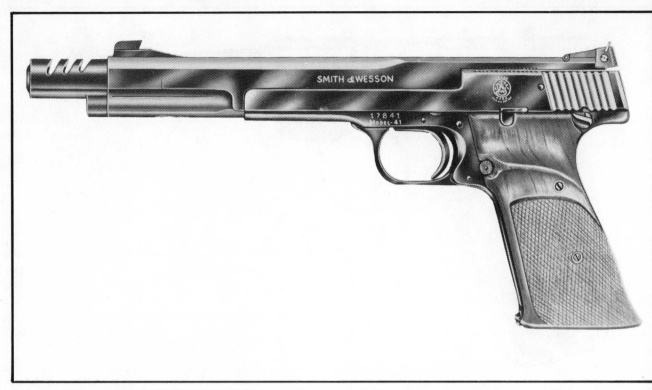

Smith and Wesson's Model 41 Long Rifle automatic pistol is also available in a 22 Short caliber model.

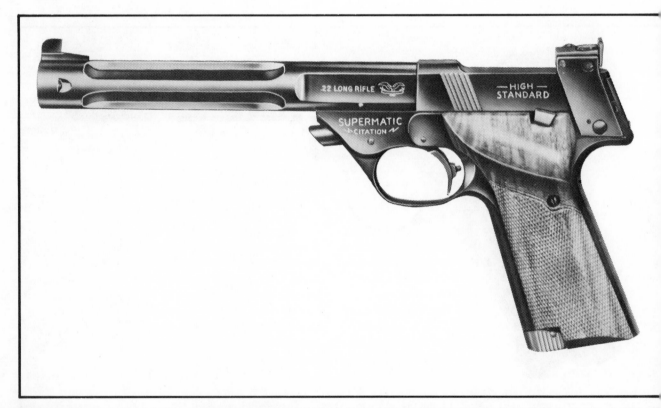

High Standard's Supermatic was intended primarily as a target pistol, but with the shorter barrel (offered as an option) it lends itself well to use for informal shooting or hunting small game.

Heckler & Koch HK-4 pocket size and weighing in the vicinity of one and one-half pounds and with barrels about three and one-half inches in length. They'll range in price from above $100 up to nearly three times as much. None have adjustable sights; in fact, most of them have poor sights with the smallest being the worst in this respect.

The smaller guns are extremely difficult to control, and their very short barrels don't generate full performance from the cartridge. The larger guns are mechanically quite accurate, but the average individual cannot shoot them as well as he can the larger 22s.

All of the guns in this class are designed more for *carrying* than they are for shooting. We simply don't recommend them as a first choice or for general-purpose use. They can make great plinking fun, but they lack the broad versatility of the larger guns, even though many of them cost considerably more.

If you're thinking of purchasing a handgun for hunting, consider carefully the game you'll be seeking. If it's strictly small game, then the bigger 22 autos are far and away the best choice. On the other hand, if you anticipate perhaps an annual foray for whitetail to produce horns for the den wall or venison for the freezer, with perhaps an occasional hunt for sheep, goat or boar on a commercial preserve, then one of the big-bore centerfire autoloaders is in order.

Only three calibers are currently available which meet the requirements for this sort of shooting, and one of them, the 38 Colt Super Auto, is handicapped in that factory-loaded cartridges are *not* supplied with a suitable hunting bullet. So, unless you plan to handload, this number is out. That's a shame, because it is actually my favorite. Properly handloaded, I consider it superior to both the 9mm Parabellum and the 45 ACP for big-game hunting. Though I've killed a good deal of game with the 9mm, I consider it marginal for the purpose and would recommend the 45.

Very few different guns are generally available in this caliber. The Colt Government Model predominates, with the Llama line-for-line copy and the Star look-alike trailing behind. The Browning/SIG/Sauer and H&K 45 models are also available, but only to a limited degree, and are much more costly. Subject to its limited availability, the H&K P9S is probably technically the best choice inasmuch as it is available with a six-inch barrel and target sights as options. The longer barrel (five inch being standard) and its polygonal rifling produce substantially higher velocity and energy than may be obtained from the other models. However, all things considered, the Colt GM

The Heckler & Koch HK4 22 LR.

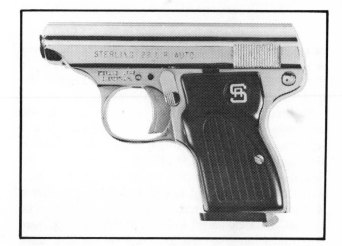

Offered in either blue or nickel finish, the Sterling 22 is a well-executed pocket pistol. Guns of this type are valued for their portability, not hair-splitting accuracy. They have the advantage of easy concealment and are sufficiently accurate for casual tin-can shooting and other varieties of plinking.

is probably the most practical choice, and since a hunting gun should possess adjustable sights, the Gold Cup Target model is the best of the several variations. Some money can be saved off the approximately $320 price by buying the standard GM model and fitting after-market sights. This saving will be especially noticeable if you're fortunate enough to locate an excellent used GM.

If you should happen to be a handloader and prefer my choice of the 38 Super, then by all means get the Colt GM, and then fit it with top-grade target sights. I'd recommend the Bo-Mar rib/sight combination,

The Walther GSP offers many shooting refinements, including adjustable sights, trigger weights and an outstanding finish. The GSP model 22 L.R. comes in either a 2.2 or a 3.0 lb. trigger. This Walther match pistol is made to conform to ISU and NRA match target-pistol regulations.

not only because of its excellence, but because its installation is so much simpler and cheaper than most others. Both the Star and Llama are available in 38 Super, but they're priced very nearly as high as the Colt, so little is to be gained by their uses.

Assuming you're willing to settle for the slightly less power of the 9mm cartridge, choosing a gun is a whole new ball game. You may select from Walther, Browning, Star, Llama, H&K, SIG, SIG/Sauer, Colt, Smith & Wesson, and other makes in several models. Actually, a choice need not be nearly that complex. Remember that a hunting gun should have the longest practical barrel so as to extract the maximum potential from the cartridge, and should also have adjustable sights. Colt, Llama and Star have the longest barrels at five inches, with the Browning HP very close behind at about $4^5/8$ inches. Of the lot, only the Browning is available from the factory with target sights. However, the less available H&K P9S may also be had in 9mm with the extra-length barrel and target sights at a rather high price. As far as factory-produced guns go, this model will produce maximum velocity from factory-loaded ammunition—a factor worthy of consideration. In the end, though, probably the best combination of economy and performance will be obtained from the 9mm Colt GM with after-market target sights added as we described in reference to the 45.

In my view, though, it seems the only valid reason one might construct for using the 9mm cartridge in preference to the 45 is to be able to hunt with a particular make/model gun that is not offered in the latter caliber. In this case, the Browning HP in the

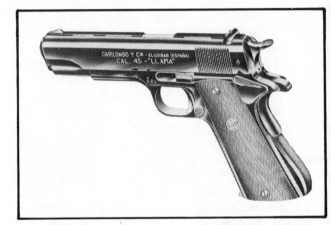

The Llama automatic pistol is priced well below a comparable Colt. Llama pistols are finely crafted but rugged. The Llama automatic pistol is available in three small-frame calibers.

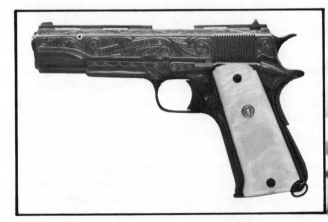

Llama makes the Super 38 Deluxe Engraved Auto.

Colt's Government Model

Colt's 45 cal. Commander Model

Colt's Gold Cup

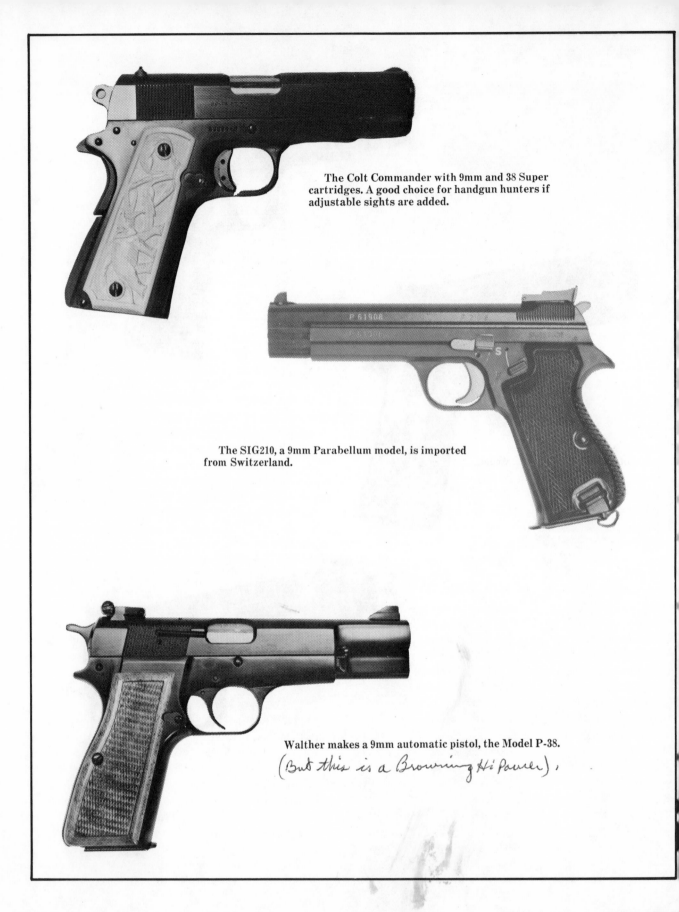

The Colt Commander with 9mm and 38 Super cartridges. A good choice for handgun hunters if adjustable sights are added.

The SIG210, a 9mm Parabellum model, is imported from Switzerland.

Walther makes a 9mm automatic pistol, the Model P-38.

(But this is a Browning Hi Power),

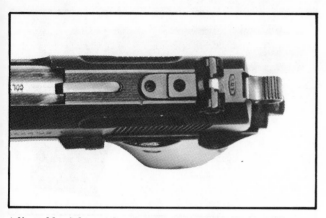

Adjustable sights, either factory installed or after-market, are essential if the pistol is to be used with any degree of accuracy. Experience has shown the square-notch sight to be far superior to a "V" for fast alignmnt and accuracy.

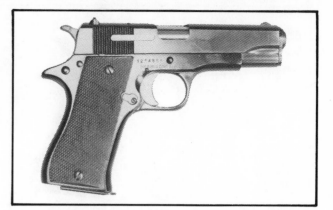

Star's Super compact 45 Model PD comes equipped with factory-installed adjustable sights. The little PD is hardly any bulkier than many guns of 9mm or even 380 caliber.

target variation wins hands-down. None of the other 9mm pistols quite come up to the Browning's reputation for accuracy, durability and reliability, nor do they have fully adjustable sights.

Choosing a defense gun involves a number of compromises. Obviously, when one is defending his own life, he will demand maximum lethality that can be obtained in the gun/ammunition combination within such other limitations as may be placed upon the size, weight and concealability of his armament. One must also consider the single-action versus double-action controversy; the latter being preferred (sometimes demanded) by individuals and departments who do not feel comfortable with the public image or safety factors involved in carrying the SA gun "cocked and locked," or with the additional operations necessary to get into action hurriedly with the same type carried in "condition two" with the hammer down on a chambered cartridge. If the gun is to be carried openly, or only moderately concealed, then the big 45 autoloaders win hands-down. In SA configuration, this gives us a choice between the Colt, Star or Llama. Again, the Colt is generally to be preferred. If the gun is to be more closely concealed, then the shorter Colt Commander and even shorter (and lighter) Star Model PD are the only logical choices. I prefer the Star, because of its lighter weight and factory-standard adjustable sights. However, you can't go wrong with the lightweight Commander. If the double-action capability is required, we have very little choice in 45 caliber, with the SIG/Browning and SIG/Sauer (identical guns) and H&K P9S constituting the entire field. However, Llama is introducing their new double-action 45 auto scheduled to go into production in the latter part of 1980. Beyond that

there are no production-model DA 45 autos, though the Seecamp DA conversion of the Colt is a semi-production item and probably more available than the models mentioned.

If size, weight or other overriding considerations preclude use of the 45, as a practical matter we drop down to the 9mm Parabellum, and a choice may be made from a large number of guns in this caliber. In the single-action field, the Browning HP is, in this scribe's opinion, the best choice. Its durability and reliability are almost legend. In the double-action field, only the S&W M39/59 is sufficiently smaller than the Colt GM to merit serious consideration. The Walther P38 is too clumsy and bulky, and the other DA models currently available are just as big if not as heavy as the Colt. The M39 in particular is unusually thin, flat and compact, and with its aluminum-alloy frame, is quite light at $26\frac{1}{2}$ ounces. It is large enough to qualify as a full-scale service sidearm, yet compact enough for full concealment under almost all but the most exacting circumstances. In fact, the only smaller and/or lighter 9mm pistol is the single-action Star BKM.

Up to this point, we've made no specific reference to magazine capacity. Most 9mm pistols have a magazine capacity of eight or nine cartridges, with one more in the chamber giving a total of nine or ten rounds. Currently, only the Browning HP and the S&W M59 deviate from this; the former carrying 13 in the magazine and the latter specifying 14, but usually capable of holding 15. Thus, fully charged, the Browning offers 14 shots and the M59 16 shots.

Many individuals and some departments lay great stress upon the desirability of large magazine capacity. Because of limitations in grip size, such large

The Colt Government Model, in the Argentine version with hammer down on chambered cartridge.

With a chambered cartridge, hammer at full cock and manual safety on.

capacity is available only in 9mm and smaller calibers. Thus, if it is demanded over all other considerations, nothing larger or more powerful may be used.

Demanding such large magazine capacity also forces one to use either the Browning or the S&W M59. The former is available only with the wide magazine, so no comparison can be made there. On the other hand, the M59 is little more than the M39 with its butt widened to accept a double-column magazine. If one compares the M59 to the M39, it becomes quite obvious that a considerable penalty in bulk of the butt is paid for the additional seven cartridges. As already mentioned, the M39 is quite concealable, while the M59 does not do nearly so well in this respect.

Technically, the large-capacity double-column magazine offers a substantial advantage in sustained fire power. Consequently, where it may be obtained without compromising any other requirements, it should by all means be chosen. If you're determined to use a 9mm single-action pistol for defense and it's to be carried openly or lightly concealed where the added bulk causes no problems, by all means choose the 14-shot Browning. If the requirement is for a double-action pistol, then I say the same of the 15–16-shot S&W M59. But don't under any circumstances compromise other desirable gun characteristics solely to obtain the larger magazine capacity. If, for example, the 45 would otherwise be your choice, but you switch to 9mm just to obtain an extra half-dozen shots per loading, you're working in the wrong direction.

Greater magazine capacity is great *after* all the other requirements have been met. In this respect, the S&W M39/59 offers a unique combination. One may carry the M59 openly or lightly concealed for its larger number of shots, then switch to the otherwise identical M39 with nine shots when more concealment becomes necessary. The two guns function in the same manner, are operated identically and differ very little in handling and feel. Thus, one is far less likely to make a mistake when switching say, from a Colt GM service gun to a Walther or Astra when being carried concealed.

Actually, the time, effort and money which one is willing to invest in achieving maximum proficiency with a defensive sidearm is far more important than the choice of the gun and the cartridge. The most powerful gun you can buy is of little value if you don't learn to get it into action in a hurry and place its bullets correctly. Looking at it from another viewpoint, a man carrying a 32 auto with which he can hit well is far more deadly than a man carrying a 45 with which he is only passingly familiar.

Any defensive arm smaller than those already described is at best a marginal choice. Below the 9mm in power, we have a wide variety of 380 ACP autos in both SA and DA types. And most of those same models are also available in 32 ACP, with a few of them offered in 22 LR as well. One is even also available in 25 ACP (the HK-4), though such a diminutive and underpowered cartridge in a gun of this size seems little short of ridiculous. A gun shooting a cartridge less powerful than the 9mm Parabellum should never be chosen for defensive use unless considerations of great concealability force you into it.

In this respect, many people attach far too much importance to mistaken concepts of concealability. They simply purchase the smallest available gun on the assumption that it will be more concealable than a larger model. Generally speaking, this isn't true—for example, the 9mm M39 and Star BKM may be

With empty chamber and the hammer at half-cock.

concealed on the average adult under street clothing equally as well as most 32 and 380 autos. Yet countless thousands of individuals choose the smaller guns.

Many individuals go even further, choosing diminutive 25 and 22 autos for concealed carrying under conditions which would actually allow them to carry the Star or S&W. The only conditions under which I can condone the selection of the very small autos and cartridges is when one is forced to wear abbreviated attire such as swimming trunks or shorts and a T-shirt. Much more suitable (and larger) guns can be concealed quite well under a sport shirt worn with the tail out, even if one's only other garment is a pair of shorts.

In the final analysis, the best choice of a defensive arm is the most powerful gun/cartridge combination which circumstances allow you to carry and the most powerful which you can handle with a high degree of proficiency. Choosing anything less makes you a poor insurance risk.

Target autos are the most precise short guns made. Fed with the finest ammunition and handled and maintained as intended, several makes and models will place ten consecutive shots into (or nearly into) a one-inch group at 50 yards/meters. Frankly, it takes a great deal of experience and training before one can even appreciate—much less extract—the accuracy potential from the better target autos.

As far as domestically produced guns are concerned, there are actually quite a few choices. In the 22 field, the several variations of the High Standard Supermatic and the S&W M41 constitute the entire field. There are even fewer choices in the centerfire field. For those matches requiring 45 caliber, there is exactly *one* such target gun manufactured in this country today; the Colt Gold Cup MKIV. However, the same gun is also acceptable in U.S. (and some foreign) competition for so-called "centerfire" matches often shot with smaller calibers. If this particular factory model doesn't meet your requirements, then you must step out of the production-gun field and spend several hundred dollars more (over the $320 Colt price) for a carefully custom-crafted product from one of the better pistolsmiths.

In the centerfire match field, we find only one production model available, the S&W "38 Master," Model 52. Priced over $320, it contains unique accuracy-producing features not found in other production autoloaders, and with flush-seated 38 Special

The unusually flat configuration of the Smith & Wesson M39 makes it easier to carry than most comparable pistols.

Smith & Wesson offers the only "centerfire match" pistol as a factory production model in the M52.

"GENTLEMEN, CHOOSE YOUR WEAPONS"

In the author's opinion, the Walther P38 9MM is too bulky and clumsy for its caliber. It is an 8-shot automatic pistol with a 4-15/16″ barrel.

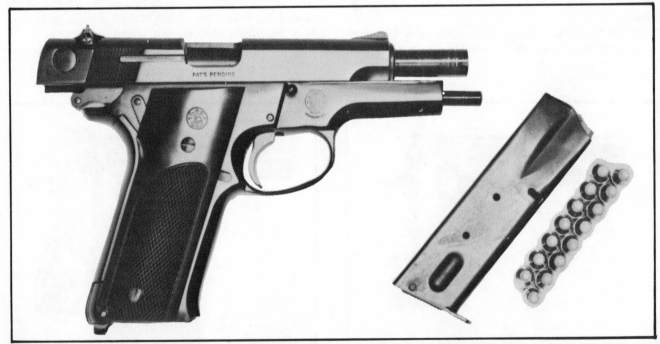

Smith & Wesson's Model 59 is usually described as a second-generation M39. Both guns share many features, but the M59 employs a 15-shot staggered magazine rather than the single-column eight-shot magazine of the M39.

wadcutter ammunition of the midrange type, it has established a most enviable world-wide reputation for superb accuracy. While I can envision few shooters who wouldn't be satisfied with this single available choice, there are several highly sophisticated foreign models from which one might choose if he wished to spend upward of $600. Walther offers its GSP model in 32 S&W caliber, and there is the SIG/Hammerli P240 in 38 Special. If none of those meet your exacting requirements, there are several custom pistolsmiths in this country who will convert the 38 Super Auto or Colt GM to 38 Special and then modify and accurize it to almost unheard-of accuracy.

After all that, though, my recommendations for a *practical,* competitive battery would be the S&W M41 in 22 caliber, the S&W M52 in 38, and the Colt Gold Cup in 45.

In this chapter, we recommended only a very small number of guns for specific purposes. As mentioned, a quick skim through SHOOTER'S BIBLE will show literally scores of other makes and models which are commercially successful and, therefore, must certainly serve useful purposes. They do, of course, and countless thousands of pistoleros choose them based upon various personal opinions, prejudices, economy, and other intangible factors. I find no fault with this at all, and, in fact, own and use several dozen such guns regularly. To me, though, they are *secondary* choices and while they are certainly a lot of fun to shoot (and for some very narrow and specific purposes they are unsurpassed), I feel that the basic selections outlined in this chapter are the best that can be made. My opinion is based upon a good many years of personal experience and association with some of the most noted pistoleros the U.S. has ever produced.

Chapter Four
Auto Handling and Marksmanship

By the time the autoloading pistol came along and was generally available to the public, both single-action and double-action revolvers were widely known and had established enviable records for practical accuracy. By the term "practical accuracy," we mean simply the degree of accuracy that is produced by the combination of both the *mechanical accuracy* of the gun and ammunition and the marksmanship skill of the shooter.

At the risk of seeming superfluous, I want to point out that the most accurate auto you can obtain (and there are those which will shoot one-inch groups at 50 yards) can't make up for the shortcomings in the shooter's skill. Conversely, even a marksman of Olympic caliber can't consistently hit a two-inch target with a gun capable of producing only five-inch groups. We must work from the assumption that the would-be marksman is using a gun capable of at least average mechanical accuracy for the type, make and

model. Even this will vary widely with 22 rimfire autoloaders *generally* being more accurate than the run-of-the-mill centerfire models—with the exception, of course, of those specially tuned and accurized target models supplied by a few makers and dozens of custom pistolsmiths.

It is for this particular reason that we strongly recommend that the neophyte pistolero begin his training with a 22 rimfire autoloader chambered for the Long Rifle cartridge. Perhaps the chambering advice is unnecessary, in view of the fact that the only successful autoloaders in this class which do not use the LR cartridge are those very costly and sophisticated models made for Olympic rapid-fire competition and chambered for the 22 Short. In view of ammunition costs, it would be nice if we could buy a Ruger MKI, a High Standard or a S&W auto for a reasonable price that would perform well with Shorts. Unhappily, we can't do that, but even the 22 LR

22 rimfire cartridges come in a variety of sizes. The BB Cap, 22 Short, 22 Long Rifle and 22 "Stinger". Of these, all but the 22 BB Cap will function in autoloaders. The BB cap may be fired, but it lacks the power to cycle the action and must be loaded singly and ejected manually.

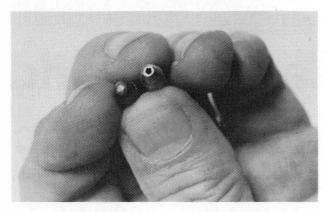

22 cartridges are available in solid or hollowpoint bullet styles. The more expensive hollow point is unnecessary for practice and may not be quite as accurate as standard velocity loading.

per-shot cost is less than 15 percent of, say, the 9mm Parabellum. For the beginner, the 22 rimfire offers other advantages over the centerfires, including but not limited to minimum recoil, minimum jump and report, simplicity of design, ease of care and maintenance, and at least in some models, lower cost.

There are two schools of thought on the selection of the beginner's gun. One is that he should purchase the very best (and, therefore, most expensive) modern and sophisticated model possible. The reasoning behind this is that if he shows respectable progress and wishes to stick with the game, he'll want the very best gun eventually, so he might as well get it from the start. That sounds great in theory, but today guns of that type range from well over $200, with more than a few priced in the $500 range. That's pretty steep for a beginner, and I personally feel that there are less expensive guns which provide a degree of accuracy that is entirely adequate to see one

through his entire training phase, and which will meet all of his needs, even if they do lack sophisticated features such as dry-firing devices, adjustable triggers, compensators, etc.

I'd also like to point out that a gun which is properly zeroed or targeted and which is thereafter used with the same loading can meet the beginner's needs with fixed sights of good design. Admittedly, initial targeting requires a bit more care and ammunition, but once that has been done, such sights will do the job quite well.

With all that in mind and at the risk of being accused of plugging a friend's product, I would suggest the Ruger 22 autoloader as a beginner's gun. If keeping the cost at a bare minimum is of paramount importance, the "Standard Model" with its fixed sights will do quite well, particularly if a bit of additional weight is added beneath the barrel in the form of a length of lead wire (the type used for swaging bullets), taped to the underside of the barrel. If a few more bucks can be spared, then the Ruger MKI with its heavier barrel and target-type adjustable sights is perhaps a slightly better choice—though quite frankly, its mechanical accuracy is no greater.

As for beginning ammunition, first of all, don't spend extra money for high-velocity or hollow-point loads. They're great for hunting, and sometimes more fun for plinking, but the standard-velocity load is the one to use because it is usually at least a little bit cheaper, often a bit more accurate and its recoil and report are slightly less. If you shop around for sales and specials at department and discount stores, you'll often find ammunition priced quite low and by laying in a thousand rounds or so, you'll be able to save a substantial amount. Likewise, don't spend extra money for "match" ammunition until you're good enough to utilize its accuracy.

However, before ever picking up the gun and long before feeding it cartridges, there are quite a few other things to be learned in preparation.

First of all comes learning proper sight alignment. One must align the front and rear sights so that the shooter's eye sees the rear notch with the front blade centered in it (that is, equal amounts of light visible between both sides of the rear notch and the front sight). In addition, the top of the front sight must be flush in the notch with the top of the rear sight. This sounds simple enough in the telling, but it takes a bit of training and experience to get the alignment exactly right and to repeat it correctly time after time.

This alignment can be learned and practiced on the gun, the only problem being that there is no way to check it against a known standard, or any way for anyone else to check it for you. No matter how well you align the sights, an observer or a coach can't view them from exactly the same distance and position and determine how well you've done—and we all know how good most of us are at checking ourselves, particularly when there's no way to retain that alignment and view it later.

Consequently, you might make a bit better progress in the beginning if you used a sighting and aiming device which is easily fabricated. This gadget costs nothing, being cut out and put together from a piece of stiff cardboard with a little bit of black ink or paint applied. The inner face of the back should be white or at least a light color to give the proper contrast.

The rectangular notch at the bottom of the front piece represents the rear sight, the separate rectangular piece represents the front sight, and the round black disc represents the bull's-eye, which we'll get to shortly.

Take the device in one hand and insert the front sight element between the two layers of cardboard at the bottom; then position the front sight so that it is properly aligned in the rear-sight notch, centered laterally, with the top flush with the top of the rear sight. Don't spend more than a few seconds doing this, then lay the device down, look away for a moment, and recheck it. If there's any slight deviation that you didn't notice originally, the second look will usually make it clear. Actually, if you've a companion around, hand the device to him for checking. He may be even more critical than you. You may think this practice is boring, but it will stand you in good stead when you pick up the gun.

Now, familiarize yourself with the *complete* sight picture which includes the two sights properly aligned but with the bull's-eye added in its proper place. The circular bull should be perfectly centered laterally above the front sight, with its lower arc just barely touching the center of the top of the front sight at exactly six o'clock. The game is the same—start with both separate parts out of the device, then insert the front sight and align it correctly, then insert the bull from the top and position it properly. When both are in place, make whatever minor adjustments are necessary to get the whole picture exactly right, then check or have it checked as before.

After a bit of practice with the sighting and aiming device, it's time to have a go with the gun—but no *shooting* yet. Make doubly certain the gun is empty, verifying that by opening the action, looking into the chamber, and then as a double-check, poking a bent piece of wire in as well. Grasp the gun, raise it to eye

This diagram shows proper alignment of front and rear sights but improper placement of target in relation to sights. At the top is shown a mock-up of the bull's-eye and three shots as they would group with the sight picture.

Sight alignment with a real handgun is more difficult than with a diagram. This shooter has a bit too much front sight for a normal hold. This much sight, in most instances, would cause a high bullet strike.

Known in military parlance as the "raise pistol" position, this is the way to start, with the gun firmly grasped and the finger out of the trigger guard. He is facing the target directly, which is *not* the proper position for shooting one-hand, NRA-style.

The body is rotated to the left (for a right-hand shooter) forty-five degrees or more, the feet spread slightly and supporting the weight evenly.

level and line up those sights. You'll discover that it's not nearly so easy to do with the sight on a two to three-pound gun out at arm's length; however, with the practice you've had on the sighting and aiming device, you'll know exactly what you must see.

Don't worry yet about a bull's-eye; concentrate on bringing the gun up, taking only a few seconds to align the front and rear sights correctly, then lower the gun for a short rest and repeat the process. You'll be surprised at the number of repetitions that it will take to tire your arm and make your eyes water; as little as 15 to 20 repetitions of such unaccustomed action may be all you can handle in the beginning. As soon as it reaches the point where you feel eye strain and it becomes difficult to hold the gun with the sights in alignment for a few seconds, it's best to take a break and relax.

After each short session on the gun, go back to the sighting and aiming device. There probably isn't much resemblance between your first efforts on the gun and the neat, sharp picture you can produce with the device. Yet in order to do the kind of shooting you're hoping for, you'll eventually need to reach the point where the sights on the gun are aligned just as neatly and precisely, and you can keep them that way for several seconds.

Next comes aligning the sights on the gun and the *keeping* them that way while you align them with bull's-eye; but still no shooting. This needn't be don on a range at a formal target, nor even done outdoors Just paint a penny or similar-sized coin flat black an tape it to the wall of your den at about shoulde height. Then, back off about ten feet, raise the gu first align the sights, and then bring the sights int their proper relation to the bull.

At this point, you'll most likely discover that whil aligning the sights was simple enough without muc attention to your body position, adding the target t the picture makes the cheese a bit more binding. S we'll digress here into the subject of stance and hold.

The function of your shooting eye is to align th sights and target; the function of your trigger finger to squeeze the trigger and fire the shot while th sights are properly aligned on target. All the rest o your body serves the single function of providing support or platform for the gun while those action are taking place. In military parlance, your entir body becomes a "gun platform." And the human bod isn't all that stable a platform when it's standing stil It's a wondrous machine for movement, but it's n worth a damn at standing upright and stationary. pulses and twitches, flutters and breathes, sways

he gun is then thrust forward and lowered, aligning
with the target. As it comes down, minor changes in
e position of the feet may be necessary to line the gun
 with the target.

As the gun levels on target, the wrist and elbow should
be "locked". Shoulders and hips should be as nearly as
level as possible, and the chin should be tucked into the
shoulder so that the shooting eye falls directly behind
the sights without any great physical effort.

he amount depends mainly upon the physique of the
ooter, but the head must be twisted or turned a good
al toward the gun to align the eye with the sights while
ill keeping the gun aligned as nearly as possible with
e long bones of the arm.

A more downward view of the subject of the last photo-
graph which illustrates the difference in alignment
between gun and forearm, and also illustrating the
straight high-thumb position.

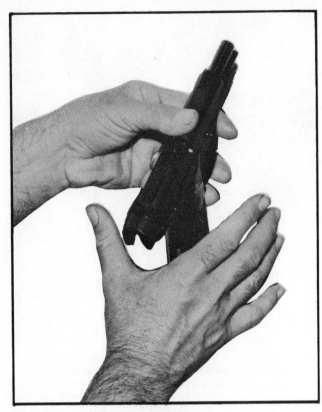

Pick up the gun with the off hand and transfer it to the shooting hand.

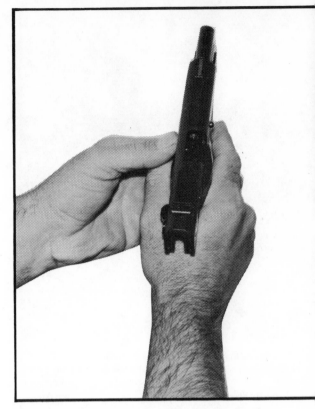

To properly position the gun in the shooting hand, use the off hand to seat it.

the wind, and under pressure, it trembles and twitches. Even rifle shooters stretched out on their bellies and laced up in leather coats and shooting slings can't hold completely still.

But it isn't all that discouraging, for by developing a proper stance and practicing it, along with a few simple breathing and body exercises, you could reach the point where the gun may be held well enough to place all of the bullets in the black with at least most of them in the ten-ring.

The idea is to plant yourself as firmly as possible on your two feet, hips fairly level, and weight balanced. At the same time, your body must be positioned with respect to the target so that you can hold the gun properly (barrel in line with the long bones of your forearm) and so that you can get your shooting eye lined up behind the sights.

Determining this position involves standing facing the target (that blackened penny on the wall) with the gun in your shooting hand. Raise the gun and point it at the target, and you'll see quite readily that there's no way you can look through the sights and still have the gun aligned with your arm. Okay, turn away from the target (to the left for a right-hander) about 45 degrees, extend the gun again, and look over the

sights at the target. Juggle the position, keep you feet some 12 to 18 inches apart, and keep juggling th position until, with the gun in line with the forearr you can look through the sights at the target. Depen ing on your build, it's quite likely you'll have to tu your chin into your shoulder—that's not bad, becau firm contact there helps steady everything.

The angle with respect to targets that allows all th is one you'll have to work with for quite a while; yc may wind up changing it slightly as you gain exper ence, but that's in the future.

Now, still with an empty gun, assume the pos tion—the "stance"—that you've discovered, bring tl gun up, align the sights a bit below the target, the raise the gun to bring the sights up into prop alignment with the bull's-eye. As soon as you feel yc have all three elements (front and rear sight ar bull's-eye) in precisely the correct alignment, low the gun, take a breather and repeat the exercise. It almost inevitable you'll find yourself getting thin *almost* right, then sweating and straining to ma those last corrections, to the point that your han start trembling, the gun starts dancing, and your ey feel like someone is working them over with a vacuu cleaner. The harder you try to squeeze out that l

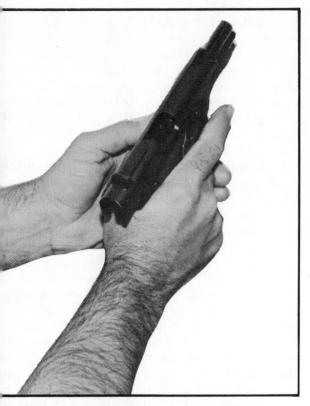

rap three fingers of the shooting hand around the ont strap.

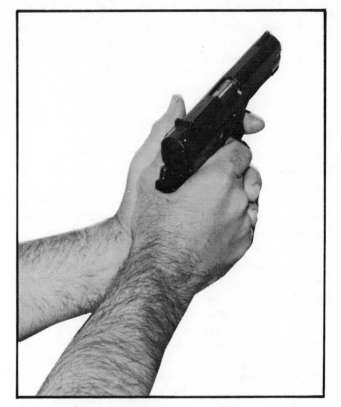

The thumb of the off hand is not used to grip the pistol but helps maintain alignment.

t of precision, the more you tremble and the worse e sight picture looks.

Don't be alarmed; this is perfectly normal. This is oided by relaxing a few moments before each tempt, breathing deeply to oxygenate your system, erhaps closing your eyes, taking one long, last, deep eath as you bring the gun up, then letting about half it out and attempting to obtain the proper sight cture in only a few seconds. Concentrate on the ghts, and if you can't obtain the proper picture in ve to ten seconds, quit, back up, relax and breathe, d try again.

Even expert shooters find themselves trying too rd and taking too long, and have to back off. eally, you should align the sights with one another the gun comes up, and then go right into alignment ith the bull, taking no more than two to four conds. Taking longer, at least in the beginning, sults in nervous and muscular tremors in the hand d arm, and the eyestrain we've already mentioned. his isn't meant to be discouraging so early in the me, but to be reminded that in shooting rapid-fire ages, you'll have considerably less than two seconds recover from recoil and obtain the proper sight cture. This is not at all difficult with practice and is

the goal toward which you're working.

You'll most likely at some point discover that you're not certain the sight alignment is correct. You'll start guessing whether the front sight is high enough or low enough or too far right or too far left in the notch. Again, when that happens, don't start sweating and straining over it, but simply put down the gun and work with the sighting and aiming device until you once again have the precisely correct sight picture fixed in your mind. The goal you're seeking is more-or-less *instinctive* alignment without conscious thought, like your feet automatically work the clutch, brake and accelerator of your car in smooth coordination with your hand on the shift lever.

Okay, now with stance and sight picture under control, it's time to get into the exercise known as "dry fire." This consists of snapping the gun on an empty chamber while keeping everything else right, especially the sight picture. It also consists of preserving momentarily the mental image of exactly where the sights were in relation to the bull at the instant the hammer fell. This is known as "calling the shot," and when actually firing, it enables you to tell approximately where each shot strikes on the target, even though you can't see the bullet hole.

Dry fire introduces trigger control and trigger squeeze, and you can't accomplish that without having the proper hold on the gun.

Work on the latter first; don't pick up the gun in your shooting hand and expect to be grasping it correctly. Instead, pick the gun up in your off hand and carefully position it firmly in the shooting hand, following the photo sequence. The upper portion of the back strap is first seated firmly against the web between the thumb and forefinger, then the butt is rotated downward against the heel of the hand; the bottom three fingers are then wrapped tightly around the front strap and the thumb extended forward without bending it down. The thumb isn't used to actively grip the gun; its role is more or less passive, aside from forming a pocket or seat for the back strap. While doing all this, remember to keep the barrel parallel to the forearm.

Position the pad of the first joint of your forefinger in approximately the center of the trigger; note that this leaves the finger fairly sharply curved with space between it and the frame of the gun. Keep it this way; the trigger finger should contact no part of the gun between the trigger and the grip. The finger should be free to move without interference.

Now, before lining up on the target, practice pulling the trigger with the gun held so that you can look

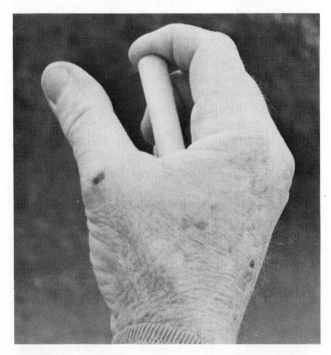

A short piece of dowel can be employed to practice trigger squeeze. It may be used in places where it's not acceptable to show a gun.

down on it from above. With the gun cocked, press the trigger *straight* to the rear, familiarizing yourself with the amount of resistance to be overcome, and watching carefully to ensure that the muzzle isn't forced to either side by incorrect trigger movement. If you allow the finger to move to the left as it comes backward, the muzzle will likely twitch left as the hammer drops; and the opposite effect will be produced if the finger moves to the right.

To achieve this degree of control over your trigger finger, you've got to educate the rest of your hand to remain completely immobile (all the time gripping the gun securely) while the trigger finger moves. This sounds easy, but, as in most things done with your hand, the thumb and other fingers instinctively react to or oppose movements of the forefinger. If those digits are allowed to do this while you're pulling the trigger, the gun will move. The essence of trigger control is keeping the gun as motionless as possible (at least with respect to the hand) as the trigger is pressed rearward. By watching the gun closely while you "feel" the trigger, you'll be able to tell when the rest of your hand is getting out of control. If the hand tenses up or resists the trigger finger, the gun will move in the hand. It's better to train your hand and trigger finger in this fashion before attempting dry fire on a target.

While the foregoing is probably best done with the gun properly grasped, you can get a lot more practice by using a short length of dowel seated between the finger tip and web of the hand. You can carry the dowel in your pocket and practice wherever you might be, something that can't be done with the gun. Taking a gun out of your pocket or briefcase and practicing the trigger squeeze while waiting in a crowded dentist's office might be cause for criticism; but you can do it with the dowel and no one will be the wiser. Anyway, position the dowel, and then practice pressing it *straight* to the rear with the trigger finger; watch the dowel in the process, and if it tips to the left or right, you know the tip of the finger has moved in the same direction rather than straight to the rear. A few minutes of this two or three times a day will do wonders for your trigger control.

Once you think you have that whipped, it's time to assume the proper stance, align the sights and target, and carefully squeeze the trigger until the hammer drops.

Follow the same procedure as before, align the sights as the gun comes up, then move into alignment with the target. However, now you should also start applying light pressure, taking up any slack as the sights are aligned, and, as they come into alignment

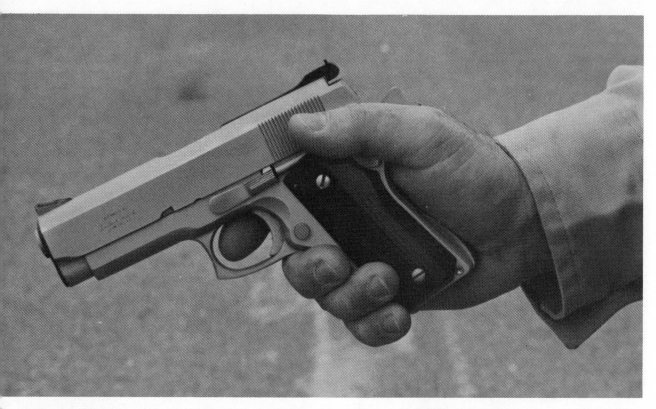

Here we have a different grasping problem: That of a lighter and smaller gun (a Behlert 45 Bobcat) intended for defensive use. A tighter and more convulsive grip is required, and in this photo the thumb has not yet been turned down and clenched inward as it should be. The short butt does not provide sufficient space for all three fingers, so they must be clenched together somewhat, and the smallest digit is clamped over the front cover.

with the bull, applying greater pressure. Then, while maintaining the correct sight picture, continue the trigger pressure until the hammer drops.

About now you'll discover that while it's not difficult to keep the two sights correctly aligned, it's impossible to hold them in rigid alignment with the bull's-eye. The sights will be in almost continuous movement around the six o'clock point of the bull; that movement will generally describe a horizontal figure eight about the six o'clock point. Don't become alarmed; this is normal, and even the best shooters experience it to some degree. In the beginning, the lateral extent of this rather regular movement may be much greater than the width of the bull. However, with continuous practice, you'll be able to narrow it substantially.

The ultimate goal is to control it within the width of the bull. The most common tendency among beginners is to break up the trigger pull, attempting to apply brief pressure only when the sights are closest to the bottom of the bull. That's wrong; pressure should be continuous and unbroken even though the

sights keep drifting back and forth. So long as the trigger pull is completed smoothly and without disturbance of the gun, the bullet will still strike the target within the limits of the visible movement. Even though the limits of this movement extend beyond the bull (at least in the beginning), the usual distribution of a series of shots will place the majority of the bullets in the black.

On the other hand, if you try to snatch the trigger at the instant of precise alignment, the gun will be substantially disturbed, twitch aside, and the bullet may not even strike the target at all. Of course, you're not shooting live ammunition, so the game at this point is to maintain the image of the sight/target relationship at the instant the hammer drops. This will give you a good idea where the bullet would have struck had one been fired, and after a few hundred "dry shots," you'll be able to go to the range and put all this into serious practice with live ammunition.

Switching to live ammunition introduces the new factors of report and recoil, but with the 22 rimfire, they are minimal and should not present any great

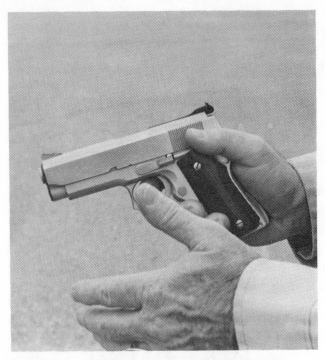

Circumstances permitting, the off hand should be used to provide additional gun support and control.

The hand moves in, the forefinger hooking over the front of the trigger guard, and the remaining fingers wrapping around those of the right hand.

The shot goes off and, in this instance, the gun is caught at the peak of recoil and lift. It may appear that the gun has no contact with the supporting hand, but there is some contact.

The empty magazine is out, the finger is clear of the trigger (remember, there's still a round in the chamber) and the charged magazine is being thrust into the beveled magazine well.

PISTOL GUID

The two-hand hold is completed, ready for the first shot, but the gun is still being raised toward eye level to permit the use of the sights if desired.

The gun is up to eye level now, sight alignment is achieved, and if it hasn't been necessary to fire earlier, the shot can now be more carefully planned.

The magazine enters the butt smoothly and, at the same time, the proper shooting grasp is being re-established on the gun.

As the magazine encounters the resistance of the magazine catch, the left hand is rolled slightly and the magazine is rammed fully home with the heel of the hand. Now the gun is rolled and pushed back into firing position.

There is no elaborate posturing as the gun hand sweeps down to grasp the butt and begins drawing the gun out of the holster.

The gun is lifted almost clear of the holster, the trigger finger has started toward the trigger and the thumb has begun cocking the hammer.

problems. The fact that you've switched to live ammunition doesn't eliminate the need for frequent use of all the exercises described up to this point. It is significant that even the best shooters usually warm up with dry-fire exercises each time before loading up to shoot for the record. Many of those same people perform the various exercises at home every day, whether or not any actual shooting is done. So, if you can only get to the range once or twice a week for live firing, stay with daily dry-fire exercises to keep in trim and to improve your control of the shooting situation.

Once you've begun shooting live ammunition, it's really just a matter of continuing practice and very careful attention to detail.

You should show slow but constant improvement in group size and numerical score on target, but this is likely to be cyclic, with scores perhaps dropping slightly one week from those before, but then climbing to represent an overall improvement the next week.

In other words, a graph of your scores against time would show a zigzag line that generally rises. When live-firing results drop badly or seem to go completely to hell, a short layoff and reversion to dry fire and the other exercises will help pull you out of the dumps.

All of the foregoing may imply that handgun shooting is entirely self-taught. Well, if no help whatsoever is available, it certainly can be. However, progress will be substantially faster and slumps can be cleaned up quicker if you have a coach. The ideal situation would be one in which the coach was himself (herself) an experienced and accomplished shooter. However, that's by no means necessary. Even a non-shooter can familiarize himself with all of the exercises, observe your performance carefully, and determine when you're not doing things quite right. An observant coach who has never fired a shot can help you a lot and can discover lapses on your part before they become apparent to you. Even your favorite girlfriend who hates guns can be of considerable help simply by reading this dissertation and then observing your actions carefully.

Perhaps we should have mentioned this at the beginning of the chapter rather than now, but a good many people today who are proponents of the "point-and-shoot" system of defensive shooting tend to belittle bull's-eye training and marksmanship. They contend that since defensive use of a handgun generally involves very rapid firing, at large, sometimes vague targets moving at unknown distances, often without the use of sights at all, that the type of

he gun is clear and cocked, the thumb is moving down
ward its proper position, the trigger finger has entered
e guard and the gun is being thrust forward.

The gun is fired! Note the fired case directly above the
gun and, in particular, the fact that the firing cycle has
been completed. The lengendary tremendous recoil and
jump of the 45 auto is not evident.

ooting we've described has no "practical value." I
isagree very strongly with this approach, for a thor-
ugh grounding in basic marksmanship has been
roven to improve one's performance in any form of
ooting. As far as it being of no "practical value," the
ility to deliberately hit a precise target is the
ssence of all types of shooting.

No matter what use you might eventually intend to
make of your autoloaders, a thorough grounding in
basic, known-distance marksmanship on ring targets
cannot help but improve your performance. Toward
that end, learn properly at the beginning and you'll
encounter a lot fewer problems along the way.

Chapter Five
Care and Maintenance

In the beginning, it was believed—and rightly so—that an autoloading pistol would not function well unless kept almost surgically clean and very carefully lubricated. Certainly this was true to varying degrees with most of the designs produced during the first three decades of the "automatic era." Some of the earliest reasonably successful designs had built-in mechanical problems which were at least partially alleviated by proper cleanliness and lubrication.

It must be remembered that, for the first couple of decades after autoloading pistols had been proved to be practical, many designers in the field actually did not understand the problems of either gun or ammunition. Further, there was a tendency (one we see often enough today in numerous fields) to place in production a design not fully developed in order to cash in on the tremendous market potential that had been uncovered by Browning and other superlative designer/inventors of the period. Then, too, many designs were overly complex. Remember that cartridges, ammunition-manufacturing techniques and guns developed more or less concurrently, and for

a few decades, people really weren't sure what an autoloading pistol *should be*.

The various principles of operations were still under development, and the most desirable ones that we know so well today had not yet been fully developed and refined to definitive form. Also, standards of reliability had not been established, and more than one design was forced into reasonable commercial success by national pride, high-class advertising and public relations work, even though it achieved substandard levels of performance. Or they were inordinately complex and costly to manufacture. Classic examples of this are the Parabellum/Luger, even in its definitive 1908 version, and the terribly impressive Mauser of 1896.

The former isn't intended to repeat information, rather to point out that the myths and legends we still encounter today regarding care and maintenance of such guns had valid roots in early designs. Early autoloaders of, say, the pre-World War I period, often did require very meticulous maintenance in order to produce even mediocre functional reliability and

A maintenance nightmare, the Mauser "Broomhandle" survived only until less complex, more easily serviced pistols became available. Now sought by collectors, the ungainly Mauser served in two major wars before retirement.

accuracy. It isn't economically practical today to go back and test those early designs, but if one studies contemporary literature carefully, it is easy to ascertain that at least some of those early guns required a good deal of babying.

Without meaning to detract from the other arms geniuses of the period, we must point out that the Browning/Colt design adopted as the "U.S. Pistol Caliber 45, M1911" by the U.S. Army achieved a record high in reliability and durability, and, at the same time, required a minimum of care and maintenance. The Browning design, as refined by Colt, outstripped its contemporary competitors by a most substantial margin in these respects. Doubtless there are those who will take issue with that statement, but to them I say simply, "Look around and tell me what other pre-World War I design autoloader is still being manufactured, is currently a significant commercial success, is still in wide military usage, is adapted to all of the major centerfire handgun cartridges, and is still widely used for virtually every purpose from highest-level marksmanship competition through plinking, hunting, law enforcement, and military service?"

The answer to that question is *none,* for all "Colt 45" contemporaries are long dead and buried. The Mauser, the Webley-Scott, the various Mannlichers, the Steyr, and their companions are all gone. Only the Mauser and the Parabellum/Luger survived World War I, and they survived this long only because of national pride and the existence of war-time tooling which made them immediately available in the early 1930s. The Mauser went first, and the Parabellum was quickly dumped as soon as adequate production capacity for the replacement Walther P38 could be built up.

Before someone points it out to me, I'll acknowledge that Mauser Werke did produce more Parabellum pistols in the late 1960s and early 1970s. But, there was never any pretense that they were intended as *service* pistols, and were made simply for the Luger enthusiasts willing to pay a very high price.

In any event, care and maintenance of modern autos (by which we mean the Colt/Browning and various copies thereof) and the big-bore service-type autoloaders designed and placed in manufacture since the early 1930s is really quite simple and easy. In fact, it's less of a problem than with a typical modern revolver.

For the job, you need just a few tools and supplies. Here are my suggestions: One or more screwdrivers of good quality with bits carefully ground and polished to fit screw slots precisely. High-quality Allen wrenches for some guns like the Auto-Mag which uses socket-head screws. Any special tools required by a particular gun, such as a barrel-bushing wrench. A few assorted needle files. Sturdy one-piece cleaning rods. A tight-fitting brass-bristle brush for cleaning the bore. An over-size brass-bristle brush for cleaning chambers. Assorted plastic or soft-metal scrapers and diggers for neglected guns. Short pin punches to fit any tight pins found in a particular gun. A good,

bore-cleaning compound (Hoppe's No. 9 is still ha[rd] to beat). A good synthetic preservative. Patche[s] wiping cloths, a plastic pouch to contain the greasy materials, a canvas or leather roll for the tools, and a piece of felt or carpeting on which to work.

A new gun that's been fired only a few hundred rounds under reasonably good conditions presents no care and maintenance problems whatever. So let's begin with something a bit more difficult, say, a well-used Colt 45 Auto you've just acquired and

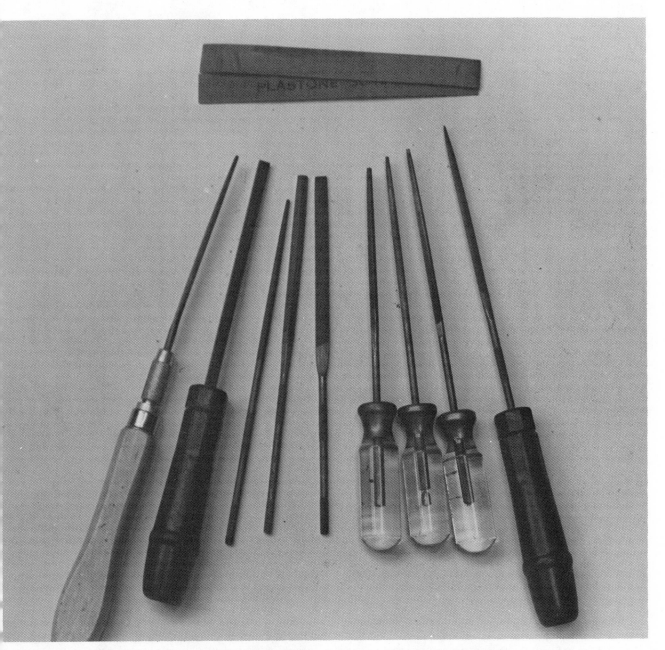

In addition to the usual solvents and patches, scrapers and needle files are a big help in cleaning up long-neglected guns. Judicious use is the key factor. Don't attack the metal, just the rust and fouling.

about whose history you know nothing. We'll assume it's been neglected a bit and thus has accumulated dirt, fouling and debris over the years. Keep in mind that while we're discussing the Colt, the procedures will apply to any centerfire autoloader.

First, check the gun thoroughly for functioning, preferably by firing a dozen or more rounds of full-charge service ammunition. Make a note of any malfunctions that occur, since more thorough cleaning may eliminate the problem.

Field-strip the gun using an exploded view as a guide, and if you're not thoroughly familiar with the gun, lay the parts out carefully in the sequence they are removed so you won't encounter problems in reassembly.

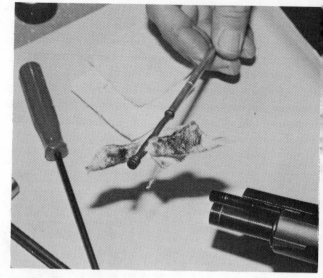

Patches that look like this indicate the need for more scrubbing inside the barrel. Even after a bore is thoroughly clean, some blackening of the patches may be noted from the deposits of gilding metal that remains in bore.

Firearms assembly handbooks published by the NRA contain exploded views and disassembly instructions for guns frequently encountered by today's shooter. They are inexpensive but a must for the gun owner who needs to know how to strip and reassemble a firearm properly.

Start with the barrel. Use a new tight-fitting brass-bristle bore brush dipped in solvent and scrub the bore thoroughly. Wipe the bore with dry patches until it is completely dry; a wet bore will look shiny and clean when it isn't. If it doesn't look clean at this stage, continue the scrubbing, but there is no need to remove all of the thin copper wash that may be present on the rifling. But if your sensibilities simply can't stand the presence of that copper wash, then use a bit of J-B Bore Polishing compound on a tight-fitting patch to polish it out rather than scrubbing with the brush. Incidentally, the bore can be thoroughly clean otherwise, while patches may still show a dark stain from the copper wash.

Once the bore is thoroughly clean, take a look at the chamber. More often than not, the chamber is over-looked, even by people who clean the bores quite well. You need a special over-sized brush for this job, and in 45 calibers I use either brass, shotgun brushes or a 50 caliber machine gun cleaning brush. Using plenty of solvent, force the brush all the way into the chamber, then rotate it while pushing it in and out. Keep this up until you've gotten all of the powder fouling out of the forward part of the chamber. A gun that's seen a lot of shooting and hasn't been properly cleaned may have a substantial accumulation of very hard powder-fouling coating the forward third or half of the chamber, and it may stubbornly resist efforts to remove it. When that happens, chuck the chamber-cleaning brush in an electric drill set on slow speed, and spin it in the chamber until all the residue is removed. Extraction and ejection problems and short-recoil malfunctions are often due to rough fouling in the chamber causing the case to grip the chamber walls more tightly than usual. In especially stubborn cases of chamber fouling, it might be necessary to wrap a bit of very fine steel wool around the brush and spin it in the chamber. The chamber won't be damaged by this; nevertheless, go easy, and quit as soon as all the fouling is gone.

Switch to the outside of the barrel and remove all dirt and fouling. Use an old toothbrush to scrub out the locking lug recesses, the barrel lug, the mouth of the chamber and the barrel tang, etc. Examine the

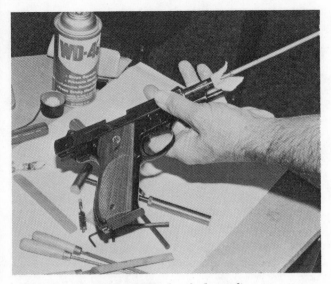

A tight-fitting patch is used to dry the bore after treatment with a solvent-soaked brass brush. At hand are files, mallet, screwdriver and solvent.

chamber mouth and muzzle for burrs, and if any are noted, remove them very carefully with a scraper or fine-cut needle file. Wipe the barrel down lightly with preservative, inside and out, and set it aside.

Take the slide and remove all the small parts from it: firing pin and spring, firing-pin stop, extractor, etc. Slosh the entire slide in a pan of solvent—or, lacking that, hot water and plenty of detergent—to make certain liquid enters all the holes and recesses. Use small brushes (small caliber, bore brushes, toothbrush, typewriter brush, etc.) to scrub out all of the small holes and recesses. If you find caked debris that won't yield to this treatment, use small plastic or brass scrapers to dig it out. Scrub out the locking lug recesses in the slide, and pay particular attention to the assorted grooves and slots in the underside at the rear. Make sure all caked debris is removed. Scrub out the front of the slide and the recoil-spring tunnel as well, using snug-fitting brushes. These areas are usually neglected. Also make certain the slide breech face (where the cartridge head is supported) is thoroughly cleaned. Look the slide over for burrs and remove any that are found, especially where they might interfere with the movement of other parts.

A final sloshing in solvent will wash away the loosened debris, then stand the slide on end to drain so none will be trapped in the holes and recesses. This can be speeded up by using an ear syringe to pump jets of air into the holes to blow out the liquid. When all the holes and recesses are free of solvent, spray

lightly with preservative, and again set the slide u▓ that the excess can either drain away or be bl▓▓▓ away.

Scrub off the small parts from the slide, including the recoil spring and guide and look especially for any kinks, foreshortening or breaks in the various springs. A kinked or bent recoil spring can cause failures to feed, and the same defects in the firing-pin spring can cause misfires or slam-fires. After all the excess preservative has drained from the slide, reassemble the small parts to it.

Occasionally the Colt mainspring (also similar models) will be gummed up with oxidized grease and oil or other debris inside its housing. This can cause poor functioning, misfires, and harsh trigger pull.

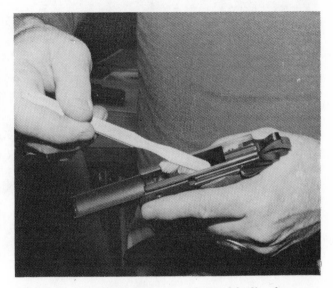

Utilize an old toothbrush to remove dirt and fouling from the mouth of the chamber.

This is especially true if the housing assembly was of military origin and dipped in melted cosmolene as was once the practice. The only way to be sure is to completely disassemble the housing and scrub the deep spring seat and all small parts completely free of grease and dirt. Then apply preservative lightly and reassemble the entire unit.

Drop the magazine into your pan of solvent and, with the stocks removed, slosh the entire receiver group in the solvent. This will flush out most of the loose debris, and if you leave the receiver submerged for a while, the solvent will loosen the hard stuff. Give the receiver group exactly the same treatment as the slide; remove all the small parts and carefully scrub or

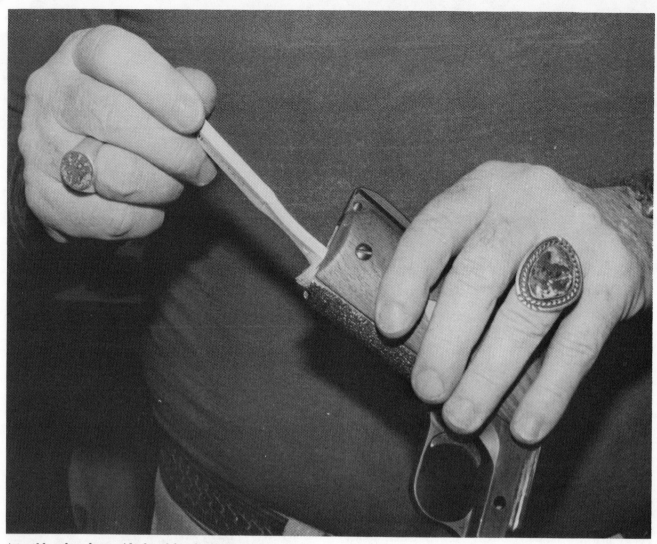

A toothbrush makes an ideal tool for cleaning.

scrape out all recesses and the interior. Clean up the small parts the same way and remove any burrs that might be found.

Once everything in the receiver group is cleaned, lightly spray the inside of the receiver with preservative and drain or blow away the excess. Leave all the small parts to dry for the moment, and after you're certain that they're all serviceable and undamaged, apply molybdenum disulfide grease very sparingly to all rubbing, sliding or rotating friction points and areas *except* the sear nose and the sear notches in the hammer. Reassemble the small parts to the receiver, then spray in only the tiniest amount of preservative.

We're now ready to put the gun back together, so assemble the barrel to the slide, then take a swab or Q-Tip wet with acetone and clean all preservative from the guide grooves in both receiver and slide.

Apply molybdenum disulfide grease sparingly in those grooves, and also apply it on the underside of the slide where it contacts the disconnector and the hammer face in cocking. If the barrel bushing is quite snug on the barrel, apply molybdenum disulfide grease sparingly around the muzzle as well. Reassemble the entire gun, and it should function much more smoothly and freely than before.

Now that you *know* the gun is thoroughly clean, it won't require such an extensive cleaning job for many hundreds of rounds.

Don't forget the magazine you dropped in the solvent. It may look good on the outside, but chances are it's clogged internally with dirt and lint caked with hardened oil. Disassemble it completely, scrub off the follower and spring, and then use whatever means are necessary to get the inside of the magazine

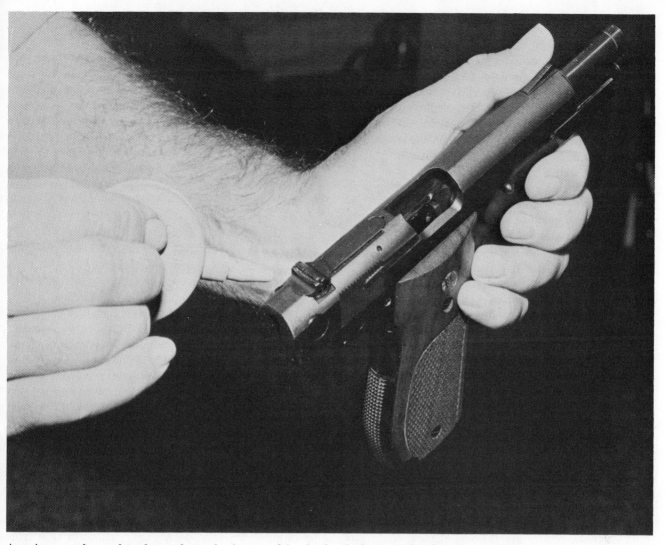

A syringe can be used to dry pockets of solvent and is also handy for removing dust from hard-to-reach places.

body completely clean. A cut-down toothbrush or even a percolator or small bottle brush can be used. Wipe the interior lightly with preservative and reassemble.

The gun is now probably cleaner than it's ever been in its life. From now on, only minor cleaning will be necessary after each shooting session. Essentially that means field-stripping the gun, cleaning the bore and chamber, and removing powder fouling and unburned propellant granules from the slide breechface and adjacent areas of the receiver with a toothbrush and patches. Wipe the cleaned areas with preservative, reassemble, and the job is done. Don't attempt to remove and replace the molybdenum disulfide lubricant between slide and receiver. Its affinity for metal is so strong that it can't be rubbed off, and a virtually invisible coating is quite adequate

for superior lubrication. Don't attempt to relubricate the gun by spraying it inside and out from an aerosol can after each cleaning. It actually requires very little lubrication, and what it is given after its thorough cleaning will be quite sufficient for many hundreds of rounds. When you do pull it apart again for a thorough scrubbing inside and out, even the solvent will not remove the working layer of molybdenum disulfide lubricant. Consequently, only the tiniest trace need be added in the appropriate areas when reassembling the gun.

What we have just gone through pertains essentially to all centerfire autoloaders; however, the very costly and sophisticated target guns share with the very small pocket guns a greater sensitivity to ammunition variations and a much-reduced tolerance for dirt and fouling. Consequently, guns of these types require more careful, more frequent, and sometimes more thorough cleaning. This is especially true of full-house customized and accurized 45 and 38 Autos wherein the original design tolerances that give the basic gun its superior reliability have been greatly reduced to improve accuracy. In regard to guns of this type, too frequent disassembly is considered by many to reduce their accuracy life, and this introduces further complications into cleaning.

While not many big-bore autoloaders are yet made of stainless steel, experience with the Auto Mag indicates that lubrication is critical. The makers of the Auto Mag (and perhaps some others as well) supply a special "space-age" lubricant with the gun and specify its use. When such a situation is encountered, by all means follow the manufacturer's instructions as to type and method of lubrication. When you come up against this sort of situation, forget what I've written here and do what the manufacturer or pistolsmith tells you. The stainless steels generally used in firearms manufacture do have a disadvantageous tendency to gall where two similar surfaces rub or slide under high contact pressures. Only the special lubricants can alleviate this problem. Fortunately, the smaller stainless autos of less powerful calibers don't seem to experience this problem, probably due to looser fits and less contact pressure.

Essentially everything we've said applies equally well to autos chambered for the various 22 rimfire cartridges. However, the rimfires introduce yet another problem. Virtually all 22 RF ammunition is loaded with swaged soft lead bullets. In addition, the bulk of these bullets are lubricated by a coating of wax or waxy grease, though some high-velocity loads are copper-plated. A good deal of the bullet lubricant is sheared or wiped off during feeding, and accumulates around the chamber mouth and on the slide breech face. In addition, when cartridges do not feed with precise accuracy, slivers of lead and lubricant combined are sheared off the bullet by the chamber mouth. Thus, it is inevitable that after only a relatively few rounds are fired we have an accumulation of lubricant and lead built up in the breech. As if this were not enough, propellant combustion is often incomplete, and unburned or partially burned granules of powder also accumulate in the breech, mixed with the usual sooty form of powder ash or residue. Most of the better guns are designed and made so that after a certain amount of this mix has accumulated, any addition is forced out.

These same guns display an amazing tolerance for this mess, and many of them will continue to function for thousands of rounds with a mass of this gook in the breech. However, if one cares for his gun at all, this debris should be carefully cleaned out after each shooting session. Done that way, it is easily removed while still soft. If allowed to accumulate for too long, it becomes quite hard from heat and pressure and then can be removed only by digging and scraping. Done regularly before this happens, it requires only a moment or two with small brushes and solvent.

Many of the better target-type 22 rimfire autoloaders are equipped with muzzle brakes or compensators. Others contain gas-escape vents at 12 o'clock in the barrel near the breech. Both vents and compensators are traps for powder fouling and bits of lead and lubricant. If allowed to accumulate over any extended period of firing, this material becomes quite hard and difficult to remove. Compensators that are not cleaned regularly will eventually fill up to the point that the hardened fouling will actually distort bullets as they exit, destroying their accuracy. When this stage has been reached, nothing less than a scraper or reamer will cut the material out. That presents no great problem with the compensator inasmuch as minor damage to its interior won't interfere with the gun's accuracy. However, if gas-escape vents near the rear of the barrel are allowed to fill up with caked residue, cutting it out may very well result in burrs being turned over in the bore. These burrs will certainly deform bullets to a slight extent and produce a deterioration in accuracy. Consequently, it is exceedingly important that gas-escape vents in the barrel be frequently and very carefully cleaned.

Don't get the impression from the foregoing that cleaning is predicated only upon shooting. Far from it, in fact, many guns which are never fired actually need cleaning quite often. The hideout gun carried in a hip pocket will accumulate all manner of lint, dirt and grit in a relatively short time. Such accumulations can cause malfunctions and may also result in excessive wear. A gun carried in this fashion should be wiped down and blown out quite frequently. If you doubt this, take a look at a gun that's been carried in this fashion for several days—you'll find lint and dirt literally clogging some of its clearance cuts and orifices. As long as the gun has not been wet, this material can be blown out quite easily with compressed air, any form of air syringe or even the exhaust from mama's vacuum cleaner.

Guns carried concealed beneath clothing and next to the skin or underclothing require even more frequent attention, even if plated or made of stainless steel. They accumulate acid body moisture and thus will deteriorate rapidly if not cared for properly. Even a first-class holster doesn't provide a great deal of protection for a gun carried under your arm beneath a shirt in the summertime. The gun will be constantly damp, if not actually wet and should receive prompt attention each time it's laid aside. A gun carried in a belt holster, especially by a police officer who's out in all sorts of weather, should be given a minor cleaning and wipedown at the end of every period of use. A gun, carried in the glove box of a farm or ranch truck, will most certainly be clogged with dust and grit in very short order. Leave that gun in there untended for a couple of weeks while the truck is working the fields, pastures and dirt roads, and it may be clogged badly enough to malfunction when you need it. Even the auto laid casually in the bureau drawer among your socks and drawers against the possibility of a late-night intruder will need periodic cleaning. I've seen "bureau drawer" guns literally filled with lint which had combined with lubricant to form a thick, soggy mass which would certainly interfere with, if not prevent, firing.

Guns carried afield for any protracted period of time, for whatever the reason, require daily attention, and may require it even more often. You'll never see a good platoon sergeant or squad leader let his men bed down for the night without checking their weapons and cleaning them as needed. It has ever been thus, for just recently I was reading again the journals of Lewis & Clark (concerning their epic expedition from St. Louis to the Pacific and back in 1804–1806), and frequent reference is made to daily cleaning of weapons or "putting our guns in order."

Care and maintenance quite naturally extends to protecting the gun from the elements, from damage and from excessive wear. When the gun is carried on one's person (or, in a vehicle for that matter), it is in need of a holster or other covering. Military establishments have always recognized the need for this protection better than most and have invariably provided commodious holsters with close-fitting flaps or covers which serve not only to keep out dirt and moisture, but to protect the gun from impact. Professional pistoleros (law officers) don't usually care for flaps or covers simply because they feel this might interfere with getting the gun into action in a hurry. Civilians seem to feel the same way, but I think the fear is more imaginary than real and that their guns would benefit substantially from holsters that enclose them entirely.

Guns taken to matches should be protected by being kept in a tightly enclosed shooting box or in the common and more economical "pistol rug." Guns kept around the house should be isolated from the dust, grease and dirt circulating in the average residence. Since most people want to keep their guns where they can be seen, a tightly built glass-fronted cabinet or display case is probably the best bet. However, it needs to be fitted with some means of ventilation so that rapid changes in temperature and

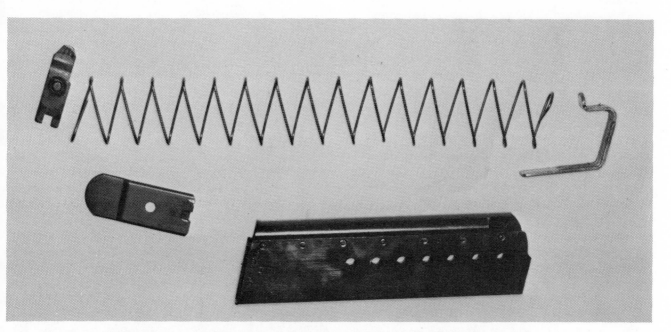

Some magazines are difficult to disassemble and must be bathed in solvent to be cleaned. Others can be disassembled and the parts cleaned by wiping. Be careful when removing the spring because it is easy to deform if allowed to bend over the magazine edge.

Silica Gel in bags or cannisters helps to prevent moisture from forming in closed spaces such as gun cabinets.

humidity won't produce rust-generating condensation inside. In areas of high humidity, some mild heat source at the bottom of the cabinet or case is particularly desirable and need be nothing more than a 15- or 20-watt light bulb.

Bags of fresh silica gel may also be placed out of sight in cabinets to prevent rust and if you don't mind the appearance, sheets of VPI (Vapor Phase Inhibitor) paper hung beneath the guns on the walls will also do the job very nicely. If guns are kept out of sight in drawers, silica gel and VPI paper should also be used. If guns are displayed openly and guests or friends are either encouraged or allowed to handle them, a silicone wiping cloth should be kept right along with them and used after every handling. The perspiration acids of some individuals will produce rust on a fine gun in a matter of only a few hours. The only sure way to guard against this is to either lock the guns up where they can't be touched, or keep a wiping cloth handy and make certain it is used every time a gun is handled.

In the final analysis, proper care and maintenance of your autoloaders requires nothing more than plain common sense. Look closely at the gun frequently, and if you see any accumulation of dirt, lint, grit, moisture, etc., then it needs at least some cleaning. And if you see that such accumulations occur frequently, then the gun needs more protection from everyday hazards.

Proper care and maintenance of any handgun actually requires very little time and hardly anything in the way of tools and supplies. Considering that one may very well invest from $175 to more than $500 in a good gun these days, it would seem that regular maintenance would be well worthwhile.

Chapter Six
Holsters and Carrying Gear

The belt holster, as a means of carrying a multi-shot sidearm, had become fairly well developed by the time the autoloading pistol became a practical reality. In centuries gone by, the various single-shot and multi-barreled pistols—ranging from the matchlock up through the cartridge revolver—had been carried in almost every imaginable manner. "Gentlemen" carried small screw-barrel pistols in cuffs, boot tops, waistcoat pockets, tucked in the waistband, and in probably every other position and manner since "discovered" by some modern pistolero. "Ladies" carried diminutive pistols in their muffs, bustles, bodices (who the hell said a bra holster was new?), and a lady of the evening, less likely to be encumbered by voluminous petticoats and overskirts, might have a small pistol tucked into a garter. Old engravings show less savory citizens such as Blackbeard and Kidd with a brace (or several brace) of flint pistols tucked in a voluminous sash and dangling from a broad shoulder belt whose primary purpose was the support of a cutlass or other edged weapon. Somewhere along the way, the belt hook developed and sees some resurgence today. Usually a simple springy brass arm

secured solidly on the off side of the gun, it served to slip inside the sash or waistband with the pistol outside, or vice versa. Among the military, pistols were large, heavy, clumsy, and single-shot. Generally only mounted troops and officers possessed them, and to be sure of being able to get off at least one shot, a pair was carried in matching holsters slung over the pommel of the saddle.

In any event, the belt holster and companion types we know today didn't become common until after the advent of the percussion revolver. The same may be said of the gun belt. At the dawning of the present century, autoloaders became practical and several types of belt holsters had become common, as had the pouch-type shoulder holster, the cross-draw holster, and a variety of gimmick designs, most of which spring up again periodically and die away nearly as quickly.

In the early days of autos, much effort was expended to devise a holster/stock combination which would allow the gun to be instantly converted for use as an autoloading carbine with much greater rapidity of fire than the bolt-action military rifles of the day;

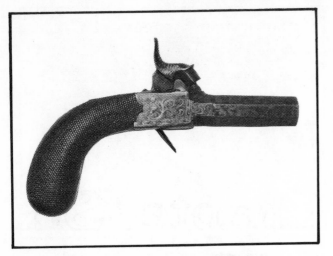

This tiny caplock dates from the mid-1800s. With its folding trigger and overall small size, it was probably intended to be concealed in the bearer's clothing.

remember, this was before the advent of the submachine gun or machine pistol at the end of World War I. Best known of this type is the wood holster/stock supplied with the Mauser M96 and later pistols. It was just that: a wooden holster shaped like a rudimentary butt stock, hollowed out to completely enclose the gun, fitted with a hinged wooden lid that doubled as a butt plate when secured, and fitted at its other end with a metal attaching device matched to a slot in the grip frame of the gun. This probably derived from the earlier Borchardt pistols manufac-

tured in Germany. Close on the heels of this came the so-called "board stock" for the Parabellum (Luger) pistol to which a more conventional leather holster was attached by straps. The Parabellum system apparently never went beyond Mauser-Werke. The earlier wood Mauser holster/stock was copied at least in principle in several places, was copied directly in Spain for the Star pistols, and for Browning pistols used by Canadian and other armed forces during World War II. The fact remains that the holster/stock, as a method of converting a belt-size pistol to a light carbine, was never very practical, and became even less so after the advent of the low-cost, compact, lightweight submachine gun. Still, the idea continues to crop up periodically, and currently Heckler & Koch (West Germany) manufactures its VP70 with a molded plastic holster/stock. With the stock detached, the gun is capable *only* of semi-automatic fire, but when the stock is installed, it automatically activates a full-auto fire-control system with limited burst length. Incidentally, to the best of this scribe's knowledge, the VP70 has the highest cyclic rate of fire in the full-auto mode of any pistol-type weapon, on the order of 2200 rounds per minute. No wonder bursts are limited to three or five rounds automatically.

Today, holsters for autoloaders are just as varied as those for revolvers. With the exception of military establishments, which generally use all-encompassing flap-type covered holsters, almost all big-bore

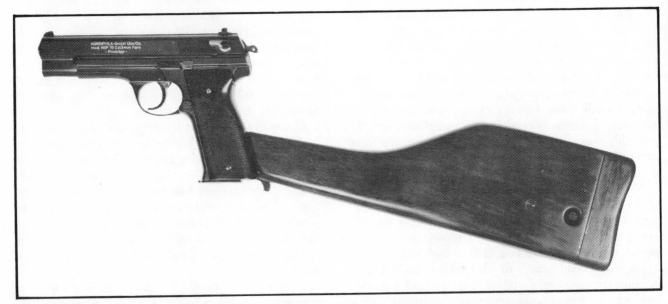

Holster/stock combinations were in vogue prior to World War I and died out for the most part with the acceptance of the machine pistol. Both the Mauser and the luger pistols were equipped with shoulder stocks during the war but few recent efforts to popularize holster/stock combos have been made. A notable exception to this is the prototype shown.

autoloaders are carried in a basic belt holster of open-top type, much more often than not fitted with a safety strap which may be disengaged quickly without extraneous motions as the draw is started. A few law enforcement agencies, notably the Illinois State Police, carry such autos in a military-type flap holster of cross-draw style.

The basic belt holsters may be classed by their vertical position with regard to the waistline (actually the gun belt or trousers belt). There is the high-ride which places the butt of the gun above the waistline; the drop-loop which generally places the butt about even with the waistline (but may place it a good deal lower since there are varying lengths of "drop" offered by different manufacturers), and last, the swivel holster in which the holster proper is permitted to rotate fore-and-aft about a metal pivot attached to a separate belt loop. Usually the swivel holster places the gun lowest of all, but it comes nowhere near the low-leg position that films and television show for 19th-century gunfighters.

Each of these three types has specific advantages.

First, the high-ride design is best suited for concealment under a coat or jacket, though a fullsome cut is needed if the bigger guns are not to announce their presence by a substantial bulge.

The conventional drop-loop holster is the best choice for ordinary exposed carrying of the bigger guns, so long as one generally remains on his feet. When seated, this type often makes the gun more

The Heckler & Koch VP70, shown here without a stock, is capable of semi-auto only unless the stock is attached. With the stock in place, a controlled limited burst capability is in operation.

or less inaccessible by jamming into the chair or seat cushion and cocking the gun at an awkward angle or trapping it in the upholstery. This is particularly true when seated in an automobile.

The swivel holster is probably best suited of all the conventional belt types for carrying the bigger guns exposed when riding in a patrol car. The holster proper can be rotated to place the gun in a readily accessible position as one sits down, and this can become very important.

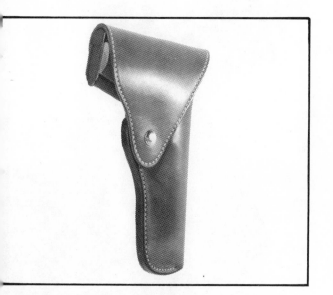

Military-style holster, such as this Bianchi, provide maximum weather and dust protection, but they make drawing slow and cumbersome. A few European police departments favor holsters similar to this and many hunters consider them to be superior to any other type.

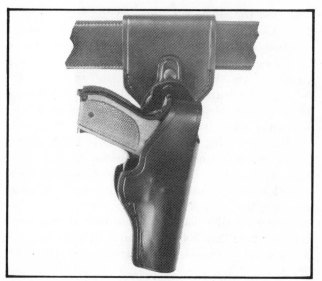

Swivel holsters, such as this Smith & Wesson Model B29, are used by many law enforcement agencies. The swivel holster places the gun in an extremely low position, but this holster can be swiveled forward for comfort when you sit.

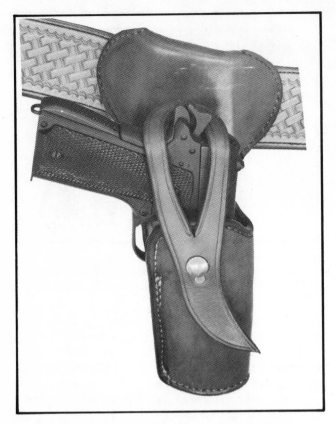

Drop-loop holsters are suitable for carrying large-frame pistols if most of the gun-toter's time is spent on his feet. Most of these holsters place the gun butt on or below the user's waistline.

One of the oldest variations on the belt holster is the cross-draw type. It's as old as the percussion revolver and was (still is) favored by military users. For a right-hander, the cross-draw holster is positioned high on the belt, over or slightly in front of the left hipbone, with the gun angled at about 45 degrees to the horizontal, but forward. It possesses one advantage over other belt holsters in that in addition to readily presenting the gun to the right hand, simply reversing the left hand allows a quick and easy draw to be made as well. Even though we've mentioned the swivel holster as being excellent for wear in an automobile, the cross-draw rig is even better. We mentioned earlier that the Illinois State Police use a military-type flap holster for carrying their Smith & Wesson autos, and it is a cross-draw type for this very reason.

For those still carrying the gun at the waist, "inside-the-pants" holsters have become fairly popular in recent years. They're usually very skimpy holsters made of relatively light leather (to reduce weight and bulk) which are slipped between the waistband and your shirt or whatever else you're wearing there. They are great for concealing the gun under an ordinary jacket, but unless the gun is quite small, this type really requires the trousers to be one to two inches larger in waist measurement than normal. Pants properly fitted for ordinary wear become uncomfortably tight when any but the smallest pistol and holster is worn in this fashion. These ISP holsters have to be held to the trousers or belt securely in some fashion, or the holster is liable to stay on the gun when you make a quick draw. The most common method is one or more snap loops hanging over the outside to be attached to the trousers belt.

That's not much help in the case of beltless slacks, so a better method uses matching velcro patches on the inside of the waistband and the outside of the holster. A simple leather-covered metal hook (I've also seen them molded of plastic) slipping over the waistband is sometimes used, but those I've seen don't grip the trousers very tightly, and I'd still be concerned with the holster staying on the gun. Admittedly, a good many people carry ISP holsters without any retention device, but when this is done, the holster and gun are likely to slither around and out of position. ISP holsters are available in ordinary style as well as the cross-draw type, and they can be positioned anywhere on the waistband, including the

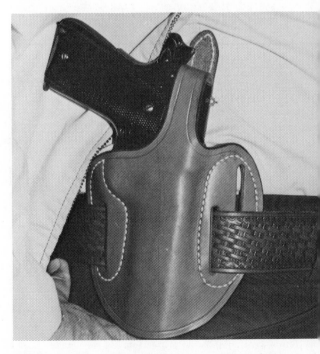

A Baker Pancake holster may be worn as a cross-draw holster or, as shown here, a high-riding standard belt holster for maximum concealment.

PISTOL GUID

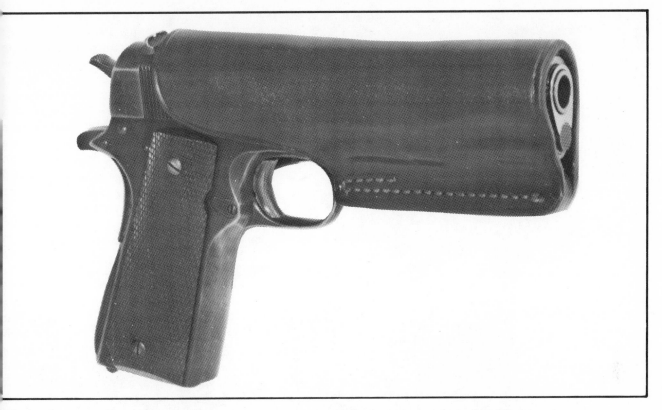

Open belt holsters, with or without retaining straps, are very popular for large-frame autoloaders. The open belt holster, such as this Bianchi, offers little protection for the pistol but provides reasonably rapid access and secure anchorage.

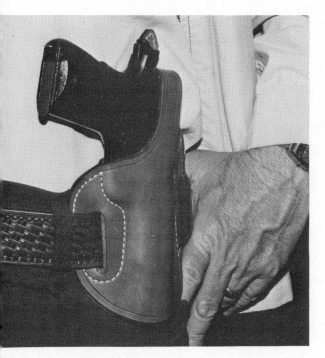

The cross-draw holster is worn on the left side of a right-handed shooter and is positioned high on the belt and slightly forward of the left hipbone.

small of the back, which is a popular concealing position for a spare gun of medium size.

Hip-pocket holsters are by no means new, but have become more popular in recent times for concealing the smaller auto loaders. Usually they consist of a stiff leather panel (which sometimes contains a soft aluminum sheet sandwiched between two layers of leather), sized and shaped to fit the pocket closely, with an abbreviated pouch for the gun attached to it. If the backing piece fits the pocket tightly enough, no additional retention device is necessary, but I prefer a snap fastener or velcro patch as added insurance. Actually, even the largest autos can be carried this way, but concealment isn't so good, especially if one bends over or sits down, causing the butt to push his coat out. Of course, the hip-pocket holster can be bought for either right- or left-hand use, and it's an excellent way to carry a medium-sized auto as a spare gun. A uniformed officer with a big gun exposed on his hip can conceal a 380 auto quite easily in his off-hip pocket against the time when his main gun is lost or out of action.

A wide variety of shoulder holsters is available for autos of all sizes. The conventional, split-front, pouch

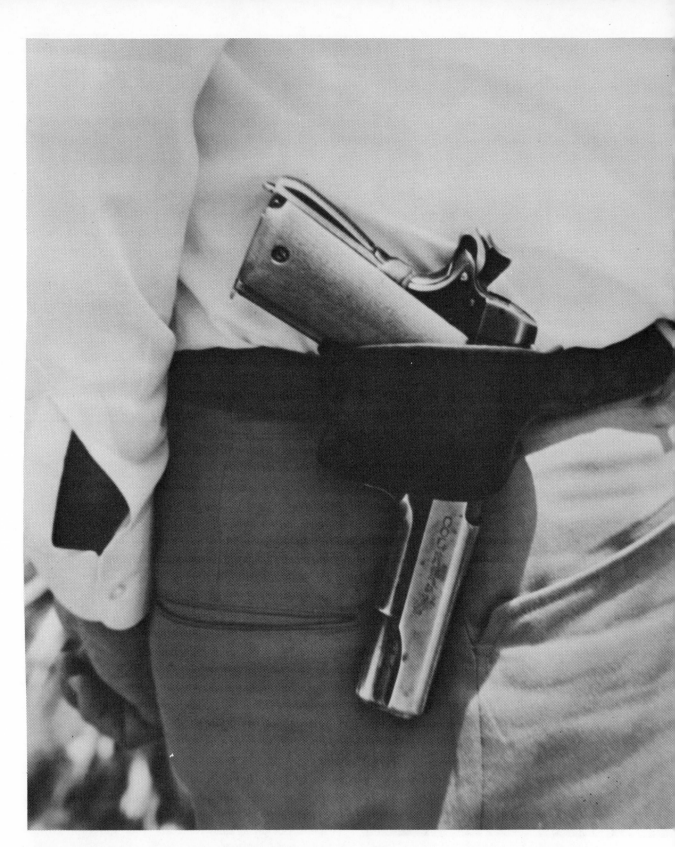

An almost holsterless carry, the belt slide uses minimum leather and provides very rapid access to the pistol. This well-used Colt belt slide is attached to the belt of a seasoned Texas Ranger who says he has tried all sorts of holsters and feels that "the least holster is the best holster."

holster, with or without a retaining spring and/or safety strap is the most common type. The shoulder holster carries the gun butt-up and forward, and is suspended from an inverted U-shaped soft leather yoke riding over the top of the same shoulder. There is an elastic or fabric strap crossing over the back and encircling the opposite shoulder as well, and there may be provisions for attaching the lower end of the holster to the trouser belt to hold it down. One problem with a very long, heavy gun in a typical shoulder holster is that it tends to bounce around a great deal if one runs or engages in any vigorous, physical activity. A more recent development of this basic shoulder holster substitutes for the across-the-back strap a second and almost identical yoke over the opposite shoulder supporting a carrier for one or two spare, loaded magazines. After all, if at least one spare magazine isn't carried, we are throwing away one of the principal advantages of the auto-loader.

A variation of the shoulder holster carries the gun horizontally, butt to the front. The first of this type I saw was made by Paris Theodore of Seventrees Limited quite a few years ago, but it is now featured in the Alessi line. This type holster can be had for any size auto, but the longer guns will bulge the coat significantly unless one is quite chesty. The horizontal shoulder holsters made by Alessi are quite closely fitted to the gun, contain a minimum of leather, with thumb-break safety strap, pull-through safety strap, or no strap at all. Both height and angle of the holster can be varied, and the holster yoke is connected in the back with a second yoke supporting a magazine carrier. The yoke holds the magazine carrier upside down, as is proper, and, again, both angle and height may be varied. Personally, I am quite fond of the horizontal shoulder holster for small autoloaders. When properly adjusted, it positions the gun for ready access and seems to me to work best.

There is another unusual form of shoulder holster which is apparently no longer available. This is the SMZ model previously offered by Seventrees. It positions the gun muzzle-up, generally vertical, by means of a folded piece of polyethelene which is wrapped around the slide and through the trigger guard, to be secured by a one-way snap which is easily disengaged by *simultaneously* twisting and pulling the gun. With a little practice, the gun comes out cleanly and smoothly, yet if grabbed by one not familiar with the proper method of release, it is quite secure. The SMZ holster hangs from a conventional shoulder yoke, and there is a retainer strap extending across the back, around the front of the opposite shoulder and down to the belt.

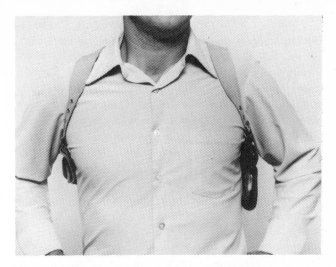

The Alessi shoulder holster features a horizontal carry, butt to the front. This design lends itself well to smaller autoloaders, and the weight of the gun is counterbalanced by a loaded magazine carried on the opposite side.

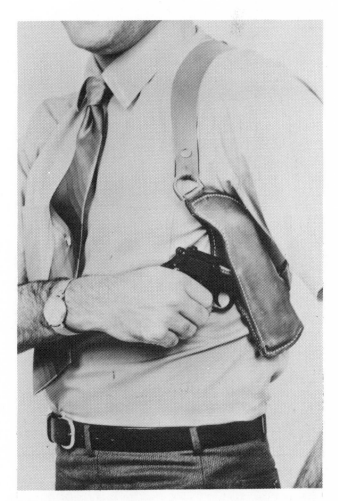

A Bianchi shoulder holster.

Now we get into the more unconventional holsters. Ankle holsters seem to be undergoing a popularity surge. I'm not fond of them myself, but once you become accustomed to the weight and bulk of a gun down there, they do offer a practical way of carrying a *small* auto where the average man on the street won't think to look for it. Officers in plain clothes and off duty, where a coat can't be worn or looks out of place, find the ankle holster an ideal solution for concealing a gun, especially now that flared trousers are widely worn and offer sufficient space. You'd have a hard time concealing the smallest gun on your ankle under a pair of old pegtops, and straightlegs won't do much better, but those flashy flares cover a gun easily without any bulge. Mechanically, the ankle holster is simple; it's merely a broad leather or elastic band encircling the leg just above the ankle bone (though it can be worn higher) and which has attached to it a bare-minimum holster of thin leather. Other variations exist, including one composed of a footless stocking of heavy knit material to which the holster proper is attached. Most likely the ankle holster is a derivation of the wrist holster for derringers that cropped up many years ago.

Things then get even more different.

You can buy a small suede bra holster for the little 22 and 25 autos which your girlfriend can tuck down between her gazongas, and if she's sufficiently stacked, the gun will be well hidden.

You'll find crotch holsters which go inside your pants, and while they offer maximum concealment, they offer minimum access to the gun. The theory behind the crotch holster is that it will pass a routine shakedown. If the wearer might find himself in danger or custody afterward, he'll eventually be allowed to relieve himself and can sneak the gun out at that time and take whatever offensive action is necessary.

Then there's the arm holster. Almost identical to the ankle holster, it's made to be worn on the arm

The ankle holster provides a practical way of carrying a small auto pistol.

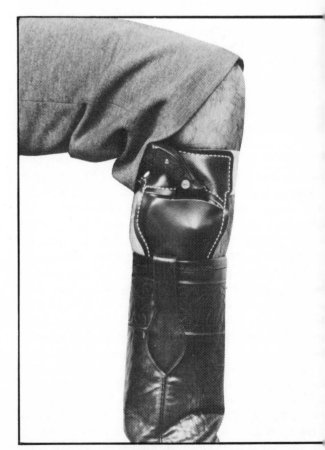

This leg holster is holding a revolver, but this kind of holster is better used for small-frame autoloaders since they are flatter than a revolver and more easily concealed in such a holster.

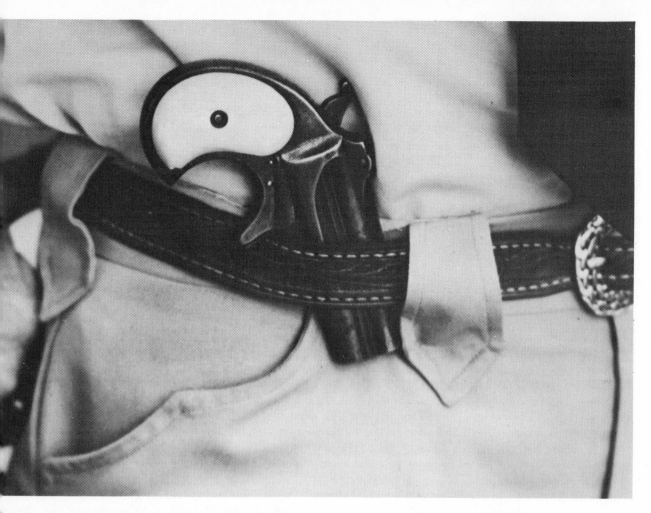

Holsterless carry is suitable for small guns such as this Remington derringer. Unless the gun has a projection in this case the trigger—it may easily slip from its place and slide inside the trouser leg to the ground. Few things are as attention-getting as the metallic clang of a handgun hitting the ground in a public place.

except for the very smallest guns, its use will probably require a very loose sleeve. If you canvass the various, small, custom makers around the country, you'll find an astounding variety of special holsters intended for maximum concealment, and you can probably find a model intended to be worn on virtually every part of the human body. Probably the oddest I've ever seen was a so-called groin holster whereby a very attractive, young lady garbed in a rather full skirt carried a cutdown Uzi submachine gun on the inside of her left thigh. Rather high up, too.

Then, of course, there are those methods of carrying which don't utilize a holster in the conventional sense. Simplest of all is merely dropping a gun in your coat or pants pocket, but this has the disadvantage of allowing the gun to get turned around or snagged in the pocket lining so that you can't get to it in a hurry.

It is much more practical to simply stick the gun in your waistband. I find it works well, especially with the larger autos, to position the gun just over the hipbone on your shooting side. I've also known guys to shove a small auto inside a boot top. Depending upon the boot, the leg and the gun, it can work fairly well, but the gun isn't always very secure.

Then there's the paperbag, laundry or towel trick. It means simply that the gun is concealed inside either of these, and carried loosely in the hand. There are two basic reasons for carrying a gun in this fashion, the first being that one might be so skimpily dressed that there's simply not enough cover to hide the gun. The second reason is that there are numerous circumstances in which one needs to be armed, but might find himself in a position where immediate disposal of the gun is essential to survival, without leaving any evidence of its presence behind. A gun in a paperbag or rolled up in a towel can be pitched under a car, into an alley or even a garbage can, leaving you clean as a hound's tooth.

Of course, holsters are only part of the game. Belt types are obviously supported by a belt; for exposed wear, they'll usually be hung from a gun belt which is carrying other equipment as well. In the case of a uniformed officer on patrol, the belt will also be carrying spare ammunition, keys, flashlight, mace, cuffs, baton, perhaps communications gear, and maybe even a few other items, depending upon local requirements. Add all these things up, and the belt may easily be carrying 10 or 12 pounds of vital equipment. This means it needs to be fairly wide in order to distribute the weight well, and stiff to prevent sagging. Of course, it requires those same characteristics in order to support the gun properly and to keep the holstered weapon in the proper position.

Consequently, the gun belt cannot be just a strip of cheap lightweight leather and do its job properly. For use with the gun alone, it needs to be at least one and one-half inches wide, and even wider when additional equipment is being hung on it. It needs to be first-grade leather and thick enough to be stiff, even if this means doubling the leather. The belt should be a tight fit in the loop on the holster, and if wear creates looseness here, keepers should be provided to prevent the holster from sliding back and forth. Belts are available with the traditional buckle fastener, and to a lesser degree the "buckleless" style, utilizing velcro patches. This makes for a lighter and more compact belt, and it also provides infinite waist adjustment, as opposed to the set positions of the holes in a conventional type. The belt should be fitted over all the clothing that will usually be worn, and in some areas, one may even need two belts; one for summer wear and one of substantially larger size to go over heavy winter clothing.

The once-popular "Sam Browne" belt utilized a diagonal shoulder strap to transfer some of the gun's weight to the shoulder and prevent its dragging at the hip. It seems strange that this design was popular among uniformed officers in the days when the gun belt carried only a holstered revolver, but that now when the belt carries 10 to 15 pounds of assorted gear, it is hardly ever used. Perhaps a return to a modernized version of the Sam Browne would be worth looking into.

All manner of belts are used for carrying concealed guns, usually doing double duty as a trouser belt as well. Concealed guns are usually lighter and more compact, and a belt as narrow as one and one-quarter

inches will do the job if of best quality and if t holster is fitted tightly to it. However, a looser fit the belt is acceptable if keepers are used to positi the holster, or if the trouser belt-loops are position so that the holster will be held in place by them. Ma individuals who carry a gun in this fashion want to able to remove it and the holster quickly as a conv nience.

After all, an external gun belt can be popped off a few seconds, but if the belt is holding up your pan removing it isn't quite so simple. In any event, t has brought about the "snap loop" holster in whi the belt loop is not sewn or riveted permanently at t bottom but is secured by a pair of heavy-duty sn fasteners. Popping the fasteners loose allows the h ster to be removed or installed on the belt wi relative ease. However, this leaves the holster ratl loose on the belt, so it becomes especially desirable use keepers or properly positioned belt loops stabilize it.

One of the major reasons for carrying an autoloa ing pistol is the greater fire power it offers, not only the form of the greater number of cartridges (than t revolver) its magazine contains, but the great rapid with which it may be reloaded under fire with fully charged magazine. With practice, a good au can thus be reloaded in as little as two secon substantially more rapidly than one may reload revolver, even with speed loaders. All this is thro away if one does not carry at least one spare magaz fully charged, and that necessitates a pro; container for the magazine(s) which protects it fr weather and damage and yet makes it immediat accessible. If you like, the magazine carrier may considered simply a "magazine holster." It is a sim rectangular leather pouch carried on the gun b and, if worn exposed, it will usually be supplied wit snap-fastened covering flap.

Magazines are carried butt up as a rule, not only protect the cartridges therein, but to position them that they may be grasped at the bottom and thus ready for immediate insertion in the gun without a changing of the grip. Like the holster, the magaz carrier must fit snugly on the belt so that its posit doesn't change, and, like the holster, it should si an angle and height best suited for the carrier. Ma zine carriers may be made of leather less thick a stiff than holsters, and while the fit should be snug should not be tight enough to interfere with ra withdrawal. Some makers offer holsters with ma zine pouches incorporated in them.

Personally, I do not care for such designs for sev reasons: they make the holster much more bulky, a

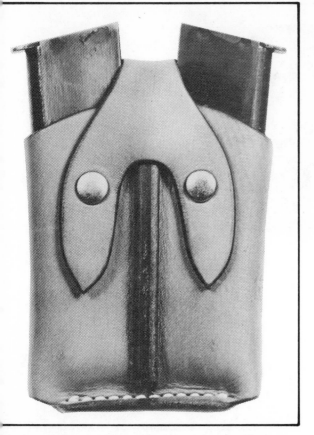

Magazine pouches come in a wide variety of styles. Various makers offer open top, flap top or stap-retained carriers.

When you are selecting the proper magazine pouch or carrier, look for the same qualities you look for in a holster.

Having the spare magazine on the shooting side greatly slows down reloading. Rapid reloading is only possible when the off hand can grab the fresh magazine easily while the shooting hand is ejecting the fired magazine and positioning the gun for reloading. When a shoulder holster is used, hanging the magazine carrier from the harness on the opposite side helps balance the gun, but even under the best of conditions, magazine access is a bit slower than when carried on the belt.

Holster construction and material are important in durability and fit. Cheap holsters are made of cheap leather. Top-grade holsters are made from the best part of the hide, the back. The rest of the hide is used for less critical items such as cuff cases, magazine pouches, keepers, and the like. Big, heavy guns require thick, strong leather of saddle-skirting type.

The typical belt holster is folded to shape from a single "blank" die-cut from the hide. The belt loop is first folded over and sewed, then the body is folded and sewed up along the rear outline. Depending on the design, gun intended, and quality level, narrow strips of leather called "welting" may be sandwiched into the seams. Welting functions as a spacer and also strengthens seams. Sewing may be done with plain cotton thread in cheap holsters, or Nylon or heavy, waxed linen thread in the better rigs. Nylon has ideal characteristics so long as it isn't so thin that it cuts through the leather. Nylon can be strong enough for the job, yet so thin it will cut through. Personally, I prefer heavy, waxed linen shoemaker's thread; it's theoretically not as good as some synthetics, but I like it.

All heavily stressed seams–at holster mouth and belt loops—should be at least double-stitched, and rivet reinforcements aren't unusual. When D-rings or other metal or plastic accessories are attached, rivets are usually better than stitching. Any metal part should be heavily plated to prevent corrosion and its weakening effect on leather.

Some holsters are made by simply folding over the blank and sewing it up. It's made big enough so that the gun can be seated without difficulty, and that is the extent to which it "fits" the gun.

A proper fit is accomplished by "blocking" which consists of wetting the holster, forcing the gun in, and

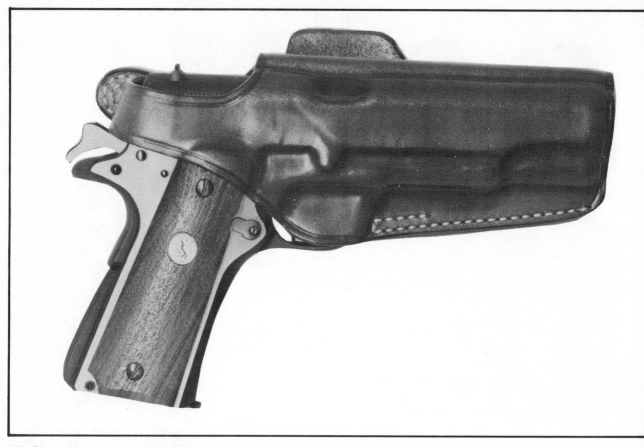

"Blocking" a holster provides an almost perfect fit and helps to keep the gun in the holster in unusual positions. Those who expect to become involved in gymnastics while they are carrying a handgun might do well to invest in one of the factory-blocked holsters, such as this Bianchi.

applying pressure to mold the leather against the gun. In volume production, a dummy gun (usually an aluminum casting) is used, with the holster placed between thick rubber blocks and pressure applied by an air or hydraulic press. The rubber forces the damp leather into close contact with the dummy gun; the dummy is removed and the holster is quickly dried under heat lamps. To speed drying, a volatile liquid, such as alcohol, is used instead of water to wet the leather.

Blocking may also be done by hand. After the gun is placed in the moist holster, smooth, shaped tools are used to force the leather into intimate contact with all the gun's surfaces. The tools are plied, stroking the leather under considerable pressure, the leather is stretched and compressed, and the surface is burnished. This produces the best fit of all; the burnishing closes the pores of the leather, smoothing the surface and increasing its resistance to scuffing and abrasion. Some makers use a small amount of hand blocking to finish holsters which have been machine blocked. It may be to improve fit, or it may

be just to give the rig a more or less phony "hand blocked" look. Some I've seen had slide outline showing on the outside as if hand-blocked, but th outlines didn't even come close to matching the gu inside.

Incidentally, a good holster that has softened an become a bit loose from use can often be salvaged fo several months' more use by being carefully hand blocked over the gun, then dried at a slightly elevate temperature to shrink it just a mite. But too muc heat will ruin the holster forever.

The tendency is all too common to try to sav money by buying cheap leather. It never ceases t amaze me that someone will spend $200–$400 for gun, then buy a poor-fitting low-grade holster just t save a few dollars. Leather gear is no different tha other commodities—you get what you pay for. Th better makers, e.g. Bianchi, Safariland and Hume, se good gear at fair prices; similar items priced lower ar likely to be of lesser quality.

Whether for sporting or professional use, the bes carrying gear is none too good—choose it carefully!

Chapter Seven
Autos and Hunting

In recent years, hunting with handguns has grown tremendously. Such hunting has taken place throughout the history of handguns, but not until the 1920s and 1930s was much ever said or written about it. When Elmer Keith began writing in the 1920s, he repeatedly told about taking all manner of game including elk with revolvers, and he still reports with regularity on such activities. Then, in the 1930s, Smith & Wesson introduced its 357 Magnum revolver, and its use for taking big game throughout North America was heavily promoted as part of the advertising game. Also, during the same general period, Colt advertised its 38 Super Auto as the ideal hunting handgun because of the cartridge's high velocity, flat trajectory, and great power.

These events encouraged hunting with handguns, but it wasn't until after World War II that significant activity in this area began to come to light. The 357 Magnum was the most powerful handgun cartridge available, and we began to see published accounts of its use on all manner of game, though the biggest species such as elk and big bears seldom figured in the story. U.S. servicemen from various parts of the world

reported taking deer, boar and similar-sized game with the ubiquitous 45 caliber Colt Goverment Model and, for the first time, serious interest began developing in taking big game with autoloaders.

During the same period, I shot my first big game with a handgun (previously having limited myself to small game with small calibers) in Europe with both the 45 and 38 Autos. I also used a 40-caliber wildcat revolver, but that's another story. At this time, handgun hunting was still essentially a revolver game, mainly because none of the autoloader cartridges could offer the velocity and power of the 357 Magnum and, also, the 44 Special when properly handloaded.

Then, in the mid 1950s, the 44 Magnum revolver cartridge was introduced, and for the first time, a really potent hunting cartridge for handguns existed. There followed a wave of hunting activity, all North American species being killed with the 44 Magnum. Bob Petersen (Petersen Publishing Company) killed a record polar bear in Alaska; someone reported taking a Kodiak and someone else a grizzly, and in a relatively short time, every other large species was reported downed with the 44 Magnum.

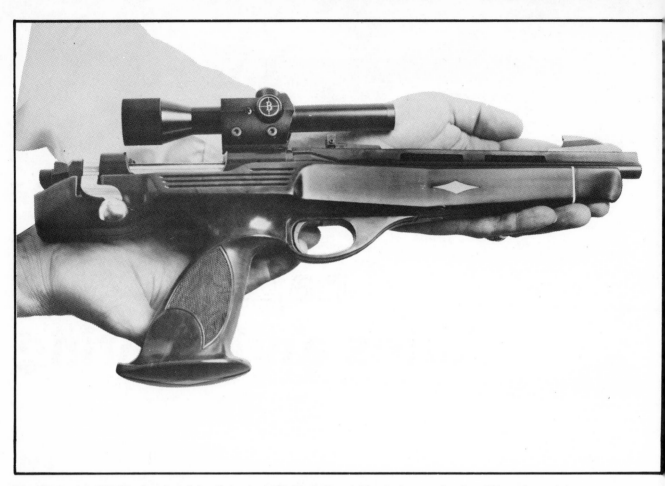

The Remington XP-100, chambered for the potent 221 Fireball cartridge is, in some hands, a 150-yard varmint rig. Most shooters choose to equip these big pistols with a scope for maximum accuracy. Basic styling of the gun is ultra-modern, with the high impact plastic stock and unusual lines.

Since then, we've been exposed to frequent magazine articles (not to mention a complete book I wrote on the subject) on hunting everything from chipmunks upward with all manner of handguns. In the early 1960s, Remington introduced its XP-100 single-shot pistol with its 221 Fireball cartridge for varmint hunting; and in the mid-to-late 1960s, Thompson Center Arms introduced its single-shot interchangeable-barrel pistol in all manner of cartridges for hunting both varmints and big game. In the late 1960s, Lee E. Jurras took off on what was probably the world's first handgun hunting safari in Africa, where he killed many head of the larger herbivorous game, though admittedly no elephant, buffalo, or lion, with the 44 Magnum.

As a result of all this, hunting with handguns became a common topic among pistoleros, and Lee Jurras and I took off together on another African handgun safari. That trip generated a good many magazine articles and culminated in the publication

of our joint book, HANDGUN HUNTING, published in hardcover by Winchester Press and in softcover by Stoeger Publishing Company.

Throughout all this, though, the bulk of emphasis was on the revolver for handgun hunting, primarily in the three magnum calibers (357, 41, 44). The reasons are obvious, for these calibers offered substantially greater power than could be obtained from any production autoloader. As a practical matter, the Colt GM in 38 Super and 45 caliber represented the most potent autos available. Not only did these calibers fall well below the magnum sixgun loads in power, but no really effective hunting loads were offered by the factories; they were traditionally loaded with full metal-jacketed bullets of round-nose form, which is the least effective type on game.

Introduction in the late 1960s and early 1970s of the first truly effective jacketed expanding-bullet loads in these calibers spurred hunting interests, as did published accounts of extensive hunting with

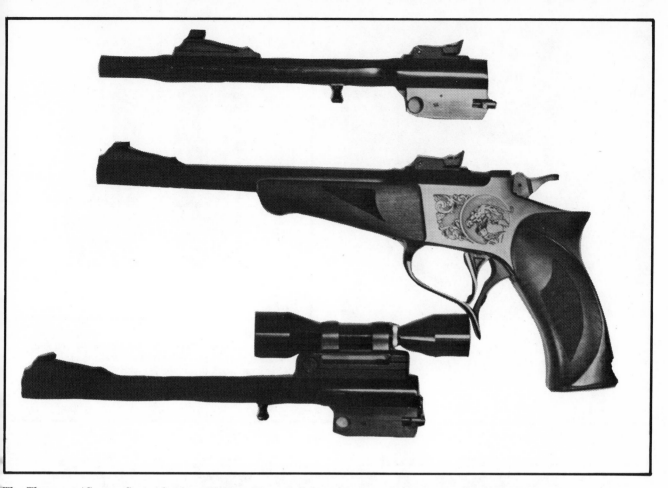

The Thompson/Center Contender is available with a profusion of barrels to handle almost any practical caliber of ammunition. Barrels are easily exchanged and render the pistol suitable for almost any type of hunting.

them by the originator, Lee E. Jurras. I participated in the field tests of this new Super Vel ammunition, killing numerous deer, bear, even antelope, with a wide variety of autoloading pistols (mainly Colt, Browning and Star) in calibers 9mm Parabellum, 38 Super and 45 ACP.

In short, by the early 1970s, it was pretty well proven that our bigger autoloading-pistol cartridges with *proper* bullets and loads were quite adequate for taking game up through deer and black bear if one simply hunted intelligently, shot accurately, and didn't try to stretch his barrel beyond 50 to 75 yards.

Then, in the mid-to-late 1960s, much was made of the introduction of the Auto-Mag pistol in 44 and 357 AMP calibers. On paper, the gun/cartridge combination produced greater power than any revolver, yet was a modern locked-breech autoloader constructed entirely of stainless steel. Unfortunately, delivery of the guns was much delayed, and the one Mexican-made lot of factory-loaded 44 AMP ammunition

simply did not live up to the claims made for the cartridge. Nevertheless, at least several thousand of the guns were eventually delivered (up to now, that is), and handloaders developed ammunition which did live up to the original claims of the designer.

Though the Auto-Mag was (is) expensive, factory-loaded ammunition is not available, and the gun is destined for a short production life (the end probably very near now). This gun did offer the aficionado a hunting handgun superior in range, power and accuracy to everything else, including the vaunted 44 Magnum revolver.

The Auto-Mag is a "finicky" piece of machinery, requiring meticulous care in tuning, cleaning, lubrication, and adaptation of ammunition. It is a gun for the specialist, the handgun-hunting aficionado who is willing to accept the gun's idiosyncrasies, including its great weight and bulk, in exchange for field performance surpassing that of any other handgun. With proper ammunition and in the hands of a superb

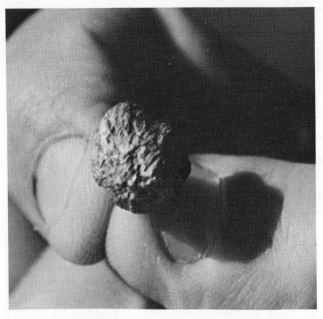

Properly designed handgun bullets will expand like this when driven at adequate velocities. This particular 357 projectile was recovered from a large African antelope.

Super-Vel introduced the first truly effective handgun bullet, shown here with a conventional round-nosed slug. The originator of Super-Vel, Lee E. Jurras, has taken much big game with these high-velocity, expanding bullets.

The mighty Automag is now defunct, but it remains much in demand by many handgun hunters. Premium prices are being paid by those who want them for shooting and by those collectors who hope to watch their investment increase in value.

marksman, many Auto-Mag pistols will shoot two and one-half-inch or smaller groups at 100 yards, and with a trajectory sufficiently flat to permit sure hits out to 200 yards or more. In fact, standing several hundred yards off to the side, I watched Lee Jurras kill an antelope at 217 yards in New Mexico. I vouch for the range because I measured it. And there were other witnesses. That performance wasn't a fluke, because others have come close to it since and the gun he was using had shown us groups under two and one-half inches on the range before the hunt.

The key to hunting with an autoloader is in selecting a gun/cartridge combination best suited to the game or class of game. Most shooters are limited to small pests or the small edible game of the squirrel and rabbit class, and for these the 22 RF auto is probably by far the best bet. A barrel length of six inches or more is needed to develop the full potential of the ammunition, and precisely adjustable target sights are desirable to permit pinpoint zeroing, but are by no means necessary beyond that point. With the gun dead-on at 50 yards, shoot it at 30 yards to determine maximum trajectory height above line of

sight. You'll encounter no difficulty in hitting targets of the size indicated above by slight *hold-under* for ranges of 20 to 40 yards as indicated by the trajectory height. Beyond 50 yards, the probability of a first-shot hit drops off rather rapidly, but with a bit of shooting you will be able to see the amount of drop and can hold over to compensate for it.

If most of your shooting will be in the woods where the light is relatively dim, I recommend a white-outlined rear sight and a red insert up front. Under better light conditions, the plain black sights that are standard on the gun will do quite well.

While speaking of sights, we should point out that if you're a squirrel-shooting buff, many of your shots may well be at angles approaching the vertical. In days gone by when my late father and I hunted squirrels in the tall hickories of the Sangamon River bottoms, shots at more than 45 degrees above the horizontal were not uncommon. At such angles, the gun will shoot well above the point of aim. There's a simple rule about high-angle shots and it applies whether you're shooting below or above the horizontal. It states in general that in order for the bullet to

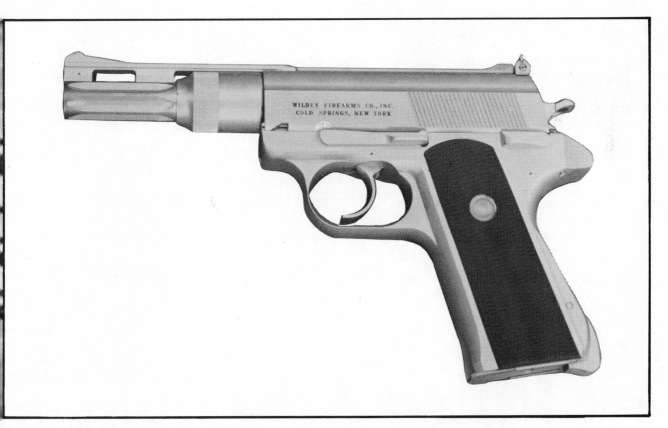

The Wildey auto manufactured by the Wildey Firearms Co. of Cold Spring, N.Y. may be a logical heir to the Automag's devotees. It is available in special 9MM and 45 Long loadings and may change the hunter's thinking as to what a hunting handgun should be.

AUTOS AND HUNTING

Lee E. Jurras has taken many varieties of American and African game with a handgun. He is posing with the Automag used extensively in Africa for medium soft-skinned game.

strike point of aim, the gun must be zeroed for the *horizontal* range, no matter what the *slant range* might be. Visualize this situation as a right triangle; slant range is the distance from the gun muzzle to the target; a vertical line drops from the target to the horizontal; the horizontal distance between the gun muzzle and that vertical line represents the *horizontal range*. Consequently, if you're shooting at 45 degrees to connect with a bushytail high in an old shag-bark hickory and the slant range is 50 yards, the horizontal range will be only a hair over 35 yards. So, if the gun were targeted for 50 yards horizontally, the bullet would skip over the head of your toothsome target. As a result of all this, for popping squirrels up in the trees, I prefer a 22 RF auto targeted at about 25–30 horizontal yards.

A choice may be made from a wide variety of 22 RF autoloaders. Personally, one's wallet permitting, I would prefer the Smith & Wesson M41 in its longest barrel length. However, at the other end of the price scale, the Ruger MKI is entirely adequate though far less sophisticated. And even the less expensive Ruger "Standard Model" with fixed sights is quite good as a field gun once the more difficult job of zeroing has been correctly accomplished. Of course, small game may be hunted with any of the larger calibers, but they possess greater power than is needed, generally have higher trajectories, are noisier, and more expensive to shoot. The bigger bores are also more destructive of meat, and if you want to enjoy those toothsome bushytails and cottontails to the fullest, head shots with the 22 RF are best.

The intermediate calibers, such as the 25, 32 and 380 centerfires, are not entirely impossible for hunting use, but their utility and effectiveness is quite low. The 25 cartridge simply isn't available in any gun of sufficient size and accuracy to be practical for hunting. Secondly, the cartridge is available only with FMJ bullets, the least effective type, and it offers little handloading potential. Some 32-caliber guns are sufficiently large and accurate for hunting use, but the ammunition is available only with FMJ bullets, and, again, the handloading potential is very small. Some of the better 380 pistols possess many of the characteristics needed for hunting, but the low energy level and high trajectory of the cartridge make them relatively ineffective. I've seen the 380 (in high-performance, JHP loads) kill small wild boar, but I'd oppose its use on general principles.

As a practical matter, the 9mm Parabellum represents the smallest least-powerful auto cartridge that should be used for taking game up through the deer and black bear class. And, as with other cartridges, it should never be used in its original "ball" loading with FMJ bullets. Their tendency is to simply penetrate cleanly, leaving a relatively small wound channel, and transmitting only a small proportion of their total energy to the game. Instead, factory high-performance loads utilizing hollow-point bullets of *proven* expansion capability must be used. I use the word "proven" here advisedly, because there are factory hollow-point loads in existence whose bullets look great, but due to an improper balance of core hardness, jacket thickness, cavity size and shape, etc., they simply do not expand well or reliably in animal tissue. Consequently, their behavior upon entering game emulates that of the FMJ bullet.

It is impractical in this book to classify the effectiveness of all the commercial loads of this type which are currently available, partly because there are so many of them, and partly because bullet design and construction frequently change without public notification. Tests by which one may determine the relative expansion capabilities of different loads are well known. If you want to obtain the maximum hunting efficiency from your 9mm pistol, the use of those tests is strongly recommended.

Actually, best results may be obtained from all of the big centerfire cartridges by handloading.

As a practical matter, for game of the deer and bear class at ranges of around 50 yards or less, bullets weighing from 110 to 90 grains and driven at velocities of 1300 to 1450 fps respectively, represent the

Hollow-point bullets may always look effective, but they may be no more potent than conventional round-nosed bullets if they fail to expand. Tests must be made to determine the usefulness of each particular bullet type.

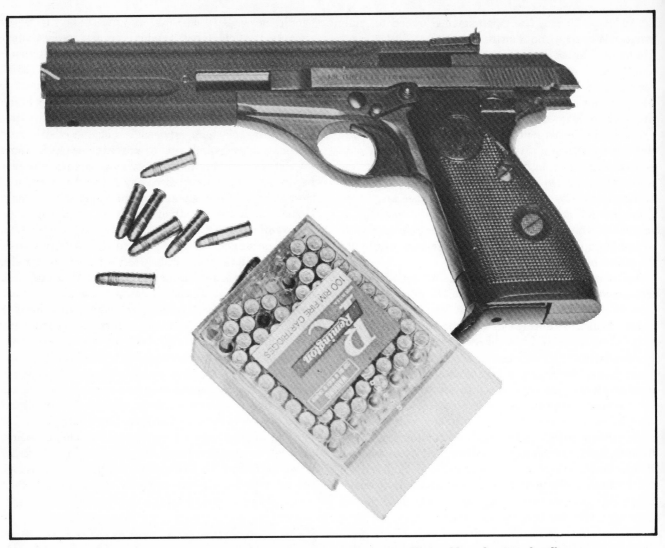

As an accurate practical 22 for small game, the Beretta is hard to beat. It's handy, durable and easy to handle. Many a bushytail has fallen to this particular Model M76.

best selections for the 9mm Parabellum cartridge. Keep in mind that these velocity values are measured at the muzzle and that game is a good deal farther away. Consequently, it is only *impact velocity* that counts, and even the best-jacketed handgun bullets will not expand significantly or consistently at velocities under about 1000 fps. At velocities under 1000 fps, even the most sophisticated expanding bullet will generally just punch on through as if it were of FMJ construction.

The 38 Super Automatic cartridge (and the dimensionally identical 38 ACP) is about ten percent more effective than the 9mm Parabellum in its traditional FMJ loading. The cartridge has tremendous potential, however, and it is most unfortunate that there are no high-performance expanding-bullet factory loads to adapt it to hunting. It exceeds the 9mm in velocity, energy and flatness of trajectory, but to use it effectively on game, one simply must handload. The most deadly load I've cooked-up drives a 90-grain JHP bullet at 1600-plus fps from a standard five-inch barrel. Bullet expansion is great, and this load is a sure killer on deer with a lung or heart shot. Due to violent expansion at shorter ranges, it may not penetrate deeply enough on a shoulder shot to kill quickly, though it will certainly put game down long enough for a follow-up shot to finish the job. It is also deadly on a neck shot, though it is generally less effective on black bear because of their greater size and bulkier bodies.

If I were loading 38 Super for bear or for big mule deer out west, I would switch to a 110–115 grain JHP bullet driven at about 1450–1500 fps. Bullet expansion would be less violent and penetration deeper, accomplishing better execution on the bigger animals. I once shot a large fallow deer with this load at 125 yards, the first bullet striking in the shoulder and penetrating deeply without significant expansion and without striking any vital organs. A second shot at about half that range (the shoulder shot anchored the animal) into the lungs expanded well and would have caused death in a very few minutes, but I ran up and finished the job at about six feet with a neck shot. Frankly, this particular kill was stretching the 38 Super's capability almost beyond the breaking point. I would have not even tried it if the animal had not been standing perfectly still and had I not been able to shoot from a perfectly solid rest in a no-wind condition. I was certain of hitting the animal within three inches of point of aim, but, without this certainty, taking such a shot would have been folly.

Frankly, of all the standard, conventional auto cartridges, the 38 Super is my hunting favorite—but only with proper handloads.

Because of its flat trajectory and high velocity, it transfers more energy to the target than the 9mm, and hitting with it at ranges beyond 40 yards or so under field conditions is substantially easier than with the 45.

Probably because it is far and away the most popular big-bore autoloading pistol cartridge in this country, the 45 ACP is also extremely popular for hunting. By virtue of having the largest cross-sectional bullet area of all, it is considered by most to be extremely effective on animals and people alike. When a comparison is based upon FMJ bullets, this is undoubtedly quite true; however, when we move into the area of expanding bullets, the 45 ACP's most serious limitation makes its presence known. The design of the guns available in this caliber limits the chamber pressures to which it may be loaded, so that with bullets of reasonable weight, it simply isn't practical to exceed a muzzle velocity of about 1100 fps. Harken back to what we said about 1000 fps being the floor for consistent bullet expansion of any degree and you see what happens. At significant ranges, the velocity drops below that critical level, and the bullet performs almost as if it were full-jacketed.

The large cross-sectional area of the 45 caliber offsets limited bullet expansion to some degree, but its relatively low velocity also reduced shock effect and the secondary-projectile effect. The latter

increases greatly with velocity; witness the tissue destruction produced by bone, muscle and cartilage fragments being hurled aside by the bullet as it passes through the animal. At high-impact velocities, these secondary projectiles often destroy more tissue than the bullet alone. At high-impact velocities, bullet fragments are often thrown off, and these also become secondary projectiles of considerable effect. We can't depend upon the 45 bullet for such effect, so under many conditions, the 38 Super may be more effective because it transfers more energy to the target and also produces greater tissue damage through secondary projectiles.

While I feel perfectly capable of killing a deer, boar or black bear out to about 50 yards with the 45 Auto, I really believe I would prefer the 38 Super for the job. Of course, we are comparing factory 45 loads with expanding bullets against maximum-performance loads in the 38 Super because factories don't offer the latter. Even with handloads, the 45 suffers from the same limitations we've already mentioned, so handloading doesn't help much.

Because standard ball ammunition in 45 has developed an excellent reputation as a man stopper, it has often been used for hunting. Because of its bullet weight and cross-sectional area, it penetrates deeply and opens a relatively large wound channel. If bullets are very carefully placed, it is a much better killer than the smaller calibers with the same type bullet. Thus, if only ball ammunition is available, I'd be much more inclined to use the 45 than either the 9mm or 38.

Because of its limited velocity, the 45 ACP is the one autoloading cartridge for which I feel effective hunting loads can be assembled with cast lead bullets. Hard lead bullets of semi-wadcutter form driven at maximum velocities create a more extensive wound than the FMJ bullet, even though no expansion may take place. This is due to the fact that the SWC shape transfers energy much more efficiently, produces greater secondary projectile effect and thus penetrates less deeply. If the lead bullet is made of a softer alloy (as soft as will permit reliable feeding in the gun) and also of hollow-point design (combined with FWC shape), then it adds at least modest expansion to its behavior and does even more damage to the target.

My personal preference for a lead-bullet hunting handload in this caliber is a SWC type of nominal 210-grain weight which is then hollow pointed with a drill. This forms a cavity at least ⅛ inch in diameter and ¼ inch deep, reducing weight below 200 grains. The bullet can then be driven at about 1100 fps, and

Animals of the deer and bear class should be taken with nothing less than a 38 Super or 45 ACP in autoloaders. In this picture, the bear is already starting to let go and fall down the tree to the dogs waiting below.

PISTOL GUIDE

Heckler & Koch P9S pistols are available here in limited numbers but are growing in popularity. They are offered in 9mm Parabellum and 45 ACP. Both are well-suited as hunting guns since they are light, easily handled and durable.

will expand substantially at velocities down to about 900 fps.

So, from the foregoing, you can see that conventional autoloaders chambered for standard factory-produced cartridges can really be considered quite effective on game up through black bear. On larger game, they won't do nearly as well as the magnum sixgun loads, but the expert stalker and careful hunter who can get close and place his bullets precisely should be able to take elk, moose and perhaps even the big bears.

Of course, as we've already implied, the big Auto-Mag in 44 or 357 AMP caliber is substantially superior to any other auto for hunting big game. It shoots flatter, develops greater energy, is generally more accurate, and transfers much, much more energy to the target. However, it is a limited-production item that will probably be available only a

short time longer, and it is purely a handloading proposition. Probably 98 percent of handgun hunters don't own an Auto-Mag and perhaps never will, so they are limited to the standard cartridges already described.

As far as gun selection goes, only the Colt GM and the Star and Llama look-alikes are readily available at a reasonable price in 45 caliber. The three are also equally available in 9mm and 38 Super and, in my experience, they are equally effective in the field. Autos in 45 caliber are also marginally available from the German Heckler & Koch and SIG/Sauer companies, and from two or three limited-production companies in the U.S. As a practical matter, though, if you want a 45 for hunting, you'll find Colt is the most widely available.

A comparable availability condition exists in 38 Super caliber. Colt, along with Llama and Star, offers

Among the pistols chambered for 9mm, the ancient Browning-designed High Power is the ultimate choice because of the factory-fitted adjustable sights and traditional reliability.

guns in 38 Super, and Browning and SIG/Sauer have announced a new model, but, at this writing, it is not generally available.

In 9mm, one may choose from a wide variety of guns by Colt, Star, Llama, Browning, SIG/Sauer, Walther, Mauser, etc., all of which currently manufacture excellent models in this caliber. Even more different makes and models are available on the used-gun market, some of them having been manufactured in the hundreds of thousands as military arms since 1900. Frankly, I'd recommend sticking with current-production guns and choosing the one which suits you best. From all the guns available, if I were forced to make one choice in 9mm Parabellum, I believe it would be the venerable and almost ubiquitous Browning High Power. With a little extra work, this model is superbly accurate, handles very well and has an excellent reputation for functional reliability. It possesses a 13-shot magazine capacity (nice to have, but, frankly, superfluous for hunting) and may be obtained with factory-fitted target-type sights, an accessory not generally available on other 9mm pistols.

In making your selection in any caliber, concentrate on the characteristics of the most practical value for hunting—that is, accuracy, reliability and good sights. Beyond that, keep in mind that both factory and handloaded ammunition in all of the calibers we've mentioned do not develop their full potential velocity and energy in standard length barrels. Consequently, other factors being equal, the gun with the longest barrel will deliver the most smashing blow.

Keep in mind also that a large percentage of guns in all centerfire makes and models may require tuning and/or modification before they will deliver adequate functional reliability with anything other than ball ammunition. Thus your selection may be tempered by the ability of some models to feed and function well with factory high-performance loads and handloads. In this respect, it's a good idea to query as many owners of the model(s) you prefer before making a decision. Find out, by question or by actual trial, just how well the model performs with the ammunition or load you want to use.

Don't feel that you will be handicapped in hunting with an auto just because you can't afford an Auto-Mag, or because most hunting pistoleros use magnum revolvers. Pick an auto that suits you, learn to stalk carefully, shoot well, keep your shots close, and you'll be right up there with the rest of the boys.

Chapter Eight
Pistol Ammunition: When and How

The revolver had been around a long time before autoloading pistols became a practical reality; in fact, more or less practical revolvers date from 1836 with the introduction of Samuel Colt's first wheelguns made at Paterson, New Jersey, and destined to find fame with the Texas Rangers fighting Mexicans.

By present-day standards, though, I suppose we can only say that practical revolvers date from the beginning of the metallic cartridge which appeared in its first genuinely practical form as the 22 Short in the mid 1850s. That diminutive cartridge of miniscule power combined with the Rollin White patent to give the fledgling firm of Smith & Wesson a virtual stranglehold on the metallic-cartridge handgun market until 1869. The 22 Rimfire Short cartridge was almost immediately scaled up and appeared in 44 caliber for the Henry rifle in 1860. By the end of the Civil War, it was made in sizes as large as 58 caliber.

The very nature of the rimfire case made it impossible to construct one strong enough to produce a really powerful and trouble-free cartridge of larger caliber. Consequently, by the late 1860s, reloadable centerfire cartridges appeared, and by 1873, such famous numbers as the 44-40 Winchester and 45-70

U.S. Government, not to mention the 45 Colt, had arrived on the scene in combination with vastly-improved firearms mechanisms of all sorts.

In reality, by the early 1870s, all of the essential elements of the modern obturating metallic cartridge had been well developed. In mechanical design, the cartridge case, primer and bullet had been developed to the form in which they are manufactured today. Ammunition of this type permitted development of the revolver to a high state of durability, reliability and accuracy.

During the 1870s, various firearms authorities and exhibition shooters made statements that the guns and ammunition then available were "perfect." Amazing—for the time—records of accuracy were established with the 44 Smith & Wesson Russian cartridge and hinged-frame Smith & Wesson revolvers evolved as a result of that company's greatly-successful Russian contract and subsequent production of around 200,000 revolvers for Czarist Russia.

By the mid 1880s, machine guns had been developed to function successfully and reliably with black-powder ammunition of the times. Even some auto-

During the heyday of rimfires, cartridges came in all sizes. Here, the 22 Short is shown beside a 41 Rimfire. Caliber as large as 58 appeared briefly during the late 1860s.

loading-rifle mechanisms had been designed, and, though none saw commercial production, they incorporated most of the elements to be used in automatic weapons design for the next five or six decades.

Thus, in retrospect, it may be somewhat surprising that the autoloading pistol did not arrive on the scene in practical and successful form until the late 1890s and did not achieve wide-scale production until 1900.

It is not so surprising when one considers the fact that revolvers and large, autoloading mechanisms—such as the Maxim and Colt machine guns—were very tolerant of ammunition variables, and of the copious ash and residue produced by the combustion of what we now call "black powder," but which was at the time known simply as "gun powder." Even though black powder was remarkably stable and capable of producing superb accuracy when all other factors were properly regulated, about 56 percent of its volume still remained behind in the form of ash after combustion. In revolvers, this posed no particular obstacle because the number of rounds that would be fired caused the accumulation on the working parts of no more residue than could be overcome by a bit more thumb or trigger-finger effort on the part of the shooter.

In the case of early machine guns, the mechanisms were large and heavy enough that provision could be made in their manufacture to accommodate the amounts of fouling or ash that might accumulate in regular use. It has become almost legend that Morman arms genius John M. Browning's first 45-caliber machine gun fired 10,000 rounds of black-powder—45-70 cartridges in one sitting without any malfunction.

Unfortunately, at least for those who wished an autoloading pistol, it apparently was not possible to produce an autoloading mechanism small enough for one-hand use that could accommodate either the fouling of black-powder propellant or the physical size that the bulk of black powder made necessary in a cartridge of adequate power. For example, the most popular revolver cartridges of the day were 44 and 45 caliber, ranging in length from 1.43 to 1.60 inches. An autoloading mechanism to handle cartridges of that size would have been too bulky and heavy to find ready acceptance as a one-hand firearm.

Consequently, the autoloading pistol had to wait for a new and better propellant which would at the very least be of substantially less volume for given energy output, and which would produce far less ash by its combustion. Though many individuals, companies and governments had been attempting to develop just such a propellant, it was the French scientist Velie who produced the first practical "smokeless powder" in the mid-to-late 1880s. Anxious to achieve military ascendancy over its potential enemies—of which there were many—France adopted the world's first smokeless-powder military-rifle cartridge in 1888. This was what we now call the 8mm Lebel cartridge, generally known in Europe under the metric designation of $8 \times 50R$.

Velie's powder (and here I should state that the term "powder" is neither descriptive nor correct, and what we call "smokeless powder" is more properly termed "smokeless small-arms propellant") was far from perfect, as explosions in French storage depots soon made evident. However, others followed Velie's lead very quickly, and far-better smokeless propellants appeared very soon on the scene. Though machine guns had proved successful with black powder, they were immediately adapted to smokeless-propellant ammunition with tremendous improvements in performance. The ideal "fuel" for the autoloading firearm had arrived.

The use of the word "fuel" is correct, for any firearm is essentially nothing more than a single-cylinder "heat engine." Your automobile engine ("motor," if you will) is a heat engine of multiple cylinders with captive pistons. Fuel is burned in the cylinders to create heat and gas under pressure which drives the pistons the length of the cylinders. During this the piston's linear motion is converted to rotary motion which is transferred ultimately to the rear wheels and makes that slick buggy zoom down the highway.

The firearm is a similar heat engine, except that it burns a *solid* rather than a *liquid* fuel, with the barrel constituting the cylinder and the bullet constituting the piston. In the firearm-heat engine, the piston is free rather than captive. The work done is in transporting the bullet/projectile a great distance through the atmosphere to strike a particular target and transmit sufficient energy to produce the desired effect. This effect ranges from a simple circular hole in a piece of paper up to the destruction of an animal or human being, or in some military firearms, the penetration of several inches of extremely tough steel armor.

Our firearm-heat engine found black powder a very inefficient fuel because of severe limitations upon the power it could develop. Smokeless propellant, on the other hand, was vastly more efficient, having a much greater energy content and the capability of actually producing more power in our firearm-heat engine than could actually be used.

Thus, smokeless propellant—which is not in fact truly smokeless, but merely produces a great deal less smoke than black powder—made possible the successful autoloading pistol. Arms designers instantly seized upon smokeless propellant and began developing concurrently cartridges and pistol mechanisms. Borchardt, Mauser, Schwarzlose, Browning, and numerous others worked away with vigor, and quite successfully, too.

Some of the earliest attempts were to design autoloading pistols around revolver-type cartridges with rimmed cases and lead bullets. The rims generated considerable difficulties in feeding and stowage in a magazine of practical size and shape, and the lead bullets caused problems in feeding from magazine to chamber. The rimless type of cartridge case had

already appeared in rifle and machine-gun ammunition in the late 1880s for the same reason, and the fully metal-jacketed bullet had been designed by Bode slightly earlier. Our pistol/cartridge designers simply scaled down the rimless centerfire case to sizes that would accommodate the diameter and bullet weight they had chosen and which would also contain a sufficient amount of existing smokeless propellant to produce the desired performance (and all this was determined more or less empirically) at 100 percent loading density.

Following this approach, designers produced cartridges much smaller in overall size but more powerful than the previous black-powder revolver numbers. For example, John M. Browning produced the 32 ACP of less than half the size of the 32-20 Winchester cartridge, yet nearly equaled its power in a handgun substantially smaller and lighter than a typical revolver. This cartridge/gun design combination was, in fact, so successful and so readily accepted by the public that by 1909, Browning was honored by Fabrique Nationale (the manufacturer) because one million of this and other Browning guns had been manufactured and sold. By the first decade of the 20th century, several designers had produced typical rimless, fully metal-cased-bullet pistol cartridges in the 9mm/38 range which far exceeded the power of existing 38-caliber revolver cartridges and yet were generally one-third shorter.

By 1908-1910, the autoloading-pistol cartridge had achieved its definitive form which remains essentially the standard today, seven decades later. By 1910, there were in existence the 32 ACP (7.65mm Browning), 380 ACP (9mm Browning Short), 9mm

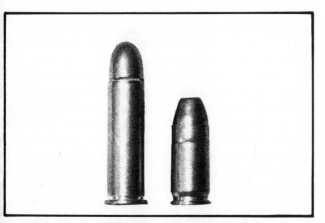

Left: 38 Special and right: 9mm Parabellum. The development of the rimless case and smokeless powder combined to make autoloading pistols practical.

Efficient smokeless powder made possible redesigned cartridges of practical size to feed through an autoloader. The 380 ACP, left, generates greater energy than the 32-20 on the right.

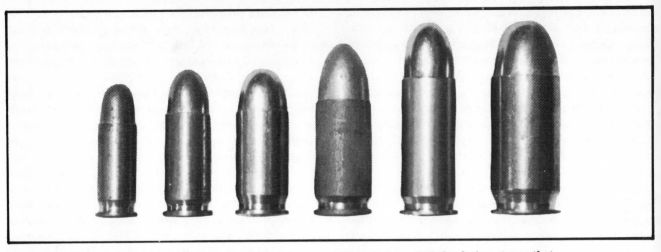

Shortly after the turn of the century, autoloading handgun cartridges had reached the design stages that they occupy today. From left to right are: the 25 ACP, 380 ACP, 9mm Parabellum, 38 Super and 45 ACP cartridges. All were in production by the year 1910 although they were known by other names in Europe.

Parabellum (Luger), 7.65mm Parabellum (30 Luger), 38 ACP (and a wide variety of exceedingly similar cartridges), 7.63mm Mauser (30 Mauser), and what is considered in this country the ubiquitous 45 ACP or 45 Colt Automatic.

All were of true rimless form except the 25, 32 and 38 ACP, which used a semi-rimless case with the rim being only slightly larger in diameter than the case head. All were assembled in relatively short cases (compared to revolver cartridges), the solid-head case virtually filled with powder and loaded with a fully metal-cased bullet. Case shape was generally cylindrical, though the 30 Luger and Mauser were of classic bottle-neck shape. The 25, 32, 380, and 45 calibers were of relatively low velocity, ranging from about 800 through 950 fps, while all of the others were considered high-velocity cartridges producing approximately 1100 fps or more. The low-velocity cartridges were loaded to chamber pressures generally under 20,000 CUP (the present standard, though presented then as PSI), while the high-velocity types were generally loaded to about 30–33,000 CUP.

And there development stopped. The majority of the autoloading-pistol ammunition manufactured today is identical, both mechanically and in performance, to the ammunition of 1910. Of course, slightly more efficient propellants have been developed, and they have generally been used more for economic reasons than any other, inasmuch as smaller amounts would produce the established pressure/velocity levels. And of course, manufacturing methods have changed; today a cartridge case or bullet may be produced with no more than half the number of operations employed 50 or 60 years ago.

From time to time from the early 1900s, half-hearted attempts had been made to improve the lethality of autoloading-pistol ammunition by designing expanding-type bullets. Unfortunately, such bullets seldom, if ever, delivered the desired results simply because designers followed rifle-bullet practices. Bullets designed along those lines simply would not expand reliably or consistently at the velocities that could be obtained safely in existing autoloading pistols. In fact, even today, the most modern *production* autoloading pistols are not genuinely capable of driving that type of bullet fast enough for reliable expansion.

However, all this is not to say that autoloading pistol buffs and law enforcement officers must still rely upon the traditional metal-cased bullet and its low level of lethality. In the late 1950s, a gentleman I call friend took it upon himself, operating alone, without backing and in nothing more than a simple basement handloading shop, to improve handgun-ammunition lethality and develop what is now known generically as "high-performance" ammunition. That gentleman was Lee E. Jurras. That he was eminently successful is evident in the fact that all major ammunition manufacturers in this country—and several abroad—have since copied his developments—some well and some poorly, but none completely—and now offer as regular production items high-performance cartridges for autoloading pistols. It should be noted that such ammunition is not available in all calibers, but generally only in calibers 380 ACP, 9mm Parabellum and 45 ACP. By far the widest variety of those loads is offered in 9mm because of its world-wide acceptance and popularity.

After having privately proved his theories and developed producible and marketable high-performance ammunition, Jurras formed the Super Vel Cartridge Corporation of Shelbyville, Indiana, and its product achieved world-wide recognition. However, in 1974, the Super Vel plant closed its doors for various reasons. By the time Super Vel operations were shut down, the major domestic ammunition manufacturers had followed Jurras' lead and began to offer their own lines of high-performance ammunition. That Super Vel had been entirely dependent upon some of these companies for the components which it assembled might well have had something to do with the fate of the Shelbyville plant. It is worthy to note that a new company is now loading similar ammunition under the Super Vel name. The current crop of Super Vel ammunition is not necessarily manufactured to the same designs or specifications that Jurras formulated in the late 1950s and early 1960s.

It may truthfully be said, then, that Lee Jurras revolutionized handgun ammunition, and autoloading-pistol ammunition in particular. The ammunition he developed was vastly more lethal than the so-called "hard ball" traditional design, and in some instances and calibers, proved itself so much more effective that a practical comparison simply could not be made.

Jurras' approach was a simple one. He designed and produced bullets that would expand substantially in animal tissue at velocities that would be safely produced in existing guns. This could only be achieved by two means. First, it was necessary to design jacketed bullets (essential to reliable feeding in autoloading mechanisms) which would expand reliably at the lowest possible impact velocity. This required very thin, soft jackets and very soft cores, much more than any that had been previously used. Secondly, he had to increase the velocity of those bullets to achieve that expansion. The latter could be accomplished within allowable chamber pressure limits (with existing propellants) only by reducing bullet weight. Thus, by driving a lighter bullet at a higher velocity and by designing the bullet specifically for expansion at those velocity levels, he was able to achieve a high degree of expansion at normal handgun ranges.

During the developmental work, Jurras found it necessary, or at least desirable, to incorporate other features to obtain maximum velocity and expansion safely in existing guns. Among these were increasing bullet pull (the amount of force required to force the bullets from the case), the use of slightly undersized (by contemporary standards) bullets to ease peak pressures, JHP (jacketed-hollow-point) and JSP (jacketed-soft-point) bullet designs which did not permit any lead to contact the feed ramp, and a distinctive truncated-cone bullet shape. Eventually he established that maximum lethality could be produced in 380 caliber with bullets of 80-grains' weight, in 9mm Parabellum with 90-grain bullets, in 38 Super Auto with 107-grain bullets, and in 45 with 190-grain bullets, all of hollow-point type. He also established that reliable expansion could not be obtained at impact velocities of less than 1000 feet per second with any practical and economically producible bullet design.

As an example of Jurras' accomplishments in this field, the classic FMJ 9mm Parabellum load with a 116–125-grain round-nose bullet at 1165–1140 fps, produces a wound cavity of very small volume, generally a simple cylindrical passage only slightly greater in diameter than the bullet. The bullet will generally penetrate a human target completely, transmitting only a small percentage of its energy to that target and expending the balance beyond. The definitive Super Vel development (Jurras) was a 90-grain jacketed-hollow-point at 1422 fps which produces a wound cavity several times greater in volume, will not usually penetrate a human target completely, and thus generally transmits virtually all of its energy (402 foot pounds) to the target.

The improvement in lethality (over FMJ ball loads) achieved by Jurras in other autoloading-pistol calibers was generally a bit less than that of the 9mm, but still quite significant. Even the 380 ACP, considered only marginally effective as a defensive cartridge in its original form, achieved quite a fair reputation among law enforcement officers with the result that pistol sales in this caliber multiplied many, many times with the availability of the Super Vel loading.

All this is not to say that the new high-performance loads were without problems. Lighter bullets meant shorter bullets, and when made with sufficient bearing surface and seated deeply enough in the case for adequate bullet pull, they produced cartridges of shorter than standard length. This introduced feeding problems with some guns, particularly those such as the Parabellum (Luger) and Walther P-38 in which the cartridge travels a relatively long distance from magazine feed lips to chamber. Cartridges of this type were also found to be less tolerant of more or less normal variations in production guns in regards to feeding. Individual guns, even brand-new ones fresh from the factory, would often feed ball ammunition perfectly, yet occasionally malfunction with this type. This occurred with some regularity in all calibers; the problem can be corrected easily with a relatively small amount of handwork, but the average shooter isn't competent to do this sort of thing, and expects *any,* standard production gun to function with *any* production ammunition in the appropriate caliber. This had no apparent effect on the marketability of Super Vel or later high-performance ammunition, inasmuch as those who purchase it for its greatly increased lethality are willing to have individual guns tuned as necessary for functional reliability.

It was this occasional feeding difficulty that caused most of the second-generation high-performance ammunition by the major manufacturers to be a bit inferior to the original Super Vel. The big makers, catering more to the mass market than the gun buff or law officer, felt it necessary to modify the bullet design for better feeding in rough guns, as well as to improve producibility and reduce costs. They certainly cannot be blamed for those changes, but they do result in ammunition which is generally just a bit less effective than the original item.

None of the things Jurras did were unknown in bullet and ammunition development. Yet no one had ever been sufficiently interested in improving handgun ammunition to spend the time and money to get the job done. The general attitude of the major manufacturers had been simply that the loads they produced were perfectly functional and, being the only ones available, would be accepted by the entire shooting public, amateur and professional alike. From a purely business viewpoint, this was quite logical. It was certainly less than fair, though, to those professional gunmen whose lives—and the lives of those they were sworn to protect—often depended upon the efficiency and lethality of their ammunition.

It goes without saying that high-performance ammunition costs a bit more than the traditional design. And one who is familiar with the problems and processes involved in producing such loads has no difficulty in understanding the reason for additional costs. It is a simple fact that the traditional standard ball ammunition, with its fully metal-jacketed bullet of standard weight and velocity, is perfectly adequate for the average shooter's use. Only those using the auto for hunting or defensive use can justify the additional cost or show any need for the greater lethality. Consequently, it's unlikely that high-performance ammunition will ever constitute more

than a relatively small segment of ammunition production. The traditional design and the performance levels may be old, but they serve quite well.

There is one other segment of the autoloading pistol cartridge story that deserves special attention. The National Rifle Association has been the governing body of pistol competition in the U.S. for nearly six decades. For most of that time, there have been two matches which require the use of the 45 ACP cartridge, and one other which allows its use. The "Centerfire" matches allow the use of the 45 autoloading pistol; the "45 Caliber Semi-Automatic Pistol" matches require the use of a gun chambered for this cartridge. For both of those matches, no limitations other than caliber and a requirement that ammunition be "safe" need be met. Then there are the "Service Pistol" matches which require that ammunition, "45 caliber, manufactured by or for the government and issued for service use," be used. In addition, ammunition for this match is required to be issued on the range by match authorities.

Over the years, shooter demand for super-accurate ammunition to meet both requirements resulted in the development of special match loads. In the service pistol, this took the form simply of ball ammunition loaded generally to military specifications, but held to extremely close tolerances and selected for match use upon the basis of accuracy testing. Amazingly accurate ammunition was developed in this fashion, the best of which has been manufactured for the U.S. Government and labeled "match." Some lots have produced accuracy as good as one-inch groups at 50 yards. Aside from its superior accuracy and (sometimes) special labeling, this ammunition does not differ from standard, military ball.

The other class of 45 match ammunition is generally referred to as "midrange" type and has been developed by all major domestic manufacturers to produce maximum accuracy out to 50 yards, as well as minimum recoil compatible with reliable functioning of the 45 auto pistol. While several different bullet types have been used in the past, this match load has reached fairly definitive form now with a fully metal jacketed bullet of modified semi-wadcutter form and weighing about 185 grains. It is loaded to produce a muzzle velocity of approximately 770 fps and is, of course, manufactured to closer tolerances than standard ball. This ammunition, too, is often capable of producing groups of one inch or less at 50 yards in the best guns.

Generally speaking, this match ammunition is intended for use in guns that have been modified or originally manufactured purely for target use. Conse-

Extremely accurate ammunition is found in boxes bearing this label. It may group as close as an inch at 50 yards. The cartridges are specially assembled to comply with "Military Match" requirements.

quently, it is likely to produce feeding problems in many standard-issue service guns, and because of its low recoil impulse (lighter-than-standard bullet and reduced velocity), it often will not fully cycle the action of a standard pistol unless a weaker recoil spring is installed.

That is just about the full story on ammunition for autoloading pistols. It has already been pointed out that autoloading pistols are designed to function properly only within a fairly sharply defined range of recoil impulse, and that recoil impulse is dependent upon a combination of bullet weight and velocity. High-performance loads achieve adequate recoil impulse by driving lighter-than-standard bullets at higher-than-standard velocity; conversely, if one chose to use abnormally heavy bullets, it would be necessary to reduce their velocity. A typical Colt Government Model 45 caliber pistol (a standard gun,

not modified in any way) will function reliably with the standard 230-grain bullet within a velocity range above 750 fps. As velocity exceeds about 900 fps, the gun continues to function reliably, but parts wear is substantially accelerated, and the probability of parts breakage from "overdriving" the mechanism increases very rapidly.

It is for this reason that within each caliber there is only a small number of loads within a narrow range of bullet weights and types. Compared to the wide variety of revolver loads, this seems a very small selection. Nevertheless, the autoloader's dependence upon prescribed limits of recoil energy for functioning severely limits the range of practical loads that can be used. As an example, in the 45 ACP, we find only three loads available: the standard ball round; a midrange match load with a 185-grain SWC bullet at about 770 fps; and a high-performance load containing a 185–190-grain JHP bullet at 950–1000 fps, depending upon manufacturer. And, among them, only the latter two may be depended upon to produce reliable functioning in *service* guns. At the other end of the scale, consider the 38 Special revolver, *not* dependent upon recoil for functioning, where we find literally dozens of different loads with bullet weights ranging from 90 grains to 200 grains and with velocities from less than 700 fps up to in excess of 1500 fps.

This isn't to imply that the autoloader is any less efficient or less desirable than the revolver. While it obviously lacks versatility in ammunition, it possesses numerous other advantages—rate of fire, magazine capacity, flatness, and compactness, etc.—and these certainly compensate quite adequately for that one basic shortcoming.

Chapter Nine
Autoloading Pistols of Today

At the time GCA'68 was enacted and went into effect, a tremendous number of makes and models of pistols were available in the U.S. Quite a large percentage of them were various, so-called "pocket guns" manufactured abroad and imported and distributed in very large quantities here. Unfortunately (at least in my opinion), the factoring criteria established for enforcement of GCA'68 prohibited further importation of virtually every auto smaller than the Walther Model PP.

As is well known by most pistoleros today, our legislators and regulators equate size with criminality, and without regard for any other factors, they continuously attempt to eliminate "readily concealable" handguns upon the assumption that a "small" gun serves no "valid sporting purpose" and is further most likely to be used in the commission of a criminal act. It is interesting to note that having in 1968 managed to prohibit *importation* of small handguns, those same legislators and regulators are now attempting to eliminate all similar guns from *domestic manufacture*. Because of GCA'68, you'll not see any foreign-

manufactured *small* pistols shown in the following pages.

While it would be quite difficult to go back through the years and count the number of makes and models that have been available from time to time, it appears that there are probably more different makes and models of autoloading pistols available today than ever before. I must point out that there are unfortunately several models on the market which serve few useful purposes and some which are of such poor design and/or manufacture so as to be unsafe under some conditions. As an example, one small autoloader (which shall remain nameless at this point) has produced several fatalities through inadvertent firing under conditions which should have been foreseen and guarded against by both the designer and the manufacturer.

On the other hand, the mere fact that we do not cover a particular model in the following pages is not meant to indicate that we condemn it or consider it unsafe; such absences are generally due simply to inability to obtain a sample, or to the manufacturer's

Astra Constable

failure to supply information. Unless otherwise indicated in the descriptive text, all of the guns listed hereafter are considered safe, durable, reliable, and suitable for the purposes for which they are sold, assuming they are handled and maintained properly. This is not necessarily meant as a recommendation, but simply a statement of the facts as we know them from personal experience and the reports of other users.

ASTRA (UNCETA): This is one of the older Spanish arms-making companies, dating from well before World War I. Over the years, Astra has produced a wide variety of both autoloading pistols and revolvers, including the very unusual, unlocked-breech, 9mm M400/600, often referred to as the "water pistol Astra." Astra is one of the few Spanish pistol-making firms that survived that nation's bloody civil war of the late 1930s. Because of the provisions and enforcement regulations of GCA'68, the only Astra autoloader currently available in this country is the "Constable," made in 22 LR, 32 ACP and 380 ACP. This model is now imported and distributed in the U.S. exclusively by Interarms.

ASTRA CONSTABLE: This is a relatively simple blowback-type medium-sized autoloading pistol possessing double-action first-shot capability. It has been obviously modeled after the successful Walther PP/PPK series, and was introduced some years ago as the first of the new-generation double-action pocket pistols brought into being by both the popularity and unusually high price of the Walther models. The Constable features a ribbed slide, fixed sights, burr-type hammer, and hammer-dropping/hammer-blocking safety of the Walther type. The recoil spring is concentric with the barrel, and field-stripping is by means of a vertically sliding disassembly latch inside the front of the trigger-guard. An auto/manual slide stop is present on the left side of the frame, and the magazine catch is in the Browning location at the left rear of the trigger guard. While the Constable copies the size, shape and appearance of the Walther PP, it is quite different internally. It features a much simpler and less costly double-action lockwork and frankly does not display quite as high a quality of fit and finish as the much more expensive Walther. Functionally, though, it has

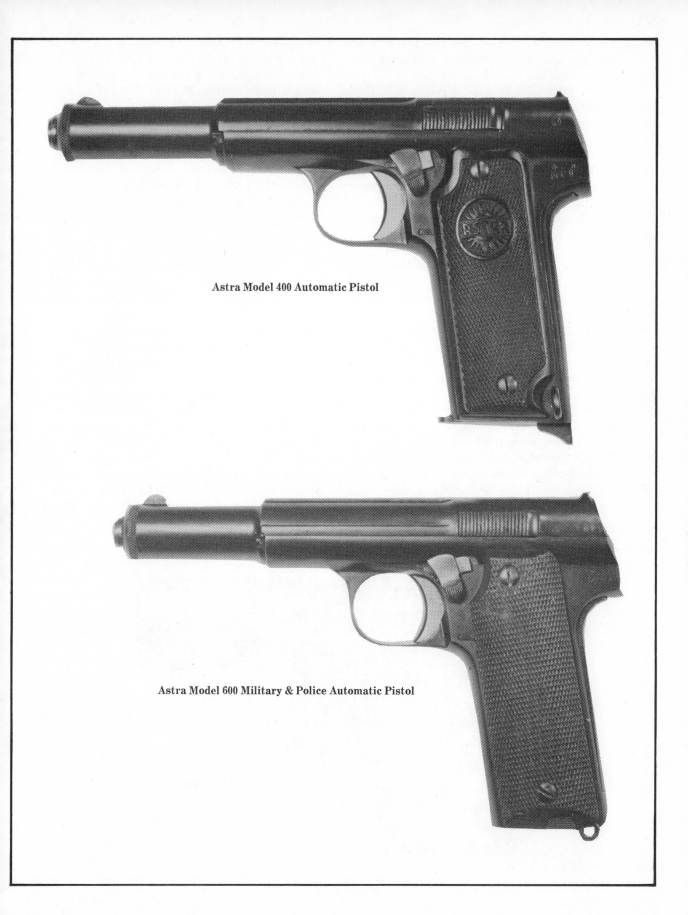

Astra Model 400 Automatic Pistol

Astra Model 600 Military & Police Automatic Pistol

developed an excellent reputation and has become reasonably popular as a secondary personal arm among police officers.

BAUER FIREARMS: A relatively small U.S. company which began during the 1960s by importing foreign arms of several types and has since progressed to domestic manufacture of a single design of very small pocket pistols. The gun is known simply as "Bauer 25 (22) Auto" and is constructed entirely of stainless steel. It is nothing more or less than a line-for-line copy of the well-known "Baby Browning" design nearly three-quarters of a century ago by John M. Browning and then manufactured in slightly different forms by both Fabrique Nationale and Colt. Being only four inches long and weighing only ten ounces, this diminutive gun has become quite popular for use where maximum concealment is required. A good many police officers carry it as a last-ditch hideout gun, and in this usage, its stainless-steel construction becomes a distinct advantage in preventing or at least limiting corrosion from perspiration acids and in reducing maintenance requirements.

While the 25 and 22 Long Rifle versions appear to be the same, they are dimensionally different in key areas. The original design accommodated only the short, 25 ACP cartridge, and lacked sufficient magazine space and recoil stroke to handle the longer 22 LR. Thus, it was necessary for Bauer to redimension these areas of the gun to permit chambering of the 22

LR. The Bauer is by a substantial margin the smallest autoloading pistol available chambered for the 22 LR cartridge. In my opinion, the high-velocity hollow-point loading of the LR is preferable to the FMJ 25 for defensive use.

BERETTA: Armi Beretta is Italy's oldest manufacturer of handguns, and a Beretta pistol has been the standard Italian service sidearm since before World War I. Beretta is one of those companies substantially affected by GCA'68 in that several of its models popular in the U.S. were prohibited importation by that legislation. Over the years, Beretta autopistol designs have been characterized by simplicity, a small number of parts, unusual sturdiness of internal parts, ease of disassembly and assembly, and high-quality workmanship. With the single exception of the M90 double-action model (no longer available in this country), all Beretta pistols since about 1914 have shared a distinctive appearance; even the newest models could have been presented without a name and be readily recognized as being Berettas. In 1977, Beretta introduced a new series of centerfire autoloaders, all quite similar in appearance, and sharing many features, in calibers 32 and 380 ACP, and 9mm Parabellum. All Beretta pistols are imported and distributed in this country by the U.S. Beretta subsidiary.

BERETTA M76: This pistol is in 22 rimfire, of target type, built around the basic single-action Beretta design of many-years standing. It presents

Bauer 25 Caliber Automatic Cartridge Pistol

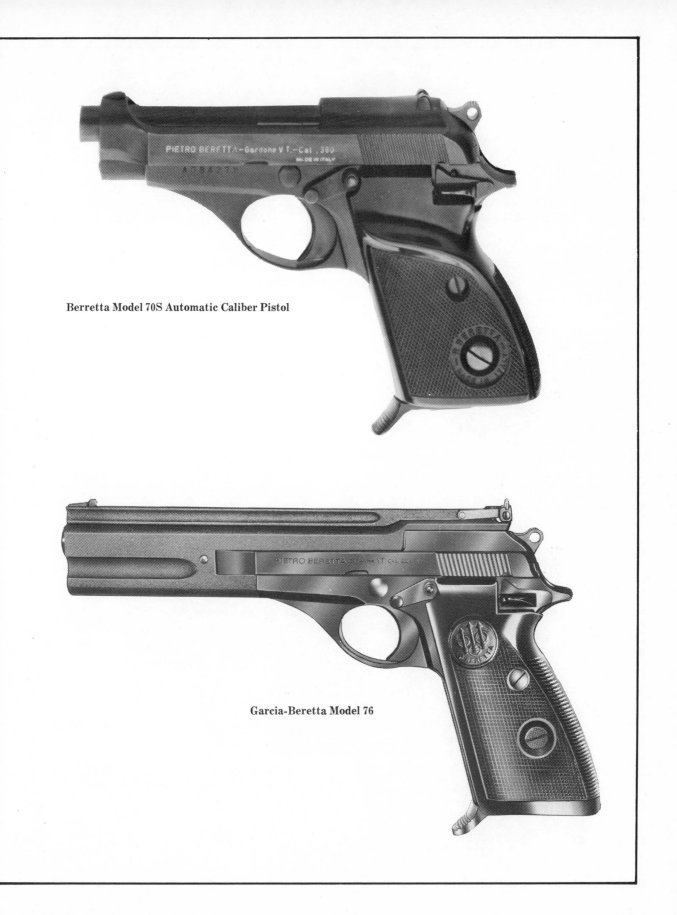

Berretta Model 70S Automatic Caliber Pistol

Garcia-Berretta Model 76

Beretta Models 81/84

Beretta Model 92 9mm Luger

quite a different appearance than the pocket models of recent years, but this would not be true except for the fact that it has a much longer barrel and that barrel is enclosed by a massive light-alloy shroud pinned to the barrel and carrying adjustable target-type sights. Interestingly, the rib on the shroud extends fully to the rear over the slide so that while maximum sight-radius is obtained, both sights are still installed upon the same bar of metal and thus have no relative motion as is found in the traditional 22 auto with front sight on the barrel and rear sight on the slide. The M76 is otherwise a thoroughly conventional unlocked-breech (blow-back), exposed-hammer, magazine-in-butt design. While technically it appears to possess the attributes of a target pistol and it is priced in the same range as High Standard and S&W models, it has not achieved any popularity for that use in this country.

BERETTA M70S: The traditional Beretta blow-back design originated with the 1914 model, was improved as the M1934, and given a further facelift after World War II. It is a very simple and sturdy design, with open-top slide and easily removed barrel. The hammer is of burr type, the manual safety is quite positive, and disassembly is easy. It possesses an unusual magazine-catch location, low on the left side of the grip, and pressed to the right to release the magazine. The catch is flush with the grip and thus cannot be inadvertently depressed, but by virtue of this location, it must be operated with the off hand, and even then is not the easiest to reach in a hurry. The M70S magazine possesses the characteristically Beretta curved, forward-sweeping finger rest incorporated into the removable floor-plate. This feature aids control, but interferes with concealment and has been eliminated in the more recent designs. While this basic design has been made in several other calibers, the 70S is offered only in 380 ACP.

BERETTA M81/84: This is the newest blow-back design from Beretta, and essentially it is the earlier design (represented by the M70S) extensively modified to provide double-action first-shot capability and to accommodate a double-column magazine containing 12 rounds in 32 caliber (M81) and 13 rounds in 380 caliber (M84). It has also been modified to carry a conventional Browning-type manual safety at the left rear of the frame and a Browning-type, automatic, slide stop above the trigger. Further, the magazine catch has been vastly improved over earlier models by placing it in the Browning position at the left rear of the trigger guard where it can be manipulated by the thumb of the shooting hand, thus allowing an empty magazine to be ejected without the use of the off hand. Beretta tradition is maintained by using relatively few parts of sturdy construction. The changes and improvements over earlier designs do not significantly alter the appearance; as a matter of fact, except for the enlarged trigger-guard and forward-positioned DA trigger, the 81/84 could easily be mistaken for the earlier M70S. The two different model designations apply to the same gun with only very minor modifications to adapt it to the two different calibers. It should be noted that the 81/84 is the only medium-sized pistol currently available in 32 and 380 caliber to feature a double-column magazine of large capacity. When this desirable feature is combined with a simple and reliable, double-action lockwork, the new Beretta design may be said to be the most advanced of the type. It should be noted that in these small calibers the use of a double-column magazine does not make the grip unusually large, so neither handling nor concealability suffer.

BERETTA M92: As a practical matter, the M92 is essentially the earlier single-action M951 extensively modified with the same type of double-action lockwork as found in the 81/84 and further modified to accommodate a double-column magazine which contains 15 9mm Parabellum cartridges. However, in this instance, Beretta has chosen to leave the magazine catch in the original M951 position at the lower left of the butt. This is subject to the same objections mentioned in regard to the M70S, and I would have much preferred the catch to be shifted to the Browning position. The M92 is of typical Beretta appearance and design otherwise, and is of locked-breech design. The locking system is quite similar to that of the M951, but is much improved to eliminate the locking-block breakage problem that existed in the earlier model. Locking is accomplished by a pivoted block seated in the underside of the barrel and being cammed upward to lock the barrel and slide securely together. During recoil, it is cammed downward into the frame to unlock and allow the slide to reciprocate independently of the barrel. Like the 81/84, the M92 carries a separate dismounting lever which simplifies disassembly, and the extractor functions as a loaded-chamber indicator to both sight and feel.

BROWNING ARMS: This firm is a bit unusual in that it was formed many years ago to market the firearms designs of an American, John M. Browning, which were manufactured abroad by the Fabrique Nationale of Herstal, Belgium. Not until the past few years did it acquire its own manufacturing facilities in this country, though from time to time modern designs (not from the great John M.) have been manufactured under contract for Browning by other firms in the U.S. as well as abroad. As this is written, the only autoloader generally available is the High Power, made by FN, and known to most of the rest of the world as P35 or G.P. Though it has been made in other calibers, the only one available is 9mm Parabellum, and the unusually sturdy construction and design of this pistol has demonstrated its ability to withstand chamber pressures well in excess of those normally employed by this cartridge.

The HP was John M. Browning's last pistol design, produced in the late 1920s, as the ultimate improvement upon his earlier locked-breech designs, but not fully developed and placed in manufacture until the mid-to-late 1930s. It was manufactured in substantial quantity before World War II, and remained in production throughout that conflict, with several hundred thousand manufactured for the Wermacht during German occupation of Belgium. Production has been continuous since, and many other nations have adopted this pistol as their standard military sidearm; among them have been Great Britain, New Zealand, Canada, Taiwan, and others. The Browning HP has developed a tremendous reputation for durability and reliability throughout the world and is quite popular among law enforcement officers in this country where departmental regulations allow its use. It was the first big-bore pistol available in this country with a double-column magazine and an unusually large (for the time) capacity of 13 rounds. In the beginning, the Browning HP was offered only with fixed open sights, but in more recent years, optional target-type sights of rather indifferent design have been added, and for a short period of time, it was offered with a military tangent-type long-range rear sight as well.

BROWNING BDA: Though this modern double-action centerfire autoloading pistol bears the Browning name, that is its only relationship with the company. In reality, it is the Swiss SIG-designed P220 pistol manufactured in West Germany by J.P. Sauer & Sohn, and otherwise designated SIG/Sauer P220. Under the latter name, it is also available in the U.S. from other sources.

COLT FIREARMS: Colt, of course, is the oldest continuously operated U.S. handgun manufacturer. It began producing percussion revolvers in the mid-1830s, went out of business for a short while, then began supplying revolvers again in 1847, and has operated continuously ever since. Colt introduced autoloading pistols to this country—and to a lesser extent to the world—with the purchase and manufacture of John M. Browning's 38 caliber locked-breech design in 1899. By 1911, it had refined Browning's designs into the M1911 45-caliber pistol adopted in that year by the U.S. Army. That model has been in continuous production ever since, for a total of 67 years. Beginning in 1903, Colt also manufactured very fine pocket-type pistols in 25, 32 and 380 calibers, also of Browning design; and in 1915, produced the first practical 22-rimfire autoloading pistol from a Browning design. Pocket pistol production termi-

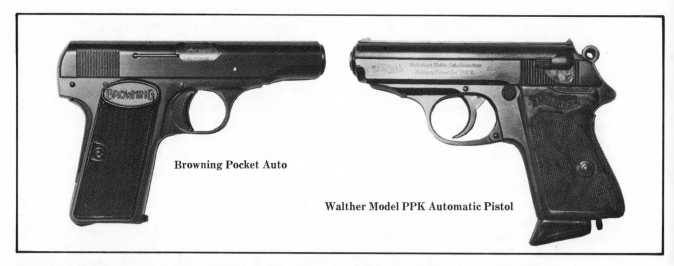

Browning Pocket Auto

Walther Model PPK Automatic Pistol

Thanks to GCA '68, many fine but compact handguns are missing from today's marketplace. Examples of these outlawed handguns are the pre-1968 Browning Pocket Auto and the extremely popular Walther PPK. Both guns are available in modified (larger) versions now, but these pocket autos of old are now available only as used guns at premium prices.

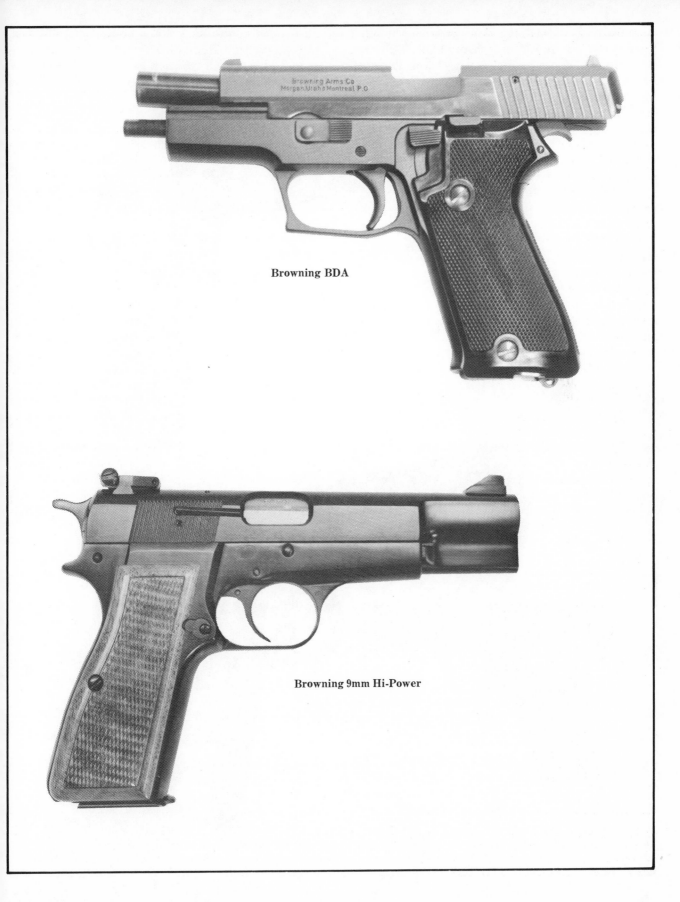

Browning BDA

Browning 9mm Hi-Power

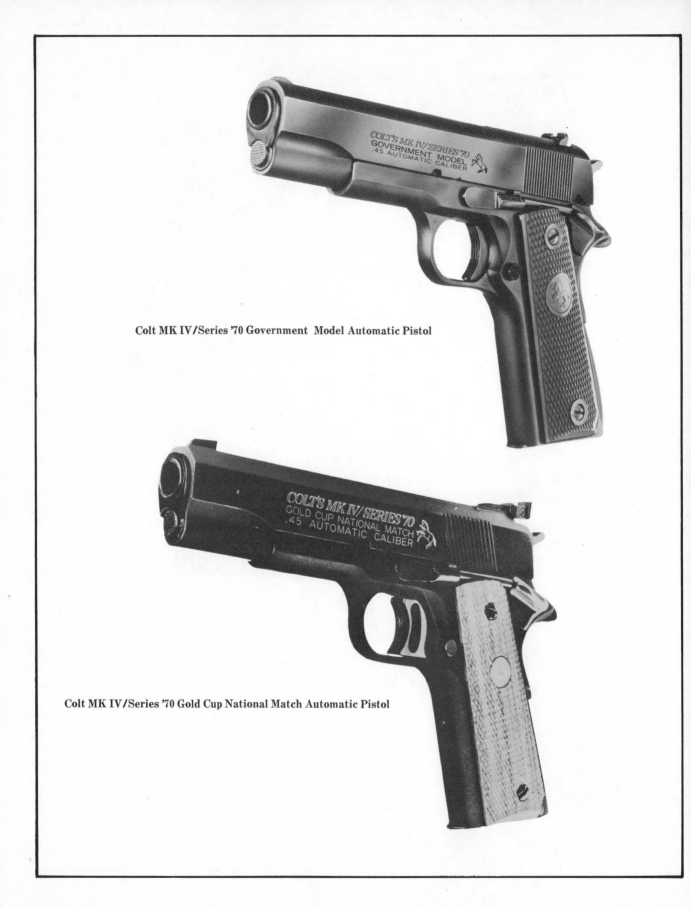

Colt MK IV/Series '70 Government Model Automatic Pistol

Colt MK IV/Series '70 Gold Cup National Match Automatic Pistol

nated in 1946, and 22 auto manufacture was finally halted in 1977. Today, Colt manufactures only the 1970 version of the original 45-caliber M1911 model in several variations. This is not to say that Colt has stagnated in the autoloading pistol field, for its R&D department has developed what appears to be a very good and quite modern big-bore double-action locked-breech auto known as the M71. Whether this new design will enter production in the foreseeable future simply can't be stated at this time; Colt authorities have refused to give us a positive answer.

COLT GOVERNMENT MODEL MK IV/SE-RIES 70: This is the latest refinement of the original M1911 45 design, and in spite of the impressive model designation, the only significant improvement upon the original is the use of a spring-fingered, collet-type barrel bushing. This supports the barrel muzzle securely and locates it consistently without the necessity for a very precise hand-fitting job as was required for maximum accuracy and reliability with the pre-1970 solid bushing. Commonly known simply as the "Colt 45 Auto" or "Government Model," this design has a tremendously good, world-wide reputation for durability and reliability under poor conditions. By the same token, among laymen its reputation for accuracy is less than it should be—a situation brought about by poor results obtained by millions of U.S. soldiers whose experience and training with the gun was too brief for them to learn how to handle it properly.

On the other hand, among pistol enthusiasts, the GM is known for good accuracy. When properly modified and set up by an expert pistolsmith, it is capable of accuracy bettering two-inch groups at 50 yards. The basic GM pistol, in addition to the 45 ACP cartridge, is also chambered for the high-performance, 38 Colt Super Auto introduced in 1929, and was adapted to the world-favorite 9mm Parabellum cartridge during the 1960s. Two modified versions (in the same three calibers) of the GM are offered; the lightweight Commander (LWC) with the barrel shortened to 4¼ inches, a rounded hammer-spur and trimmed grip safety, and an aluminum-alloy frame. The other version is physically identical, but has a steel frame and is designated "Combat Commander."

COLT GOLD CUP NATIONAL MATCH MK IV/SERIES 70: This is the definitive development of the target-model version of the Colt GM. It shares all the basic, mechanical features of the standard GM, but carries a sighting rib on the slide and Colt/Ellia-son micrometer-adjustable target-type sights; all parts critical to accuracy are carefully hand-fitted. In addition, it is fitted with a wider match-type trigger

and trigger stop, and modified sear and hammer to permit a better trigger pull to be obtained. It is also supplied with a softer recoil-spring to permit better functioning with light target loads, and the slide is somewhat lightened toward that same end. This is the only factory-made 45-caliber autoloading target pistol manufactured in the U.S., and it is the only one of that type generally available throughout the world, though other 45 autoloaders do exist.

HECKLER & KOCH: This is a relatively new company which arose in Germany following World War II and began its arms activities by producing the roller-locked G-1 7.62mm service rifle and related automatic weapons for the West German military establishment. In the mid-to-late 1960s, H&K introduced a very advanced locked-breech big-bore double-action pistol design featuring the unusual Vorgrimmler locking system developed in Germany during the latter part of the war. This locking system allows the use of a barrel fixed rigidly to the frame, thus eliminating the accuracy-reducing clearances and movement necessary in movable-barrel designs. As this is written, the P9S is the only big-bore locked-breech pistol operating with a fixed barrel. H&K also utilizes hammer-forged parabolic rifling of slightly smaller-than-standard dimensions, thus causing an increase in chamber pressure and velocity from standard ammunition.

Most unusual of the P9S is the fact that both the slide and frame are manufactured from sheet-steel stampings welded and spot-welded into solid assemblies with assorted spacers and functional cast parts. A separate breech-block is pinned into the slide, and the trigger guard and front strap are a single molding of a very tough plastic. The double-action lockwork of the P9S is unusual, featuring a fully enclosed, rotating hammer and a manual cocking and decocking lever on the left side which is also used to engage or disengage the slide stop manually.

A rather large pistol, the P9S is dimensioned around the 45 ACP cartridge and is currently offered in that caliber as well as the 9mm Parabellum.

HECKLER & KOCH HK-4: During about the same period, H&K also introduced its HK-4 blow-back pistol of unusual interchangeable caliber design. Developed from the prewar Mauser HSc, this gun also utilizes a stamped steel slide but in conjunction with a light-alloy frame of conventional form. It possesses double-action lockwork, the slide stop is entirely automatic, and is unusual in that it is disengaged to run the slide forward when the magazine is empty or removed by simply pulling the trigger. The stop also engages automatically as the slide is

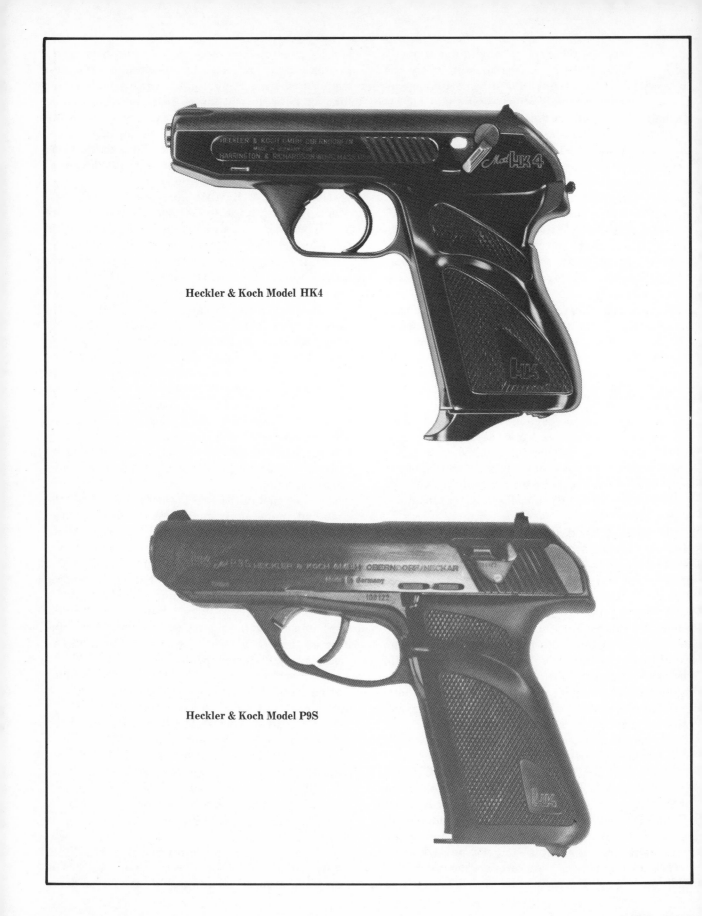

Heckler & Koch Model HK4

Heckler & Koch Model P9S

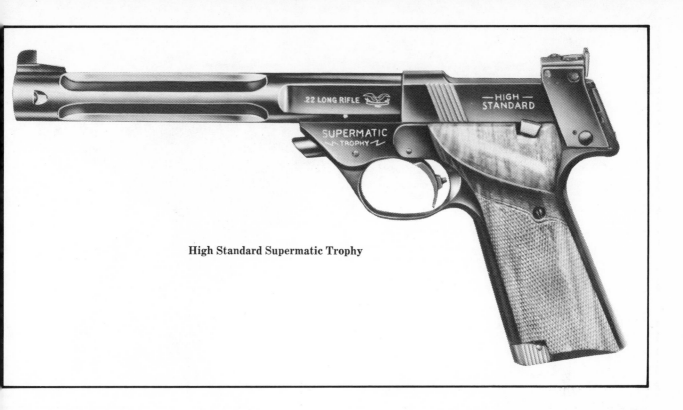

High Standard Supermatic Trophy

retracted when the magazine is out. An unusual feature of the lockwork is that when the hammer is cocked and the manual safety on the slide is engaged, the hammer is lowered *safely* by simply pulling the trigger. When a charged magazine is inserted with the slide-in battery, retracting the slide causes the stop to engage and hold to the rear, after which the trigger is pulled to disengage the stop and allow the slide to run forward. This initial trigger-pull will not fire the gun, but a second pull of the trigger will. While this is a rather sophisticated system, it can be confusing, perhaps even potentially dangerous, to an individual who has not made himself thoroughly familiar with the operating characteristics of the design.

HIGH STANDARD: The High Standard Corporation has been manufacturing 22 rimfire autoloading pistols, which were initially developed from the old Hartford designs, since the late 1920s/early 1930s. Prior to World War II, the designs remained relatively prosaic, being full-size but relatively light in weight, and even when designated as target types, not competitive with the reigning Colt Match Target Woodsman of the period. After the war, High Standard refined the basic design extensively, incorporating a removable (interchangeable) barrel system, and adding many refinements desired by the serious target shooter. After several years of refinement, the present "Supermatic" design emerged and is presently produced in several minor variations. The design incorporates a rigidly mounted but detachable barrel; a short slide containing its own recoil spring, a concealed, rotating hammer, trigger-pull adjustments, and fully adjustable target sights. In standard form, the rear sight is installed upon the reciprocating slide (therefore, creating relative movement between the two sights), while in the military model, the rear sight is installed upon a massive yoke attached to the frame so that there is no relative movement between the two sights, and the slide is free to reciprocate through the center of the yoke. Barrels are somewhat interchangeable among the different models, and a highly refined version chambered for the 22 Short cartridge is available for International Rapid-Fire shooting.

LLAMA (GABILONDO): "Llama" is the trade name placed upon the autoloading pistols (and revolvers) manufactured by Gabilondo y Cia of Vitoria, Spain. Gabilondo is one of those few Spanish pistol-makers privileged to resume regular operations after the civil war of the mid-to-late 1930s. Prior to World War II, other names were sometimes placed upon the same guns, but since large-scale importation into this country began in the early 1950s, only the name Llama has been used. Incidentally, the same guns are sold widely throughout the rest of the world, though it would appear that more are sold here.

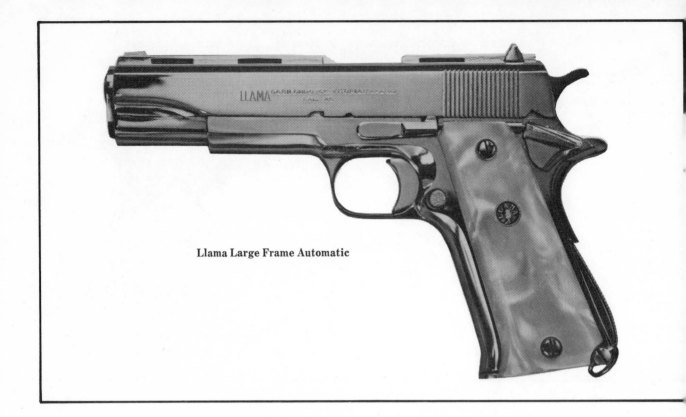

Llama Large Frame Automatic

About 1927, Gabilondo began to copy very closely the Colt/Browning M1911/A1 in calibers 45 and 9mm/38. Even though the resulting gun is a very close copy, there are minor differences, and U.S. parts will not usually interchange. For example, the ejector has sometimes been made as an integral part of the Llama frame whereas it is a separate part riveted and pinned in place on the Colt; the Llama spring and plunger housing on the left side of the frame is attached by screws rather than being riveted as in the Colt. Today the large, 45-sized frame, Llama auto has been dressed up a bit and modified further with the addition of a low ventilated rib and a few other small changes. It is offered in calibers 9mm Parabellum, 38 Colt Super Auto (9mm/38 in Spanish terminology), and 45 ACP. Incidentally, Gabilondo specializes in supplying all of its guns elaborately decorated with engraving and gold damascening.

The most unusual feature about the Llama line of autos is that the large-frame locked-breech pistol has been scaled down to accommodate the 380 ACP cartridge. The 380 model is substantially smaller and lighter, while retaining all of the features of the big gun. This model is often favored by handloaders because its locked-breech construction allows some upgrading of the 380 cartridge by loading to higher pressures; however, this must be done carefully, or

damage will result. Gabilondo also manufactures the small-frame gun in 32 ACP and 22 LR caliber with the locked-breech feature eliminated, converting the design to straight blowback, but otherwise possessing all the features of the 380 and 45 ACP.

In this respect, Gabilondo has made the maximum use of a single basic design well-proven in advance; it has been produced full-sized then scaled down to a smaller caliber, and finally modified only slightly as necessary to accommodate two, additional, small calibers. The result is a total of six models in two sizes, all of identical appearance, having maximum parts interchangeability and maximum use of all original features. All six models of Llama pistols are imported and distributed exclusively in this country by Stoeger Industries.

MAUSER: The post-World War II resurrection of the original Mauser Werke which manufactured German service rifles, pistols and machine guns (among other products) from 1871 on. Mauser has manufactured pistols since the mid-1890s, beginning with the famous "Broomhandle" and continuing with the Parabellum/Luger and finishing-up during World War II with the Walther P38 and HSc. During the mid-to-late 1930s, Mauser developed a new double-action, medium-size, blowback pistol of advanced design in 32 and 380 ACP caliber. Little commercial

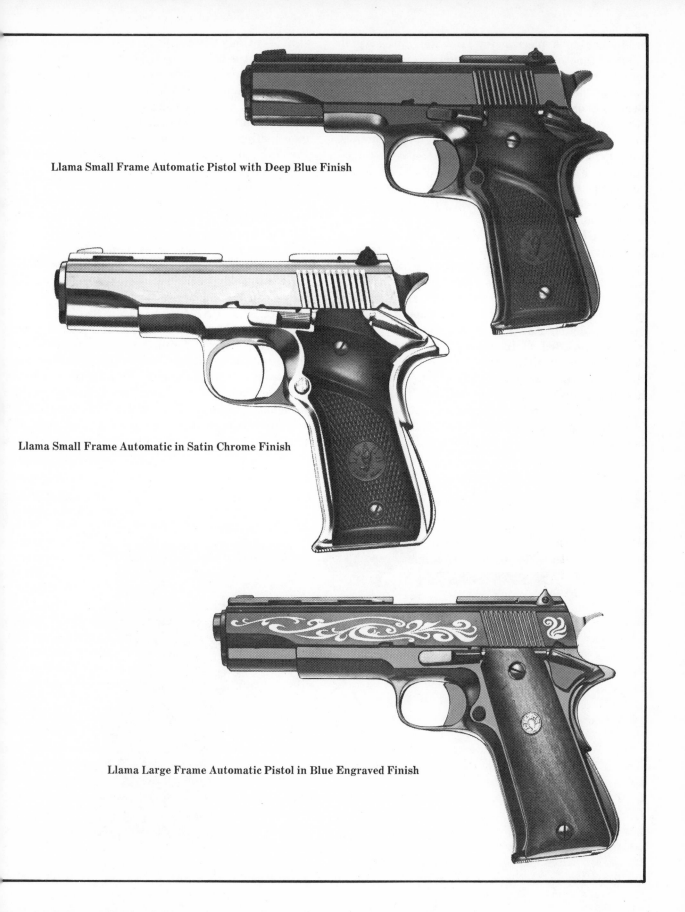

Llama Small Frame Automatic Pistol with Deep Blue Finish

Llama Small Frame Automatic in Satin Chrome Finish

Llama Large Frame Automatic Pistol in Blue Engraved Finish

production took place before the war, but several hundred thousands of this HSc model were manufactured for German military use before the famous plant was dismantled in 1945. In the 1960s, Mauser elected to again produce this excellent pistol in its new plant. Minor changes to facilitate production were incorporated in the new HSc, but its appearance and characteristics were not changed. It was introduced in 32 and 380 ACP caliber, with the latter becoming the U.S. favorite as professional gun carriers became more concerned with lethality and ammunition performance.

MAUSER HSc: The Mauser HSc carries a conventional tubular slide with concentric recoil-spring and fixed sights. While it is essentially an exposed-hammer design, only the tip of the hammer spur protrudes beyond the rear of the frame and slide in order to permit manual cocking when desired. It possesses double-action first-shot capability and is actually intended to be carried with the hammer down, in which position the rear of the hammer closes the slot in the frame and slide through which the hammer spur protrudes for cocking. The double-action lockwork is relatively efficient, but its mechanical advantage is apparently not all that it could be, because the DA trigger pull is rather stiff. The slide stop is entirely automatic, no part of it exposed, and, therefore, the breech may be closed only by inserting an empty magazine, or a full magazine, in which case the top round is automatically chambered. Field stripping is accomplished by pulling downward on a small cylindrical latch inside the front of the trigger-guard, after which the slide and barrel may be eased forward and lifted off the frame. The HSc is generally quite well made (and priced accordingly) and is functionally quite reliable. About the only criticism I can make of it is in the handling department. The rearward extension of the frame is poorly shaped and jams into the web of the shooting hand. When firing only a few rounds, this poses no problem, other than making the gun point low. But if a great deal of firing is done in a short period of time, the web of the hand may easily become bruised or blistered.

MAUSER PARABELLUM: Also in the 1960s Mauser determined to resume production of a variation of the original Parabellum/Luger pistol which it produced from the early 1900s until 1942. This pistol is so well and widely known as to require hardly any comment here. The first model offered by Mauser was designated "Mauser Parabellum," and was, in fact, the Swiss service model adopted in the 1920s, with grip safety and reverse manual safety and without

Mauser Model P38

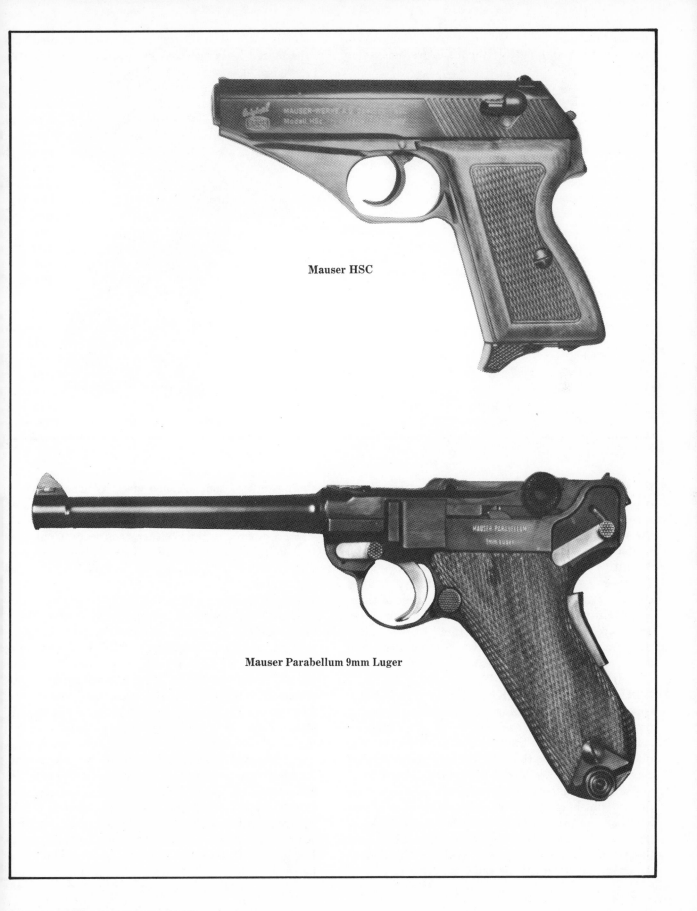

Mauser HSC

Mauser Parabellum 9mm Luger

MKE Kirikkale Double Action Automatic Pistol

the distinctive swell of the P08 at the bottom of the front strap. Of more than casual interest, this model was marked with the American eagle stamped over the chamber. Later, Mauser re-introduced the P08 model possessing all of the features of the original, definitive "Luger." This model was designated "Mauser Parabellum P08." Interestingly, Mauser could not apply the name "Luger" to either of these pistols since the exclusive right to use that name had been purchased by Stoeger Arms (now Stoeger Industries) many years ago when it was importing and distributing Parabellum pistols manufactured by DWM/Mauser.

MKE: The initials MKE stand for the Turkish Government Firearms Manufacturing facility, and it produces one autoloading pistol model, the TPK, also sometimes known as the "Kirikkale." This pistol is nothing more or less than the Turkish-manufactured copy of the Walther Model PP and is offered in 32 and 380 ACP calibers. While it cannot be said that the fit and finish of the TPK approaches that of the Walther, the price differential makes a slight roughness reasonably acceptable. While the TPK does possess all the features of the Walther PP, it does suffer in that the magazine catch is at the butt (after

the pattern of some French-made Walthers) rather than in the Browning position of current Walther production. While these guns appear a little rough when compared to the Walther, they seem to perform well in the field. The MKE TPK is imported and distributed exclusively in this country by Firearms Center, Inc.

RUGER: Sturm, Ruger is the most successful of firearms manufacturers formed in the post-World War II period, and it was also the first to rise during that period. The first product of Bill Ruger's inventive talents (since followed by many more) was the Ruger "Standard Model" 22 LR autoloader. At its introduction in 1949, it displayed many innovative features, mainly a frame welded from two stamped-steel halves and a steel-tube barrel extension enclosing a cylindrical bolt. It is a relatively simple and uncomplicated design, composed of few parts and designed specifically for low-cost manufacture on simple tooling. That this approach was successful is clearly evident in the fact that it still remains today, by a very substantial margin, the lowest-cost 22 RF auto on the market. Styled to resemble the famous Luger pistol (perhaps because of the similarity between "Luger" and "Ruger"), the Standard Model

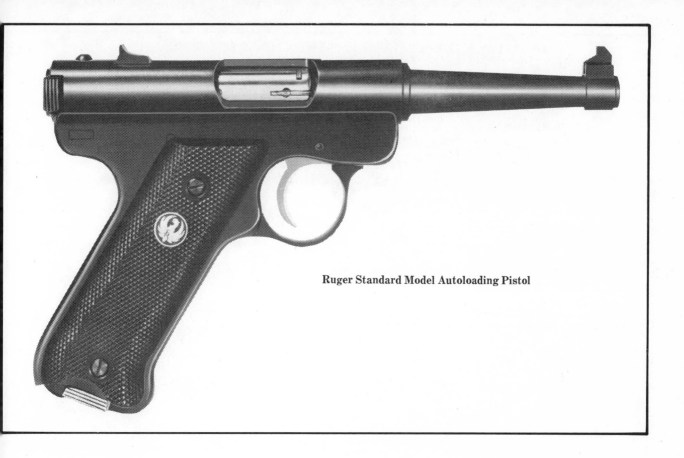

Ruger Standard Model Autoloading Pistol

remains in production without change to this date, and its popularity has not diminished in the least. As from the beginning, it remains the lowest-cost full-sized 22 LR auto available. Since its introduction, a target version has been introduced, featuring heavy and/or longer barrels and fully adjustable micrometer-type target sights. It is known simply as the "Ruger MKI," and while priced modestly above the Standard Model, it, too, still costs less than virtually all other full-sized 22 autos. Ruger introduced the welded and stamped, sheet-metal frame on this gun nearly 30 years ago, and yet today only one additional gun (the H&K P9S) has employed this same type of advanced construction. It should not be overlooked that the low-cost Ruger Standard Model struck the market at a most opportune time to encourage a great many new shooters.

SIG: Initials for Suisse Industrie Gesellschaft, an industrial combine which produces all manner of products, of which firearms represent only a small part. Currently SIG offers the very highly developed and specialized SIG/Hammerli P240 Centerfire Target pistol. The gun is generally conventional in appearance and apparently available in this country only in 38 Special caliber, though foreign shooters report using it in 32 S&W Long. It utilizes a highly refined basic Browning slide/barrel locking system, and an unusual sear/hammer relationship whereby the working edges of the engaging surfaces are under load only at the time of firing. This avoids the wear and chipping problems encountered with most other rotating-hammer designs. The P240 is very finely made and fitted. Aside from the refinements of sear/hammer and locking-system design, the P240 is fairly conventional and is distinguished primarily by the very high order of workmanship which enables it to produce superb accuracy. Such quality does not come cheap, and, to this author's knowledge, this gun is the most expensive autoloading target pistol on the market at over $750. All SIG and SIG/Hammerli pistols are available through Gil Hebard Guns and Mandall Shooter's Supplies. The SIG/Sauer P220 is available through Hawes International.

SIG/HAMMERLI P208/211/230: Also available are the SIG/Hammerli 22 Rimfire Target pistols, the fairly conventional P208 and P211 in 22 LR and intended for both American- and International-type 22 matches. Much more sophisticated and of substantially different design is the P230 International Rapid-Fire pistol chambered only for the 22 Short.

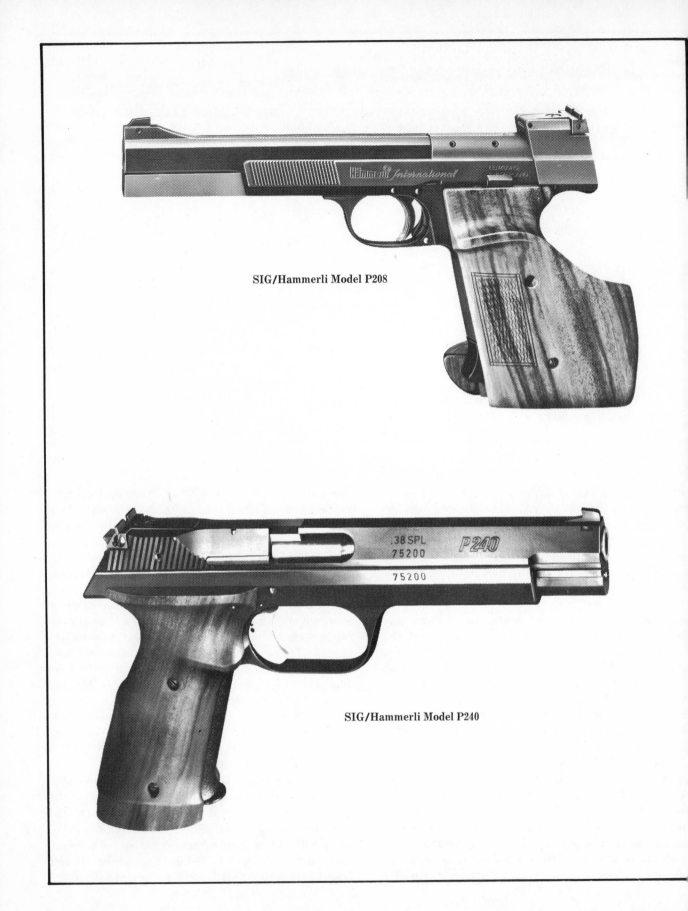

SIG/Hammerli Model P208

SIG/Hammerli Model P240

The 230 features a light-alloy subframe containing the grip and magazine, a steel upper receiver group containing the barrel and small reciprocating bolt or breech block at the rear. It also features gas-escape ports in the top of the barrel to be used to regulate muzzle velocity to the minimum that will produce reliable functioning.

SIG/SAUER P220: SIG is also responsible for the design and testing and development of what is now known as the SIG/Sauer P220. This dual name is due simply to the fact that the gun is manufactured under license by J. P. Sauer & Sohn in West Germany. This is a full-sized military and police-type pistol utilizing a highly refined, cam-operated, Browning-type locking system with tubular slide and recoil spring beneath the barrel. It is unusual in that the slide is a stamped and welded sheet-steel shell into which is pinned a separate breech block. It is quite unconventional in that it deletes entirely the traditional manual safety to which we are all accustomed, and substitutes a fully automatic internal firing-pin safety operated by the trigger through an intermediate lever. It is set up so that the firing pin is blocked securely to the rear except when the trigger is pulled deliberately rearward to fire.

The lockwork is of double-action type, simple and sturdy, and a separate manually operated decocking lever is provided to ensure that the hammer can be lowered safely without disengaging the firing-pin safety as would be required if the hammer were let down in the conventional manner. Once the hammer has been lowered, firing may be double-action by a simple pull of the trigger, or in deliberate SA fashion after manually cocking the hammer.

Construction of the balance of the gun is fairly conventional, with a light-alloy frame and wrap-around grips. The P220 is dimensioned around the 45 ACP cartridge, and is designed for easy change to smaller calibers by substitution of barrels, magazines and slides. It is currently offered in only 9mm Parabellum, 38 Super and 45 ACP, though catalogs and brochures also list the 22 LR and 7.65mm Parabellum. In theory, one may purchase the gun in any of the available calibers, then as they become available, obtain the correct parts for easy conversion to any of the other four calibers.

SMITH & WESSON: Smith & Wesson's early attempts at developing an autoloading pistol were not successful, the result being overly complex and over-priced—so it died during the 1930s. Consequently, when S&W decided after World War II to re-enter the field, particular care was taken to produce a simple yet superbly efficient design which at the same time retained cosmetic S&W identity. The first auto of the new generation to be introduced was the M41 target pistol in 22 LR caliber. It features a cutaway slide with recoil spring beneath the barrel and a detachable barrel secured by a trigger-guard lock. In addition, the barrel carries an integral rib which extends rearward over the slide and supports the micrometer-adjustable rear sight there so that there is no relative movement between the two sight units. The M41, in the several minor variations that have been made, has incorporated all of the refinements desired by the serious target shooter, and the gun has developed a superb reputation for reliability and accuracy at the highest level of competitive shooting. Even a conversion unit to adapt it to 22 Short caliber for international rapid-fire matches is available.

S&W M39: Following the success of the M41, Smith & Wesson introduced its first full-sized big-bore autoloader. This was the M39, with a simple but extremely smooth and sturdy double-action lock-work and incorporating a variation of the basic Browning barrel/slide locking system. The M39 also features a hammer-dropping/hammer-blocking safety, and an unusual magazine safety operating through the ejector but which may be easily removed without interfering with regular functioning. It was the first domestic-production service pistol to incorporate click windage adjustment in its standard sights. The gun was designed for maximum compactness around the 9mm Parabellum cartridge and employs an aluminum-alloy receiver. As a result, it is the most compact lightweight full-bore service pistol available.

S&W M59: In the early 1970s, Smith & Wesson modified the M39 design to accommodate a Browning-like double-column magazine with a design capacity of 14 9mm cartridges and designated it M59. In production form, the magazine will generally hold 15 cartridges, giving the M59 the largest total capacity of any production pistol available as this is written. As a practical matter, the 16-shot M59 is simply the M39 with the frame widened to accept the double-column magazine. Other parts have undergone minor changes to accommodate the widened frame, but the design is otherwise identical.

S&W M52: Smith & Wesson went on to develop a pure target version of the basic M39 design, incorporating a heavier steel frame, longer and heavier barrel and slide, and precisely adjustable trigger and sights. The M39 also featured a unique barrel bushing threaded into the slide and making only line contact with a raised bead just behind the barrel muzzle; this permitted much closer fitting on a production basis than previous bushing designs. To suit the prefer-

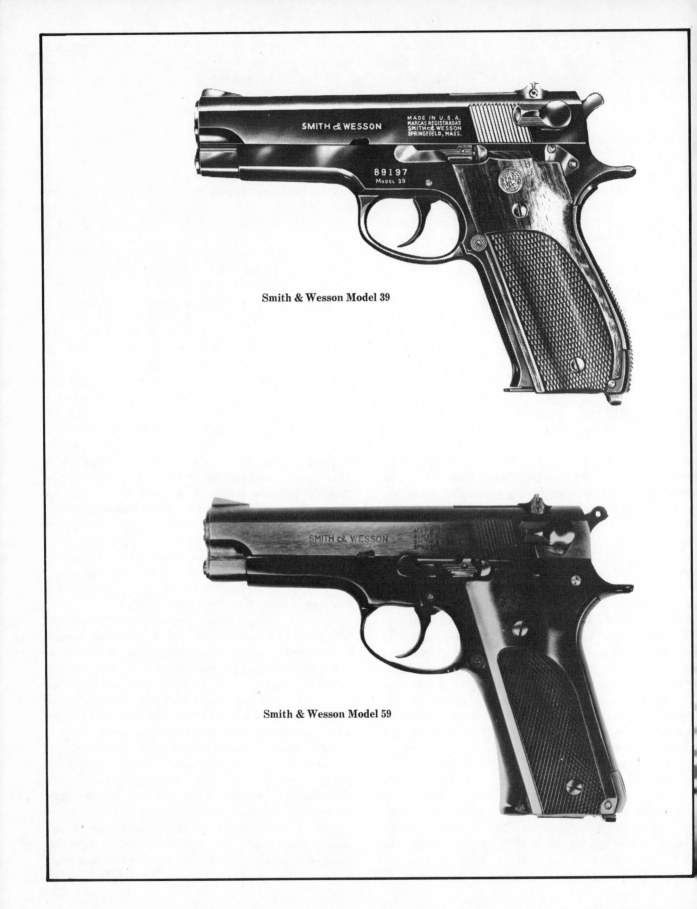

Smith & Wesson Model 39

Smith & Wesson Model 59

Smith & Wesson Model 52

nces of U.S. shooters and the best centerfire ammu-
ition available, the M52 was further designed to
ccommodate and feed positively with the flush-
eated, midrange, 38 Special, wadcutter, target loads.

STAR (BONIFACIO ECHEVERRIA): Star
istols are manufactured in Spain in the north-coast
own of Eibar, in the Echeverria plant which was
ermitted to resume operations after the Spanish
ivil War. Echeverria began manufacture of hand-
uns in the early 1900s and, during World War I,
ade hundreds of thousands of 32-caliber autos for
e French government. Following that conflict, it
eveloped a large-frame big-bore autoloader employ-
g the Browning locking system of the Colt GM,
ombined with a simplified lockwork and frame. By
922, the design had reached mechanically definitive
rm, and the guns being manufactured today are
ssentially the same except for cosmetics and materi-
ls. Largest of the series are the Model AS and Model
, chambered for the 38 Colt Super Auto (9mm/38)
nd 45 ACP cartridges respectively. They are essen-
ally the same size as the Colt GM. The Model B is
nly very slightly reduced in some areas and is cham-
ered to the 9mm Parabellum.

During the past decade, Star took the Model B,
ortened the barrel and slide, pared down the gun
enerally, and substituted aluminum alloy for steel as

the frame material, to produce the Model BKM—
otherwise known as the Starlight. This is the smallest
and lightest caliber 9mm Parabellum pistol currently
available and has become quite popular for concealed
use. Following that success, Star made essentially the
same modifications on the 45 Model P to produce the
Model PD which is currently the smallest and lightest
production 45 auto offered by a major manufacturer.
The PD is approximately ten percent smaller and
lighter than the Colt LW Commander.

Following World War II, Star scaled its big-frame
design down to match the 380 ACP cartridge, retaining the full breech-locking system. This produced a
gun nearly two inches shorter and 15 ounces lighter
than the big model, yet retained all of its desirable
features. The resulting development moved through
several stages, with the current form probably repre-
senting final development and known as the "Super
SM." Of all-steel construction, it is considered by
many to be the finest single-action exposed-
hammer 380 pistol available, even though it is somewhat larger than some other popular models. All Star
pistols are now distributed exclusively by Interarms.

STERLING ARMS: Another new pistol-making
firm which came up in the 1960s and has thus far
limited its activities to autoloaders of service and
sporting type. After initial and unfortunate develop-

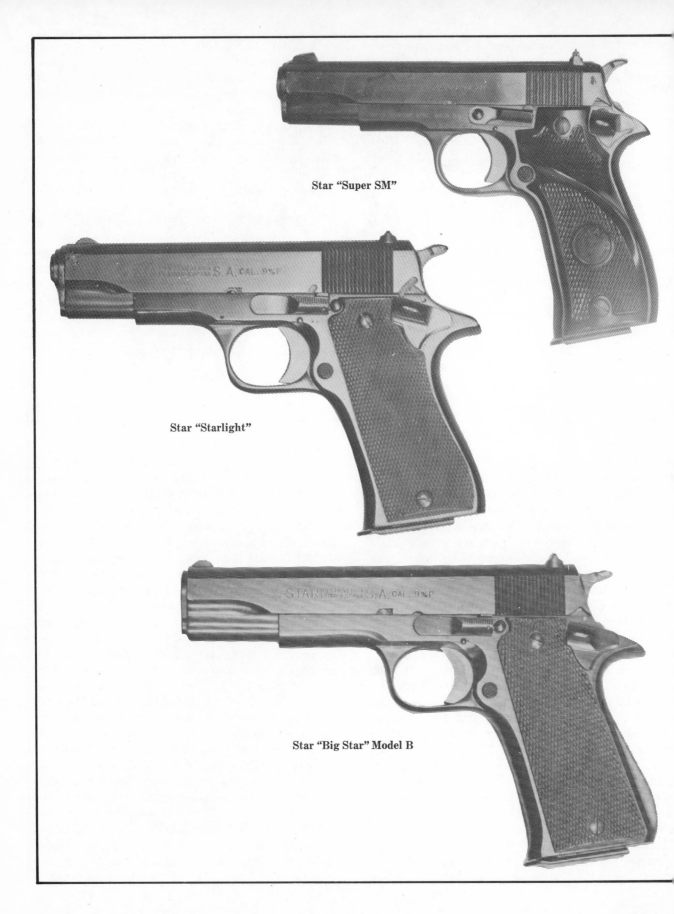

Star "Super SM"

Star "Starlight"

Star "Big Star" Model B

ment and production of odd-looking and unsuccessful 22 rimfire and small 380 pistols, the company changed hands, and the new staff concentrated on development of small, pocket autos in 22 and 25 caliber, and a medium-sized, double-action 380 pistol. Since then, Sterling has also developed an unusual full-sized, 45-caliber, double-action autoloader with large magazine capacity and several other unique features.

STERLING M301/302: The smallest of the Sterling pistols is the Model 300 series, a very basic blowback autoloader, employing a tubular slide, concentric recoil spring and a striker-type firing mechanism. The design is quite simple, composed of the minimum number of parts and intended for manufacture by investment casting and minimal machining. This design is quite small, light in weight, available in both 22 LR and 25 ACP, and very reasonably priced; therefore, it has become quite popular for concealed use.

STERLING M400: Following the success of the small pocket pistols, Sterling designed and placed in production a medium-size 380 autoloader bearing a great external resemblance to the Walther PP series, employing a Walther-type safety and concentric recoil spring inside a tubular slide, and possessing double-action first-shot capability. Produced initially in carbon steel, it has now been refined and lightened and is offered as the Model 400 MKII constructed entirely of stainless steel.

STERLING M450: M450 represents Sterling's most ambitious project to date, and is a full-sized, exposed-hammer locked-breech double-action autoloader with ambidextrous safety and partially staggered magazine to obtain a capacity of eight cartridges (plus one in the chamber) without exceeding the butt length and width of the Colt GM. A manual safety, easily converted to left-hand use, is featured, as in an adjustable barrel bushing.

Star Model PD

Sterling Arms Model 301/302

Sterling Arms Model 400 MK II Double Action Pistol

Sterling Arms Model 400

Sterling Arms Model 450

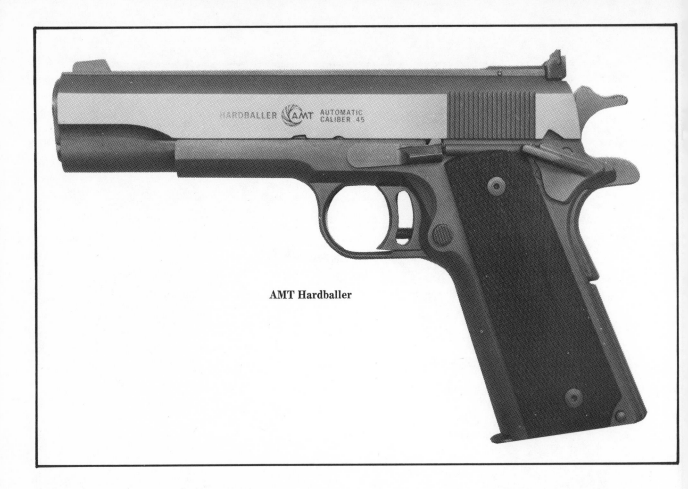

AMT Hardballer

TDE/OMC: Actually these are two designations for the same basic organization which produces two rather unusual pistols. As a matter of fact, the same parties were involved in the manufacture of the now-discontinued Auto Mag pistol. Under the TDE name we have the "Backup" stainless-steel 380 autoloader. This is the smallest centerfire auto made above 25 caliber and is of unusual design in that it employs a separate breech-block T-slotted vertically into the slide and which is removed at the first stage of disassembly. It is a straight blowback design, employing an enclosed hammer, and is designed primarily for maximum concealment and, therefore, smallest possible size and minimum number of parts for the 380 cartridge. Because it is by far the smallest 380-caliber pistol available and also because of its stainless-steel construction, the Backup has become exceedingly popular as a hideout gun for uniformed officers and as an off-duty gun under those conditions where a larger and more powerful gun simply can't be hidden.

Under the OMC name, we have the "Hardballer" pistol which is nothing more or less than a complete, line-for-line and dimension-for-dimension copy of the Colt pre-1970 Government Model 45 auto. At present, two-variations are available, the first featuring a ribbed slide and fully adjustable target sight, while the second is identical except for use of conventional, fixed sights. All other characteristics are identical to those of the Colt Government Model.

WALTHER: The Carl Walther plant has continuously manufactured autoloading pistols since before World War II, with the single exception of temporary cessations following German defeat in two major wars. Only two basic models of Walther pistols are available in the U.S. today, the PP-PPK/S series first introduced in the late 1920s, and the P38 finalized in the mid-to-late 1930s and adopted as the standard German service arm in 1938. A medium-sized pocket-type pistol, the PP (for pistole polizie, "police pistol") was the first successful double-action pistol of its type. It represented the ultimate development of the type at the time of its introduction and is still considered by most users and authorities to be the best. Other German companies introduced comparable guns a decade later, but it was not until the 1960s that other double-action pistols of this type were

Walther Model PPK/S Auto Pistol

Walther Model OSP

Walther Model PPK Automatic Pistol

developed to compete with the Walther PP, and even today they usually run second best behind it.

The hinged trigger-guard takedown, the automatic firing-pin safety, the hammer-dropping/hammer-blocking manual safety, the pin-type loaded-chamber indicator, and the unusual revolver-like double-action lockwork (incorporating a secondary cocking lever functioning like the revolver trigger) of the PP were all Walther innovations that have survived unchanged for 50 years now, and have all subsequently been copied except for the double-action mechanism.

The P38 followed the PP and incorporated many of the PP features, in fact, all of them except the tubular slide, blowback system, and trigger-guard takedown. Instead, the P38 used a cutaway slide and rear-mounted recoil springs, combined with a pivoted-block locking system and exposed barrel, plus a rotating-lever, takedown system similar in function and location to that of the earlier Parabellum pistol. Like the PP, the Walther P38 set the pace, and it was nearly 20 years before another double-action service-type full-size autoloader was developed to compete with it.

While the P38 is made primarily in 9mm Parabellum caliber, it is also somewhat available in 7.65mm Parabellum (30 Luger) and in a modified form, in 22 LR. The PP and PPK/S are both available in calibers 22LR, 32 ACP and 380 ACP. Demand for the 32 is relatively light, since it lacks the virtues of either of the other two calibers.

Following the enactment of GCA'68, Walther introduced a new model, the PPK/S, which is simply the PP with the barrel and slide shortened to the minimum length that could qualify for importation under the new law and regulations.

WALTHER GSP/OSP: Over the years Walther has produced a number of 22 rimfire target pistols of considerable sophistication. The one currently available represents the highest refinement of all they have learned in this field. It is identified as the GSP model and is of unusual configuration, placing the removable magazine ahead of the trigger guard in the light-alloy frame. A unitized removable firing mechanism, including trigger and hammer, fits in the top of the frame, and there is also a dry-fire firing mechanism available as an accessory and it may be installed for practice. An upper receiver portion is rectangular in section, houses the round reciprocating bolt, and accepts the slab-sided relatively heavy barrel at the front, where it is pinned removably in place.

This gun is fitted with orthopedic-type grips with adjustable shelf and very precisely adjustable target sights of typically European pattern. It is manufactured in 22 LR caliber, but a variation designated GSP-C is also produced in 32 S&W caliber, intended only for flush-seated, wadcutter-bullet cartridges. Additionally, the same basic design is offered in 22 Short caliber for rapid-fire competition and is then designated OPS.

Chapter Ten
Choosing a Used Gun

It has been said that more than two-and-one-half million *new* handguns are sold in this country each year. Of course, this includes imports as well as domestic production. We have no way of knowing what percentage of these guns are autoloaders, but on the surface, it would appear that by far the greater majority of imports are autoloading types, while the majority of domestic production are revolvers. Actually, it doesn't matter either way, for we are concerned with new guns only as their tremendous production generates *used* guns which may be encountered in even the smallest shop. This annual rate of some two-and-one-half million handguns has been going on for a number of years, and if I were to hazard a personal estimate of the number produced since World War II (roughly 33 years), I'd say it would have to fall somewhere in excess of 40 million, perhaps a good deal more.

Prior to that, the figures become more vague, and it's simply impossible to come up with any reasonably accurate number. However, I think that it can be stated without fear of contradiction that countless tens of millions have been produced. For example,

there are several basic models by major manufacturers, the production of each of which has exceeded several million. Even some models, introduced back before the turn of the century, were produced in hundreds of thousands before being discontinued in the 1930s.

Then, to all these accumulations of new guns, we must add the many hundreds of thousands of surplus military handguns imported legitimately into this country before the infamous GCA'68 (Gun Control Act of late 1968). And, of course, there are hundreds of thousands brought back both legitimately and clandestinely by millions of U.S. servicemen returning from several wars.

A generally accepted figure for the number of handguns currently in private hands throughout this nation is given at 50 million. That's almost one gun for every four men, women and children alive in this country today. Personally, I feel the true number is much higher, simply because the survival rate of handguns is quite high. A handgun may, of course, be destroyed by fire or calamity, but the *average* pistol or revolver simply never wears out with use. An avid target shooter may buy a new gun and put as many as 50,000 rounds through it in a short time, but it will be maintained superbly, and when the owner becomes dissatisfied with its performance, he certainly doesn't toss it in the nearest trash can. Instead, he trades or sells it to someone else who keeps it in service for many more years. The average handgun is purchased at least partially for home-defense and remains in the home or homes for generations, all the while seeing very little use. As people die, homes are broken up, families move, etc., these guns are sold or given away and become part of the massive used-gun market. Police departments buy hundreds of thousands of new guns each year, and in most instances, they trade in large numbers of old guns on the new models. These trade-ins also enter the used market. Hundreds of thousands of gun enthusiasts each buy dozens of new guns each year. There is constant turnover among them as they enter the used market.

There have been both private and governmental efforts to determine the size of the used-handgun market, but to date, there has simply been no credible estimate possible of the total number of annual sales.

Doubtless, it will eventually become possible through the careful machinations of the anti-gun forces, Congress and the Treasury Department to computerize and record all so-called "legitimate" used-gun sales made through licensed dealers. Interesting though that information would be, the "big brother" system which would make it possible must be regarded as anathema by private citizens who value their rights. But, even if that information were known, the figure wouldn't mean much. Surely even more handguns change hands between individuals, with no records whatever being kept. There is almost no possibility of accurately estimating their numbers.

So, all I could really say is that we *know* that several millions of used handguns of all types and ages, ranging from antique muzzle-loaders up to the most sophisticated target autoloaders are bought and sold as used guns each year. Their condition ranges from pure, useless junk better suited as a trotline weight up through the finest modern autos valued at several hundred dollars, and on to priceless antiques and objects of art demanding five- and even six-figure prices from moneyed collectors.

The question posed and hopefully answered by this chapter is how *you* can make an intelligent selection

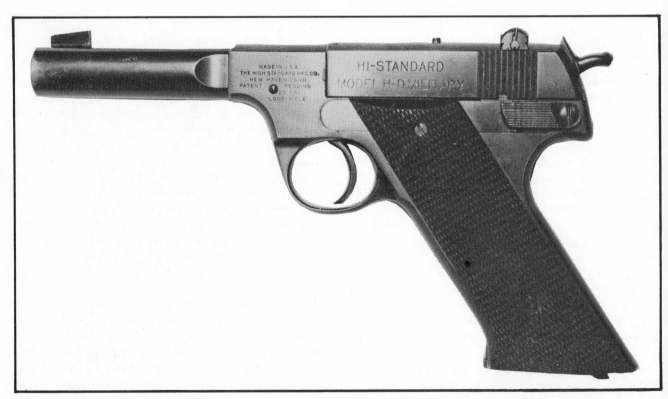

The High Standard HD Military Model was made in considerable numbers but has nearly vanished from today's market. This and other sporting-type 22s are less common on the used gun counter than are larger caliber, more expensive pistols.

from this vast supply of used guns to obtain an autoloader that will meet your needs at the most economical price.

The autoloading pistols available on the used market (and by that we mean those which you see in the showcases of the typical gun shop) may be broken down into several classes, exclusive of collector's items. First, and probably the least common these days, are the sporting-type 22 rimfire models. Generally speaking, these are mostly of domestic manufacture and include all of the non-target Colt Woodsman models and variations plus the similar products of High Standard and Ruger, with a smattering of foreign models. Then come the so-called "pocket pistols," consisting of a tremendous variety of makes, models and designs ranging from tiny palm-sized pistols in 22 Short and 25 ACP, up through the larger and more modern 32 and 380 ACP pistols by Walther, Mauser and many other makers, most of which are foreign. Beyond that we encounter the military and police types typified by the 1911 Colt Government Model and the S&W M39 of domestic production, and the Browning HP and Walther P38 of European manufacture.

I think perhaps the first factors to be considered in selecting a used auto are its origin, age and availability of parts. With respect to origin, one should stick with guns made by a company still in existence and still in the firearms-manufacturing business. Even that isn't an infallible guide. For example, hundreds of thousands of the fine Sauer M38 pistols were made during the very short period of 1938–1945, many of them from the latter part of that period being of dubious quality. And, even though the J. P. Sauer Company still manufactures firearms, it is not in a position to provide any assistance whatever regarding the M38; replacement parts are totally unavailable except in used form from those shops that specialize in cannibalizing junk guns. While I personally cherish an early-production M38 in very fine condition, I wouldn't recommend it as a working gun to anyone because parts are not available and also because the odds are not good of obtaining one made of good materials and adequate standards of quality.

On the other hand, we have the excellent Walther PP series of pistols introduced in the late 1920s and manufactured in tremendous quantities during World War II. Walther still manufactures the series, albeit

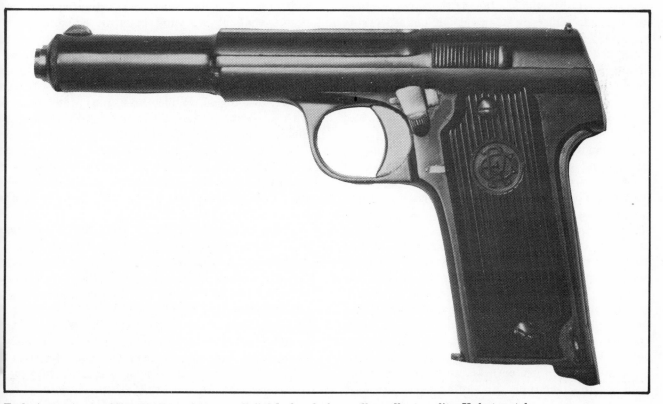

Early Astra pistols of the 400/600 series are well-finished and of overall excellent quality. Unfortunately, parts are no longer available.

slightly improved, so parts and assistance are still available (as are new guns), and a used wartime Walther can be a good buy as a working gun.

If at all possible, choose a gun whose original manufacturer is still in business and from whom parts are still available. An alternative is to choose a gun which has been discontinued and for which parts are no longer produced, but are still available at the time of purchase. Under those conditions, you can acquire the most-likely needed parts for the future and lay them aside: a spare magazine or two, firing pin, extractor, and such other parts as one may determine from the design and experience and references might require replacement in the future.

Most of us tend to ignore reality occasionally and want to purchase a gun based on appeal rather than utility. Unfortunately, such a gun often turns out to be a long-obsolete design containing assorted defects. Remember, the autoloading pistol is a relatively new mechanism. First introduced in the 1890s, it went through much experimentation and development until after World War I. During that 20-odd-year period, literally hundreds of inefficient and defective designs and models were manufactured in substantial quantities which continue to show up as used guns today. If they're in good working condition— complete and functional—buying them as objects of conversation and study is fair enough; but as working guns, they are very poor bargains. Some such models continued in production or military service up until World War II, and so may give the appearance of being relatively modern. However, when a gun with which you are not familiar shows up and seems like a good buy, your best bet is to dig back into books and magazine articles and identify it properly. Pin it down as to manufacture, design vintage, performance history, and other factors we've mentioned.

One particular class of autos should be generally avoided. These are Spanish autos manufactured under innumerable names by countless companies (most no longer in existence) from about 1910 until the beginning of the Spanish Civil War in the middle 1930s. During that period, there were innumerable small shops making parts or complete guns in the north of Spain where the arms industry is concentrated. One shop might make rough frames and slides, another barrels, another magazines, and so forth. Other shops might buy these parts either finished or in the rough from several sources, assemble the basic guns, and stamp them with whatever name they felt appropriate at the time. Quite often, such guns were very crudely made and contained the cheapest materials available. Dimensional control of critical areas

like chambers and bores was very poor, with the tendency to be oversized to avoid high pressures and to facilitate functioning. Such guns were generally modified copies of basic Browning designs, though some ingenuity was shown, and even a few uniquely Spanish designs surfaced, such as the JO-LO-AR and the Astra M400 "water pistol." The principal problems encountered with these guns are poor design, soft working parts, which wear rapidly or damage easily, very poor workmanship and consequently poor functioning, short service life, and low durability.

This cannot be construed as a blanket condemnation of all Spanish autos made during the period. Three Spanish makers stood above all the rest, producing guns of excellent quality then, just as they do now. We should also point out that the Spanish Civil War wiped out that segment of the arms industry producing what we call today "junk guns." "Astra" pistols of uniquely native design and excellent quality have been produced from about 1920 on. Astra 9mm pistols of the entire period display unusually fine workmanship and materials and are sought after even today. The Astra trademark was used by Unceta y Cia. The firm of Star Bonifacio Echeverria, presently located in Vitoria, Spain, also produced excellent autos during that period. It is well known today for its fine line based upon extensive modifications to the Colt/Browning that achieved more-or-less definitive form in 1922 and has been manufactured continuously ever since. Gabilondo y Cia manufactured excellent, big-bore autoloaders during the same period, most of them close copies of the Colt/Browning 45. While these guns were marked with a variety of names (names usually chosen by quantity buyers and distributors or exporters), since World War II, they have been made almost exclusively under the name Llama. Slightly modified and improved since, they are available today exclusively from Stoeger Industries in the U.S., and are highly regarded.

There is another class of auto that should be avoided insofar as purchase for any extensive use is concerned. Up through World War II, there were literally millions of Browning and other type pistols manufactured abroad. Of the Browning types, only the Browning HP, M1910 and "Baby" 25/22 are still in production; of the others, only the Walther later models are still manufactured in significant quantity. Even those two makers have changed the models substantially, so parts of modern manufacture may not always fit. All of the others, including the Austrian Steyr M12, the Radom P35, the Tokarev M33, the Lahti, Ballister-Molina, Luger/Parabellum,

The Jo-Lo-Ar has a unique design and may be interesting to some collectors, but it is of poor quality. Parts are soft and replacements are not available. For even casual shooting, it should be avoided.

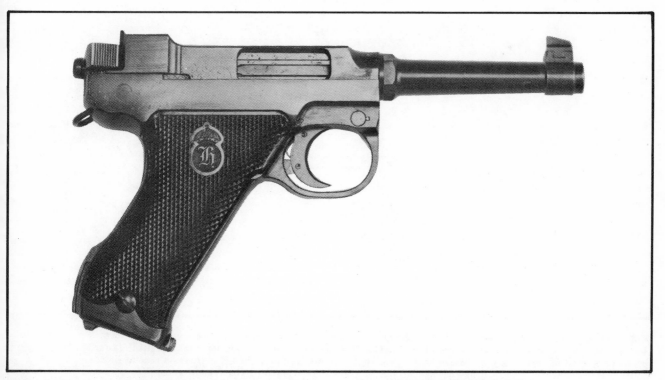

Military pistols from World War II may be well-designed and reasonably well-finished like this Lahti. They may also need unobtainable parts or may be chambered for unusual cartridges.

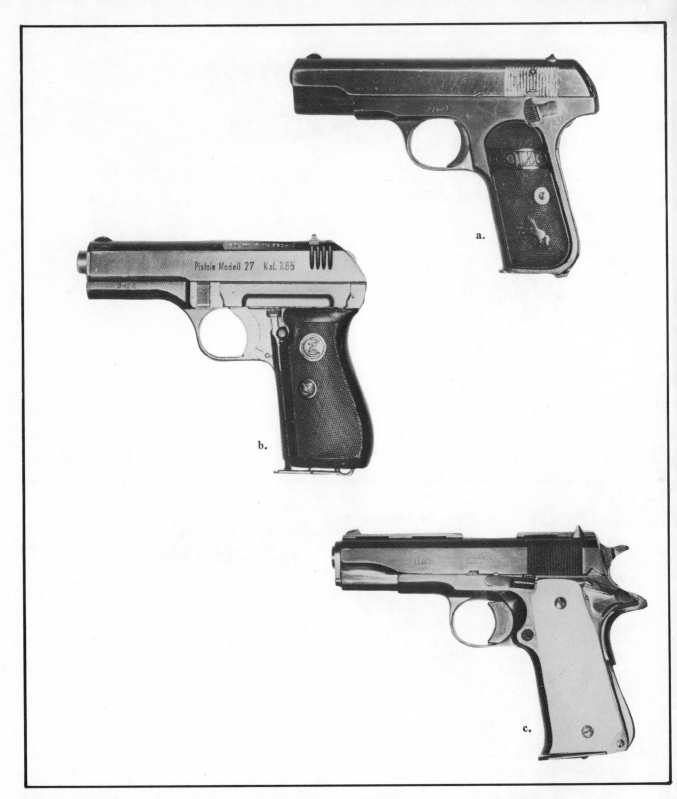

Mid-sized autoloaders are frequently found on the used gun counter. Some are more appealing to collectors than to shooters and command unrealistic prices. a.The Colt 380 was produced in large numbers, but the few examples offered for sale today are priced as if only a few were produced. b.The CZ M27 was a second-line military pistol of World War II. It has become a collector's item like everything else from that conflict. c.The Llama (22,32 and 380) is still also available as a new gun and probably represents the best buy of the three pistols shown.

These two Colt pistols are sometimes found on the used gun market and pose two different kinds of problems for the prospective shooter. The 1903 Pocket 380 (right) was widely distributed, but parts are now difficult to obtain. The little 25 cal. "Junior" (left) wasn't actually made by Colt and repair parts must be obtained from firms which handle Astra parts.

Astra M600, Browning M1908, and several others have been discontinued.

Most of these guns are of at least reasonably good design. However, not only did production terminate at the end of World War II, but late war production often left much to be desired in the way of materials and workmanship, and the only parts available today are those cannibalized by specialists from junk and surplus guns. In addition, some of these guns are chambered for cartridges such as the 9mm Bayard, 9mm Steyr, 7.62mm Tokarev, and others which are either no longer available, or available only in limited quantities on an indifferent basis at high prices.

In the final analysis, your best bet in a used gun in any of the categories we've listed is one still in production (even if in revised and improved form). It is manufactured by a company still in the same business; for which parts are still manufactured or expected to be available in substantial quantity in new form for a good many years, and preferrably of domestic manufacture. Once you get outside of those areas, the probability of problems increases rapidly to

the point where you might find yourself with a gun that won't work and can't be repaired in short order.

Once a decision has been made to buy a used gun, the principal problem is to determine the condition of a particular example to assess its future life and performance, and whether it's worth the price being asked.

The first thing you'll notice on a used gun is the condition of its external finish and its grips. Actually, unless the gun is pitted by rust, I don't really consider the finish all that important. Considering that a badly worn finish has the greatest effect in reducing the price, it's often possible to have a gun refinished for substantially less than the price differential; and if the finish isn't too bad, for a couple bucks worth of material, you can do a good touch-up job yourself.

Grips are much the same way; there are several sources of good replacement grips at reasonable prices. Obviously bad original grips will usually allow you to obtain the gun for sufficiently less money so that you can come out ahead even after replacing them.

Assuming you're one of those fellows who wants his gun to shoot where he looks, I'd consider the condition of the bore most important mechanically. Over years of looking through used barrels, I've formulated a couple of opinions about used-gun dealers. First, if they show you a gun with what appears to be simply a dirty bore with the statement, "I ain't had time to clean it yet," then they probably haven't cleaned it thoroughly because they suspect or know that it is either badly worn and eroded or pitted beneath that apparent dirt and fouling. Don't ever buy a gun like this with the thought that, "I'll clean it up at home and if the bore's not good, the dealer will take it back." Insist on a thorough cleaning of the bore before any money changes hands. My second opinion is that dealers usually liberally apply oil or grease in the bore so that when you look through you see a shiny reflective surface produced by the oil and not the steel. That reflection obscures wear and pits. If a dealer hands you a shiny, oily bore, insist on scrubbing it thoroughly dry before examining it closely.

Up until recently, there were vast quantities of surplus military pistol ammunition on the market, most of which contained so-called "corrosive" primers. Countless thousands of otherwise-perfect guns have had their bores ruined or at least significantly damaged by failing to clean well after the use of such ammunition. Look closely for this.

Obviously, a perfect, unworn bore is preferable and often will be found on a used gun. Look closely at the muzzle for nicks and burrs which will interfere with accuracy; if they are small, you can remove them. Large ones can be removed also, but this requires costly counterboring. Look throughout the bore for light etching caused by surface rust which has the effect of causing the bore to look a bit dark, though distinct pits may not be visible.

Also look at the throat (origin of the rifling) ahead of the chamber for darkening and rounding of the edges of the lands, all of which indicate excessive firing. Also, examine the chamber closely for roughness or pitting which has a decidedly deleterious

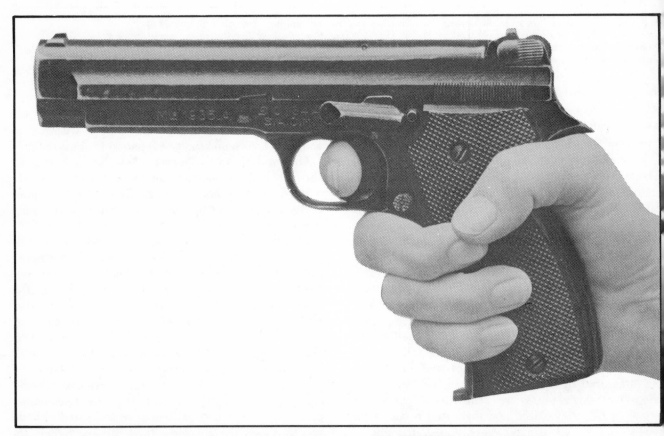

This French M1935A has sleek lines. Most shooters find it comfortable to hold. But it is chambered for a 32 Long cartridge which has never been available in this country and was only imported as military surplus for a brief period. Such guns should be avoided by anyone who expects to do some shooting.

effect on functioning because it increases extraction loads. You'll have to be careful in this area, because chamber roughness may sometimes be simply the result of a hard coating of powder fouling which is built up there, with the roughness being on its surface rather than the chamber proper. The chamber surface may be perfect under the layer of fouling, but there's no way of knowing until it's removed, and that removal can be difficult. You may also encounter a bulged barrel, particularly in military models, and this obviously calls for costly replacement. If the price is cheap enough, and a replacement barrel can be obtained, such a gun may represent a worthwhile buy.

The extractor, ejector and firing pin are essential for functioning. If they are battered or bent, excessively worn or, at worst, broken, the gun is worth a lot less. Firing pins and extractors are easily replaced if available, but ejectors in some models can be quite difficult to obtain. For example, some guns have the ejector cast integrally with the frame, and repair must therefore consist of an expensive welding and reshaping job. If the firing pin is straight, smoothly rounded at its tip, and protrudes adequately, it's okay. If the extractor has a clean sharp hook where it engages the cartridge, and if its spring seems to be stiff and vigorous, then it is all right.

Sights will generally be of the fixed type and probably show evidence of being banged around a bit. If they're banged up and perhaps even loose, it's cause for arguing the price down; but repair isn't difficult and can usually be done at home. If the sights are badly battered but solidly installed, usually no more than a little file work is needed to put them in first-class shape.

If at all possible, disassemble the gun and look closely at the lockwork parts. If they show no signs of breakage, excessive rust-pitting or wear, but are simply dirty, then they should be okay. Watch particularly, though, for the condition of the smaller springs. They may have taken a set or be bent out of shape. Check the recoil spring(s) for breakage or kinking, either of which would make replacement necessary.

Cycle the gun manually to make certain everything functions correctly. Check the safety(s) by cocking the gun and attempting to fire it with the safety engaged. Check the slide stop to make sure it does its job, and pay particular attention to any unusual sounds during cycling. If you hear gravelly grating inside the gun, something is wrong.

Always take particular pains to check the disconnector function of any auto. This is done by cocking the gun, then retracting the slide slightly and pulling the trigger; if the hammer falls, the disconnector is probably defective. The gun should fire only when the slide is in battery or within about 1/8 inch of battery. Malfunctioning is usually due to burrs or dirt, because there is little to wear in most disconnector systems and they are not subjected to forces that are likely to cause breakage.

In Browning-type locked-breech pistols, check the locking ribs on the barrel and their corresponding shoulders in the top of the slide for any significant peening or battering. If such is present, I'd be leery of the gun. In those guns such as the P38 and Beretta Brigadier series with separate locking blocks, examine the block, as well as its seat in both frame, barrel or slide very carefully for hairline cracks or peening and battering. The Beretta system, at least in the single-action models, is prone to breakage of the block.

Care should be taken to ascertain that all of the disassembly and assembly operations can be done easily. This may sound superfluous, but I've often encountered used guns in which the disassembly features and parts had been damaged by improper and forceful attempts by previous owners who didn't follow correct procedure. Also, it's not unusual to find a gun that has gone for decades without disassembly, and whose maintenance has been poor enough that the disassembly parts might be rusted solidly in place.

The majority of autoloading pistol malfunctions are caused by poor quality or worn, damaged magazines. Pay particular attention to this. Actually, you can't be certain a magazine will feed correctly without firing the gun. While some shops have facilities for this (a bullet trap or backstop in the back room), most do not, and unless you know the shop owner well, it isn't likely he'll let you take the gun out for a weekend to give it a try. Almost as good a substitute is manually cycling the gun with *dummy* cartridges. Any respectable gun shop *should* have dummy cartridges available for this purpose, but if they don't, you can be prepared by having a handful which you made up at your hand-loading bench, using properly resized cases and new bullets, but no powder or primer. Incidentally, if you make up such dummies, always drill a hole clear through the case so that it will not get mixed up with live ammunition.

Theoretically, of course, a conscientious dealer should have already checked all of the used guns in his showcase, repaired any safety defects and priced the guns according to their condition. Laugh now if you wish.

If you read and study thoroughly the chapters on

maintenance, repair and pistolsmithing, you'll get an excellent idea of the amount of repair work that might be practical for you to perform at home without any substantial investment. Always keep this in mind when you're shopping for a used gun. As far as common models are concerned, guns in need of at least slight repair are generally priced lowest. If you can find a low-priced gun of the type you want which needs repairs that you can perform, then it will most likely be a better bargain in the long run than paying 75 to 100 percent of new list price for a slightly used model in first-class condition. There's one more item I'd like to mention. In this day of tremendous demand for especially desirable new handguns, it is the rule rather than the exception that *used* examples of those scarce models are priced above new-gun retail prices. I think the classic examples of this are the M29 and certain other magnum S&W revolvers, and the S&W M59 auto. I have received literally hundreds of complaints from readers about this aspect of the used-gun market, and it is interesting to note that the majority of those complaints were written by individuals who had *already* paid as much as $100 to $200 over new, retail prices for a slightly used gun of the same model. If you want a particular model that badly, so badly that you are willing to pay a substantial premium, far be it from me to tell you how to spend your money.

On the other hand, this so-called "black market" pricing is made possibly *only* by those of you who *do* pay such exorbitant prices. As any first-semester economist will tell you, prices are determined by the immutable law of supply and demand—that is, as long as those customers are willing to pay extra, any item will sell at premium prices. When there are more items than customers, prices go down, even below established retail levels. In effect, then, the people who are paying—and complaining about—those inflated prices are the ones who are directly responsible for those prices. The manufacturers *do not* control retail prices; that is done only by the retail seller *and* the buyer.

Chapter Eleven
Military Pistols

In the early days of the auto pistol, it was apparently a point of national pride and honor that all major world powers have their soldiers and officers armed with a gun of native design and manufacture. Thus, in the U.S. the M1911 45 Auto was adopted. In Germany, the Parabellum P08 (Luger) armed German troops. Italy adopted the Beretta and to a far lesser extent the Glisenti. Great Britain held out and continued to use the Webley and Enfield revolvers after the failure of its native Webley-Scott 455 auto. Belgium adopted the M1910/22 Browning and later the P35. Spain had its Star; Austria had its Steyr-Hahn M12. France and Soviet Russia replaced their revolvers in the 1930s with native developments of the M1911 Browning, and even Japan developed and adopted its unusual Nambu. Smaller nations bought or manufactured under license those major-power designs they felt best suited to their own needs. Examples include the 9mm M1903 Browning produced for Sweden by Husqvarna, the Colt M1911 manufactured in Argentina, Swiss manufacture of the Parabellum (and wide sales of the same design of German manufacture to numerous nations), and world-wide sales of the M1896 Mauser to several nations.

Of course, during wartime, all bets were off. France bought hundreds of thousands of Spanish pistols; Great Britain and Norway bought Colts; Portugal and France bought Savage pocket autos, and, during World War II, Germany even purchased 9mm Star pistols from Spain. During the several wars, the conquerors almost invariably kept captured manufacturing facilities in operation to produce large quantities of whatever pistols could be made. At the height of its territorial expansion, the Nazi regime was issuing more than a dozen different models manufactured in France, Poland, Belgium, Czechoslovakia, and elsewhere. It's also been the practice during wartime for nations to impress to military service all manner of civilian pistols for which production facilities exist.

Following World War II, the world was literally flooded with the most horrendous hodgepodge of military pistols and calibers that could be imagined. This applied not only to autoloaders, but also every existing revolver production-facility contributed several years' output to the confusion. Many nations had issued captured enemy materiel as well as everything they could buy. France was one of the captured nations which finished the war with its own 1935-design U.S. 45 autos, several different revolver designs, newly manufactured German P38 and Sauer M38 pistols, along with captured supplies of virtually every other model the Werhmacht had used. Though France may be an extreme example, ammunition supply was a nightmare—no less than five autoloading pistol calibers and at least two revolver calibers were in use.

Following that war, most nations decided to clear up this mess. Within the Soviet Bloc, this presented no problems: Mother Russia simply decreed that standard Soviet arms be either supplied to or produced by the new satellite nations. The result was massive production and issue of the Soviet TT M1933 7.62mm pistol. Millions were produced to rearm Soviet forces and those nations behind the Iron Curtain. In the 1950s, this model was officially replaced by the 9mm Makarov (Model PM) with much the same result. The second time around, though, Czechoslovakia chose a native design designated M52. The M52 is chambered for the original Soviet 7.62mm cartridge loaded,to a muzzle velocity of 1600 fps, the highest velocity of all contemporary, military-pistol ammunition. Thus, the U.S.S.R. enforced standardization of military pistols within its sphere of influence, replacing more than a dozen models with one.

In the West, things were a bit different. National pride still played a substantial role, but the tremendously increased costs of tooling up for large-scale production helped hold things down. Those nations which survived the war with production facilities for modern designs found a ready market. For example, Belgium finished the war with Fabrique Nationale able to produce large quantities of the very fine P35 9mm pistol. An aggressive sales effort resulted in adoption of this pistol by many nations; as this is written, the P35 (under various designations) is the standard military sidearm of Canada, Great Britain, Australia, New Zealand, Belgium, Taiwan, Cuba, and numerous others.

France, ever the individualist, developed from its 1935 pistol the 9mm M1950, which eventually replaced the earlier hodgepodge. Italy's Armi Beretta developed a new, locked-breech, 9mm pistol designated M1951, which eventually replaced all of the earlier designs for first-line issue. Interestingly enough, the state of Israel chose this pistol as its standard, military sidearm. It was also chosen by the United Arab Republic, which has by now fought several unsuccessful wars against Israel. The Swiss SIG Company developed its P210 series of pistols, which was adopted by the Swiss Army and by a few other small nations.

Some nations attempted development of new native designs, but for various reasons—usually cost—gave up and went to licensed production or purchase.

The U.S., on the other hand, after examining the situation carefully and conducting trials of new lightweight pistols, decided the large inventory of M1911 45 pistols ruled out the tremendous cost of a change to a light 9mm.

A few years after World War II, the German arms industry began developing again, and the Walther plant resumed production of the P38. It was adopted by the new German Army, and subsequently by a number of other nations.

As should be apparent by now, two trends developed in the West in military pistols. The first was a drastic reduction in the number of designs, essentially the result of economic consideration. The second was the reduction in the number of different calibers, and while this was partially an economic consideration, it was also the product of NATO standardization efforts. As a result, all the major Western-world nations except the U.S. have adopted the 9mm Parabellum cartridge; the only other exceptions are those small nations which are for economic reasons still utilizing earlier designs in other calibers. Among them are a few nations still equipped with U.S. 45 pistols supplied to them during the war or acquired during postwar re-equipment. Some of the latter have explored conversion of the M1911 to 9mm to provide at least partial compliance with NATO standardization goals.

Where dozens of models once armed the West, today that task is accomplished mainly by the Browning/FN P35, Walther P38, Beretta M951, SIG P210, French M1950 and, of course, our ubiquitous Colt/Browning M1911/A1.

These guns represent the first postwar generation of modern military pistols. While some are postwar designs (the most popular P35 is not), all are designed for 1935-ish materials and technology. And that means that their manufacture is costly. During World War II, German industry, particularly Walther, did considerable research into lower-cost manufacture from stamped sheet-metal parts combined with cast and machined spacers and other assembly methods. Although this died with the end of the war in 1945, it was resurrected by Heckler & Koch in the early 1960s.

This FN Browning military model 1935 Hi-Power 9mm automatic pistol takes a 13-shot magazine.

The SIG/Sauer P210-6 is an ultra-modern pistol manufactured in Germany. It includes an investment-cast frame and a welded sheet-metal slide.

The outgrowth of all this was the introduction in the mid-to-late 1960s of the H&K P9S. This pistol was designed from the beginning to be manufactured to the maximum extent possible from stamped sheet metal. The slide was constructed from a sheet-metal shell into which were welded muzzle and breech closures in combination with a separate breech block pinned in place. The frame was formed from a single complex sheet-steel stamping folded to shape, spot-welded together, and with investment-cast spacers and supports welded in place where necessary. To further simplify production, the trigger guard and front strap were molded from a very tough plastic, and sights were also made from plastic. Thus, the P9S became the first of the second-generation modern military pistols designed from the outset for the most rapid and economical production current technology will permit. As a result, it was also designed for production with the least number of machine tools made from the least amount of raw material. One further benefit gained from these features is light weight.

Internally, the P9S was designed for minimum-cost high-volume production, and also for simplified operation. It employs a concealed hammer, double-action lockwork, both chamber and cocking indicators, and a manual cocking and decocking lever which may also be used to operate the slide stop. It was further designed for simplified disassembly and for maximum interchangeability of parts. This new approach to big-bore pistol design by Heckler & Koch departs heavily from tradition, and, while it increases costs in small production quantities, the ultimate unit cost in large-scale production is reduced.

Following Heckler & Koch's lead, the Swiss SIG Company developed its new P220 design. SIG's goal was the same as that of H&K, and the approach differed only in that an investment-cast aluminum-alloy frame was used. Slide construction and internal parts followed H&K practice. In one respect, SIG departed from tradition even farther, eliminating the familiar, manual safety; choosing to perform its functions with a fully automatic, internal, firing-pin safety actuated by the trigger, and by a manual decocking lever. SIG also chose to make the P220 in double-action form.

Another feature shared by the P9S and P220 is the fact that they are dimensioned around the 45 ACP cartridge, and are designed so that they may be made in smaller calibers with minimum tooling changes. They may, in fact, even be converted to other calibers by relatively simple parts substitution.

Both the SIG P220 and H&K P9S represent the latest developments in military pistols. As this is written, neither has been widely adopted by other nations. However, it seems quite obvious that both companies have gambled a great deal of development and production money on such adoption. Certainly it is unlikely that domestic sales alone would justify these developments. Incidentally, it may be significant to note that *both* the P9S and the P220 are currently manufactured *only* in West Germany.

During the period immediately following World War II, military use of the pistol was de-emphasized. Typical ivory-tower study groups announced profoundly that the result of military actions had not been significantly affected by pistols. No doubt such conclusions were entirely correct, inasmuch as there is no record of any battle worthy of the name being won or lost with sidearms. Considering the assault rifles, rocket launchers, submachine guns, grenades, and other weapons with which the infantryman is ordinarily equipped, one can hardly consider the pistol an offensive weapon of war. It lost that capability with the death of the horse cavalry, a use in which it was decidedly an offensive weapon upon which the outcome of the action could depend.

However, those studies which tended to downgrade the pistol dealt only with the surface. They gave no consideration to the fact that there are countless military duties and situations in which the pistol can be the deciding factor in the survival of the individual or a small group of soldiers. The studies also completely ignored the psychological effect upon a soldier of always having an effective weapon immediately available—no matter what his duties or circumstances—in the form of a reliable pistol at his belt.

The jeep driver, even with a rifle or submachine gun racked at his side, may not have a chance to grab it when he comes under fire and has to bail out. Lying in a ditch with no weapon at all while under fire can be a terrifying experience. With a pistol on his hip that driver at least *feels* that he has a good defensive capability. With no weapon at all, he feels totally helpless and vulnerable. A tank or APC crewman is in an even worse position; he *can't* keep a shoulder weapon immediately at hand, and if he is forced to bail out, he'll be completely unarmed unless there's a pistol at his belt. The machine gunner or mortar man simply *can't* carry any other weapon larger than a pistol, and he can't use the big gun to defend himself at close range.

In fact, the only man in uniform who can depend upon having his primary weapon available at all times is the rifleman. The result is that anybody in a combat zone who's not a rifleman—and that includes one helluva lot of troopers—actually *needs* a pistol.

There are ample indications that some armies are again recognizing the value of the pistol. Unfortunately, the U.S. Army does not appear to have yet reached that conclusion.

Pistols designed primarily for military use have always been quite popular among civilians. Some of the many reasons for this are purely emotional. For example, the trooper who carried (or envied those who did) a 45 M1911 during military service will quite often obtain one afterward as a useful memento of his service. Others simply take justifiable pride in owning the pistol which arms the defenders of his nation.

Less true now than during the 1950s and 1960s, countless thousands of shooters chose to buy military pistols (surplus in the millions following World War II) for their low cost. Before GCA'68, one could often buy a fine-condition 9mm military auto for $\frac{1}{5}$ to $\frac{1}{3}$ the price of a comparable new civilian model. When 45 M1911s cost a hundred bucks new, I bought many ex-military examples for $20–$25. A military P38 could be had for $50–$75 when new ones cost around $200. Cheapness of ammunition also influenced buyers. In the early 1960s, military-surplus 9mm Parabellum ammunition could be had for one and one-half cents per round while fresh factory-loads cost many times that.

In fact, I believe strongly that the wide availability of surplus military pistols and ammunition in the 1950s and 1960s did more to promote and increase handgun shooting and ownership than any other factor before or since. Countless thousands of today's confirmed pistoleros were introduced to the game by those low-cost guns and ammunition.

Purely military pistols possess other appealing advantages. Most important is the fact that they have passed the most rigorous tests imaginable to ensure functional reliability under the worst possible conditions. The average owner doesn't expect to shoot at −65°F. or +135°F., nor after the gun has been immersed in mud or exposed to sea spray for many hours—but military pistols have demonstrated their ability to do so. That makes the owner feel better. Such pistols have also passed extensive tests to ensure that they will function reliably for many thousands of rounds; that they can be repaired quickly and easily; that neophytes can be easily and quickly trained in their use, and that they are as mechanically safe as possible.

Military pistols are as durable, reliable and safe as technology can make them. The fact that they may be a bit heavy and bulky as a result does not detract from their desirability and normally generates substantial civilian sales. Even those lesser guns pressed into military service in times of need acquire additional prestige and an aura of excellence which may not necessarily be earned. They, too, achieve additional popularity by virtue of military use.

Chapter Twelve
Repair and Modification

Most people who have attempted parts replacements and even relatively minor repairs on revolvers know the job can get pretty hairy. Often what appears to be a simple parts replacement, with the new item dropping right into place, turns out to be an impossible task that has to be finished by a competent pistolsmith.

Autoloaders are generally a good deal simpler in this respect. Most of the more prominent and popular big-bore autoloaders of today were designed with the military market in mind, if not specifically for it. The result of those considerations was that simplicity of maintenance and repair *in the field* was uppermost in the designers' minds. There have been notable exceptions, such as the Parabellum P08 (Luger), but in the main, such guns are usually capable of tool-less disassembly and assembly, and feature a very high order of parts interchangeability. Some, particularly the Colt GM, require no tools except punch and screwdriver for replacement of any part.

While many of the medium-sized autos, commonly but erroneously referred to as "pocket pistols," were not designed to military requirements, they still usually share this ease of disassembly and parts replacement. With the exception of barrel replacement on those models where it is permanently installed, a screwdriver and pin punch or drift is usually all that's required to replace any part. Even the tiny, *true* pocket pistols, the smallest 25 and 22 caliber autos, are usually quite simple in design and seldom require more than a screwdriver and punch for complete teardown and reassembly.

The most common functional problems are caused by damaged or defective magazines. If a gun has a butterfingered owner, the magazine may be dropped (either empty or charged); it seems to have an exasperating proclivity for always landing on its feed lips. Even a slight amount of distortion or a small dent, can cause serious feeding problems, and if not otherwise obvious, can best be identified by comparison with another magazine *known* to be undamaged and to produce correct functioning.

Without considerable experience, it's difficult for the layman to straighten bent feed lips. I advise against any attempt until a replacement magazine is available; then careful manipulation of pliers may be

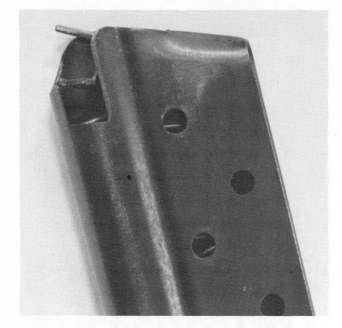

Close-up of feed lips. The magazine follower must move smoothly to the upper limit of its travel. The lip or shelf on the follower which engages the slide stop may become bent, particularly in the unreinforced stamped follower of this type, so that it does not exert sufficient upward pressure. This portion of the follower may also be bent inward or come from the manufacturer slightly undersize so that under some circumstances it can slip past the slide-top extension, thus preventing removel of the magazine.

employed to copy the shapes shown on the good magazine. Nicks, burrs or sharp edges on the feed lips should be carefully removed with needle files and the area then stoned or polished smooth. If a magazine has seen extensive use, the feed lips may be cracked loose from the rear wall of the body where they were originally welded or silver-soldered. A very careful and skilled torch artist can reweld these cracks, but usually it's easier and cheaper in the long run to simply replace the magazine. Incidentally, if the gun in question is one for which replacement magazines are not readily available through the usual channels, we have the Triple-K Corporation which is prepared to supply replacement magazines for virtually every autoloader that ever saw commercial success. Triple-K can also custom-make new magazines or modify existing ones to fit almost any old pistol you might possess.

Magazine bodies often become dented, and even though the dent appears to be slight, it may prevent cartridges from rising smoothly, if at all. Shallow dents are best repaired by removing the floor plate, following spring and follower, then working through the open bottom to file down the intruding dent. Even if the dent is deep enough that filing it off inside actually cuts completely through the thin metal of the body, the magazine will still function correctly until you can find a replacement.

Alternatively, if the dent appears quite deep and yet not too broad in area, it may be simply drilled out from the outside. This may leave an unsightly hole, but it will permit the magazine to be used. Many older magazines have the floor plate permanently assembled by either silver soldering or pins. If the soldered joints crack, a temporary repair can be affected with modern cyanoacrylate (Super Glue) adhesives. The joint must be first thoroughly degreased with a solvent such as acetone, then the smallest amount of adhesive flowed into the crack. If the crack is of significant width, it should be forced nearly shut in a C-clamp or vise inasmuch as this type adhesive has virtually no gap-filling capability. Of course, if you have a torch, then apply low-temperature silver-solder *paste* into the crack after cleaning, and apply just enough heat to melt the solder. The low-temperature solder will melt before the original joint, and if you work carefully, what remains of the original joint will not be melted in the process. If pins holding the floor plate in place have become loose, simply peen or rivet their ends to tighten them up.

Sometimes you'll find a heavily used magazine in which the notch engaged by the catch has become worn oversize so that the magazine is not held high enough in the gun to produce reliable feeding. In such cases, the upper portion of the notch in the body is simply worn away. If the condition isn't too bad, the stripped body can be placed over a shaped bar of steel held securely in a heavy vise, and the area just above the notch carefully peened to move metal downward and compensate for the wear. Afterward, the notch may require truing with needle files. Since peening thins the metal at a critical area, this is at best a temporary repair. If the magazine affected is irreplaceable, then a first-class shielded arc-welder can build up the area, after which you'll have to very carefully file it to shape. If on disassembly you discover a kinked follower spring, simply grasp the wire on both sides of the kink with smooth-jawed pliers and carefully straighten it. Be particularly careful that you don't simply substitute a new kink for the old.

The slide and the several parts it houses don't often give much trouble, but fortunately when it does, repairs are usually fairly simple. The Browning-type, firing-pin stop, as found in the Colt GM and

Browning HP, is a marvel of simplicity. If from wear or other causes it fits too loosely in its vertical T-slot, it may drop downward slightly as a shot is fired, become disengaged from the firing pin to fall out as the slide recoils, and allow the firing pin and the spring to be thrown out the rear of the slide. This puts the gun completely out of action and the flying parts can seriously injure the shooter. The simplest cure for this condition is to peen the sides of the stop until it fits tightly enough in its slot that moderate force is required to press it into position. Alternatively, thin, steel shim stock can be sweated to the stop's front face with soft solder and then stoned down until it can just barely be pressed into place.

Long, slender firing pins, typical of Browning-type autos, easily become bent. Even a slight bend can cause the pin to bind or jam in the forward position; at best this can cause a feeding problem, and at worst, can cause the gun to fire as the slide slams into battery. Not good. If a bent firing pin is suspected, remove the pin and roll it across a smooth, flat surface (a piece of old, plate glass is ideal) while observing it carefully. Any bend will be obvious. Mark the highest point of the bend with a piece of chalk, then lay the pin on a smooth block of lead with that point upper-most and tap the chalk mark smartly with a light hammer until the pin is straight. A firing pin straightened in this way contains severe stresses, and may well break later. Consequently, it's a good idea to secure a replacement and install it at the earliest opportunity; however, the straightened pin will get the gun back in service immediately.

A broken or badly kinked firing-pin retracting spring can also cause forward jamming of the pin. Springs are cheap and readily available, and should be replaced if there is the slightest visible distortion or breakage. Occasionally the head of a firing pin may be found to be peened or riveted where struck by the hammer, and this is a clear indication of improper heat treatment or material. Such a pin can be restored to service by filing away the distorted metal, but it should be replaced immediately with a proper new pin.

The hole in the slide breech through which the firing pin protrudes may develop considerable burrs around its perimeter with heavy use; a bent firing pin will accelerate this development. Such burrs will eventually interfere with feeding so should be very carefully removed with stones or needle files in such a manner as to not distort the breech face. In a well-worn gun, it may also be discovered that this hole is substantially larger than the firing pin, thus allowing the metal of the primer cup to flow back into the gap

Nicks, burrs or sharp edges on the feed lips should be carefully removed with a needle file.

around the firing pin. This can cause serious functional problems, particularly in extraction and ejection, and can tie up the gun completely. At its worst, it may allow the primer cup to rupture, releasing hot gases to come back through the firing-pin hole and toward the shooter's face.

Proper repair requires either welding up and redrilling the hole, or drilling it out and turning in a hardened, steel, threaded bushing containing a hole that fits the firing pin closely. Both methods are beyond the capabilities of the average kitchen-table pistolsmith, and should be entrusted to a competent professional workman. Alternatively, you may turn a replacement firing pin out of drill rod on a miniature lathe, or even on a drill press with files, leaving it oversized at the tip to properly fit the enlarged hole.

Long, spring-type, one-piece extractors of the Browning type, as found in the GM, may sometimes lose their spring tension and no longer grip the case rim securely enough for positive extraction and ejection. If the extractor is easily flexed with the fingers, this is probably the case. Unless you're a heat-treating

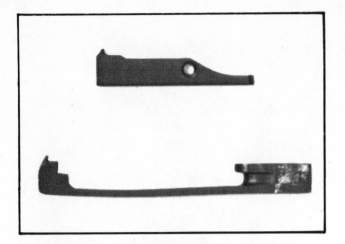

In any kind of extractor (these are the two types that have been employed in the S&W M39), the claw (the portion which actually engages a case rim) should be smooth and free from burrs. It should especially be polished smooth on the angled surface which strikes the case rim and cams the extractor outward to snap over the rim when the slide has dropped on a manually chambered cartridge. In those designs where the case rim moves up behind the claw during feeding, a slight bevel on the underside will facilitate feeding.

expert, this extractor should be replaced at the earliest possible date. However, a temporary repair can be effected by simply bending the forward portion of the extractor (ahead of the circular section at about its midpoint) inward 1/16 to 1/8 inch. The front of this type extractor is subjected to a considerable load in many guns because it strikes the forward bevel of the case extractor groove forceably as the gun goes into battery. This can over-stress the hook which draws the case from the chamber and cause all or part of it to break off. If only part breaks off, a temporary repair can usually be effected by smoothing up the broken surface of the hook and beveling it slightly, then deepening the hook with needle files. This, however, is a purely temporary repair.

Pivoted hook extractors with separate springs sometimes wear badly on the inner face of the hook. When it wears to a forward slope, it may slip off the case rim instead of pulling it properly to the rear. This can be repaired by filing the inner face of the hook forward to restore the proper angle. A weak spring beneath the rear of the extractor will exaggerate this condition and should be replaced. Because of the severe side loads placed on such an extractor, the hole through which its pin fits may be worn into an egg shape, and this can cause problems. The part should be replaced, though it can be repaired by drilling out the holes in both extractor and slide, and fitting an

oversized pin. Unfortunately, this spoils the slide for later replacement with a correct extractor and pin, so should be reserved for last-ditch conditions.

If the removable barrel bushing in the muzzle of the slide becomes very loose, accuracy will suffer even if functioning does not. The bushing should be replaced with a new one that fits snugly, but a temporary fix can be accomplished by dimpling the outer surface of the bushing with a sharp center punch. This dimpling raises burrs which increase the effective diameter of the bushing to center and hold it more securely in the slide. The bushing should be solidly supported by being placed over a steel rod that nearly fills its bore or it may be deformed by the impact of the punch. Where there is no bushing to support the barrel or where it is permanently installed, as in the Browning HP, repair can be accomplished only by drilling out the slide muzzle and pressing or soldering in a new, steel bushing which fits the barrel closely. This is a job for the professional.

In the case of locked-breech pistols, locking lug seats in the slide sometimes become peened, battered or burred. This condition can interfere with functioning and can usually be repaired in that respect *temporarily* by careful stoning and filing of the burred edges so that they no longer interfere with movement. However, actual repair consists of welding the offending areas, re-machining the seat, and perhaps even heat-treating the slide. This is not only a job for a first-class professional, but may often be more costly than replacing the entire slide.

Occasionally, one may encounter a *cracked* slide. This is most likely to occur in Colt GM slides of war-time manufacture, and the crack is usually vertical, on the right side in the vicinity of the ejection port. Such a slide is best discarded and replaced, though technically it is possible for a first-class welder to repair the crack, after which the adjacent areas must be re-machined, both inside and out. A new slide is cheaper.

When such a crack is encountered, don't continue shooting the gun—the slide may break in half during the next shot, allowing the rear portion to fly back and strike the shooter in the head. If a gun is dropped or struck severely, it's possible for one side of the slide to be bent inward slightly over the guide grooves. This will prevent free movement on the frame, and if the damage is severe, repair probably isn't practical. If the damage is slight, though, clamping the slide inverted in a heavy bench vise will allow the bent-in portion to be worked back into proper position with a heavy *brass* drift and hammer. Take note, however, that the metal will be heavily stressed by this and

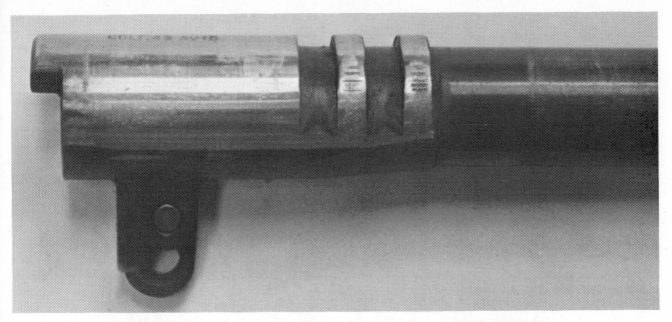

Locking lugs on Browning-type pistols are often overlooked in tuning for maximum reliability. If the lugs bind in their corresponding slide recesses, they can prevent the slide from going fully into battery, even though it moves far enough forward to fire safely. More important, if binding exists, too much of the recoil energy will be absorbed during unlocking, and perhaps an insufficient amount will remain for reliable functioning.

may crack. I once had the entire front third of the portion below the guide groove split free from the rest of the slide after such a repair job.

Sights (either front or rear) dovetailed into the slide can work loose from the shock of recoil, perhaps somewhat aided by various movements required for zeroing. If not too loose, they can be secured without removal by simply staking the edge of the dovetail ahead or behind the sight with a sharp, center punch. One fairly deep indentation at each point, centered laterally, will do the job nicely, and does not usually appear offensive. If the sight is quite loose, or if you wish to avoid the exposed stake mark, remove the sight, peen the edges of the dovetail very lightly, then dimple the bottom of the slide dovetail with a sharp center punch. Degrease the area, drift the sight back into the proper position, then put a drop or two of cyanoacrylate adhesive into the joint and the sight will be in position to stay. If a brazed and/or riveted-in-place front sight comes loose, it should be removed, the entire joint area thoroughly cleaned, the sight clamped in position, and silver solder flowed-in to fill the joint. Unfortunately, this will usually spoil the finish on the gun, making further work necessary to restore its appearance.

Over the years, most guns that are extensively carried will pick up assorted nicks, dings and burrs which might interfere with free parts movement.

Sometimes a single nick and burr on the edge of the slide can convert a marginally functional gun into one that doesn't work at all well. Careful removal of such burrs—wherever they appear—with needle files and stones is essential.

The frame and the lockwork parts it houses constitute the most complex part of the gun. Fortunately, as I've already said, complete disassembly is usually quite easy with nothing more than a screwdriver to remove the grips, and pin punches to drift out those pins holding other parts in place.

Disconnector function is essential for safety, and if it does not move freely (whether a separate part as in the GM or formed on a trigger bar as in the Star) any binding or hesitancy can usually be attributed to dirt or burrs in the recess in which it moves. Careful cleaning and stoning will correct this. If movement is still not brisk enough, the spring may be weakened or bent. Replacement is usually a good bit better than attempting to repair the spring.

If full-cock notch engagement is not positive and if the trigger pull is too light, then it's most likely that the sear nose and the corresponding surface on the hammer form an incorrect angle; this may be due either to wear or previous attempts to improve trigger pull. Once this condition is reached, doubling may also occur, and repair of existing parts is beyond the capability of the home pistolsmith unless he has prepared himself with the appropriate jigs and blocks for recutting those surfaces with abrasive stones. Better trust repair of the original parts to a professional, and/or install replacements.

If trigger return after the shot is hesitant or incomplete, check first the trigger-return spring (which may be combined with another spring function, as in the three-armed sear spring of the GM) for proper tension. If the spring appears to be weak, a temporary fix may be accomplished by stretching a coil spring, bending the leaf type, or putting a spacer beneath the former. In either case, don't rely on this permanently, but obtain a new replacement as soon as possible.

More often trigger return is inhibited by burrs and/or binding inside the frame. This is particularly true with the GM where the trigger slides rather than rotates and is fixed to a long, hollow yoke which passes back through the magazine well. Carefully inspect all areas where the trigger or connected parts can rub in the frame, and smooth them with needle files and stones. For deep recesses, a short piece of file or stone broken off and epoxied to a wood handle will allow working inside without too much difficulty. Pay particular attention to those Browning-type designs where the magazine passes through a hollow trigger-yoke. Often the yoke will be bent inward slightly so

that it rubs on the magazine body. This is usually the case if trigger return is poor with the magazine in place and correct with the magazine removed. To correct this condition, carefully remove burrs from the yoke, expand the yoke, and smoothly polish that portion of the magazine over which it passes.

Misfires or poor ignition may be caused by a weakened mainspring, a spring that is kinked or broken, or impeded by dirt, debris and rust that have accumulated in the recess in which the spring operates. This is particularly true in the case of the Colt/Browning and Star designs where the mainspring is seated in a close-fitting hole which seldom gets attention because it is difficult to reach. Removal of the spring and thorough cleaning of its recess will help a great deal.

Hammer, sear and other rotating parts are pinned to the frame. The pins are usually quite hard and do not wear significantly of themselves. In most instances, the internal parts are also hard enough that it's unlikely their pivot holes will wear oversize. However, the frame is usually of a less-hard material—especially true of the lightweight guns with aluminum-alloy frames—and so the hole in the frame may wear oversize. This usually doesn't progress to the point where it produces any functional difficulties, but it can produce a lot of slop in the fit of

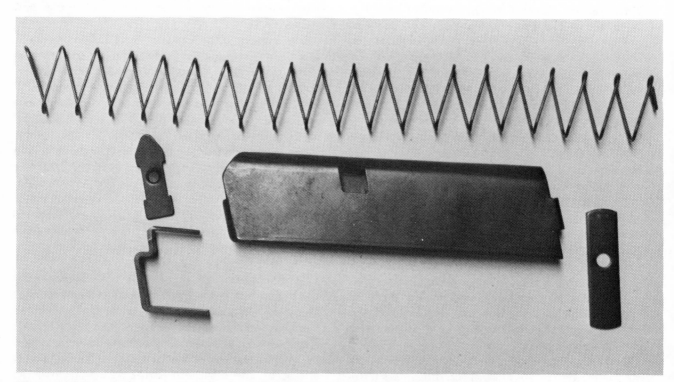

The most common dysfunctions in autoloaders originate in damaged or defective magazine parts.

internal parts. Pins may be temporarily tightened by simply peening around the outer edges of the holes in the frame.

If a more permanent fix is required, then new, oversize pins must be fitted. This is practical only for single-unit pins, and not for those which are part of a safety, slide stop, etc. Oversize pins are easily made of drill rod, after which they must be fitted to the hole in the frame, and this will ordinarily result in them being too large to pass through the rotating parts. The holes in those parts must then be carefully polished until just large enough to admit the pins freely. This is not an easy job and shouldn't be taken lightly; it's easy enough to enlarge the holes, but in polishing them out by hand, it's very easy to make them egg-shaped, funneled and no longer at the correct angle. So, as a practical matter, this job should probably be left to a professional.

The safety, slide stop and perhaps other controls are held in their engaged and disengaged positions by spring-plunger detents of one sort or another. Failure of the slide stop to properly engage after the last shot has been fired can often be traced to excessive friction between it and the detent plunger. Original-manufacture plungers are usually properly smoothed and profiled, but some of the replacement parts offered are not and they simply do not permit free operation. Careful polishing and deburring of the plunger end, with perhaps a bit of polishing on the surface engaged, will usually make for much smoother operation. Actually, a very rough plunger can actually lock the part in position. If the plunger is soft, even polishing will constitute only a temporary repair, because the rubbing surfaces will wear rapidly. You can harden the plungers at home, simply laying them on a fairly thick piece of sheet steel and heating the latter until it is red hot, thus heating the plunger to the same temperature without burning it. Then immediately knock the plunger off into light engine-oil and let it cool. This won't be the ideal form of heat-treatment, but it will harden the part somewhat, and give it some wear resistance. Of course, burrs or bends can also interfere with controls movement, and if any are present, correct them.

Safeties are essential to *safe* use of the gun. Check by attempting to fire with them engaged, and if they fail to hold, remove them and examine the engaging surfaces very closely. Defective safeties can sometimes be repaired if the problem is only one of wear, but I recommend against it unless you're experienced. On the other hand, slipping in a new replacement part is falling-down easy.

Some of the more modern autos use a stamped sheet-metal mainspring seat which merely engages a lip in an angled cut in the back of the frame, and is then held in position by spring pressure. These seats are quite tough, but if one does become damaged, you'll be better served by replacing it than attempting repair. The seat can become burred and interfere with installation or functioning; simply file off the burrs.

Grip-screw bushings on Colt and S&W autos have a habit of working loose, especially in the aluminum-alloy frame models. If caught while they are merely loose, turning the bushings back in snugly and applying a drop of Loctite or cyanoacrylate adhesive will generally cure the problem. Unfortunately, all too often these bushings are put back in place indifferently, and the very fine threads in the frame are damaged or ruined entirely. If you go to the trouble and expense of buying a special tap from Brownells, the holes may be rethreaded after peening around the edges, and the bushing very carefully reinstalled. The bushing should then be restaked from the inside, using either the special punch available from Brownells, or a punch with a pyramidal point inserted through the bushing hole on the opposite side of the frame. On *steel* frames, an effective, permanent repair can be accomplished by simply reseating the bushing, then flowing silver solder into the joint. Unbushed grip-screw threads in the frame require different treatment. If thread damage is slight, peen around the edges of the hole and then retap. If the damage is serious, simply retap for the next larger thread size and open up the hole in the grips to accept the larger screw.

Some autoloaders have some rather thin frame sections which can be dented or bent inward easily by a solid impact; this is especially true of the aluminum-alloy models. If enough deformation is present to interfere with functioning, but the metal is not cracked, it can usually be reshaped with a brass drift and hammer while the frame is held tightly in a vise, properly supported by fitted hardwood or lead blocks. As mentioned in reference to slides, the metal may crack during straightening. Slight deformation left after straightening can be filed down to provide moving-parts clearance.

Grips are often split or cracked, whether of wood or some plastic material. If no fragments are lost, wood grips are easily repaired with any really good adhesive. The main object is to align the pieces carefully until the adhesive is set. This is usually best done on the gun, positioning the parts and holding them with any screws that are not involved in the break, then wrapping with masking tape until the glue is set. Keep the glue from adhering to the frame with a layer of plastic film; don't use oil or grease or it might prevent the cement from holding. Plastic grips can be repaired with the *proper* plastic solvent/cement, but since most often the proper material won't be known, use cyanoacrylate adhesive instead, taking particular care to ensure that it is prevented from bonding the grip to the frame. Plastic film is probably best for this purpose, but make certain all metal surfaces are covered because the adhesive has remarkable penetrating capability and will sneak into places you don't suspect.

After broken or cracked grips have been repaired, a bit of touch-up with needle files in the checkered area and perhaps a bit of sanding elsewhere to clean them up will finish the job nicely. If there are small fragments or slivers missing, position the rest of the parts as accurately as possible, then fill in the gap with epoxy or glass-bedding compound, preferably tinted to match the color of the grips.

Grips, especially those of wood or of cheap lightweight plastic, will often work loose on the gun either due to aging and shrinkage, or from the pounding of repeated recoil impulses. Loose grips will cause inaccuracy, particularly excess vertical spread on target, because they prevent the recoil impulse from being transferred smoothly from the gun to your hand and arm. Flat-plate grips such as those found on the Colt GM manifest such looseness only in the oversize holes which fit over the grip-screw bushings. You may either plug the holes with epoxy or glass-bedding compound, then when cured, drill new holes that are a snug fit over the bushings. Or you may coat all of the related metal areas with release compound, put a dab of epoxy on the inner surface of each hole, then tape the grips in place until it is cured.

Grips which are inletted into recesses in the frame may be given the same treatment; however, a more secure repair results if a bead of epoxy is run around the inletted wood before pressing the grip into place, with release compound applied to the metal. Thin, fragile segments of wood grips which are hollowed-out to overlap safeties and the like may also be substantially reinforced and thus prevented from splitting by a thin backside coating of epoxy or glass-bedding compound.

We've left until last one repair operation that probably occurs to the average pistolero more often than any other—refinishing. First of all, we don't have the space here to go into the complete refinishing operation in detail. To do that, we'd have to cover rust removal, elimination of pits and mars, proper polishing to several levels, restoring markings, refitting parts, degreasing, cleaning and etching, the various

solutions and compounds for producing a new finish, and, of course, the equipment for doing all that. There are low-cost rebluing and refinishing kits on the market, and they are accompanied by rather well-written and comprehensive instructions. If you feel you want to get into complete refinishing, we'd suggest you look over one of those kits, and also consider purchasing one of the better references on refinishing such as *Firearms Blueing and Browning*, by Angier.

For our purposes we'll just dwell somewhat briefly on touching up the original finish. Guns which were originally finished in a glossy blue will usually show wear where the gun rubs against a holster, and where the hand makes frequent contact with it. Over the years, I've noticed that on a gun which is carried a good deal, the finish usually disappears first on the back strap—partly from friction of handling it, but probably more from the corrosive effect of perspiration acids. Areas in close contact with the holster will go next, particularly around the muzzle, the edges of a revolver cylinder, and the trigger guard of an autoloader.

Assuming there is no rust pitting and perhaps only very minor (almost invisible) surface etching, the worn areas should be carefully polished by hand with small pieces of the finest aluminum-oxide abrasive cloth or paper you can obtain. Once all discoloration and roughness are removed, finish the area by stroking it lightly in one direction only (along the longest dimension of the part) with a well-worn piece of that abrasive cloth moistened with light oil. If that doesn't produce a surface smooth enough to match the rest of the gun, repeat with crocus cloth and light oil.

There are a number of touch-up bluing compounds on the market, most of which will do the job quite well. Those I've had the best luck with are Numrich's 44-40 and G-66 Paste Blue. Results are about equal, but the paste is more convenient. Regardless of the type you use, you'll be doing yourself a favor if you read the instructions at least three times and then follow them *explicitly*. The instructions will generally say to thoroughly remove all oil and grease, which I prefer to do with acetone since it leaves no residue. The surface is then warmed to a bit above room temperature, and the compound applied gently with a clean, grease-free cotton swab or cloth. Several applications will usually be necessary to make the color dark enough, but even then the odds are against any touch-up job actually *matching* the original finish on the rest of the gun.

No matter how well the compound is applied, it will not have the durability and depth of the original finish. Consequently, after the job has been finished, and the proper oil (specified in the instructions) has been applied, let the gun set a few days for the finish to age. Then, clean the oil off and give the area (preferably the entire part, such as barrel, frame, etc.) a good coat of hard paste wax. Though I suppose there are plenty of waxes that are suitable, plain old Johnson's Paste Floor Wax has always worked well for me. Let a thin, uniform coat of the wax harden, then buff it well with a grease-free cloth. This will give an added layer of protection over the touched-up area.

Guns which have an original, sandblasted or matte blued-finish don't respond quite so well to the same treatment. The polishing necessary to remove rust and etching also smooths the matte surface, so even after bluing, the area won't match. About the only thing you can do about this is to use a soft wire brush to remove any rust, then degrease the area thoroughly, and apply the touch-up bluing compound per the balance of instructions. The same applies to military arms with a parkerized finish. There's no way you can touch up that grey phosphate-finish so it will match the original. Applying a touch-up bluing compound to the worn area will give it some protection, and if you apply it over the entire part without polishing it, it will darken the original finish somewhat so that the touched-up area doesn't look quite so out of place.

It is quite difficult to do anything with a damaged plated finish. A small area that has worn through can be touched up with a "brush plating" outfit such as that sold by Texas Plater's Supply. This is simply a minimal electroplating outfit where the plating solution is applied with a brush. This may sound great, but it's almost impossible to match the original plating or to obtain a uniform coating over any significantly large area. About the best that it will allow is to thinly replate a worn spot so that the base metal will not rust. The patch won't match exactly in texture or color, and it won't be possible to get the coating as thick as the original finish, but it's a helluva lot better than doing nothing.

Doubtless if you put your mind to it, you could probably come up with other repair operations that you can perform. However, the foregoing constitute those which are likely to be necessary most often, and which you can do with the least amount of tools and equipment. Certainly they'll enable you to save a lot of gunsmithing bills and to keep your guns perking correctly for a long, long time.

Chapter Thirteen
Grips, Stocks and Handles

Most autos are shipped from the factory with plain checkered grips of either walnut (or some similar hardwood), or plastic. Considering that the plastics usually used have a slickish feeling and a glossy-smooth surface (even over the checkering), wood is much to be preferred. It offers a more secure hold, especially when hands are sweaty, greasy or bloody. Standard grips of either material usually are of plain shape, with at most a rudimentary thumb-rest ridge, sometimes on both sides for ambidextrous use.

Aside from ordinary plastic and wood we find numerous other materials used for custom-made and after-market replacement grips. Among them are rare woods, micarta, ivory, horn, bone, even silver and other previous metals. Frankly, no matter how nice they look or how much they cost, none of them are functionally as good as wood. The unique texture and feel of checkered (stippling is a good second choice) wood is ideally and traditionally suited to handguns of all sorts.

There is one material and type grip I prefer to wood for service (meaning combat) use. This is the rubber-like synthetic (probably neoprene) Pachmayr "Signa-ture" grip. A one-piece design, it wraps around the front strap and incorporates steel plates molded into the sides for stiffness. It is checkered but also has an almost "tacky" feel and texture that produces a superb hold—and the material also yields very slightly to a tight hold, which I find advantageous. At present, Pachmayr makes this Signature grip for the Colt GM (all versions), Browning HP, S&W M39, S & W M59. The Colt model fits Llama as well. Other models are in the making, but these cover the service-gun field fairly well. This is a superb grip and should not be overlooked if you are obtaining or setting up a big auto for serious social intercourse.

It seems as if every shooter owns a couple of old autoloaders with broken stocks. More letters come in asking about sources of replacement grips than about any other parts. While several manufacturers offer replacements for numerous obsolete guns, there are still many others for which replacements are almost impossible to obtain.

Replacements are made easily for many models by using the slab-type design. My favorite method is to rough out a grip plate of ⅛-inch thick wood or plastic

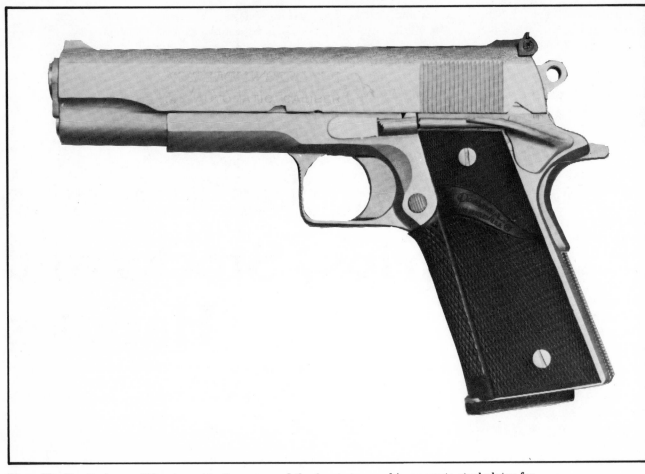

The rubberlike Pachmayr "Signature grips" wraparound the front strap and incorporate steel plates for stiffness.

and then carefully mark and drill mounting-screw holes. The blank is then screwed to the gun and carefully sanded and filed down to a workable shape, using masking tape over adjacent metal surfaces to prevent ruining the gun's finish. After rough shaping, the replacement grip may be removed and finished to suit. This procedure won't make exact duplicates of original grips, but the name of the game is to make the gun functional, and this will do it economically. If there is a recess in the grip frame as on the Colt GM, the grip plate can be strengthened by gluing to its inner surface a thin piece of wood trimmed to fit closely into the recess.

Cracked or split grips are easily repaired if you will remove all grease and dirt first. If the crack does not extend full length, go ahead and break the grip and clean the pieces in acetone to dissolve all grease; save all splinters or small pieces. Then coat metal surfaces adjacent to the repair lightly with grease, wax or release compound. Give all broken surfaces a thin

coat of five-minute epoxy and clamp them together in proper alignment. This is most easily done by screwing the grip on the gun and wrapping it securely with rubber bands or tape. After the epoxy has cured, the grip may be removed, excess epoxy dressed down, and the entire grip refinished as desired.

Grips often become loose because their mounting holes or inletted surfaces have become worn or have shrunk. This problem, too, is easily corrected and the procedure is the same for either plastic or wood: First degrease and clean the grips and the metal surfaces which they contact. Coat all metal surfaces with grease or a release compound. Next, apply a surplus of epoxy or fiberglass bedding compound to the loose fitting areas of the grips and clamp into place with both mounting screws and tape or rubber bands. Be sure, though, that the grips are aligned properly. Allow the epoxy to cure and trim away any excess.

Many grips have small bearing-surfaces that are subject to rapid wear. For those, build up additional surfaces of epoxy into or against various surface irregularities of the gun. Most often there will be cutouts in the side of the butt into which beads of epoxy may be fitted. When this is properly done, grips are not likely to loosen in a lifetime of service. In addition, this epoxy reinforcement greatly reduces the probability of splitting or shrinkage. I regularly apply beads of epoxy to inner surfaces of grips around the outlines of the butt cutouts when preparing a new gun such as a Colt Government Model or Smith & Wesson M39 for service. It's also a good idea when installing new after-market grips.

It's probable you have a gun with sound grips, but with badly worn checkering. Quite often the wear will be only on one grip—the side exposed when the gun is carried. If a replacement is not readily available, recutting the original checkering with a single-line checkering tool, such as the excellent and economical Dembart line, will greatly improve the grip's appearance and function. If traces of the original checkering remain, then it is simply a matter of carefully deepening the grooves with the checkering tool until clean sharply pointed diamonds are formed. Brush vigorously with an old toothbrush to burnish the surface and remove the fuzz, then apply a couple of coats of good quick-drying stock finish.

Screws and bushings which hold the stocks to the autoloading pistols often cause difficulties. The best installation method is that used in the big Colt and S&W autos which have separate bushings threaded and staked into the frame. The bushing fits into a hole in the grip and provides a much larger surface for absorbing recoil and other loads than the shank of a small screw. In addition, if the bushing's threads become stripped, replacing the bushing is much easier than repairing threads cut in the frame.

Many other autoloading pistols secure the grips simply by screws entering threaded holes in their butts. When these holes become excessively worn or stripped, the best repair is to install Colt or S&W bushings and alter the grips to fit over them. The bushings should be turned in tightly and secured permanently. You can stake them, but not as well as the factory without special tools, thus silver-soldering is the most practical method. Cleaning the threads (of both the bushings and holes), put paste solder on the threads, screw the bushing in as tightly as possible, and heat until solder flows freely. Use a small torch flame and keep the heat localized so there will be no need for refinishing. This method is by far the best I've found for tightening loose bushings on guns originally equipped with them. Staking or peening is seldom satisfactory, except as a temporary measure.

Unfortunately, the several models having aluminum-alloy frames do not lend themselves to silver-soldering. For these, use only those special solders that will adhere to aluminum, as well as to steel.

When soldering is not possible, clean the threads (both in the bushing and in the frame) and use Loctite or cyanoacrylate adhesive compound. If you're in the field and without other equipment, a grip–screw bushing may be tightened by hammering a sharp-pointed object closely around the mouth of the hole in the frame, which closes it slightly so that it grips the bushing tightly. Be careful, though, to avoid closing the hole so much that the bushing will not enter.

Making new replacement stocks is often not at all difficult, depending upon the type of gun. Simplest is the slab-sided type mentioned earlier and found on most big-bore autoloaders such as the various Colts. This grip is a simple piece of wood (plastic), flat on the inner side and slightly rounded on the outer with a pair of holes drilled for attachment screws.

For this type, trace the outline and hole spacing on a piece of $1/8$–$3/16$-inch-thick wood, drill the screw holes, then saw and file to profile. File and sand in the proper curvature, bevel the edges, and the job is done unless you wish to add checkering or other decoration, and we won't go into that here.

If original grips aren't available for tracing, cut holes in a piece of cardboard to match the screw holes or bushings, fit it in place on the gun butt, then trim to the shape that looks right. This will then be your pattern, and it can usually be simply flipped over to serve for the other side.

It's a good idea to reinforce home-made grips a bit on the inside, especially if they are very thin. For this, cut thin plywood—$1/16$- to $1/8$-inch thick—to fit as snugly as possible inside the cutouts in the sides of the gun butt. Then, glue firmly to the inner surface of the grips where they'll not only add stiffness, but will help absorb recoil loads. Make sure these panels don't interfere with the magazine or other parts.

Wraparound style grips such as are found on the Walther P38 and PPK pistols are more difficult. Ideally, they should be carved from thickwood blocks that will meet on the centerline at the rear. If you are good enough at wood-carving to accomplish that, you probably don't need my help. If you aren't, then try this much simpler method.

Prepare a pattern as before, extending it rearward to form either the original grip profile (take it from a photo if the original grips are missing) or whatever shape you prefer. Make sure you allow enough room at the rear to house the gun's working parts and still leave a fairly thick layer of wood over them.

Cut and fit the two side pieces from ¼-inch or thicker wood to include the extension mentioned, but leave them flat. Drill for attaching-screw and alignment-pin holes and secure to frame.

Measure the space between the rear edges of the grips and trim two equal-thickness blocks to fit in this gap. With hand grinder, knife and file, shape the front edges of these blocks to barely clear all working parts. Also, shape the top and/or bottom edges to butt closely against the frame where necessary.

Glue one of these blocks to the inner face of each side piece, aligning them carefully, and making certain that the glue doesn't run between the two blocks. Use a piece of plastic film between them if the prospect worries you. Use a good-quality water and oil-resistant glue, not common white glue or household adhesive—I prefer Titebond or two-part epoxies.

When the glue is cured, with the rough grips still on the gun, cycle the action to make certain the blocks haven't slipped to interfere with parts movement. If they have, remove wood from the inside to eliminate any problems.

Now, shape the grips the way you want them. Do it on the gun as much as possible, protecting exposed metal with masking tape, unless the gun is to be refinished. If you've used matching wood and fitted the joints closely, the glue lines will hardly be visible after the final finish is applied. Using this method, you can make a set of wrap-around grips in one-third the time necessary to carve and inlet them from solid blocks.

Incidentally, the Browning HP pistol uses semi-wraparound grips, and the same method works well for it.

Oversize or target-type grips for autos can be carved from solid wood, but, again, you'll save time and temper (and probably do a much better fitting job), if laminations are used as described for the wraparound variety. Here it will often be a matter of fitting blocks between both front and rear, perhaps even the bottom, of separate side pieces. Shape the inner faces of these blocks as closely as possible to front and backstraps—obtaining final precise fit by epoxy or glass-bedding if your carving needs it.

Thumb rests and finger ledges or butt flares can also be either carved from solid blocks with much

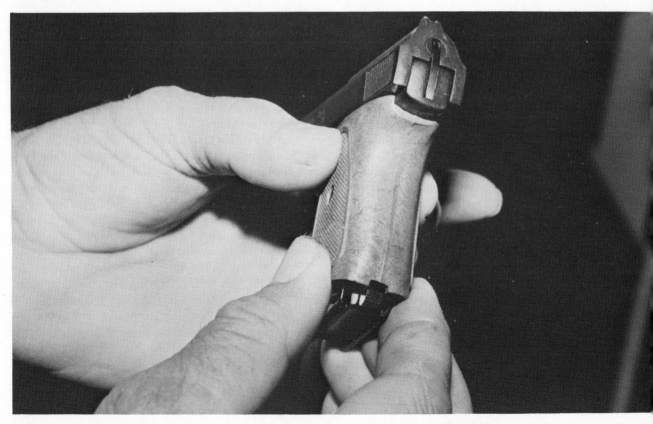

Wood grips, such as this wraparound wood grip, are preferable to plastic grips. Plastic grips usually feel too slick.

work, or shaped from glued-on pieces. I prefer the latter, and you'd be well advised to try it first. The result may not be pretty, but will save lots of time.

After you've made a set or two of grips by the laminating method, you'll have more carving experience and can do a better job of shaping them from solid blocks, in the event you decide to try. When working with grips which require complicated inletting, a Dremel Moto-Tool set up in its router attachment will be a tremendous help.

Shaping the outside of the bigger grips can be speeded greatly with a one-inch belt sander, or a two-inch Stanley Sur-Form drum chucked in the drill press. Both are desirable, the Sur-Form drum for fast-cutting, rough-shaping, and the sanding belt for smoothing and final shaping.

Finishing wood grips is really simple. If you like them smooth and bright, just sand as smoothly as possible, then apply any good stock finish according to its directions. I usually use GB Linspeed, but there are others you may prefer. If a rougher finish is desired and you don't want to try checkering, apply a couple of good coats of urethane varnish and let it harden thoroughly. Then apply a thick third coat, let it half-dry to the tacky state, and sprinkle on it all the finely ground pumice that will adhere to it. When that is dry, lightly brush off the loose pumice, and add a final, thin coat of varnish. This will give a sandpapery feel, which in some respects is more secure than checkering. Another roughening technique you can use is stippling. Do it as described elsewhere for metal surfaces.

If you prefer plastic to wood grips, they can be made in exactly the same way. Laminating is by far the simplest, but the joints will be obvious. Some amateur smiths turn this to a virtue by using contrasting-color laminations.

When original grips are in good condition for patterns, duplicates may be cast from liquid plastic. This involves coating the pattern with a latex material which forms a flexible mold, then using that mold to cast a new part from liquid plastic which hardens quickly. This will usually produce a good copy of plastic grips, but does less well with checkered wood due to fuzziness in the checkering. Several hobby-supply companies advertise plastic-casting outfits for this type of work. The nearest large hobby or craft shop should also be able to supply kits.

Fortunately, as the handgun population has increased, several firms have begun supplying replacement grips. They not only offer standard grips for most popular current models, but many special types and styles as well. In addition, they usually offer grips for a wide variety of obsolete and foreign guns. Thus, if you need new grips for an old Ortgies or a Mauser pistol of World War I vintage, or whatever, chances are one of these firms can supply them in plastic and/or wood, and often in more than one style, color or finish. Several sources for such grips are listed in the appendix.

Chapter Fourteen
Accuracy and Accurizing

Bullet velocity and energy are held down by consideration of weight, size and recoil; magazine capacity is limited by bulk. Accuracy in particular is limited in production guns by considerations of functional reliability in the field and by the economic realities of manufacturing costs.

All of the centerfire autoloaders which have been used widely for target shooting are one variation or another of the basic Browning design with reciprocating, tubular slide and mobile barrel. Since reliable function of these designs, which were originally intended for severe military service, depends upon adequate clearance between the frame and all recoiling parts, a certain amount of "slop" must be built in. Add ordinary manufacturing tolerances to this, and we have the situation where even a brand-new gun can be shaken to produce a disturbing rattle as the major recoiling parts shimmy about on the frame. Guns built with this sort of clearance will function reliably in rain, sandstorms, dry desert, rain forests, sub-zero arctic temperatures, without lubrication, and even when clogged with mud and dirt. They achieve that degree of reliability at the expense of

accuracy. All things considered, such guns actually shoot remarkably well—some of them keeping all of their shots within three inches at 50 yards, though the average won't do quite that well.

But, that kind of accuracy comes nowhere near satisfying the serious target shooter. He demands a gun with the mechanical accuracy capability of keeping all of its shots well within the 1.695-inch diameter X-ring of the Standard American 50-yard target.

This degree of accuracy can be obtained only by tightening up the relationship between barrel, slide and frame; that is, fitting parts more closely so that relative movement is substantially reduced. This process is known as "accurizing" when done after the fact on a production gun. On the other hand, the manufacturer may simply tighten up tolerances and selectively hand-fit parts, both of which substantially increase costs, and thus produce a "target" model of a particular gun. Such target models will usually include numerous other refinements, but they don't necessarily increase the mechanical accuracy.

Perhaps at this point we should explain the meaning of "mechanical accuracy." Mechanical accuracy is

The target-shooting performance of your Colt 45 automatic, or any auto, can be improved with a process called accurizing.

that degree of accuracy, generally measured as the distances between centers of the two widest shots of a 10-shot group at 50 yards, which the gun can produce with first-class ammunition when the human element is eliminated. The mechanical accuracy of a particular gun can be determined by firing it from a precision-built machine rest so that there is no shooter influence upon its performance. No individual can extract all of a particular gun's mechanical accuracy. Shooter error combines with gun error, so that the average group even the best shooter can obtain with a particular gun will be at least somewhat larger than the average group the gun can produce from a machine rest—that is, its mechanical accuracy capability. For the sake of convenience, I always refer to this shooter-plus-gun accuracy as "practical accuracy." Thus you might wind up in possession of a 45 auto which has a mechanical accuracy capability of 1.25-inch groups at 50 yards, yet, the practical accu-

racy which you can produce with that gun may be 2.5-inch groups at the same range.

In any event, tightening up the gun to improve its accuracy reduces its ability to produce completely reliable functioning under less-than-ideal conditions. Thus, a highly accurized 45 auto would be a poor bet in a foxhole or jungle, but this doesn't bother the serious target shooter in the least, because he will shoot under nearly ideal conditions. He will be able to baby the gun and thus achieve a degree of reliability that is satisfactory on the range.

While other centerfire autoloaders are occasionally accurized, probably 90 percent of those given such treatment in this country is the ubiquitous cost 45 Auto, otherwise known as "GI 45," and by numerous other nicknames, some of which are not very complimentary. For that reason, we'll describe hereafter the basic procedures utilized to make a tack-driver out of a typical 45 Colt auto. The operations remain essen-

Use copper or other protective jaws in the vise for the slide.

tially the same whether you're dealing with a well-used, World War II military-contract gun or the latest commercial production fresh out of the box.

In its purest sense, accurizing consists of those operations which increase the mechanical accuracy of the gun. However, the term is often broadened to include those additional operations and added accessories which make it easier or simpler for the shooter to extract that mechanical accuracy.

Begin by completely disassembling the 45. Separate all parts except the ejector, plunger-spring housing, and grip-screw bushings which are permanently assembled to the frame. Slip the stripped slide on the frame, and note that there is considerable vertical and horizontal play between the two. We start by reducing this play to a minimum, by narrowing the grooves on the receiver, and by squeezing the rails on the slide closer together.

The frame is clamped very tightly upright in a heavy bench vise, using shaped hardwood blocks to protect protrusions. It's also a good idea to support the frame from beneath with more blocks. Professional pistolsmiths make up special fixtures for this, but they're out of the question for the home job.

We must now peen the tops of the guide rails, slightly narrowing the vertical dimension of the grooves beneath them and thus reducing vertical play of the slide on the frame. This is done with smart blows of a medium-weight machinist's hammer with a smoothly polished striking face. If the blows are struck too hard, the surface will be dented, and you don't want that. The blows should be overlapped at least by half and all struck with the same force. Make one pass the length of the rail on each side, then slip the slide back in place and note if there's been any significant reduction in vertical play. Remove the slide and repeat the peening operation.

It may take quite a few passes (especially if you've

never done this before), to close up that groove enough to eliminate vertical slide play. However, before you've reached that point, the peening will have produced some sideward growth of the rails, mostly in the form of shallow burrs at the upper edges. As these burrs show up, remove them by very light filing to prevent them from binding on the slide. Continue peening of the rails until the slide becomes tight upon the frame and displays no vertical looseness. It shouldn't be so tight that you can't slide it on and off with both hands.

Now it's time for the slide; with copper or other protective jaws in the vise, very carefully position the slide upright and parallel to the jaws and clamp it lightly in the vise. Position it so that the full length of the guide rails are between the jaws, but no deeper into the jaws than the upper edge of the inner guide-groove. Apply pressure with the vise handle until the lower edges of the slide are squeezed together only very slightly. You'll feel a very slight amount of give when this amount of pressure has been applied. Take care, and don't overdo it. Try the slide on the frame, and check for lateral play. If it's too tight to go on at all, you've overdone the vise bit, and you're in trouble; if it can't be driven on with a soft mallet, it'll take a good bit of careful stoning and filing to correct your error.

Assuming that the slide does go on without too much trouble, check it for lateral play, and if any still exists, give it just a bit more of the vise. When you've gotten the slide tight enough to require modest urging with a soft mallet to move it over the frame, it's about right. Naturally, you'll have applied oil to those guide ribs to prevent galling. Drive the slide back and forth a few times so that it frees up just a bit, then remove it, wipe off the oil, and apply machninist's layout blue to all the rubbing surfaces you can reach on both the slide and frame. Then, move the slide once through its full travel on the frame, remove it and note where the blue is rubbed off. These bright areas indicate the high spots that are binding, and very carefully they should be stoned down slightly, then reapply the blue and try again.

By the time you've worked the high spots down so that there's fairly uniform contact, the slide will probably be a bit loose on the frame again. Lateral looseness should be taken up with another modest squeeze in the vise, and if there's any vertical play, another light pass or two with the peening hammer should cure it. You want to finish this part of the job with no discernible play in either direction, and the slide tight enough on the frame to require considerable urging by hand, but not quite so tight that the

hammer will be needed to move it.

Fitting the barrel and bushing to the slide comes next, and though all this can be done with the original barrel and bushing, you'll be far better off to begin the job with a new match-grade barrel and bushing to match. Several suppliers offer them, but I personally have a fondness for the stainless-steel barrel and collet-type or spring-finger bushing offered by Bar-Sto. This unusual bushing actually does a better job of controlling barrel muzzle position than does the solid type, and, in addition, requires no hand-fitting to the barrel. The spring fingers do the job. To avoid confusion later, fit the bushing into the front of the slide first. You'll need a bushing wrench; then press the bushing into place and rotate it into the locked position with the wrench. It should be quite tight, but still capable of being tapped into the slide with a length of dowel or plastic hammer, then rotated with the wrench without great effort.

If it's tighter than that, polish down the bearing surface very slightly with fine abrasive cloth until it will enter. Even though tight upon the barrel, the bushing will not produce maximum accuracy if there is any relative movement between it and the slide. It must be tight in the slide, just free enough to permit disassembly with the use of a wrench when thorough cleaning becomes necessary. Once the bushing is fitted, we can proceed to fit the barrel to the slide.

Match-grade barrels, the Bar-Sto in particular, are made with the tang a bit wider and longer than standard to permit obtaining a very close fit in the slide breech. First make certain that there are no burrs or other damage in the rectangular slide recess at the upper rear of the ejection port. True-up this recess with needle files, if necessary, but take particular care that it is not enlarged unnecessarily. Now, insert the barrel in the slide and attempt to position the tang in this recess; it should be just a bit too wide. *Very carefully* file and stone the sides of the tang until it will just *barely* enter the recess from beneath. Be particularly careful that the sides of the tang are kept parallel, not tapered in either width or thickness. The side-to-side fit of the tang in the recess determines the consistency with which the barrel will be positioned laterally and radially from shot to shot.

Now, check the locking-lug recesses inside the roof of the slide and ascertain that there are no burrs or other deformations present. The recesses must be free to accept the locking ribs on the top of the barrel. Insert the barrel, positioning the tang in the breech recess, press the barrel fully to the rear, and attempt to seat the locking lugs in the recesses. They should not quite seat, being held just a bit too far forward by the extra length of the barrel tang. Commence carefully and slowly filing and stoning the rear face of the tang, taking care that it is kept square in both planes, until the locking ribs will just barely enter their recesses in the slide. Now, very lightly bevel all of the edges of the barrel tang, clean off all grit and filings, and install the barrel bushing. You should be able to push the rear of the barrel up and down, engaging and disengaging the locking surfaces without too much effort, and without any detectable fore-and-aft or sideward play.

The barrel is now fitted to the slide, and the slide has already been fitted to the frame, so it remains only to fit the barrel properly to the frame, tying the three components into a functional, homogeneous unit capable of delivering maximum accuracy.

The ordinary 45 auto depends upon the swinging link connecting the barrel to the frame to lift the barrel into the locked position as the slide runs into battery. Additional metal has been left in the barrel lug so that in accurizing we may fit it to also be cammed upward by the slide-stop pin which is capable of providing far greater vertical support than that skinny barrel link.

With the barrel link in place, slip the slide/barrel unit on the frame, insert the slide stop, then push the slide forward; you'll find that it will not go fully into battery, being prevented by the oversized barrel lug coming up against the slide-stop pin. Retract the slide and slam it forward several times, then withdraw the slide stop and examine the lower forward surface of the barrel lug. You should be able to see a slight bright spot where the lug has contacted the pin; if not, apply machinist's blue to the lug, and repeat the process. This will quite clearly show the contact area where the blue has been rubbed away. Commence very carefully filing and stoning away the excess metal at the point of contact, maintaining the approximate cam shape and angle, repeatedly assembling the components and attempting to seat the slide in battery. As metal is removed, the lug will be able to move farther forward over the slide-stop pin, and eventually you'll reach a point where the slide will go fully into battery. Approach this point very carefully, and stop filing on the barrel lug while the slide still lacks a tiny bit of going home. At this stage of the game, reapply machinist's blue to the lug, check it for contact with the slide-stop pin, then lightly polish the engaging area to smooth the file marks. Don't remove any more metal than necessary. Remove any burrs that were turned up during the reshaping.

Now, clean the gun thoroughly, lubricate the barrel/slide/frame contact areas copiously, and assemble the gun completely. Remember, the slide should still fail by a very tiny margin from going into battery under hand pressure.

The gun should be function-fired at this stage, before going further with the work. Load up with ball ammunition, chamber the first round, and fire (in a safe area, of course). After the first round, under the impetus of recoil and the recoil spring, the slide will chamber the next round, and it may or may not go fully into battery. If it does, continue firing. If it does not, hold the hammer back with your thumb (finger clear of the trigger) and rap the rear of the slide smartly with a plastic hammer to seat it as far as it will go; then fire the second round. It may be necessary to fire a number of rounds in this manner before the slide will go fully into battery unassisted. This break-in firing is necessary if we are to have the slide and barrel locking up tight in battery with a minimum of looseness.

The tightness with which these parts lock up determines the consistency of vertical position of the rear of the barrel from shot to shot. By fitting the barrel lug tightly against the slide-stop pin so that the barrel is wedged securely into the roof of the slide in battery, we eliminate excessive vertical play at the barrel breech and ensure consistent positioning for each shot. Take note that inasmuch as the rear of the barrel is raised and lowered for locking and unlocking, its angular relationship to the line of sight will vary by the amount of vertical looseness that remains. Certainly if the relationship of the barrel centerline to the line of sight is allowed to vary vertically, we can expect the gun to string its shots up and down on the target.

If you do not wish to go to all the trouble of this careful fitting of the barrel lug to the slide-stop pin, much the same effect can be obtained—to a somewhat lesser degree—by replacing the original barrel link and recoil-spring guide with a device known as the "Group Gripper." It replaces the barrel link with one specially shaped so that a heavy leaf-spring placed inside the rear of the guide puts stiff upward pressure on the barrel when the slide is in battery. It serves to greatly increase shot-to-shot consistency of the barrel's vertical position. It won't do the job quite as well as a very carefully fitted lug/pin relationship, but it will produce a very substantial improvement in the average unaccurized gun.

There is another alternative, albeit somewhat more costly, to ensuring consistent vertical position of the barrel breech. This is the Bo-Mar "Accuracy Block," which is incorporated into the base of the very precise Bo-Mar target rear sight. It consists first of a base, which is actually a short rib extending from the rear of the ejection port back along the upper surface of the slide. The rear sight is inletted into the rear of this base, and up front is inletted an L-shaped member with a short vertical finger which extends downward into the slide recess that accepts the barrel tang. The base is attached securely to the slide by screws, then the vertical barrel position is regulated by additional screws so that the down-thrust member forms a stop for upward movement of the barrel breech. This accessory should be used with a "long link," a replacement barrel link available from Gil Hebard and other suppliers. The long link is available in several lengths, and the center-to-center distance between its two pin holes is slightly greater than in the original.

When a long link is installed, its greater length raises the barrel higher as the slide runs into battery, taking out some vertical play, and also engaging the locking ribs on the barrel deeper in their recesses in the slide. Proper adjustment of the accuracy block is that vertical position which causes the barrel to be held tightly against it when the slide is in battery, but yet which does not prevent the slide and barrel from going fully into battery. When this condition is set up, the rear of the barrel is more or less clamped between the link and the accuracy block, thus assuring consistent vertical positioning for every shot.

There is a secondary benefit to all three of these barrel-positioning methods which is often overlooked. As the slide and barrel move into battery, the barrel is forced tightly against the roof of the slide, or, in the third method, against the accuracy block which is firmly attached to the slide. This has the effect of also raising the slide with respect to the frame, so if there is any vertical play between those two parts, it is removed or at least greatly reduced as the full-battery position is reached. It is for this reason that use of the accuracy block or the Group Gripper will produce a substantial increase in accuracy, even on a gun in which there is considerable vertical play between slide and frame. In fact, I have been advised by a well-known target-pistol authority that for this reason the Group Gripper produces a greater accuracy improvement than any other device or operation which may be applied by the inexperienced non-pistolsmith shooter.

The operations we've described are those which improve mechanical accuracy. They constitute the heart of an "accuracy job," or the accurizing process. Many other things are done to the 45 auto in conjunction with the basic accurizing processes, but they don't have any significant effect upon the gun's mechanical accuracy. Rather, they take the form of better sights, better trigger pull, improved functional reliability, hand-fitting grips, trigger stop, stippling on front and back straps to improve one's hold, etc. These are things which make it easier for the shooter to aim and control the gun and thus reduce the human error.

First of all, with the gun tightened up, its functional reliability will have been seriously decreased. The details of improving reliability, especially with light target loads, are covered in our chapter on tuning for maximum reliability. The entire gun should be given very careful attention in this respect, for if it malfunctions during an important match, you're in trouble. Even if the "alibi rule" allows you to re-fire a string during which a malfunction occurred, you'll be under a psychological disadvantage which will surely reduce the score you might have obtained had the gun not screwed up.

Most shooters consider installation of top-quality micrometer-adjustable sights part and parcel of an accuracy job. They are certainly essential if maximum accuracy is to be obtained and if one is to be able to change sight settings for different loads and ranges and to meet changing conditions.

A proper trigger pull—proper in weight as well as other characteristic—is exceedingly important to obtaining top accuracy. A lousy pull will screw up even a good shooter. The pull should not only be of the proper weight—four to five pounds static load—but smooth, crisp and consistent, without excessive over-travel. Unfortunately, most pistoleros seem to believe that the most may be done for the trigger pull by jumping in feet first and working over the sear and hammer engaging surfaces. Nothing could be further from the truth; the average gun buff without considerable experience in this art will most likely either ruin the parts or make the pull worse than before, or even make the gun unsafe. The odds are better than 1000-to-1 against success.

Instead, the proper approach is first to smooth up all parts and areas that affect trigger pull, then install a trigger stop and/or trigger shoe. If all that is done correctly, the pull will surely be much improved, often sufficiently so that there won't be any need to start ripping up the sear and hammer.

Begin this by removing all the lockwork parts and examining them for burrs or roughness. With needle files and stones, smooth the grooves in which the trigger slides. If need by, break off short sections of stone or file and epoxy them to wood handles to reach all the way in. Smooth the edges of the trigger yoke the same way, spreading the sides slightly if necessary to eliminate lateral play in the frame. If there is ignificant vertical play in the front of the trigger when installed, soft-solder shim stock to the top and/or bottom surfaces of the finger-piece, then file and stone them down until the trigger moves smoothly fore-and-aft without vertical slop. Polish the angled rear-surface of the trigger yoke smooth where it bears on the sear spring and disconnector foot.

Check the disconnector for smooth operation in its hole in the frame. Remove any roughness in either the hole or the disconnector and polish the foot where it contacts the trigger yoke, sear spring and sear. Pressed down where it protrudes above the frame, the disconnector should pop back up smoothly and positively.

Look carefully inside the frame in the vicinity of the sear and remove any burrs or roughness which might impede smooth sear movement. Polish the upper ends of the sear-spring limbs where they contact the trigger yoke and sear; there are often burrs on the ends which can cause problems. Check also to make certain that the limbs do not rub on the frame walls or upon any other nearby parts. It may be necessary to narrow the spring limbs a bit to avoid this; if so, do it carefully on a straight taper with a fine-cut file or hand grinder, then be sure to deburr the edges.

Examine the insides of the grip and manual safeties to make certain that there are not any burrs or roughness that can interfere with the hammer, sear or other parts' smooth movement. It is not unusual, especially on military-contract guns, for these parts to rub somewhat on others, and that can play hob with an otherwise perfect trigger pull. Check the hammer strut to make certain it moves freely on the hammer and that it does not drag on the grip safety or the mouth of the mainspring housing; use those files and stones if it does.

The effect of the mainspring and its housing on trigger pull is often overlooked. Disassemble the entire unit, then carefully scrub all the crud and rust out of the housing and off the spring. Polish the inside of the housing where spring movement might be impeded by roughness. Clip two coils off the mainspring, making certain that the cut doesn't leave a protruding burr which will drag on the inside of the housing when all is reassembled.

After all this, reassemble the entire firing mechanism (after, of course, thoroughly cleaning and deburring all other related parts) and try the trigger pull. Almost invariably you'll find that the pull has improved considerably in smoothness and that it has become at least somewhat lighter. It may well have improved to the point that you can live with it without doing any further work.

The principal objection now will probably be too much over-travel. To correct this, obtain a trigger shoe which incorporates a trigger stop and install it correctly. The stop is clamped to the trigger (usually) by a pair of tiny pointed socket-head screws. To ensure that the shoe will stay securely in place, punch or grind small dimples for the screw points, turn the screws in tightly, then apply a drop of Loctite over their heads. This will keep them from working loose, yet they may still be loosened without trouble when you want to remove the shoe.

Now, turn the trigger-stop screw in until it prevents firing by halting the trigger before the sear is disengaged; follow by backing out the screw in ¼-turn increments until rearward trigger movement will just barely drop the hammer *every time*. Secure the screw with Loctite or by the clamp screw provided for this purpose in some trigger shoes. If the shoe is to be a permanent installation, it will do no harm to run a drop or two of Loctite or cyanoacrylate adhesive in between the shoe and trigger.

If after all this you still aren't satisfied with the trigger pull and are determined to do the work yourself, begin by obtaining a gunsmith's jig for the stoning of sears and hammer notches. These devices are available from Brownells and other gunsmithing supply houses at a reasonable price. Without such a jig, you'll probably ruin parts on the first attempt, and replacements will cost more than the jig. Proper stones are supplied with the jig, along with detailed instructions. Be sure to use the former and follow the latter explicitly.

Generally, they call for positioning the part in the body of the jig, securing it there with the same pin as used in the gun, then rotating the part against a stop. The surface to be stoned then protrudes very slightly above the surface of the jig which is intended to function as a guide for the stone. The stone is simply applied to the surface until it comes to rest flat upon the top of the jig. This ensures that the proper angle has been formed on the part and that too much metal has not been removed. In the case of the sear, both a primary and a secondary angle must be stoned and this requires repositioning the part after the first has been completed. Don't overlook the secondary angle; it is essential to safety and to maintaining a consistent weight of pull. If it is not properly formed, the sharp edge left on the tip of the sear by the primary angle will chip and crumble under pressure of the hammer and mainspring.

After the hammer notch and sear nose have been

properly stoned, the sear should engage the notch to a depth of no more than .040 inch and no less (for safety) than .020 inch. If engagement is too shallow, the hammer notch must be stoned deeper; if engagement is too much, then some sort of stop to limit sear entry must be formed on the hammer just below the notch. Good pistolsmiths often drill the hammer for a $\frac{1}{16}$-inch drill-rod pin, press a pin in place, then cut the pin back until the desired depth-of-sear engagement is obtained. This is a bit complex for the kitchen-table workman, so a simpler fix is needed. Using low-temperature paste solder, simply attach a small piece of shim stock below the hammer notch. Take care not to heat the hammer any more than is actually necessary to melt the solder and obtain a satisfactory bond. Then, stone or file the shim back until sear engagement falls within the proper limits.

If sear engagement is too deep by only a small amount, say, no more than about .020 inch, then it may be safely reduced by stoning off metal above and in front of the hammer notch. If more is removed there, the sear nose may be struck by the safety notch as the hammer falls, chipping away those beautiful angles that you stoned and polished, thus ruining the pull.

After all the foregoing has been done carefully, you should have a good trigger pull. Weight may be varied slightly by bending the appropriate limbs of the sear spring, but if the pull is still not to your liking, you can either start fresh and do the job over, or turn it over to someone with a good deal of experience in this sort of thing.

About all that remains to be done of the typical accuracy job is to roughen the front strap in some manner so as to provide for a more secure hold; you don't want the gun shifting in the hand during rapid-fire. Stippling is the simplest method of accomplishing this and can be done with only a center punch, hammer and some means of holding the frame solidly. Stone or grind the point of the punch to a pyramidal form, then polish it as smooth as possible. Remove all oil or grease from the front strap, then clamp the gun solidly in a vise, strap up. Rest your forearm on something solid and grip the punch tightly, poised about $\frac{1}{8}$ to $\frac{1}{4}$ inch above the front strap, then tense the hand and wrist. Strike the punch smartly, but not too hard, so that the point digs into the strap and turns up a burr as well as making a depression. The tenseness of your wrist will cause the punch to rebound to its original position, ready for the next hammer below. Move the punch so that the next impression will slightly overlap the first. Keep this up until the entire strap has been uniformly roughened.

The height and sharpness of the burrs can be varied by changing the angle of impact; at 90 degrees to the surface, hardly any burrs will be raised, while at 45 degrees, the burr may be too sharp and prominent. Best experiment on scrap metal to see exactly what you want. If the burrs do turn out to be too sharp, burnish the area heavily with a wire brush to trim them down.

That's about it as far as a home-brewed accuracy job is concerned. The professionals have many other refinements to offer and will often use different techniques and accessories. Usually they have developed their own favorite methods and labor-saving tools and fixtures, but such things aren't practical for the pistol ero who just wants to upgrade one or two guns.

Actually, there isn't any quick, simple and easy way to infuse a big-bore autoloader with first-class accuracy. It's a long and arduous task for even the professionals.

Chapter Fifteen
Handloading for Autos

There was a time not too many years ago when it wasn't terribly difficult to shop around a bit and pick up quantities of military-ball pistol ammunition for mere pennies per round. To be sure, the quality, condition and ancestry of the ammunition varied a good bit—but I only recall one particular lot of 45 ACP (which had somehow gotten water-logged in storage) which didn't usually perform fairly well. The bulk of the 45 ammunition was of U.S. military-contract manufacture, but the 9mm and other calibers came from plants all over the world since the 1930s. Most shooters shied away from the Berdan-primed foreign stuff when U.S. and Canadian boxer-primed was available, but it was in the minority. Then, though, they shot the European ammo without qualms. They bitched a bit about the brass which couldn't be reloaded easily, but they still had relatively cheap shooting without resorting to extensive handloading.

Nowadays, you can still find good surplus military ammunition from time to time, but the price is five to ten times what it was some years back. And, if you think the price of military ammunition has soared, take a look at the latest price list from Remington-Peters or Winchester-Western. By the time you read this, a single shot fired with fresh commercial ammunition might easily cost 25 cents or more. Whether you are shooting for fun, simply to make noise, or in serious contention for a national trophy, this is a helluva lot of money to pay each time you pull the trigger.

The logical solution to this most vexing economic problem (which becomes even worse as coffee and scotch prices skyrocket) is to handload. The experienced and reasonably well-equipped handloader possessed of a penurious bent can still crank out perfectly serviceable ammunition that duplicates ball-cartridge performance at a cost barely exceeding one cent per round. Naturally, he can't do this by buying all of his components and operating purely as an ammunition assembler. But, by casting bullets from scrounged free lead and shopping carefully for powder and primers, and by keeping close track of his fired cases, he can keep the price close to that level. Special-purpose ammunition will cost a bit more, of course, and that which is loaded with jacketed expanding bullets at high velocities for defense or hunting will cost the most.

Even there, utilizing factory-made bullets and fired cases, the price still need not exceed five or six cents per round if one shops carefully for powder, primers and bullets. Local gun shops occasionally run special sales on components, and it's not unusual to find a discount store offering the same at prices substantially lower than the recommended list you see in catalogs and such.

This isn't intended to be a first-semester text, so I'll begin by assuming that you already have a good loading press and dies, along with the requisite shell holder, priming equipment, and a powder measure as well as a scale to check the accuracy of that measure. We'll also assume that you are familiar with at least the rudiments of handloading and that such things as resizing and neck expansion will not require detailed explanation.

First, a brief look at your equipment. Almost any well-made loading press will do, but the reloading dies should be of the best quality. If you intend to load a good deal, by all means count your pennies and see if you can't afford a sizing die with a tungsten-carbide insert, commonly called a "carbide die." It will do a better job of resizing, and it will not be damaged by the inadvertent running of a dirty, gritty or unlubricated case into it. As a matter of fact, as long as cases are reasonably clean and uncorroded, you can dispense with pre-sizing lubrication when using a carbide die. Such dies have an amazingly long life, and it's doubtful that any individual can ever wear one out. I once ran more than one-and-one-half million cases through a carbide die, and it was still serviceable.

Your loading press is probably set up to reprime cases in conjunction with decapping and neck expansion, or perhaps during resizing, dependent upon its make. This is an entirely acceptable method, but in the long run, you'll obtain more uniform primer seating, and probably spend a little less time at it, if you obtain one of the separate bench-type priming tools—preferably one with a magazine feed and semi-automatic operation. I've obtained excellent results from the latest RCBS semi-automatic tool, and also from the Bonanza unit which has an adjustable shell-holder composed of three, eccentric, steel discs and thus doesn't require shifting holders back and forth to change calibers.

Your average adjustable powder measure will work quite well, but should be fitted with a *pistol* metering chamber. The small, light weight, fixed-charge pistol-type measures make for faster operation

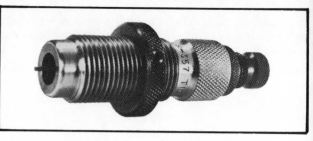

Titanium carbide pistol dies are made of the hardest carbide.

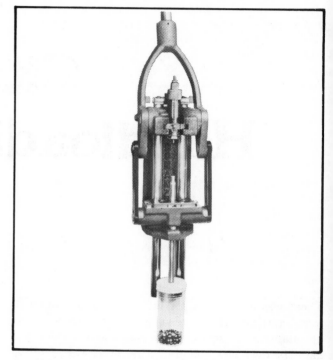

A positive spent primer catcher is a feature of the Co-Ax Press.

and do not require the use of a scale to verify their settings. For this reason, I lean toward their use.

Of course, you'll need loading blocks to hold the cases while charging them with powder, some primer trays, and some shallow boxes for keeping components handy and in good order. Other accessories you'll think of as things rock along.

It all starts with the cases. It's unlikely—and unnecessary—you'll be shelling out 10 cents each for new cases, so you'll surely be working with a wide assortment of fired brass, part of which has been generated by your own guns, and parts of which you acquire from various sources. Case condition will probably range from like-new to cruddy and dirty and a fair percentage will be bent or mutilated. Regardless, the major step—one I consider indispensable—

n preparing it for reloading, is the necessity to clean by tumbling or washing. Tumbling is by far the most convenient, though an electrically driven tumbler costs a helluva lot more than a bucket of soap and water. Recently I've been using one of the best tumblers I've encountered, by Lortone, available directly from Gil Hebard (Knoxville, Illinois 61448). It holds several hundred 45 auto cases and when used with ground nut hulls, it does a beautiful job of cleaning them inside and out.

Once cases are cleaned, spread them out and pick out and set aside all of those with significant mouth dents and/or feed-ramp bulges back near the head. If you're short on brass, most of them can be salvaged later, but otherwise you probably might just as well pitch them. Also, discard any cases which show evidence of primer leaks in the form of blackened areas around the primer or loose primers. Unless you're certain the cases were originally fired only in a pistol, keep a close eye out for bulges ahead of the web.

From time to time, a good bit of submachine-gun brass turns up, and often it is so heavily bulged in this area that the case is cracked internally and will be badly weakened even if the sizing die is successful in ironing out the bulge. If there are any *steel* cases in the lot, set them aside. Those steel U.S. 45s head-stamped in the 1940s are most likely to be rusted and weakened, and, even if not, are very difficult to resize. Those headstamped in the 1950s actually reload rather well, being much softer and more ductile, but resizing breaks their protective coating, and they'll eventually rust. Foreign steel cases aren't worth the bother so I'd suggest pitching them unless they are of a scarce caliber which you might need someday, like, maybe, 7.65mm French Long.

Install the appropriate shell holder and adjust the resizing die so that the holder seats solidly against the die mouth when the ram is at the top of its stroke. If your die incorporates a decapping stem, check its adjustment so that the stem itself does not strike the inside of the head when the case is forced fully into the die. Make sure the decapping pin is straight, held tightly in place, and aligns closely with the flash hole to punch out the fired primer. A pin that runs into the case head will surely be broken, and it may ruin the case as well.

If you're using a regular hardened steel die, make sure it is wiped clean and that the cases are equally clean and free of grit. Then very lightly lubricate the cases by dribbling a small amount of resizing lube on an old towel and tumble the cases around in it. Only a trace of lubricant is needed, so don't overdo the job. If a carbide die is to be used, then forget the lubrication unless you simply prefer it for the reduction of effort it offers. I prefer to do without and thus avoid having to remove the lubricant later.

Run the entire batch of cases through the resizing die, taking care you don't crumple the mouths against the die and making certain all the primers are eventually removed. In very old brass, you may occasionally encounter a primer held so tightly that the decapping pin will punch through the cup without removing it. Also, you may find an occasional primer from which the decapping pin will simply remove the top of the cup, leaving a thin ring of brass in the pocket. With reasonable luck, none of this will happen, but it's best to know it might. If it does, set those cases aside. Then someday if you run very short of brass, they can be salvaged by prying or pricking out the primer remains.

If the cases were lubed, the lubricant should be cleaned off at this point. If not removed, it introduces the possibility of contaminating powder and primers, and it will also collect dust and grit. This can be done by moistening a towel with lighter fluid or similar solvent, then tumbling the cases in it for four or five minutes. They'll come out dry and free of lubricant—with the exception that there might be traces still held in the extractor groove. Don't worry about that, because it won't cause any trouble.

However, I prefer to get rid of the lubricant by tossing all the cases back in the tumbler and running it for a half hour or so with a small amount of solvent added to the tumbling medium. The medium shouldn't be wet, just slightly damp. If time permits, let the tumbler run several hours, and the primer pockets will be cleaned also. For ordinary loading, I don't believe it's necessary to clean the pockets, but

The Lyman Little Grain Dribbler is a reloading accessory.

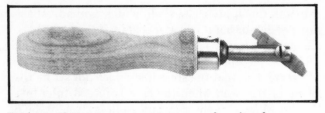

Primer pocket reamers serve to remove the crimp from primer pockets.

it's convenient and easy to do so in this fashion, and it certainly can't do any harm.

At this point, decide whether the next operation should be priming or neck (mouth) expansion. It makes no difference in the quality of the finished ammunition, but I prefer to expand the necks first, simply because if I decide to stop work and finish loading later, I'll be storing unprimed cases and will thus avoid the possibility of any primer contamination.

Assuming expansion is next, you'll have to consider the bullet that is to be loaded. Assuming a fairly hard cast-lead bullet, you'll want the mouth of the case flared just enough to permit the bullet base to start into the case without shaving lead, yet the balance of the mouth should have an inside diameter of approximately .003–.005 inch *less* than bullet diameter. If your expander plug produces a greater inside diameter than this, then you'll be well advised to polish it down a bit. Unless the case grips the bullet very tightly, you may run into feeding problems later. Also, the case mouth should be expanded only to a depth of about $\frac{1}{32}$ inch (even $\frac{1}{16}$ inch isn't too much) above the point where the bullet base will come to rest when it is seated. By stopping expansion at this point, we leave a very slight shoulder there, and the base of the bullet forces this shoulder deeper into the case as it is seated, leaving the bullet resting on it. This provides added resistance to feeding and recoil impacts, and prevents bullets from being shoved back into the case.

In checking out the matter, inside mouth diameter, you may find that your resizing die does not reduce the neck sufficiently. The expander plug must expand the case at least slightly to produce a small enough diameter to hold the bullets tightly. While this will often be the fault of an oversized die, it can also be caused, at least in part, by cases with thinner-than-usual walls. If the case is the problem, you'll either have to discard it, cannelure it (of which more later), or obtain an undersize resizing die. If it develops that your resizing die is simply oversized, then a new one is in order, and if you haven't screwed it up, the manufacturer will probably replace it without charge.

Back to expanding the necks. You'll note that the typical expander plug or rod carries a short conical section which flares the case mouth. The portion of the rod below the flare will be too long and, therefore, will expand the case deeper than we want. You'll simply have to measure this portion of the rod, then polish or grind the remainder down so that actual expansion takes place only to that point we've mentioned—just above the position of the bullet base after assembly.

Expander rods are quite hard; it might take forever for you to polish this section down by hand. It might be cheaper in the long run to take it to a machine shop and have the job done on a toolpost grinder. Or, you might chuck the rod in a drill press or electric drill, then while it is spinning, carefully apply a hand grinder such as the Dremel Moto-Tool to the section to be reduced.

Once you have the expanding die set up so that it expands the case properly, run all the cases through. The more cases upon which you can complete a single operation at any given time, the less time you'll have involved in the loading of a given number of rounds. The time consumed in frequent changing and adjusting of dies adds up very quickly.

Priming comes next. Using a bench tool fitted with a shell holder that encloses the rim snugly (and it'll pay you to select from several to achieve this close fit) and a separate priming tool which has good "feel," you'll be able to do a better and more uniform priming job than can be done on the loading press. And, if you're processing several hundred cases at one sitting, you'll get it done faster.

Look closely at the primer pockets. Some military cases have a very slight crimp around the primer pocket. It may be in the form of a ring or separate stab marks. Often it will not be heavy enough to interfere with the seating of a fresh primer; but, if it does, you have no alternative but to remove it. It usually is not nearly as extensive as the crimp found on military rifle-ammunition, so only a very small amount of metal need be removed. This can be done with the hand-held Lyman "Primer Pocket Reamer," or it can be done almost as quickly with a sharply-pointed and edged knife. Simply hold the case in one hand; insert the point of the knife blade at an angle and exert slight pressure; then twirl the case to peel out a thin, uniform shaving of brass. Such a crimp can also be removed with the swaging tool sold for use on rifle cases, but because of the small amount encountered on pistol cases, doing it by hand is usually quicker and easier.

With the primer positioned mouth-up in the priming tool, slip the case into the shell holder and keep your thumb lightly against it to ensure that the vibration of tool operation doesn't cause it to creep outward a bit and thus become misaligned with the advancing primer. Exert enough pressure on the tool handle so that the primer is pushed into the pocket, and note the slight increase in resistance as the primer anvil seats on the bottom of the pocket. It will take a little practice to develop a specific feel for this job, but maximum uniformity of ignition will be obtained with the primers seated so that the anvil bottoms solidly in the pocket. If the primer is forced in too deeply, the anvil will be jammed back into the cup, fracturing the pellet of priming compound, and thus causing erratic ignition.

On the other hand, if the primer is not seated deeply enough, the entire primer assembly may be driven forward by the firing-pin impact, absorbing a good deal of the firing-pin energy, and resulting in weak and erratic ignition. In some guns, this can even cause misfires, but because of the almost unlimited firing-pin protrusion of the 45 auto, you need not worry about it there. In any event, simply seating the primer flush with the surface of the case head, or just a few thousandths of an inch below, will not produce the best ignition unless the anvil rests on the bottom of the pocket.

With the cases sized, expanded, flared and primed, we're getting close to producing shootable cartridges.

Select the powder and charge weight desired. If your measure is an adjustable one, set it up, checking it with an accurate powder scale. *Don't* try to set the measure by simply fiddling with it until it shows one or two charges of the correct weight. Instead, check ten-charge lots, dumping ten consecutive charges into the scale pan, weighing them, and dividing by ten to obtain the average charge weight. Once the measure is adjusted so that the average weight is right on the button, you'll have the most consistent ammunition possible. Remember, too, that maximum uniformity of measure manipulation is essential if you want consistent-weight charges. It's a simpler matter then to pass 50-hole loading blocks under the powder measure and drop a single charge in each case. Make sure you drop exactly one, no more and no less, charge into each case. This is not an unwarranted precaution. On more than one occasion, I have discovered two charges in one case and none in another when I allowed myself to be distracted. A case with no powder will certainly tie up the gun, and while a double charge for some loads might not wreck the gun, with other loads it certainly will. With a new Colt 45 Auto worth $250 or more these days, inattention to powder charges can be damned expensive.

Personally, I prefer to use the small fixed-charge "pistol-type," powder measure. Being light and compact, it can be held in one hand and operated with the other, passing it from case to case over a 50-round loading block in far less time than the job can be done with a bench-mounted adjustable measure. And, I do not find that the fixed-charge measure drops any less uniform charges when handled in this fashion. Still, it does require a bit of practice and particular attention to uniform operation.

Regardless of the method used to drop powder charges, once all the cases in a loading block have been processed, hold the block at an angle under strong light and visually check *each* and *every* charge. With a little practice, you'll be able to tell whether a particular charge is significantly more or less than its neighbors. And, of course, you'll be able to see that there is no charge in a case or that it contains a double charge. Charges that appear to be just a wee bit higher or lower than the others may be light or heavy charges caused by bridging in the drop tube or they may be caused simply by mixed lots of brass with varying capacities.

When I'm checking powder charges and I see one of these, I empty and recharge the case. If the fresh one presents the same appearance, then I'm certain that the difference in powder level is due to case variation, and I don't worry about it. On the other hand, if the fresh charge bulks up differently, I know that the original charge was in error and that the error occurred at the expense of either the powder charge before or the one after. Consequently, I dump and replace them as well.

Now we come to capping the bottle. With charged cases setting in the loading block, take bullets and carefully start them in each case, aligning them as straight as possible. Press the bullet down firmly so that it wedges in the case mouth and won't fall out

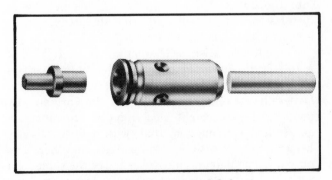

Cases can be lubricated with a resizing lubricant.

when you transfer it to the press for seating. Make certain that the seating stem of the bullet-seating die you'll be using fits the nose of the chosen bullet closely. If it doesn't, and you can't obtain one that does, simply put a dab of five-minute epoxy in the degreased cavity, then press it over the oiled nose of a bullet and let the epoxy harden. Trim off any excess, and you have a perfectly fitted seating punch. Bullets seated with a fitted punch will not only look much better, but in the case of expanding bullets, they'll perform better with undeformed noses. This is especially true of hollow-point bullets, whose cavities are often squeezed nearly shut by poorly fitted seating punches.

With the seating-die body 1/16 inch short of being touched by the ram in its uppermost position, turn in the seating screw until a bullet is seated to the correct depth or overall cartridge length. Then, back the seating screw out several turns and begin advancing the die, alternately running the cartridge in until a satisfactory degree of crimp is obtained.

"Satisfactory" can mean different things to different people. If the case is quite tight upon the bullet and if there is that small shoulder mentioned earlier supporting the base of the bullet, the crimp is not really important to proper feeding. Therefore, we need only sufficient crimp to remove the original flare from the case mouth and to turn it in slightly so that there is no possibility of it catching on the mouth of the chamber during feeding. This happens with lead bullets or uncannelured jacketed bullets.

With cannelured jacketed bullets, such a small amount of crimp may leave an unsightly gap at the case mouth, so just a wee bit more crimp should be applied until no visible gap exists. If, however, the cases do not hold the bullets quite as tightly as we'd wish, then a stiff crimp may be necessary to further secure the bullet against recoil and feeding impacts. In the past, I've even seen it recommended that the otherwise-completed cartridge be run into the resizing die a short distance to squeeze the mouth tightly into the bullet. I don't approve of this because it distorts the bullet badly, and that distortion can be eccentric and thus reduce accuracy.

The question arises as to whether we are talking of a *roll crimp* or *taper crimp*. Different authorities have stated in print that each is superior to the other. Generally speaking, I'm convinced they are equally good, but one might occasionally encounter a gun/bullet combination that will deliver slightly better accuracy with one crimp than the other. The only way you'll determine this is to try the same load with both crimps in the same gun. And even then,

without a machine rest you may not be able to prove anything. So, as a practical matter, I think either crimp will be equally satisfactory. It probably makes no difference at all—though I personally use a taper crimp because I feel it is more likely to be concentric (less likely to be lopsided) than a roll crimp.

Keep in mind that all but the 25 and 32 ACP and the 38 ACP/Super are intended to headspace on the mouth; too much crimp will create an excess-headspace condition. Personally, I don't apply any significant crimp, even in those calibers crimped by the factories.

Regardless of the crimp used, once the die has been adjusted to produce the desired amount, screw the seating punch down until it contacts the bullet firmly, then lock it in place with its jam nut. From this point on, simply run the case with bullet started fully into the die and proper seating-depth and crimp will be produced simultaneously. You may very well note slight differences in degree of crimp, but this will be due to variations in case length. Obviously, since the crimp section of the die is fixed in position, a longer case will be crimped more than a shorter one. Even though cases vary considerably in length—and I've seen them vary as much as .040 inch within a single lot—the crimp variations that result will not have any significant effect on practical accuracy. If you happen to be shooting in an important match for an expensive trophy, it will certainly do no harm to select cases of uniform length for your record-shooting ammunition. In doing this, always select the longest cases rather than the shortest. The shorter cases will come to rest in the chamber slightly farther from the headspacing shoulder, and therefore, when struck by the firing pin, they will yield slightly more than the longer cases. Theoretically—though the practical value is subject to argument—the longer cases will produce more consistent ignition. The absolute maximum consistency of ignition would be achieved if you could obtain cases long enough to actually seat solidly against the headspacing shoulder when the gun is fully in battery. However, due to manufacturing tolerances in both gun and ammunition, you aren't likely to encounter any cases quite that long.

As a final operation, the fully loaded cartridge should be wiped clean of any bullet lubricant or any other debris which it has accumulated, then carefully inspected for dents, canted bullets, shaved bullets, lopsided crimp, split necks, bent rims, protruding primers, dented or deformed primers or any other visible defect which might interfere with feeding or chambering. If you have a few hundred rounds loaded, wiping each one will take a lot of time; a perfectly satisfactory job of cleaning can be done by tumbling them a few moments in medium which has been very slightly moistened with solvent.

One precaution, though; don't tumble hollow-point bullets in granular material or the cavity will likely become clogged with it and expansion and penetration will then become erratic.

It's also a good idea, after loading a substantial batch of ammunition, to select a few rounds at random and either manually cycle them through the gun to ensure feeding, or fire them to ensure complete, functional reliability. I prefer to test by shooting, because this answers all questions that might arise. If the loads have been assembled for defensive use, then I always make it a practice to manually cycle *every* cartridge that I'll be carrying through the gun. This ensures against the chance—however remote—that I might have overlooked a defect that will interfere with feeding and chambering.

The foregoing applies to all auto-pistol loading, but there are a few additional points deserving special attention when assembling particular types of loads. With modern high-performance jacketed expanding bullets, you may find that it is impossible to obtain an adequately tight fit of case upon the bullet in assembly. When this occurs, at least with a standard resizing die, don't immediately blame the die or the cases—such bullets are often somewhat smaller in diameter than what is considered standard for the caliber. Some lightweight JHP 45 bullets run as small as .449 inch (in contrast to the .451-.452 inch generally considered correct), and some 9mms run as small as .354 inch. These bullets are made undersized for a specific purpose—that of reducing pressures and increasing accuracy at high-velocity levels—and they will upset upon firing to fill the rifling and seal the bore.

It may be necessary to obtain an undersized die to assemble such loads properly. If that's not possible, though some manufacturers do supply them, then you'll have to roll a cannelure in the case to support the base of the bullet to prevent feeding and recoil forces from driving the bullet backward. The process is simple and easy with the tools supplied by C-H Tool & Die Manufacturing Co. or D.R. Corbin Manufacturing Co. Don't make the cannelure too deep—this only weakens the case, and only a few thousandths of an inch is necessary to support the bullet

solidly. Also, if the cannelure is made too deep, the case may elongate upon firing and become too long. After cannelured cases have been fired and you're reloading them, take care that the expander plug does not iron out the cannelure or collapse the case.

All of the above has dealt with the use of fired cases in good condition. No matter how good the condition, cases fired one or more times can never be quite as good as new cases for full-charge high-performance loads with jacketed bullets. This is due to the fact that the hardness of the case mouth increases with firing, resizing, neck expansion, crimping, and bullet seating; the brass becomes work-hardened. Thus, after even the very first firing, the ability of the case to hold the bullet tightly and consistently is reduced. As a result, bullet pull (the force necessary to extract the bullet from the case) is reduced, and so less efficient use is made of the power. In laboratory tests, cases have shown a small, but, nevertheless, positive reduction in velocity with each loading.

Other defects can crop up as a case is exposed to the wear and tear of repeated loadings. A minor malfunction is of no consequence for most uses, but if you are carrying the gun and ammunition to defend yourself or others, every possible cause for a malfunction must be eliminated beforehand. This is best done by using new cases for defensive loads. After all, you aren't going to be doing that much gunfighting, so the additional cost of 50 or 100 new cases won't break you. It's cheap life insurance.

In closing, I should mention that we could write a dozen pages on bullet selection, bullet casting and other related subjects. That isn't really necessary and would, I think, even tend to confuse the issue. Certain bullets have, by many years of exemplary service, shown themselves admirably suited to particular uses that are regularly made of different autoloader calibers. In spite of the hundreds of bullet/powder combustions published in numerous manuals, books and magazine articles, we really need only four basic loads and bullets to cover the entire range of autoloader use. Those are: minimum-cost target and plinking; a low-cost load duplicating service-ball performance; a lead-bullet, defensive load; and a jacketed, expanding-bullet, defense/hunting load. The bullets we consider best for those purposes and loads are listed in the small loading-data table. We feel that a dozen pages full of additional information wouldn't help beyond that.

Chapter Sixteen
Police and Autos

As any experienced person or reference book will inform you, the revolver has traditionally been the principal police sidearm in the U.S. Perhaps because European law enforcement agencies are much more military in thinking and organization, they began adopting the autoloader just as quickly as it achieved military acceptance. Not so in America. While I'm sure there are many reasons that American police have chosen the revolver almost exclusively in preference to the auto, I'm reasonably certain that the principal reason is that even today an old wives' tale persists that autoloaders are far less functionally reliable than revolvers. That story may have been true back when the self-loader was in its swaddling clothes, nearly three-quarters of a century ago, but it certainly has not been true since the first generation of military autos proved itself in World War I.

Anyone who has ever taken the trouble to read over the tests conducted by the U.S. Army prior to adoption of the Colt/Browning M1911 (over a wide variety of other designs) will not doubt the reliability of a well-designed and made self-loader. The remarkable reliability and durability demonstrated by the Colt in those tests, and by various others in tests conducted in other countries, was certainly underscored by service under the incredibly severe conditions of 1914–1918 trench warfare. In fact, it was British complaints about poor functioning in the mud and dirt of the trenches that caused the famous Smith & Wesson Triple-Lock sixgun to be modified for military service, and for those modifications to become permanent and thus terminate production of that gun.

Even the best of today's modern revolvers won't pass some of the adverse-condition tests to which military autoloaders are routinely subjected. Of course, most western nations have used large quantities of revolvers in various armed conflicts, but if the record be checked carefully, it will be readily seen that such usage was forced because of severe shortages of autos. The hundreds of thousands of Colt and S&W revolvers employed by Allied forces during World War II were purchased only because sufficient autos couldn't be made rapidly enough; yet, at the same time, production facilities for revolvers were in existence and ready to roll. In fact, by the beginning of World War II, every major nation of the world had switched to the autoloading pistol, with the single exception of diehard Great Britain where Webley and Enfield sixguns of unusual design remained standard until the 1950s.

All of this should indicate quite clearly that the autoloader has demonstrated superior functional reliability in the field. Yet, the story persists that it is less reliable than the revolver, and that is one of the main reasons that the U.S. cop continues to be mainly armed with the latter type.

It was not until the 1960s that the auto saw any significant use as a basic cop sidearm. During that period, a few smaller city departments (Providence, Rhode Island, being the first, according to my information), adopted the S&W M39, and the Illinois State Police followed suit. The latter became the first major law enforcement agency to switch from the traditional revolver to a modern autoloader. It was also during the early 1960s that law officers began to concern themselves with massive firepower and sustained fire. Prior to that, if an officer (or a chief) thought about reloading and carrying extra ammunition at all, it was probably sort of, "if the fight isn't finished in six rounds, more won't help."

The massive violence that erupted during the '60s decade and the emergence of deliberate ambushes directed at law enforcement officers caused some serious rethinking along these lines. Officers were no longer confident that the six rounds in a service revolver would suffice for a typical shooting encounter. Street cops and their superiors alike (more of the former than the latter) began to feel the need for more shots per loading and faster reloading under fire. The big-bore, military-type auto solved both of those problems, simply by virtue of its detachable

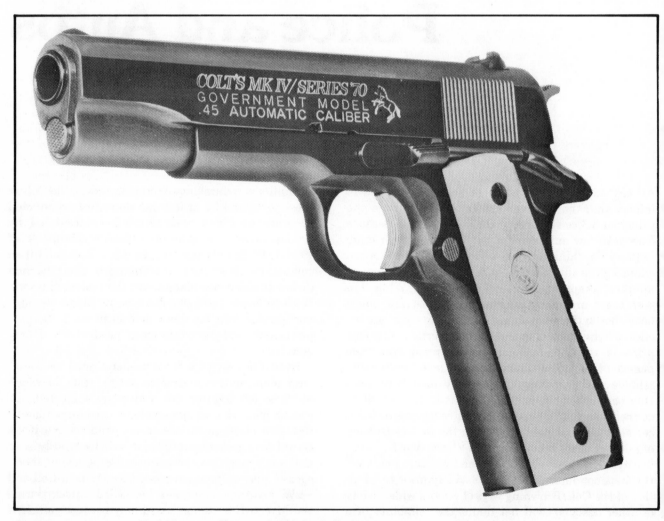

The Colt 45 Government Model is an excellent autoloader for police use.

magazine which contained anywhere from one-third to twice as many cartridges as the typical revolver, and which could be replaced to allow continuing fire in only a couple of seconds.

There are other advantages to the autoloader, once we have disposed of its unearned reputation for poor reliability. Insofar as factory-loaded ammunition is concerned, the most powerful and effective autoloader suitable for police use is the Colt 45 Government Model. With jacketed, hollow-point high-performance ammunition, this gun offers a higher degree of lethality than even the 357 Magnum revolver; it is exceeded only by the 41 and 44 Magnum cartridges, which can be had only in the big N-frame S&W revolvers. Those guns, in the relatively handy, four-inch barrel length, are $^{11}/_{16}$ inch longer, $^{7}/_{16}$ inch thicker, and two ounces heavier than the 45 auto. Furthermore, the recoil, jump and blast they produce are substantially heavier than the GM. Because of these factors, the average rookie officer can be trained much more quickly and economically to an acceptable level with the 45 Auto. An individual can be trained much more quickly to deliver accurate rapid-fire with the autoloader than with the heavy-recoiling revolvers which must be fired double action.

Let's get back to the size and weight. Being flat and relatively thin, the 45 auto is much more compact in a belt holster than the big revolvers. It is far less likely to get hung up in tight quarters or to protrude invitingly where someone might be tempted to snatch it out of the officer's holster.

There's another factor about the big auto that I feel is significant, though I've heard no one else mention it. The proper way to carry this gun (and any other single-action auto) is in what Jeff Cooper calls "condition one," with a round chambered, the hammer at full-cock and the manual safety engaged. There is something about the sight of that big gun on an officer's hip, with the hammer obviously cocked, that makes the layman or potential adversary tread lightly. Purely and simply, it *intimidates*. A revolver—or, for that matter, a double-action auto—with the hammer down simply doesn't exude the aura of deadliness and readiness generated by that big cocked hammer.

Even some shooters are intimidated by the cocked auto—many of them won't carry the gun that way, even though they know that it is mechanically quite safe. Even though the manual safety is engaged and the grip safety is backing it up, they fear to carry the gun cocked because it *"looks dangerous."* I've investigated this matter a good deal, deliberately showing up before individuals and groups of people who are not

gun-wise, wearing the big 45 auto cocked and locked; invariably they will edge away, and almost always someone in the group will eventually get around to asking, "Is that thing really loaded? Are you expecting trouble? Do you really want to carry the thing that way?" Given equal training, an officer is fully as ready for a fight with the cocked auto as he is with the double-action revolver carried hammer-down, yet observers somehow feel much more threatened by the former.

On the other hand, when the big 45 auto is carried in "condition two," with the hammer fully down on a chambered cartridge, observers pay it no mind and seem to be not in the least concerned. I think the root of this feeling is that the general public is revolver-oriented. For nearly a century, they have been accustomed to seeing double-action revolvers carried in the safe, hammer-down condition by cops. They associate that condition with safety, while they have always viewed a cocked revolver as a distinct hazard (as one should). I don't mean to dwell on this particular aspect of the single-action exposed-hammer auto, but I do feel that it is significant and that departments utilizing such guns should capitalize upon it.

The 45 is certainly not the only choice available for law-enforcement. The same gun is available in 38 Super and 9mm Parabellum calibers of less power and recoil, and there is the Browning HP in 9mm with its much greater magazine capacity. We include the Browning here, even though it is manufactured abroad (by Fabrique Nationale in Belgium) simply because it is a native, American design by John M. Browning and is sold by an American company. There is also a wide variety of other foreign-made autoloaders in calibers 9mm, 38 and 45. While few departments would consider adopting a gun of foreign manufacture, departmental regulations often permit individual officers to purchase such guns if they wish. In this category, the Spanish Star and Llama pistols are offered in all three calibers, and there is the big Beretta and the Swiss SIG.

Traditionally, the single-action auto typified by the Colt GM is the favorite. It has been adopted by quite a number of city departments around the country, and when properly utilized by people who have been correctly trained, it is highly efficient for the purpose. As we've already mentioned, it may be carried ready for action in two ways. "Condition One" is with a round chambered, the hammer at full-cock, the manual safety engaged, and, as in all other conditions, the grip safety functioning normally. "Condition Two" is with a round chambered, the hammer lowered fully against the firing-pin stop, and the manual safety disengaged (which is a superfluous statement, inasmuch as the manual safety *cannot* be engaged with the hammer down).

Talk will also be heard of two other carrying conditions, but they are not appropriate for law enforcement use. The first is with a round chambered, and the hammer engaged in the safety or intercept notch, commonly called "half-cock." Contrary to popular belief, this is not a safe method of carrying the big gun, and this position of the hammer was never intended by the designers as a carrying safety feature. Rather, the so-called half-cock notch was designed as an intercept or safety-interlock to prevent the hammer from striking the firing pin if it should inadvertently slip from beneath the shooter's thumb during cocking or un-cocking, or should drop from the full-cock position for any other reason when firing was not intended.

So long as the trigger is not held to the rear, any time the hammer moves forward, the sear will snap into this intercept notch and halt the hammer short of striking the firing pin. This notch in the hammer is *not* intended as a carrying safety and should never be so used.

The other condition not suitable for this use is the "military carry," with the chamber empty and the hammer fully down. Getting the gun into action from this condition requires the use of both hands, one to draw the gun and the other to retract the slide and let it run forward to chamber a round. This is not only totally impractical for police use, but it also reduces the gun's capacity by one round. In the other carrying conditions, the magazine is filled, and there is an additional round in the chamber. Carried with the chamber empty, the gun is limited to only those cartridges contained in the magazine. In the Colt 45, this means only seven rounds instead of the eight that might otherwise be available.

For the average individual, particularly those with small hands or short thumbs, the "condition one" method allows getting the gun into action with maximum speed and convenience. As the gun is drawn, the thumb falls naturally over the manual safety and needs only to be curled down as the gun clears leather to disengage the safety. There is absolutely no delay, and the gun can be fired just as quickly as it comes to bear on target.

Carried in "condition two," the officer must thumb the hammer back to full-cock during the draw. This generally requires more training than "condition one," and cocking the hammer can become a bit difficult for those with small hands. There is also greater possibility of fumbling or obtaining an incorrect hold on the gun under pressure when drawing and cocking from condition two. When all factors are considered, the "condition one" method is by far the most practical and convenient, and it also offers the intimidation factor of that cocked and readily visible hammer that we mentioned earlier.

Though there are relatively minor design differences between all of the single-action big-bore autos suitable for police use, everything that has been said regarding the Colt applies to them all—Star, Browning, Llama, SIG, etc.

It has been mentioned that the Smith & Wesson M39 pistol has been adopted by a number of agencies. This is a double-action 9mm pistol, so it becomes obvious that departments are not limited to the single-action gun of the Colt GM type. There has been a good deal of controversy around the use of the double-action auto for defensive and law enforcement use. In this scribe's considered opinion, most of that controversy has been generated by firearms authors who simply needed something to write about. Personally, I prefer the double-action type over the single-action. In firing countless thousands of rounds (15,000 rounds once in two days while testing DA autos) under all sorts of conditions, I have yet to find any sound basis for criticism.

The criticism of the double-action type is generally based upon the fact that when the gun is carried with the hammer down (as intended), firing the first shot from draw requires a long double-action trigger pull (just as in the DA revolver). Then, for immediate follow-up shots, firing is in the single-action mode, with the trigger in a more rearward position and presenting a much lighter and shorter pull. Admittedly, one must become accustomed to this particular characteristic of the DA auto, just as he must become accustomed to manipulating the safety of the SA type. This is simply a basic characteristic of the double-action type for which the officer must be trained. I have not noted that it presents any problems whatever to a trainee who approaches it with an open mind.

In order for the SA auto to be carried safely, it must be holstered with either the manual safety engaged or the hammer fully down; either requires an additional operation during the draw to prepare the gun for firing the first shot. On the other hand, the DA auto shares those characteristics of the revolver which allow it to be carried safely with the hammer down, safety not engaged, immediately ready for action without the necessity of any other actions or movements. The S&W M39/59 pistols do contain a manual safety, but once it has been employed safely to lower

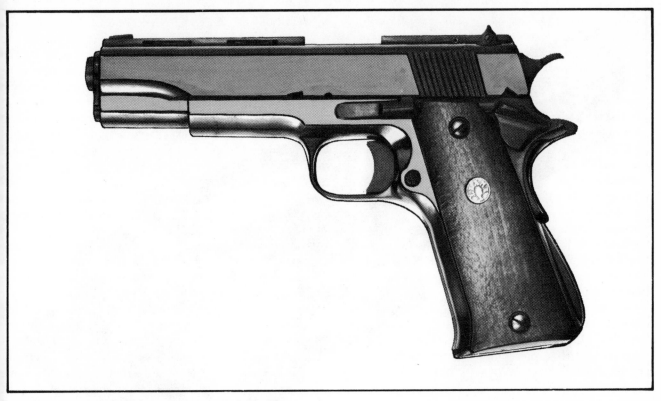

Llama autoloaders are offered in 9mm, 38 and 45 calibers.

Smith & Wesson's M39 is a double-action pistol that has been adopted by a number of law enforcement agencies.

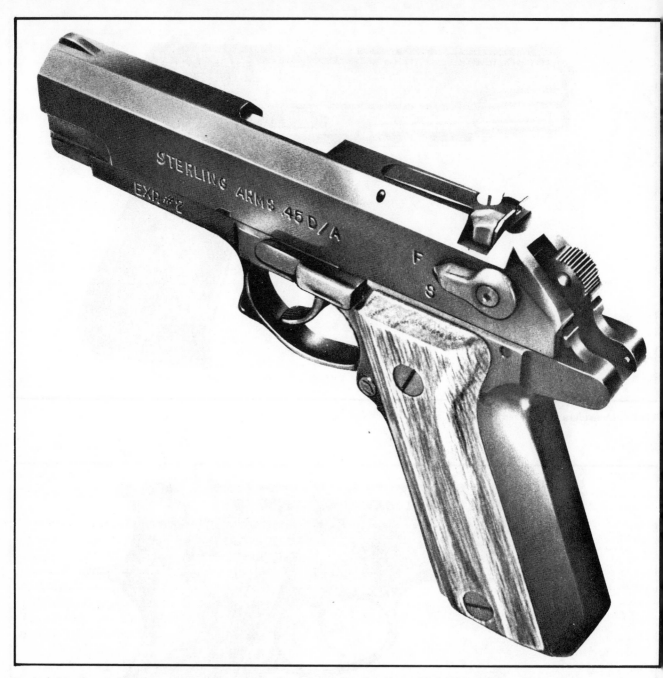

Designed to the specifications of law enforcement officers is the Sterling Arms Model 450 double-action autoloader.

the hammer, it may (and should) be disengaged before the gun is holstered, leaving it ready for instant action by simply grabbing it and pulling the trigger. Since the DA system requires no extraneous actions during the draw, it may be gotten into play just as quickly and conveniently by a left-handed as by a right-handed person. In order for a SA auto to be drawn and fired quickly and conveniently by a left-hander, it must be carried in "condition two," with

the hammer down. This is due to the simple fact that all controls on autoloaders (and revolvers as well) are located on the left side for operation by the thumb of a right-handed shooter. Admittedly, this left-handed capability of the DA auto exists only for the first shot and the balance of the cartridges in the magazine. Once reloading becomes necessary, those left-sided controls force the shooter to change hands. Again, this is no worse than the situation with SA autos or revolv-

The Heckler & Koch P9S has a sliding delayed roller-locked system which reduces recoil.

ers, for they all share this southpaw problem with right-handed controls.

Once the differences between the SA and DA systems are viewed objectively, the latter becomes the more desirable of the two. A man already trained on the SA type will no doubt resist change, but if the DA auto is presented to him in the proper light, he will soon see its advantages. A man trained only on the DA revolver will also resist change to any auto, but will in reality encounter fewer problems in switching to the DA type than the SA auto.

There are numerous other factors to be considered in comparing the DA auto to the SA. Probably the first is that at present, the only domestically manufactured DA autos available in quantity are the S&W M39/59 made only in 9mm Parabellum caliber. If departmental need or policy specifies a larger or more powerful cartridge, then there simply is no choice but to go to the 45- or 38-caliber single-action auto. However, this condition is of a temporary nature; we expect very shortly to see the Sterling Arms M450 45-caliber double-action autoloader in full production. There is also the Seecamp conversion of the 45 GM to double-action, and while it is available in relatively small quantitites and at a premium price, it

still represents a viable alternative selection when both the larger caliber and double-action capability are required.

In the case of foreign guns, and it is not inconceivable that a department might adopt such, both the H&K P9S and the SIG/Sauer P220 (the latter also manufactured under the Browning name) have also just become available in 45 and 38 caliber. Again, both of these guns command a premium price well above that of the S&W and Colt models, but they do offer the combination of double-action capability and the largest possible caliber.

There is another area in which the DA auto offers an advantage over the SA type: There are conditions under which it becomes necessary or at least highly desirable for an officer to switch the gun to his weak hand to cover a suspect while performing some other function with his strong hand. The DA auto remains fully as ready and yet as safe for a quick shot under these conditions as if it were still in the right hand. This cannot be said of the SA auto, because, once switched to the left hand, either the safety must be first disengaged, or if it is not, it becomes impossible to fire quickly. If you doubt this, take a cocked and locked GM in your left hand and attempt to fire it quickly. Manipulation of the safety is almost impossible even under good conditions.

Increased firepower is often touted as the major advantage of the auto over the revolver. To be sure, this does represent a significant advantage, but its use must be tempered with discretion. Officers trained on a revolver have fire discipline built in; they have been faced from the very beginning with the simple fact that they are limited to six rounds before reloading, and that reloading is generally a slow and clumsy process. When men so trained switch to the auto, they're usually so impressed with the greater number of shots per loading, and the ease and rapidity of reloading, that they almost forget about fire discipline. They develop a tendency to fire more shots more rapidly simply because the capability exists. This tendency must be curbed in training, whether the man involved is a rookie picking up a handgun for the first time, or an old-timer who's carried a revolver for 20 years. Increased firepower, like a nuclear weapon, serves its purpose best when it is kept in reserve and used only when absolutely necessary.

In my opinion, even though I prefer the largest, practical magazine capacity, the value of this capacity (eight to 16 shots) is more psychological than real. An officer who knows that his gun contains a large number of cartridges, and also knows that he can reload it in two seconds, feels more secure in a fire fight than if he were limited to five or six rounds and laborious, slow reloading.

Aside from that, the advantage of firepower and of sustaining that fire lies decidely with the autoloader. The smallest-capacity auto to be considered as a service sidearm is the 45 GM, containing seven rounds in the magazine and one in the chamber for a total of eight. From there, capacity ranges upward, with the same gun in 9mm and 38 containing a total of 10 rounds, and the 9mm, S&W M59 (with double-column magazine) carrying 15 cartridges in the magazine and one in the chamber, for a total of 16. A man armed with the M59 and carrying two fully charged spare magazines is prepared to lay down a tremendous volume of fire if the circumstances warrant it.

This is where fire discipline becomes terribly important, for too many shots fired too hurriedly can present a considerable hazard to bystanders or other officers. Nevertheless, if the occasion demands massive firepower, the M59 carrier can sweep an alley, street or room with 46 rounds in as little as seven to ten seconds. On the other hand, some circumstances warrant sustained fire over a long period of time. Large magazine capacity is advantageous under those conditions, and the M59 officer

with his spare magazines can lay down leisurely covering fire for quite a spell without requiring ammunition resupply. He carries almost three times as much ammunition as the man armed with the revolver, and with no more inconvenience.

It would be a big mistake to select a police auto loader based purely upon magazine capacity. All requirements must be balanced: cartridge power and lethality, size and weight, convenience of operation durability and reliability, and also any other particular requirements that an individual department might have. Desirable though large magazine capacity might seem, we must recognize the fact that it will very seldom actually be used. I do not think it wise to choose a gun purely for the largest possible magazine capacity against the possible once-in-a-lifetime encounter in which more than a few rounds will be fired. If large magazine capacity can be obtained

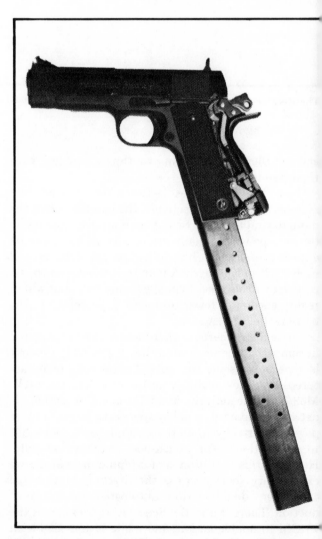

Sometimes a large magazine is an asset for law officers.

without reducing the gun's ability to meet the other important requirements, then, by all means, it should be chosen. At present—and as far as can be foreseen in the future—magazine capacities in excess of eight rounds cannot be obtained in any caliber larger than 9mm/38. In 45, seven rounds is the magazine limit at the moment; however, the soon-to-be introduced Sterling M450 does carry eight rounds in the magazine, plus one in the chamber. If your other requirements can best be met by the 45 caliber, then it would be foolish to go to the much smaller 9mm/38 just to obtain greater magazine capacity.

Let's put it another way. If your other requirements can be met by the 9mm cartridge, then it's possible to have large magazine capacity in either the S&W M59 or Browning HP, and either would be a good choice. A decision between the two would depend upon your preference for single action, (Browning) or double action (M59).

Once an autoloader has been chosen, very careful consideration must be given to magazines, particularly to spares to be carried loaded and to replacements. People accustomed to revolvers almost invariably fail to recognize the extreme importance of magazines to the autoloader.

First of all, functional reliability of the auto is highly dependent upon the magazine. A worn or damaged magazine will almost invariably cause feeding malfunctions which at best put the gun out of action for a few seconds and at worst will put it out for much longer.

Second, if an autoloader is carried with only the magazine in the butt, then it actually becomes inferior in firepower to the revolver, even if you carry a pocket full of loose spare cartridges. Once the magazine in the gun is emptied, the gun becomes essentially useless in a fight unless extra fully-charged magazines are at hand and *immediately accessible* for reloading.

Two spare magazines should be carried, and the manner in which they are carried should be given just as much careful thought as the holster for the gun. Simply tucking the magazine inside a belt won't do, and carrying it in a pocket can cause it to pick up lint and other foreign material which will cause failures to feed. They should be in a close-fitting pouch on the belt, that pouch being fixed at the position and angle which makes the magazine most accessible to the shooter's off hand. They are naturally placed in the pouch butt-up, and virtually all of the professional gunmen I have queried say that having the magazine face forward makes for the simplest and quickest reloading.

Several carriers on the market position two magazines back to back, and it would appear to me that this would inject confusion into the use of the second spare magazine under pressure and under fire. The first one will come out of the pouch and go into the gun easily, but then when you reach for the second one, you'll have to remember that it must be rotated 180 degrees in addition to inverting it as it moves from pouch to gun. This could very easily result in a fumbled reloading.

One must also remember that when the gun is hurriedly reloaded in action, the empty magazine is allowed to fall to the ground in the process. When recovering this magazine(s) after the fight, it must be very carefully inspected before re-use. If it falls on earth or grass, it may pick up dirt, mud or vegetation which could cause a later malfunction, and if it falls on concrete (most likely) the feed lips may be struck and damaged so that malfunctions are sure to follow. Don't take a chance: always inspect the magazine carefully and clean it well after such use. If there's any doubt about its condition, test it by running a full load through the gun.

We don't mean to imply by all the foregoing that the autoloading pistol is the perfect police sidearm. It does have its limitations. Fortunately, those limitations are not serious—the principal one being that it will function reliably only with full-charge ammunition or with a very limited number of lighter target-type loads. It isn't possible to use very light loads for training, a practice employed by most departments with revolvers. Many departments have also utilized light handloads for training as an economic measure. Many such departments are of the mistaken opinion that they cannot produce perfectly satisfactory, cheap handloads for training with autoloaders. Admitting that heavier powder charges must be used to ensure reliable functioning, handloading training ammunition for autoloaders is no more difficult than for revolvers. In fact, departments possessing equipment to load revolver ammunition will be able to convert it at a very reasonable cost to prepare ammunition for autos. The techniques for producing autoloader ammunition vary somewhat from those for revolvers.

It can be said fairly that the autoloader must be kept clean and properly lubricated if it is to provide the necessary degree of functional reliability for use as an officer's primary weapon. Many people place undue emphasis on this, apparently pretending that the revolver does not require equal treatment—which it does.

As a practical matter, whether routine cleaning, care and maintenance is given by the carrier or by a departmental armorer, it is easier and cheaper to maintain an auto than a revolver. For example, replacing a worn or damaged barrel in a revolver is a job for a competent professional gunsmith, while an auto barrel may be replaced in minutes by the user or semi-skilled armorer without any special tools or equipment.

The parts and labor costs of replacing a revolver barrel will usually run two to three times that of doing the same job on an auto. The small inner parts of an auto can generally be replaced without special tools by a reasonably experienced armorer or individual; doing the same in a revolver often turns out to require the services of a competent pistolsmith. While either type is certainly susceptible to damage when dropped on a hard surface such as concrete (and in my experience, this happens to quite a few police guns in scuffles), revolvers frequently suffer serious damage in the crane/cylinder area. A good auto will suffer nothing more than scratches and surface damage which do not put it out of action.

While the revolver has certainly served well as the standard police sidearm of the U.S., the auto is beginning to give it serious competition. It seems certain we may look forward to more and more departments switching to the auto, though I expect revolvers will remain plentiful at uniformed officers' belts past the end of my interesting lifetime. As far as a personal preference is concerned, if I were to don a blue uniform and walk the streets to keep the peace, and were permitted to choose my own sidearm, it would be a big-bore autoloader. It would be supplemented by two spare magazines and most likely a spare gun in the form of a smaller auto of similar type chambered for the same cartridge. And it would also be at least partially concealed somewhere else on my person.

Chapter Seventeen
You, Handguns and the Law

There are still a few states in the Union where one may wear or carry a handgun openly without being in violation of the law. In these states, an individual may also keep a loaded hand gun in the glove or map compartment of his car, ready for legitimate defensive use should it arise.

Arizona is one of those enlightened states which has not yet destroyed the rights of the individual to own and use firearms without excessive restrictions or control, as long as he does not attempt to use them for unlawful purposes. Those western lawmakers apparently still adhere to the obviously true principle that guns—like other inanimate objects—do not have minds of their own and do not commit offensive or criminal acts. They recognize the fact that objects become involved in criminal activity only when they are used by people with criminal intentions.

The fact that citizens may own and carry handguns openly in Arizona should not in any way be interpreted to mean that the law looks kindly upon their misuse. In fact, the criminal use of any firearm will cause the law to come down on a person even harder than in many eastern metropolitan areas where gun ownership is severely restricted.

There are few refuges like Arizona left today. Most metropolitan areas and many states have enacted severe gun-control laws over the years. Most notorious of them all is the infamous "Sullivan Law" enacted by New York City before World War II. It was presented as a crime-control measure to the public, though in reality it was enacted and employed to ensure that only the hoodlums of the incumbent political machine would be armed. In spite of much controversy and objection, NYC has clung steadfastly to the Sullivan Law in the name of crime-prevention, and, in fact, has enacted other ordinances to make it even more restrictive. Though the law contains technical provisions which allow private citizens to purchase, possess and use handguns, it is administered and enforced in such a manner as to effectively prohibit private ownership. A relatively recent report from New York City indicates that less than 2000 private citizens are currently permitted under the Sullivan Law to possess handguns. There's not room for a lengthy discussion of the Sullivan Law here, but it is sufficient to say that it generates de facto prohibition of private handgun ownership.

The average community's firearms control laws and ordinances generally range somewhere between the two extremes cited. However, the trend over the past several decades has been toward the elimination of individual rights and constant movement toward Sullivan-Law types of legislation.

At last count, there were in excess of 22,000 statutes and ordinances in effect which in one way or another place taxes and various restrictions on manufacture, sale, purchase, possession, transportation, and use of firearms of all sorts. The majority of those laws have a far greater effect on handguns than on shotguns or rifles.

An individual who travels interstate, and often even intrastate, can easily violate dozens of laws and ordinances without ever knowing it. Simply crossing a county line with a handgun can easily place one in jeopardy. A simple thing like moving one's residence from suburbia or from the country into the city (regardless of size) can put a handgun owner in violation of laws severe enough for him to be indicted for a felony.

Generally speaking, the firearms law situation is so confusing and the laws themselves so numerous that the BATF (Bureau of Alcohol, Tobacco & Firearms) of the U.S. Treasury Department (periodically) attempts to compile a complete list of all statutes and ordinances pertaining to firearms. This compilation is published in a thick book titled *Published Firearms Ordinances,* which is issued more or less annually without charge to federally licensed firearms dealers. Other interested parties may purchase this booklet from the U.S. Government Printing Office at a nominal price. However, even when this book is hot off the press, it already contains errors of fact and omission, simply because legislative bodies at all levels are continuously amending old legislation and enacting new laws and ordinances. It is, as a practical matter, totally impossible for even the professionals to keep entirely up to date on this situation.

Even *Published Firearms Ordinances* simply reprints a summary of the legalistic provisions of the laws. It does not contain any case law or interpretations and certainly no advice on how to stay out of trouble. Nevertheless, any handgun enthusiast should obtain a copy of this document for the time when he might be traveling with one or more of his guns and thus be highly vulnerable.

This book will not provide you adequately with all the information on firearms laws and advances in any particular locality. Because of the time lag, it may not contain all the ordinances that apply in a given place, or there may have been changes or amendments since it was set in type. Also there may be ordinances that apply which simply did not come to light when the book was being compiled. So, useful though it may be, don't depend upon *Published Firearms Ordinances* to keep you "clean."

The only way you can be absolutely certain of what ordinances apply and to what extent they'll affect your ownership and use of handguns in a given locality is to inquire of the senior, law enforcement agency. You should first ask for a general explanation of policy and second for copies of all the pertinent ordinances. It is not a rare occurrence, though, for those authorities to be simply "too busy" to comply with such requests. When that occasion arises, your only recourse is either to have a gun-buff attorney research the problem, or contact your favorite local legislator and ask him to obtain the information for you. Even if a legislator is anti-gun in thinking, he does not want it said that he did not at least attempt to aid a constituent in learning what laws affect him. Generally, your local legislator can be of considerable assistance in this matter, but, even so, there are limits to the amount of research that his staff can accomplish. This is especially true where there may be laws or ordinances whose titles do not permit them to be identified as having effect upon firearms, and which otherwise may not be sufficiently indexed to be located without a very extensive search.

It is unfortunate but true that when queried on this subject some law enforcement agencies will tell you "Yeah, we have a couple of laws on registration and permits, but we don't pay much attention to them unless a fellow gets into some trouble." Or you might get an answer, "There's an old law on the books but we don't enforce it any more." When you get that kind of an answer, beware! Even if the sheriff or the chief of police isn't enforcing an old ordinance now, he may decide to do so next week for one reason or another (political expediency being the most common) or he may be succeeded by someone whose views are quite different.

Under these circumstances, don't take any chances, don't ever assume that you need not comply with laws and ordinances simply because they aren't being enforced or may be enforced (selectively) for the moment and against only certain elements of society. Comply with the local rules to the maximum extent possible, and you'll be reasonably certain of staying out of jail. You won't like the rules—but if you don't comply with them, an irritated cop or a routine traffic stop can lead to big trouble.

Most likely there is a gun or shooting club of one sort or another in your city, or not too far away. Well-run and well-informed clubs can be your best source of information on local rules. If you've never supported a local club, it's time you began thinking about it—even if your particular interests are such that you won't ever be using their facilities. Such clubs usually contain a fair percentage of professional people, attorneys in particular, who have the facilities and clout to learn what's going on. They can be of immense help in both avoiding trouble and coping with it if (when) it comes.

You're not likely to have any great amount of trouble in determining what state laws apply to firearms ownership. A call to your state senator or representative will usually produce an explanation of the basic requirements of the law, and copies of the statutes as well. Also, there will usually be one or more individuals in the local club who keep up with state law rather well. As we mentioned earlier, you'll find state laws ranging from those which place virtually no restrictions upon possession and use of firearms up to those which in effect flatly prohibit same. It would be impractical for us to attempt to print a summary of basic state laws here, mainly because of the difficulty in obtaining the laws to begin with, and secondarily because they are in a constant state of change. Anything compiled now is certain to be partially outdated by the time you read these pages.

Federal law is another matter. In 1968, what we now call "The Gun Control Act of '68 " was enacted by the U.S. Congress and became effective in early December of that year. Its effects on handgun purchase, possession and use by individual citizens are clearly defined except in the area where an individual buys and/or sells a number of guns and therefore might in some circumstances be considered a "dealer" in firearms. This area has never been satisfactorily clarified by the BATF authorities, and different interpretations by local BATF agents have caused considerable trouble.

In simple fact, GCA '68 requires that "dealers" be federally licensed as "firearms dealers." The word "dealer" has never been properly defined and appears to be interpreted differently according to the circumstances and the whims of individual agents. In a great many instances, the gun buff who owns a number of guns will be more or less constantly trading and buying and selling to either upgrade his hobby or to accommodate changing interests. If he turns over more than a few guns within a single year, and that fact comes to the attention of BATF, he might well find himself being accused of acting as a "dealer" without the proper "Federal Firearms Dealers License." This has happened, and not just a few times.

Aside from that, federal law is fairly precise and understandable. It requires that all dealers be federally licensed, and also provides for a special "collector's license" for individuals who find themselves turning over a substantial number of guns in assembling and maintaining permanent records of sale. Those records must be maintained in a "bound book," and each individual sale or transfer be recorded on a form 4473 which is also to be permanently retained. The law also prohibits sale by a dealer to persons under indictment for a felony or convicted of a felony within the previous five years, drug addicts, those adjudged mentally incompetent, and chronic alcoholics. This places some burden upon the dealer of ascertaining that a potential buyer does not fall in any of the prohibited categories and that he is properly identified.

The law prohibits licensed dealers, and individuals as well, from selling a firearm directly to persons residing outside the state in which the seller resides, and further prohibits a dealer from selling a firearm in violation of any state or local statute or ordinance. It also prohibits handgun sale to or possession by any person less than 21 years old.

As a practical matter, the only additional requirements (over and above those which existed previously in federal law) that GCA '68 places upon individuals wishing to purchase handguns is the filling out and signing of transfer form 4473, and a prohibition on purchasing any firearm outside the boundaries of the state in which one resides (and this from either an individual or dealer).

The aforementioned two requirements are the basis for most violent objections to GCA '68. Though it is denied vigorously by federal authorities and supporters, the requirements for individual purchasers to fill out form 4473 and for the selling dealer to maintain a permanent record of the sale amounts purely and simply to de facto registration. In short, every legitimate firearms sale made since the enactment of GCA '68 is permanently recorded in federal government records.

No matter what legalistic gobbledygook may be used to rationalize or justify this, it still amounts to registration of both gun and purchaser. Federal authorities refuse to admit that this is registration, claiming that the records are simply a vehicle for tracing firearms that are identified as being used in a crime or to identify stolen firearms.

But, by any reasonable definition, permanent federal records identifying individual purchasers and each and every gun they have purchased constitutes an all-encompassing registration system.

The other objection is that the GCA '68 prohibits the ordering of a gun directly by mail or any other purchases outside the state of one's residence. Prior to GCA '68 it was possible to select a gun from any one of countless mail-order dealer and importer catalogs, and have it shipped directly to the purchaser anywhere in the country. This permitted an individual to obtain items not generally available locally, and also to shop around for the best price among competitive suppliers. But all that was stopped by GCA '68, and now one is restricted to buying what can be found locally or can be specially ordered.

Even the mail-order prohibition isn't quite as bad as it seemed in the beginning. It is still possible to order a gun by mail from anywhere in the country, but it cannot be shipped by the seller directly to the buyer. Instead, it must be shipped to a federally licensed firearms dealer from whom the purchaser can personally pick it up. In short, if someone in Seattle, Washington, has a gun I wish to buy, I can make a deal with him and then give him the name of a dealer in my state to whom he may ship the gun marked for me. Then, when the gun arrives at that dealer's shop, it is picked up on the shop's records (just like any other new-gun acquisition), and I may go in and pick it up just as if it were an ordinary purchase from that dealer. Of course, this injects considerable delay into any transaction, and the local dealers must receive some compensation for the time and effort they put into the transaction.

GCA '68 is law and we all must comply with it to stay out of jail. However, after ten years, there is not one iota of evidence to indicate that it has in any way contributed to a reduction in the crime rate or to any reduction in the use of firearms by the criminal element. In fact, crime rates and the use of firearms by criminals have both escalated since GCA '68 became effective.

While there is no question that we must comply with existing laws at all levels regarding purchase, possession and use of handguns, it is equally certain that if enough of us exert enough pressure on the legislators, the situation will improve. There are tens of millions of handgun owners in this country, and if even only a small percentage of them keeps pressure on their legislators, existing laws can eventually be repealed or amended to a more favorable form. On the other hand, if you and I and other owners do not keep up that constant pressure, then there is no question whatever but that additional laws will be passed. There is the danger that such laws would apply more and more restrictions upon handgun ownership until the point could be reached wherein not a single citizen may own a handgun, and all existing handguns could eventually be confiscated and destroyed.

I, for one, am violently opposed to such action ever taking place, even after my lifetime. Both professionally and personally I devote a great deal of my time, effort and money to exerting continuous pressure upon legislators. Each and every reader of these pages must do the same or eventually there will be no privately owned handgun in this country.

Chapter Eighteen
Competition and Autoloaders

For all practical purposes, the autoloader is THE competitive pistol type. In international handgun competition, including the shooting portions of the Olympic games, only the "International Slow Fire" matches are fired with another type of pistol. That particular match demands a single-shot pistol chambered for the 22 LR cartridge and made to an unusually high order of precision and specialization. All other matches, whether for rimfire or centerfire ammunition, are fired with autoloaders, with the single exception that occasionally one will see the Czechoslovakian Brno revolver (usually in the Soviet, 7.62mm Nagant, gas-seal cartridge) used in the "International Centerfire" match by Soviet Bloc competitors. This is undoubtedly due to the fact that to date the U.S.S.R. has not produced a centerfire autoloading target pistol of performance comparable to those found in the West. In most instances, Soviet-Bloc competitors use native designs wherever possible as a matter of national pride.

The International Centerfire Match consists of firing single shots, from the downward ready position, at individual turning targets which face the competitor for only short periods of time. Targets are silhouette type, with vertically oval scoring rings, and the range is 25 meters.

Competitors from the rest of the world generally shoot this match with either a Colt or Smith & Wesson target autoloader or a custom-built auto of one sort or another. However, in the past couple of years, European designs by Walther and Hammerli have appeared in 32 S&W Long and 38 Special caliber, and it is to be expected that these guns will see increasing use for the International Centerfire Matches. While the time intervals allowed in this match permit the use of the revolver, the autoloader is certainly superior.

The other international match is known simply as "International Rapid-Fire," and it requires a degree of rapidity of fire that simply cannot be obtained with anything other than a highly specialized autoloader. Twenty-two caliber is specified, and while either the Long Rifle or Short cartridge may be used, the latter is generally chosen because of its lighter recoil and report. The match consists of firing five consecutive shots in proper sequence at five silhouette-targets (with scoring ring) in the proper sequence from left to right, the bank of targets being exposed to the shooter for a very short period of time. The longest stage of fire encountered allows eight seconds for the firing of one shot on each of the five targets, the middle stage allows six seconds, and the real bearcat, the fastest stage, allows only four seconds for the firing of those five shots at five different targets. Sixty shots are fired altogether, 20 at each time limit.

It should be quite apparent to anyone that such rapid, aimed fire cannot be achieved with anything but a finely tuned autoloader. The guns generally used for the International Rapid-Fire Match are highly refined 22 rimfire designs modified to function correctly—and with 100 percent functional reliability—with the 22 Short cartridge. Such guns are generally fitted with compensators or ported barrels to reduce recoil and jump to the absolute minimum. When getting off five aimed shots in only four seconds, there simply is no time for conscious recovery from jump or recoil between shots.

Smith & Wesson's 9mm Double Action Automatic packs a mean wallop.

The 45 caliber autoloader is *the* gun in American matches.

Incidentally, we should take note of the fact that the rapid-fire pistol has been most highly developed in Europe. Even though both Smith & Wesson and High Standard offer models of this type, they are basically minor modifications of other models. In Europe, Hammerli, Unique, Walther, and perhaps one or two more offer much more highly specialized, rapid-fire pistols designed specifically for this match. Produced in only limited quantities, they are quite costly, ranging upward from around $500.

International competition also includes what is known as the "Standard Pistol" Match. This match resembles American-type 22 matches more closely than the others, but it requires a degree of rapidity of fire that cannot be obtained as a practical matter with the revolver. Consequently, it is fired exclusively with 22 LR autos. Because of the similarity of this match to 22 U.S. matches, it is interesting to note that the pistol which meets the rules for one will do so for the other. This is certainly a convenience for the U.S. shooter who wishes to branch out and get into international competition; he may use his standard U.S. 22 auto and thus avoid buying a costly, special gun.

While most other countries in the world have structured their handgun competition around international-type matches, things have developed differently in the U.S. Handgun competition developed principally around the revolver because of that gun's prominence in military and police use, and probably also because of the simple fact that so many sixguns were in the hands of private citizens at the time competition began to develop. Consequently, by the time a national program had evolved and had come under the aegis of the National Rifle Association, the revolver dominated all U.S. matches with the single exception of the "Service Pistol" match. The latter, of course, required the use of our standard military sidearm, the 45 Colt/Browning M1911/A1.

As a consequence, both targets and courses of fire were generally adapted to the revolver. There were no multiple-target stages as in International Rapid-Fire, nor was there a slow-fire target with scoring rings nearly as small as the international target. Our slow-fire targets were developed to be compatible with the

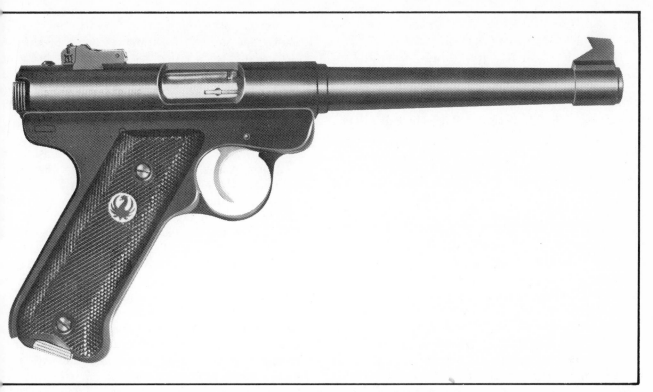

utoloading pistols such as this Ruger Mark I 22 caliber Target Model, replaced revolvers in 22 matches.

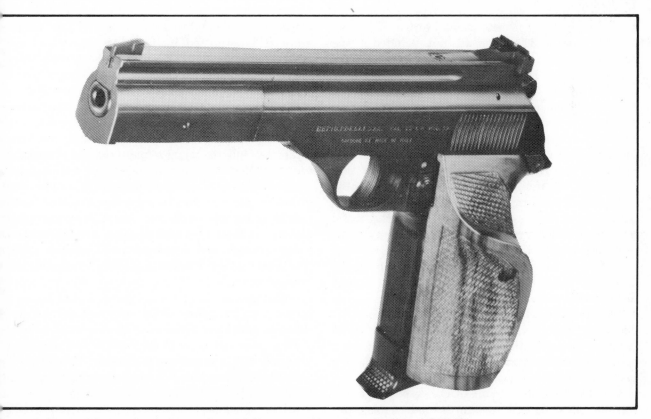

ternational match competitors often utilize 22 L.R. automatics such as this Bernardelli 100.

accuracy capabilities of the revolver rather than the precise single-shot arm of the Europeans.

The result of all this was simply that all U.S. competition involved the so-called "National Match Course," consisting of ten shots, "slow fire" at 50 yards; ten shots, "timed fire" at 25 yards, and ten shots, "rapid fire" at 25 yards, all fired on ring targets. Over the years this evolved to the point that the 30-shot, National Match Course just described was fired with three different guns: 22 caliber, centerfire caliber (32 or larger) and 45 caliber. Then to expand the number of matches even further, separate 20-shot matches were established with each caliber in slow, timed and rapid fire. Slow fire permitted a maximum full minute per shot, timed fire permitted 20 seconds per five-shot string, and rapid fire permitted ten seconds per five-shot string. Matches for the auto-loading 45 caliber service pistol were fired over the same National Match Course.

Thus, a competitor might shoot only in 22 caliber matches, only in centerfire, only 45, or in any combination thereof. With each gun or caliber, there would be four fired matches: the NMC, Slow Fire, Timed Fire, and Rapid Fire, for a total possible aggregate score of 900. If the shooter competed in all three calibers, the total possible aggregate score was 2700. If one also competed with the service pistol, then this was a completely separate event, with a maximum possible score of 300 which was not included in the National Match aggregate.

By the mid-to-late 1930s, the revolver began to be replaced by the autoloader in 22 matches; by the 1950s, the changeover was almost complete. Today, one would be hard put to find a serious competitor in 22 matches shooting anything but an autoloader. By the early-to-mid 1960s, centerfire autoloaders in 38 Special caliber had been developed to the point that they were superior to the revolver. Consequently, there came a fairly rapid changeover from revolver to autoloader in all centerfire matches, and today it is a rare thing to see a revolver on the line in a serious centerfire match. During this same period of time, perhaps a bit earlier, carefully tuned versions of the 45 service pistol became available and very rapidly displaced 45 revolvers in those 45 matches.

The result of all this is simply that for the past decade or more, formal competition in the U.S., as regulated by the National Rifle Association, has been conducted almost exclusively with autoloading pistols.

The NRA-regulated competition described above was the only organized program existing in this country until the late 1950s and early 1960s. At that time, organized police competition began to develop an soon came under the regulatory wing of the NR Because of the fact that the revolver has been (an still is) the dominant police sidearm, only revolve were permitted in police competition. This still hold true, and though some departments and organiza tions hold informal police matches where autoloade are permitted, the formal program is restricted to caliber revolvers. This is a subject of considerab controversy, and we expect that in the near futu autoloaders will be permitted in police competitio though probably only as a separate class or categor so that they are not competing directly with revolver The reason for the latter should be fairly obviou particularly if you read closely the chapter on poli guns. The auto is vastly superior to the revolver f rapidity of fire and speed of reloading, both of whic are dominant in police competition.

During the same general time frame, there arose i California what was called for a long time "We Coast Style Combat Shooting." Today this form competition has spread throughout the nation an quite a number of foreign countries, mostly because the great efforts of one Jeff Cooper. It is regulated the International Practical Pistol Confederation, which Cooper happens to be director. During th formative years of what is now IPSC competition, bot revolvers and autoloaders were used; in fact, revolve are still permitted by the rules, but the type shooting involved makes them substantially inferi to the autoloader for the job.

IPSC shooting does not conform to fixed courses fire and targets as in International and NRA matche To avoid stereotyping, courses of fire change fro match to match, as do distances and numbers targets. Only the target remains the same throughou a stylized-man silhouette sometimes with and som times without scoring or areas. IPSC courses of fi feature drawing and firing from a belted holste firing combined with movement, surprise target unknown distances, both multiple and single target both aimed and unaimed fire, rapidity of fir required actions which interrupt firing, and reloadir while firing.

The essence of IPSC-type matches and training "practical" shooting which will prepare one to th maximum extent possible to engage an armed opp nent under all types of conditions. An open mind kept at all times in regard to courses of fire, and ne ideas are incorporated so long as they have any pract cal shooting application. Courses are generally estal lished for a given match by the host organization, ar may even include firing while seated at a table or fro an automobile. There are virtually no restrictions on the gun that may be used, though ammunition is restricted to full-charge loadings of 9mm Parabellum and 45 ACP or their equivalents.

Ammunition is divided into major and minor categories, with the latter being the least powerful and penalized in scoring. This categorization and limitation of ammunition is explained by the fact that the goal of IPSC shooting is to prepare one for an armed encounter. Therefore, ammuniton of the highest lethality-capability gains a scoring advantage over that which is less adequate. This puts the shooter in the position of being forced to choose between a major-caliber gun which will produce the highest score per hit, or a minor-caliber gun which will produce a lesser score for each hit, but which by virtue of lighter recoil may allow him to obtain more hits.

Ammunition is not limited to those two calibers, but only to their equivalent energy as determined on site by a ballistic pendulum. Consequently, any caliber, whether revolver or auto, may be used and qualify as a major caliber if it equals or exceeds the energy of the service 45 ACP load tested on a ballistic pendulum. Any caliber may qualify as a minor caliber if it equals or exceeds the performance of the 9mm Parabellum service load under those same conditions.

While, as we said, revolvers and smaller-caliber auto pistols may be used in IPSC matches, they have disappeared from the scene by the process of natural selection. Because of their superior firepower and easier control in rapid fire, autos have pushed revolvers out; and, because of the scoring setup, the 45 caliber autoloader has become almost the universal choice in this country. In other countries where IPSC matches are conducted, various 9mm autoloaders are more popular than the 45. I suspect that this is more because of availability than deliberate choice. The 9mm pistols are far more plentiful and available than the 45 in most other countries.

Most forms of shooting competition, long guns as well as short, lack movement and action, as well as spectator appeal. This is not so in IPSC shooting, for it is a lively game and there is plenty of visual interest.

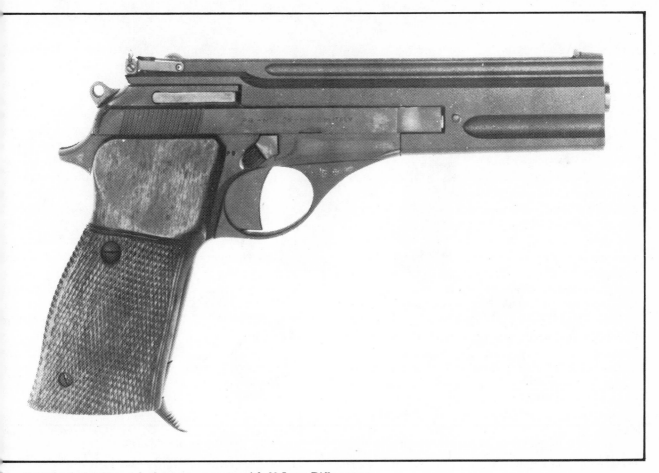

At a "standard pistol" match shooters compete with 22 Long Rifle autos.

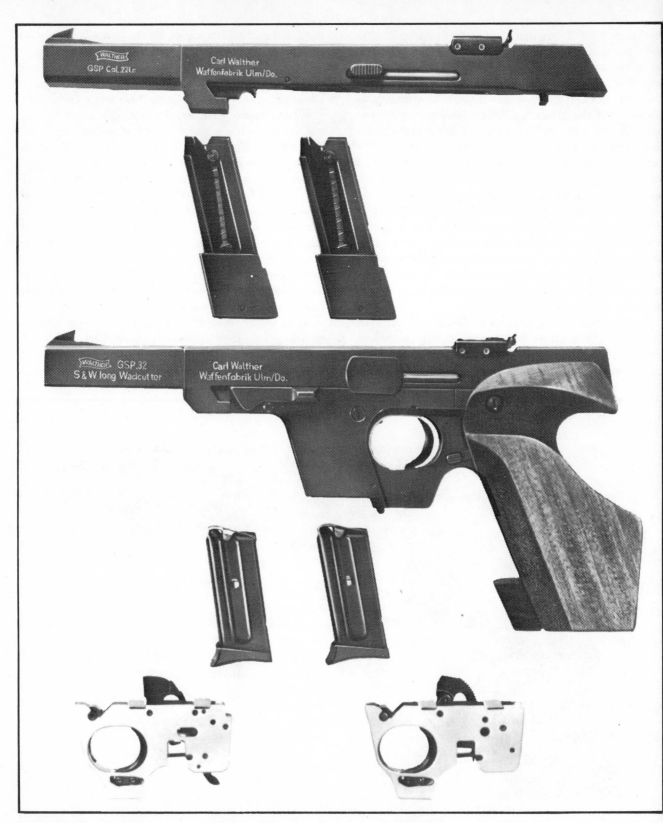

The GSP-C 22 L.R. conversion unit at the top consists of an inter-changeable barrel/slide assembly and two magazines, which enables you to convert from centerfire to rimfire in seconds.
The Walther Model GSP-C 32 cal. Centerfire Match pistol below accepts Walther's innovative "dry-fire" practice trigger.

In fact, it offers by far the most action to be found in any shooting activity. There is no comparison at all between it and a typical NRA match where one simply marches up to a firing point, fires five rounds, reloads casually, fires five additional rounds, then picks up his gear and walks back off the line. In this scribe's opinion, IPSC competitive shooting has more to offer the vigorous pistolero than any other game.

Other forms of handgun competition have sprung up in more recent years. One is the "National Shooter's League" which conducts but one type of match which consists of firing 20 shots (two at each of ten targets), and requires running between firing points, with the entire course to be finished by returning to the starting point in no more than two minutes 30 seconds. The targets are fired upon at various ranges and angles, both vertical and horizontal, all from the standing position, but some from the barricade position and some from the weak hand.

The NSL home range is at Laramie, Wyoming, and here the shortest target is shot at 16 yards, the longest at 60 yards, and the total distance that must be traversed in the process is 216 yards. Other ranges have been built around the country, and while they conform loosely to this layout, the exact distance and angles do vary. It is intended that no two ranges be precisely identical, and that the layout be adapted to the terrain available. This is another case where the stereotyped setup is deliberately avoided and an individual competing in the various places will be faced with different ranges and different shooting conditions. In reality, this is as it should be and must not be considered a disadvantage; after all, tournament golfers don't complain that the courses on which they play are all different.

As this is written, the National Shooter's League has been in existence only a little over three years, and so distinct patterns and preferences in guns and cartridges haven't yet developed. The 1975 and 1977 winners shot revolvers, while the 1976 winner shot the 45 Colt GM. Thus far there have probably been more revolvers used than autos, but in my opinion, the course of fire is better suited to the auto.

In any event, an individual wishing to compete in NSL matches will certainly not be handicapped if he chooses to use a finely accurate 38 or 45 auto. This is particularly true since a premium is placed upon rapidity of fire, and a good deal of importance is attached to hurried reloading. One must fire 20 shots and with a revolver this will require reloading three times. An auto will be reloaded only once or twice, depending upon the gun chosen and its magazine capacity. Personally, I feel that the next few years will

see the revolver displaced by the autoloader in NSL competition.

In the 1970s, we saw the rise of another form of handgun competition, Handgun Metallic Silhouette Matches. This competition is derived from Rifle Silhouette Matches originating in Mexico, and involves shooting at steel-plate game-target silhouettes at ranges of 50, 100, 150, and 200 meters. Only hits count, and for a hit to be scored, it must knock the target completely off its stand. Considering the great weight of the targets and the long ranges, this requires a cartridge possessing a great deal of energy. To date, autoloaders have been found inferior to magnum sixguns, with the single exception of the big Auto-Mag pistol. Unfortunately, the Auto-Mag has already passed out of production, and it is not expected to be available in the future except rarely on the used-gun market. As a result, we could only say that this is one form of competition (like the police matches) for which the auto is poorly suited.

One more form of handgun competition has cropped up in the past five years. It is generally known as the "Bowling Pin Shoot," originated by the Second Chance Company which produces flexible body-armor (bullet-proof vests) for law enforcement use. The target in this match is a bowling pin, five of them being placed in a row on a table or bench, with the goal being to hit and knock each of the targets off the table in a minimum amount of time. There are virtually no limitations on the gun or cartridge that may be used, nor upon the number of shots that may be fired. The shooter must simply begin upon signal and continue firing until all five pins have been swept from the table. He is then scored upon the length of time required to accomplish that feat, regardless of the number of shots fired, and he may even use a second gun in order to speed up the process.

While quite a few shooters have used revolvers in this game, it is tailor-made for the big-bore autoloader. The auto offers not only better rapid-fire control, but greater magazine capacity and speed of reloading, both of which are of extreme importance. Even though the 1977 championship match was won with a Smith & Wesson 44 Magnum revolver, the average competitor will do better under these unusual conditions with a 45 autoloader. Smaller calibers will knock the pins off the table with perfectly centered hits, but only the biggest bore can be depended upon to do so when hits are less than perfect. Ideally, the table should be cleaned with five shots, since theoretically this would allow getting the job done in the minimum amount of time and thus securing the highest score. If one shoots a smaller caliber of less power, more shots will be required. Time will go up, and score will go down—thus I expect the dominant choice soon to be the 45 auto. Certainly anyone thinking of entering this game would be most wise to plan on using the big 45 GM.

From time to time, other forms of handgun competition crop up, most of which are at least moderately well suited to use of the autoloader. None have achieved any prominence as yet, but I feel certain that in the next few years we will see new competitions, all of which will be best handled by autoloaders of one sort or another. In the meantime, I think we have already demonstrated quite clearly in these pages that the modern autoloading pistol, in both rimfire and centerfire persuasion, is the dominant arm in handgun competition.

Chapter Nineteen
Air Pistols

n these days of ever-expanding urban sprawl, it becomes increasingly difficult to find a place where one might fire a few pistol shots without either running afoul of the law or endangering persons or property. After all, the typical pistol bullet may be traveling from 700 to 1500 feet per second, and if unimpeded, may not come to earth harmlessly for as much as a mile or more. The areas where one may simply step up to the back-porch door and shoot with impunity (as I did when a youngster) are fast diminishing. Even in rural areas, farmhouses, livestock, workers, outbuildings, and other structures greatly limit shooting. Even there, simply shooting in what appears to be a safe direction doesn't always solve the problem, for bullets striking the earth will often ricochet, being deflected as much as 90 degrees from their original path, and then traveling hundreds of yards farther.

Thus, if you shoot on your own property, and that property is large enough to encompass the longest possible bullet flight, you can stay out of trouble with the law and the neighbors, but there is still the possibility of damage to buildings, equipment and

stock. In the cities, handgun enthusiasts may very well find that it is impossible or at least impractical to identify and reach an open area where one may shoot safely. Generally, it is simply no longer possible to take the streetcar to the end of the tracks, then step out into a safe shooting area. While most of the larger cities do contain one or more commercially operated indoor ranges, they never seem to be adequate to the tasks; their use is expensive and even they may not be readily accessible.

As a result of all this, many handgun enthusiasts actually have very little opportunity to shoot. In fact, except for occasional weekends in the country or vacations, they may never be able to pop a cap in practice. Frankly, I'd get little enjoyment out of owning a batch of good handguns if I couldn't shoot frequently and if I didn't know that in ten minutes or so I could be on a range or other places where I could shoot to my heart's content. Countless thousands of handgun enthusiasts are not so fortunate and are frustrated by lack of an accessible shooting place.

There is a solution to this dilemma, admittedly only a partial solution, but one that is applicable to

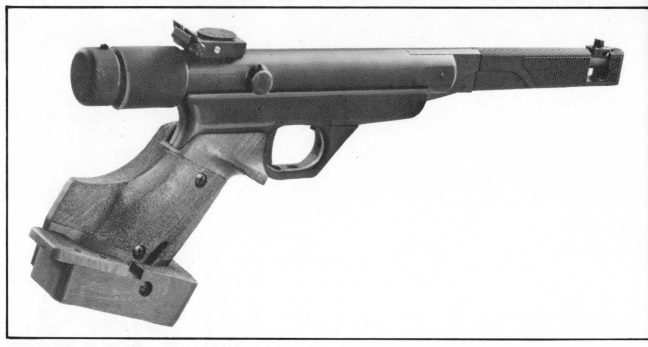

An air pistol, perhaps this Beeman Model 10 is ideal for people who have a limited area in which to practice their shooting.

everyone. This solution would allow a reasonable amount of handgun shooting even if nothing more than a small apartment is available. Air pistols are the answer. When we say "air pistols," we mean all of those one-hand guns which employ any form of compressed air or gas to drive a projectile down the bore. A quick perusal of the pages of SHOOTER'S BIBLE or similar publications will disclose a score or more of different makes and models of air pistols, very nearly all of which are appropriate for developing and practicing good marksmanship and gun handling. It is true that most of these guns do not provide the autoloading functioning to duplicate the powder-burning autos, but the only effect that has is to reduce the rate of fire without interfering with other important factors.

The air gun is ideal for practice in limited space and where the reports of firearms may be objectionable or attract undue attention. In addition, the cost of shooting a spring-air or pneumatic pistol is far lower than that of even the cheapest handload or rimfire cartridge. Guns of this type consume only a lead pellet or steel BB shot, both of which cost only a mere fraction of one cent per shot. This matter of economy has prompted many a pistolero to do much of his practice with an air gun, even though adequate facilities for shooting firearms were immediately available. CO_2 pistols, utilizing cartridges of compressed gas, are a bit more expensive to shoot, but still far more economical than powder cartridges, even the minimum-cost 22 rimfire. In fact, a dollar's worth of waisted pellets or an even smaller investment in BB's can provide a whole afternoon of shooting pleasure for an entire family. The same amount of shooting with a 22 might easily cost 10 to 20 dollars, and several times that amount with a centerfire autoloader.

The air gun is virtually silent and can therefore be shot in the home without stirring up the neighbors even though that home be a mere efficiency apartment separated from others by paper-thin walls. By use of a proper bullet trap, one can shoot almost any pistol safely indoors, but the noise of discharge is certain to bring on the wrath of neighbors and police. Not so with the air pistol; its whispering voice simply doesn't attract attention.

As we've mentioned, most air pistols are not semiautomatic in functioning. Most are single-shot, requiring an individual projectile to be loaded into the barrel or breech for each shot. There are also some of repeating type with magazines containing as many as ten waisted pellets or up to a couple of hundred steel shot. Though you may prefer the rapidity of fire offered by the autoloader, sacrificing this single capability is a cheap enough price to pay for being able to shoot when and where you please. Any type of shooting except rapid fire may be practiced quite well with a single-shot gun. Deliberate pin-point accuracy and instinctive "point-and-shoot" marksmanship and gun

Benjamin 22 cal. Super Single-Shot CO2 Rocket Gas Pistol

Benjamin 422 Semi-Automatic Pistol

Benjamin Super Single-Shot Air Pistol

Shooting with BBs is a lot cheaper than firing 22 cartridges.

Many pistoleros do much of their practice with an air gun and pellets.

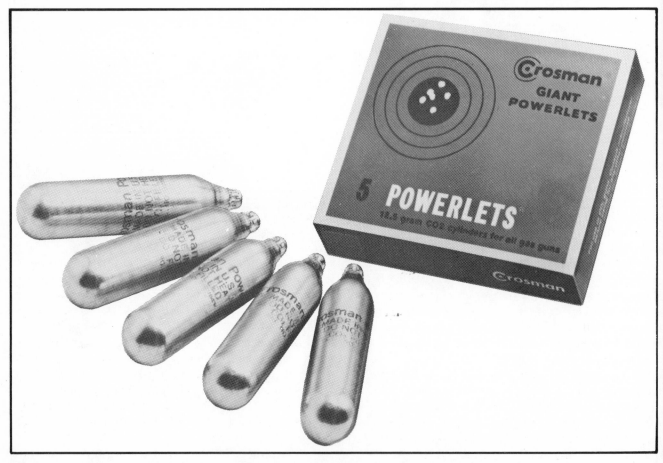

The CO_2 or compressed-gas pistol utilizes small metal compressed-gas cartridges to propel the ammo from the gun.

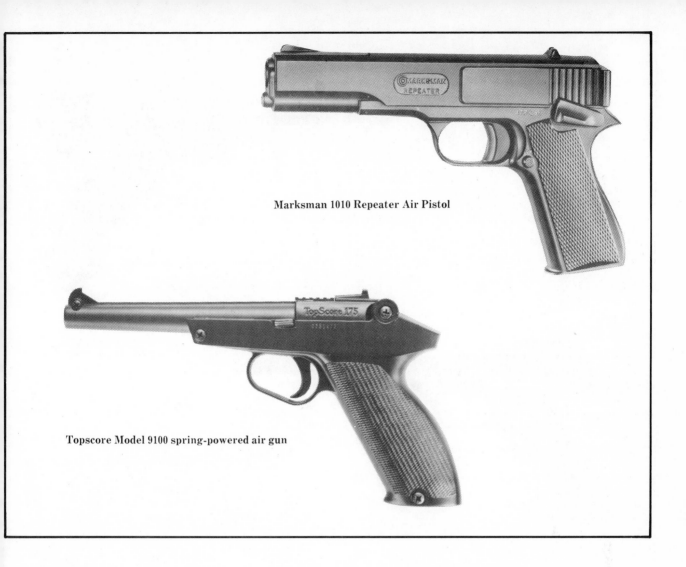

Marksman 1010 Repeater Air Pistol

Topscore Model 9100 spring-powered air gun

handling can be developed quite well with the single-shot. And, perhaps coincidentally, the majority of the air pistols available are made in the general configuration and image of a typical autoloader.

Accuracy of one degree or another is required, even for shooting indoors at a range of ten feet. The smooth-bored guns shooting spherical steel balls (BB shot) do not deliver a high degree of accuracy in the usual sense. Nevertheless, the dispersion on target at ten feet is sufficiently small to make them of considerable training and practice value. A much higher degree of accuracy is offered by those with rifled barrels shooting waisted-lead pellets. As a matter of fact, some guns of this type cost several hundreds of dollars, and at the standard international competitive range of ten meters, they will put all of their shots through the same hole in the target. It is a matter of demonstrable fact that the better rifled-barrel air pistols of target quality are more accurate than the

typical centerfire autoloader, and will usually outshoot a 22 RF target pistol at short indoor ranges. Even the lower-priced rifled air pistols are often fully as accurate as most of the big guns at short indoor ranges.

Three basic types of pistols are available. Most common is the spring-air type, in which a piston rides in a cylinder, supported by a very heavy spring. The piston is forced back to compress the spring and is then caught in the held by a sear; upon firing, the piston is released to be driven forward very rapidly by the spring, compressing the air within the cylinder. This forces the air through a small orifice into the barrel breech to expand behind the projecticle within and drive it from the barrel. This type is of relatively low power, producing velocities that usually won't exceed about 300 fps.

Next up the line we have the pneumatic pistol, in which air is compressed into a reservoir or pressure

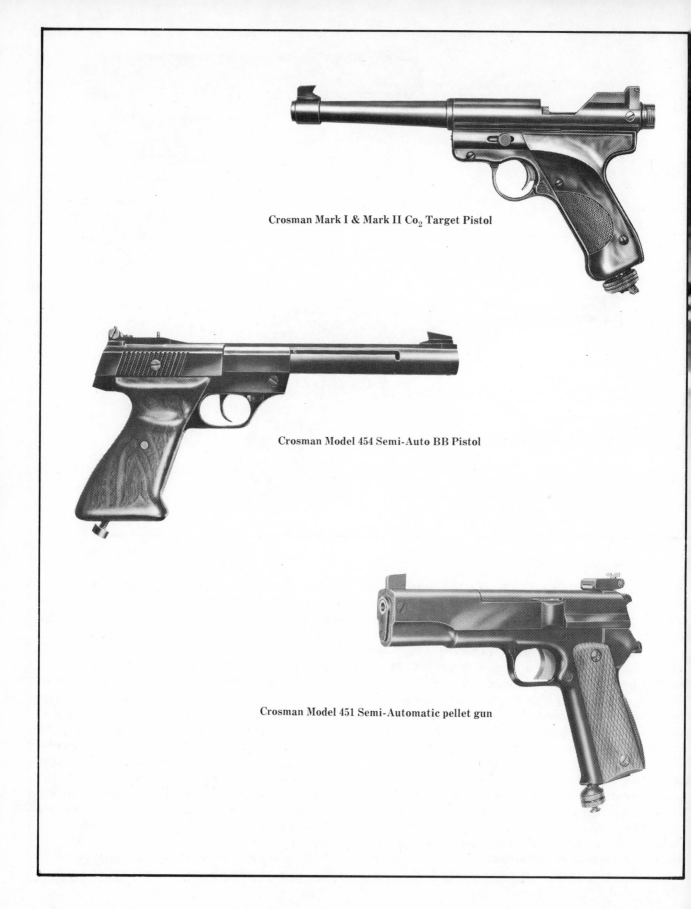

Crosman Mark I & Mark II Co_2 Target Pistol

Crosman Model 454 Semi-Auto BB Pistol

Crosman Model 451 Semi-Automatic pellet gun

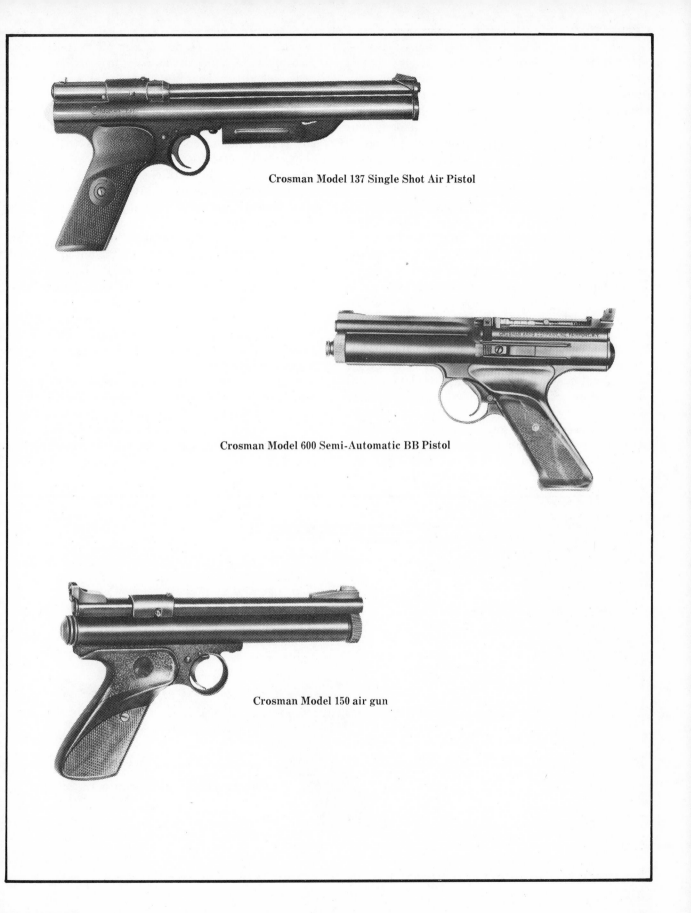

Crosman Model 137 Single Shot Air Pistol

Crosman Model 600 Semi-Automatic BB Pistol

Crosman Model 150 air gun

vessel by means of a hand-operated pump. Once the reservoir is filled with compressed air by several strokes of the pump, pressing the trigger opens a dump valve which allows that air to expand into the barrel breech and drive out the projectile. The pneumatic pistol is capable of much higher velocity, but shot-to-shot velocity may vary a good deal, depending primarily upon the consistency with which the pump is operated and the length of time that has elapsed since the reservoir was charged.

The third type is the CO_2 or compressed-gas pistol. In this type, the gun contains provisions for installing a compressed-gas cartridge. Small sealed-metal ampules filled with CO_2 under high pressure constitute this cartridge, and upon insertion into the gun in the proper manner, the seal is broken, and the gas is retained by a multiple-discharge valve. Thereafter, pressing the trigger opens the valve for a very short period of time, permitting only a portion of the gas to flow into the barrel breech and drive out the projectile. Subsequent functions of the trigger valve release essentially the same amount of gas, and this continues until pressure within the cartridge drops to a fairly low level, after which projectile velocity falls off very rapidly. Repeating and semi-auto pistols are most often this type, inasmuch as no hand-pumping or piston-cocking operations must be performed be-

tween shots. The CO_2 design also offers the greatest possibility of efficient autoloading action simply because additional gas is always available and may be tapped to operate the autoloading mechanism.

If your goal is maximum economy in choice of an air gun for in-home pistol practice, then one of the spring-air smooth-bore BB pistols is the obvious choice. Initial cost is least, and ammunition cost is the lowest, but you'll be sacrificing somewhat in durability, reliability and accuracy. At the other end of the scale, if maximum accuracy is of primary importance, then one of the high-quality spring-air rifled-barrel pistols shooting waisted pellets is the way to go. This is expensive, though, with prices on top-grade guns from as the Feinwerkbau M-65 and Beeman 10 Match Model going upward from around $275. However, as we've already pointed out, guns in this category are probably more accurate than any other pistols you own, and will produce one-hole groups hardly distinguishable from a single-shot hole in the target—if you learn to do your part.

In between those two extremes we find the excellent rifled-barrel spring-air Webley pistols in both 177 and 22 caliber at prices ranging from as little as $50 to more than $100 and capable of delivering all the accuracy you can probably use. At slightly lesser cost and equally suitable, you'll find the Benjamin

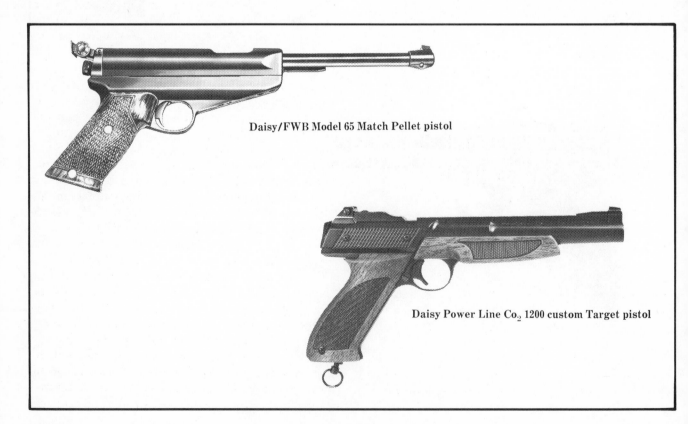

Daisy/FWB Model 65 Match Pellet pistol

Daisy Power Line Co₂ 1200 custom Target pistol

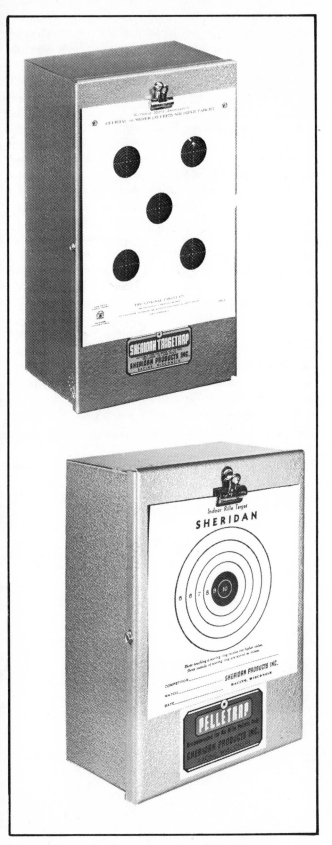

Indoor BB or pellet shooting requires a bullet trap.

and Crosman pneumatic pistols with rifled barrels in 177 and 22 caliber, both of which are quite adequate for ordinary indoor pistol practice. By virtue of their hand-pump design, they may also be pumped to the hilt to provide greater velocity and power for outdoor use at longer ranges, and, perhaps, even taking small game.

Most convenient of all the air pistols are the CO_2 types. Once the CO_2 cartridge is inserted, they're good for many shots—whether BB or rifled-barrel—without pumping or piston-cocking. The rifled-barrel models using waisted pellets are more than sufficiently accurate for exacting practice at indoor ranges, and will help all of the basic marksmanship skills. Those with smooth-bore barrels firing BB's are less accurate, but still adequate for practice at 10 feet. If you really want to practice rapid fire, there are semi-automatic models available from Daisy, Precise Imports, and Healthways. Setting up for rapid-fire practice doesn't really require a big investment. These semi-automatic pistols may offer as many as 50 to 75 shots from each CO_2 cartridge, and if you're shooting into a proper "soft" bullet trap, the steel BB shot may be reused many times over. Thus, the gas cartridges become virtually the only ammunition cost.

You may well ask why I've not mentioned any semi-automatic air pistols shooting the waisted pellet through a rifled barrel. There have been some, but at present none are generally available, at least to the best of my knowledge. Crosman once manufactured such an autoloader in the general image of the 45 GM pistol, and its unique mechanism even included a recoil simulation system. Unfortunately, the gun which worked well enough in the laboratory simply didn't stand up under ordinary field service and was discontinued. There was also available at one time a rather costly semi-auto manufactured by the Swiss Hammerli firm especially for reduced-range international rapid-fire indoor practice. My latest brochures from SIG/Hammerli do not list this gun, so apparently it is no longer available. Having no experience with it, we simply can't say whether this is because of funtional problems or simply insufficient demand to support production.

The apparent problem in producing a semi-auto pistol for waisted pellets lies in the feed mechanism. The pellets are very fragile, quite soft and easily deformed, and any workable feed system will not handle deformed pellets. Pellets are generally supplied in bulk pack, and invariably most will be slightly deformed by the time the shooter opens the package. When loading and feeding are performed manually, this presents no problem—but no practical auto-feed system will handle such deformed pellets. Match-grade pellets are packed individually in holes in a foam sheet, but even they are not entirely free from minor deformation (which may even be produced by simply removing them from the package and putting them in the gun) which will tie up the delicate feed system.

Thus far we've discussed only the guns and ammunition. Shooting them in den, living room or basement certainly requires some form of safe bullet-trap or backstop. Even though BB's and waisted pellets travel at only a few hundred feet per second, they do ricochet easily from hard surfaces, can break windows or bric-a-brac, or even cause a painful welt or serious eye injury. A perfectly practical backstop consists of a large cardboard box stuffed snugly, but not tightly, with wadded-up newspaper. Select such a box, preferably about 24×24×24 inches, stuff it well with crumpled newspaper, tape the top shut, and tape or staple targets to one side. So long as you keep your shots within that two-foot-square face, projectiles will be brought to a safe halt by the newspaper inside, with one possible exception—that of a pneumatic pistol pumped up the maximum number of strokes. Obviously, there is no need for such a powerful load indoors where no more than three pump strokes are entirely adequate.

A somewhat more sophisticated trap or stop can be made by hanging panels of heavy cloth or canvas, even carpet samples, inside a box of sufficient size. BB's and pellets strike the flexible cloth or carpet, are brought safely to a halt, and fall to the bottom of the box.

So long as a soft backstop of the two types described is used, steel BB's may be salvaged and reused many times. It's a bit difficult to dig them out from the stuffed-paper stop, but if cloth or carpeting is used, they can be simply scooped up from the bottom of the box with a minimum of fuss and bother. The fragile waisted-pellets can't be salvaged by any practical means, no matter how gently they are brought to a stop. With them, your best bet is to collect them periodically and simply set them aside until the next time you want to cast bullets. They are pure lead and can be mixed right into your bullet metal.

However you look at it, unless you're affluent enough and ambitious enough to have built your own indoor range capable of handling all of your pistols, you can benefit quite substantially from home practice with air pistols. You can invest as little as $25 or as much as the price of a good used Volkswagen.

Chapter Twenty
Single-Shot Pistols

All handguns were single-shot in the beginning, and in one form or another the single-shot pistol has been in continuous manufacture and use from the time of the first one-hand cannon-lock of the 1300s until now. Of course, there are those who will say that no true pistol existed prior to the trigger-fired matchlock for the very simple reason that although the earlier types could be held and aimed (directed) with one hand, the other was required to ignite the propelling charge with glowing coal, hot wire or rod, or slow match. Be that as it may, the single-shot pistol antedates all other forms of one-hand guns by several centuries.

Of course, we've been in the metallic-cartridge era for quite awhile now, and so our primary concern is for breech loaders. I'd hate to have to identify the very first single-shot cartridge pistol, but during the formative years of the metallic cartridge, countless designs cropped up to handle it, just as they did in the long-gun field. They ranged from the cheapest and simplest Folbert up through wondrously complex adaptations of the Martini and other rifle designs.

The single-shot pistol was never terribly popular in the U.S., perhaps because most people equated hand-guns with defensive use and could not understand who would choose a one-shot arm over a six-shot revolver for that purpose. Many small single-shots were manufactured during the transition period from muzzle to breech-loading, with the majority of them being small and low-cost extensions of the thinking that produced the percussion derringer. Most of the small early cartridge single-shots were referred to generically as "derringers." Most were chambered for cartridges of relatively low power, and their principal recommendation was that they could be very easily concealed, even several of them, on one's person where the much bulkier revolver could not. Then, of course, there was the simple matter of cost—a palm-sized Colt derringer cost only a fraction of what one might pay for a much larger revolver of the same marque. Of the many single-shot derringers, hardly any survived more than a few years. Most metamorphosed into almost equally small revolvers just as quickly as designers could develop them. The basic single-shots developed in another direction, producing a unique form of handgun that is still with us in both ancient and modern design. This was the multi-

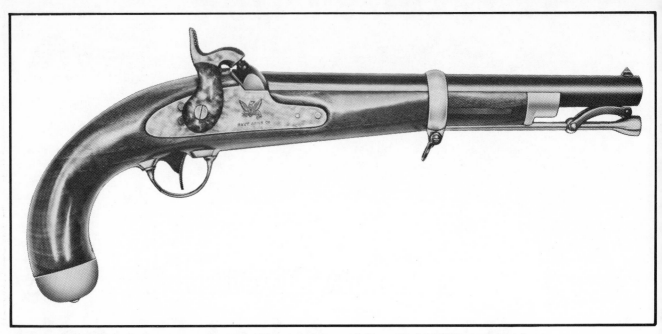

The magnum of all muzzle-loading pistols, this is Navy Arms' Harper's Ferry Model 1855 Dragon Pistol in 58 caliber.

ple-barrel pistol which had long existed during the muzzle-loading era. The basic idea was adapted to the metallic cartridge, producing tiny concealable guns of usually two or four barrels. Most successful of the lot was the Elliot-designed Remington "double derringer" manufactured by Remington for nearly 30 years after its introduction in 1866. Though Remington discontinued this model in the mid 1930s, it was resurrected by foreign manufacturers after World War II and sold rather widely in this country. It has also been manufacured in recent years in the U.S., and the type is fairly common today. Those manufactured now differ from the original only in manufacturing shortcuts and in being modified to accommodate centerfire cartridges rather than the 41-caliber rimfire of the original.

Though the Remington (and later copies) contains two barrels, it is still essentially a single-shot mechanism over which has been superimposed a method of sequentially firing both barrels by actions of a single hammer and trigger.

Other single-shot pistols developed in this country for less lethal purposes. Remington's famous rolling-block rifle action was adapted to pistol configuration, and produced for a short period of time. Smith & Wesson adapted its hinged-frame revolver system to single-shot function by replacing the cylinder and barrel with a single-shot barrel whose breech occupied the place normally filled by the cylinder. In 1925, Smith & Wesson introduced a unique single-shot

target pistol commonly called the "Straight-Line Model." In it, the long barrel pivoted on the frame through a horizontal arc, the rear coming up against a standing breech into which was fitted a straight-line, striker-actuated firing mechanism.

At a later date, Colt attempted to produce a single-shot target pistol by substituting a flat block of steel, containing only a single chamber, for the cylinder in its solid-frame double-action revolver design.

Other single shots appeared by lesser makers, intended primarily for pure target use, but none of them achieved commercial success. Those by S & W and Colt also passed from the scene after only very limited production, simply because the American shooter wasn't interested in a gun that fired only once between reloadings. Nurtured on the firepower of first the revolver and after 1900 the autoloader, the single-shot simply didn't appeal to him, even though in some instances it might offer superior accuracy.

The last of the early single-shots was the Colt "Camp Perry" model last manufactured in 1941 after a total production of only 2525 pieces. Some indication of the type's popularity may be gleaned from the fact that during this same period of time, hundreds of thousands of each of many other makes and models were sold. None of our major handgun manufacturers have shown the slightest interest in the single-shot pistol since.

In Europe, much greater emphasis was placed on precise accuracy in slow-fire competition. Conse-

Thompson/Center single-shot pistols can be changed quickly from centerfire to rimfire, and the barrels are interchangeable.

quently, a good many very sophisticated single-shot pistols were developed there. The type was commonly know as "free pistol," because it was developed for the international slow-fire matches wherein the gun was relatively "free" of restrictions. The gun was invariably of 22 LR caliber and more often than not was built upon one variation or another of the Martini action scaled down to suit the purpose and fitted with a complex multiple-lever set trigger. This general type survived World War II and is still made to a very high degree of precision and development by the Swiss Hammerli company. Probably the most accurate handgun in the world today is the highly specialized Hammerli M150 whose appearance almost defies identification as a pistol. It is currently available from Gil Hebard Guns at a price in the $800 range. Hammerli also offers its M120, reportedly capable of the same degree of accuracy, but a much simpler toggle-joint design, and therefore less costly.

Interesting though the international-type single-shot pistols may be, the typical pistolero will never encounter one. They are made in small quantities to exacting specifications and are employed only by highly dedicated marksmen in international competition. They are so highly specialized, for example, with trigger pulls adjustable down to as little $\frac{1}{2}$ ounces, they simply can't be safely employed for any other type of shooting.

At the beginning of the 6th decade of this century, Remington Arms again introduced a single-shot pistol having a most unusual configuration. In reality, it was a short rifle. This gun employed the Mauser-like rotating-bolt front-locking action developed from the earlier M721/722 rifle series for short cartridges. To make up the pistol, designated "XP-100," Remington used this action in single-shot form combined with a $10\frac{1}{2}$-inch barrel, a molded plastic stock, and a bull-pup-type trigger installed forward on the underside of the barrel and connected to the firing mechanism by a rod extending rearward. The M600 rifle introduced during the same period of time featured the same action fitted with a magazine and conventional trigger.

The XP-100 was introduced along with a new cartridge designed specifically for it, the "221 Remington Fireball." This was nothing more or less than the 22 Remington rifle cartridge shortened to reduce its power capacity, loaded with a 50-grain bullet and driven at the phenomenal (for a handgun) velocity of 2650 fps.

The pistol/cartridge combination was intended purely for hunting and primarily for taking varmints at long range. It was not intended for any type of formal target competition that existed then or now; because of its great size and somewhat unhandy configuration, it could hardly have been expected to have any value as a defensive weapon.

The XP-100 pistol is unique in design, configuration and its cartridge in that it produces a higher velocity and flatter trajectory than any other pistol/cartridge combination available as a production item. Even though this model is not really in great demand, selling in substantially less volume than any other Remington sporting firearm, it still enjoys a steady demand and has now been in production roughly 15 years.

We make particular reference to the XP-100 here because it is a specialized gun producing a level and type of performance far beyond the capability of any existing or anticipated autoloading pistol. We recognize the fact, of course, that as much as we like the autoloader, there are most assuredly things that it and its cartridge cannot do. This Remington single-shot will exceed the autoloader in accuracy by a substantial margin (being capable of groups measuring less than 1 inch across at 100 yards). It offers a long range trajectory (to 200 yards and beyond) far flatter than can be obtained from any autoloader. By virtue of its velocity it produces explosive expansion in animal targets that no autoloader can boast. And it functions at normal working chamber pressures far in excess of what any currently manufactured autoloader can handle. As a result of all this, the Remington XP-100 deserves a position in the handgun enthusiast's battery whereby it augments the autoloader for special purposes.

However, the XP-100 is not the only American single-shot pistol currently manufactured in quantity. Back in the mid 1960s, Thompson/Center Arms was formed primarily to produce an interchangeable-barrel single-shot pistol of generally traditional appearance (which the XP-100 certainly is not) and designed by Warren Center. Actually, Thompson/Center was not a new company, but rather a division formed within an old-line investment casting company purely to manufacture firearms.

The design that emerged—and is still manufactured virtually unchanged—is traditional in appearance and of the hinged-barrel type. The barrel is locked in the closed position by a variation of the traditional horizontal sliding-bolt shotgun lock, differing mainly in that it is disengaged to permit opening the breech by pulling rearward and upward on a spur attached to the trigger guard. It employs an exposed manually cocked hammer and a frame-mounted firing pin, with provisions incorporated to change quickly and simply from centerfire to rimfire and vice versa. In addition to this, barrels are readily interchangeable. Simply removing the wood forend and pressing out the hinge pin allows the barrel to be removed and replaced, if desired, by one of different length or configuration, in any one of over 40 calibers.

Insofar as versatility is concerned (within the limitations of any single-shot pistol) the Contender is the ultimate. Barrels of any practical length or weight, and fitted with virtually any type of sight (including telescopic) may be freely interchanged upon the basic action. In addition, barrels have been and are being chambered by Thompson/Center for a tremendous variety of cartridges, including some of rifle type which no other pistol can accommodate. A shooter may purchase a single Contender pistol, then add spare barrels in calibers ranging upward from 22 rimfire. Virtually the entire range of pistol and revolver cartridges is available, as are barrels chambered for the 222 Remington class, 30-30, 308

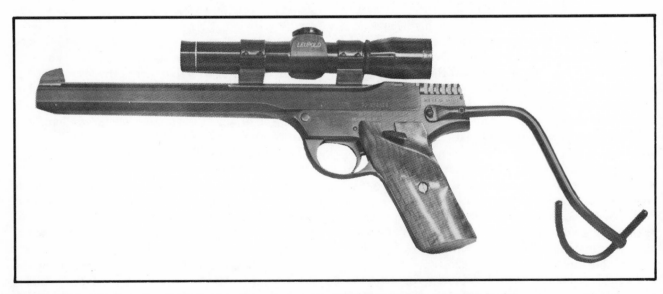

The Merrill is a single-action pistol that has the appearance and handling qualities of an autoloader.

Winchester, and others of both factory and wildcat type. Some wildcats, such as the 30 Herrett, have been developed specifically for the Contender pistol, and such chamberings are standard T/C offerings.

Though autoloading pistols do permit some interchange of calibers—as witness the Colt 22/45 conversion unit and the just-introduced SIG/Sauer P220—they cannot even begin to approach the caliber and power versatility of the T/C Contender single-shot in this respect. It is for this reason, like the Remington XP-100, that the T/C Contender deserves a place alongside autoloading pistols where it will serve to perform specialized jobs no other handgun can do.

Some other single-shot handguns exist in this country today, notably the Merrill with its hinged barrel swinging in a horizontal arc to open and close the breech. While of entirely different design than the other two mentioned, the Merrill offers the versatility of interchangeable barrels combined with appearance and handling characteristics similar to those of autoloaders. Unfortunately the Merrill is made in a very small shop in limited quantities and is not nearly so available as the XP-100 and the Contender.

Single-shot pistols do serve particular handgunning purposes that cannot be met by autoloaders (or, for that matter, revolvers) and thus should not be overlooked. In international slow-fire comeptition, even the finest and most expensive autoloader cannot quite match the scoring ability of the proper single-shot in the hands of a superior marksman. For long-range varmint-hunting, no autoloader can even approach the performance of a scoped Remington XP-100. For rapid interchange of calibers, lengths and weights, no autoloader can compare in the least with the Contender, or to a lesser extent, the Merrill. For these reasons, we include single-shots here, and hope that you'll be able to work them into your shooting activities.

Chapter Twenty-One
Combat Conversions

The term "combat conversions" is relatively new, and as far as this scribe knows, came into being around the beginning of the 1960s. While it apparently originated in reference only to big-bore autoloading pistols, I note that in the last couple of years, it has occasionally been used to describe revolvers which have been customized for carrying as combat weapons. Essentially combat conversion refers to an autoloader which has been modified to some degree. This modification adapts it better to the requirements of urban combat and to meet the specific personal requirements and desires of the gentleman (lady) who will be carrying it in anticipation of a fight.

As a practical matter, combat-conversion modifications fall into several functional categories. First are the modifications necessary to reduce the weight and bulk of the gun. Most common in this area is the shortening of the barrel and slide, followed by shortening the butt and magazine, and last by removing further metal from frame and/or slide to reduce weight. The latter is sometimes augmented by replacing certain steel parts with identical or modified parts made of lighter aluminum-alloy. The latter is not common yet, consisting mainly of replacing the mainspring housing and/or grip safety with comparable parts investment-cast from aluminum. These various metal-removing operations will often, particularly when carried to an extreme degree, make necessary internal modifications to maintain functional reliability. We'll have more on that shortly, but suffice it to say at this point that in extreme shortening jobs, extensive internal modifications, and sometimes even re-design, are required to provide sufficent space and power in recoil springs and mainsprings.

A second category of functional modifications consists mainly of improving the accuracy of the altered gun, either to maintain the level it produced in its original form, or to achieve a higher degree of accuracy. Generally speaking, the operations performed toward this end are the same as those applied to full-sized guns in accurizing them for serious target work. Unfortunately, the general tightening up of all moving parts which does the most to improve accuracy is not compatible past a certain point with the *total* functional reliability that we must have in a combat pistol.

I think perhaps we should dwell a bit on this subject. A handgun of any type carried by an individual for defense of himself and others (whether he be private citizen or commissioned officer) must function with *absolute reliability* under all conditions which may be anticipated for its use. Military pistols—such as the Browning HP and Colt GM—are designed and manufactured to produce this degree of reliability, but in doing so, they are made with generous clearances between moving parts, massive and heavy parts, and long recoil stroke. Parts clearances limit the accuracy that may be obtained, and when the gun is shortened and lightened, the weight and recoil stroke that ensure top reliability are both reduced and reliability suffers. Thereafter, if the altered gun is tightened up in conventional fashion to improve accuracy, the loss of those generous clearances further cuts reliability.

The pistolsmith specializing in combat conversions faces unique problems which are aggravated when the customer demands maximum weight and size reduction and at the same time demands the target-grade 50-yard accuracy. It is unfortunate many pistoleros refuse to accept the long-established fact that even in the original full-sized guns, maximum accuracy and total reliability simply do not go hand in hand; if we demand one, we must give up some of the other, or else compromise on a lesser degree of both.

Much of the combat-conversion smith's work is directed toward improving accuracy. And, to avoid unacceptable reductions in reliability, various new methods have been developed. They are generally aimed at consistent positioning of the barrel within the slide and the barrel/slide unit upon the frame for every shot, while avoiding the exceedingly close tolerances traditionally relied upon to accomplish these goals.

A third category of combat-conversion modifications consists of sighting refinements to improve practical accuracy under conditions of poor light and/or hurried use, yet without presenting handling and carrying problems. Generally such work consists of fitting target-type sights containing micrometer adjustments but fitted with wider-than-usual front blade and rear notch accompanied by spots, inlays or outlines of contrasting colors to improve visibility. A rib or serrated-top slide surface is also often included. The major problems encountered in the work is that sights possessing the precision adjustment that shooters currently demand are usually large and sharp-cornered, thus interfering with holstering and handling and posing the probability of snagging on clothing in a hurried engagement.

There exists yet another category of work aimed primarily at increasing speed and ease of handling, and at the same time improving rapid-fire control of the gun under adverse conditions. These modifications consist of: checkering, serrating or stippling front and back straps to improve hold, and sometimes reshaping those areas as well; funneling the mouth of the magazine well to facilitate rapid reloading; extending the thumbpieces on safeties and slide stops; squaring or hooking the front of the trigger guard to provide a seat for the off-hand forefinger; installation of special grips or stocks; installation of a recoil buffer to speed up recovery and perhaps aid in feeding; installation of reshaped parts such as triggers and grip safeties to suit the individual, and even the complete reworking of the action to provide double-action capability in pistols of originally single-action design, as in the Seecamp DA conversion of the Colt GM.

Last, (at least in my opinion, though others may have different ideas) we have the cosmetic category of work. Generally this consists of minor reshaping and resurfacing of metal in some areas and also includes the application of special or unusual surface finishes. It would also include the seldom-seen installation of decorative inlays, engraving, rare-wood grips, etc. Cosmetic modifications seldom have any significant effect upon accuracy, reliability or handling, though pistoleros often justify an additional expense of custom work by convincing themselves otherwise. For example, a metal-checkering job on the rear face of the slide may be touted for its glare-reducing capability as an aid to sighting, but in reality it's purely a cosmetic addition that the shooter wants to further set his gun aside from those of his compatriots.

Special finishes and stainless-steel replacement parts fall in the same category. Carbon-steel parts, nicely blued, contribute just as much to accuracy, handling and reliability as stainless-steel replacements or a hundred-dollar exotic surface-finish guaranteed to be as hard as a diamond and to last until judgment day. If a fellow wants this type of work and is willing to pay for it, fine. It's good for the pistolsmith's wallet, and great for the shooter's ego; but he should not delude himself into believing that such features will in any way improve the gun's performance (or the shooter's) when a fight erupts some night in a wet and dimly lit alley.

Combat conversions were first performed on Colt GM autos, and even today, this model probably accounts for the bulk of such work. However, the methods developed on this gun have since been applied to most other big-bore autoloaders, including Star and Llama, Browning, and Smith & Wesson models. Consequently, we will run through the basic modifications as they apply to the GM pistol, with an occasional remark concerning their application to other models.

Shortening the slide and barrel comes first and is the most common operation. Barrel and slide are removed and completely stripped, with the former laid aside and the latter accurately scribed all the way around where the excess at the muzzle is to be cut off. With the full-length GM, more than one inch of the front of the slide should not be removed if the original type of recoil spring is to be retained. More shortening than that will reduce spring space to the point where proper slide-into-battery load and feeding cannot be obtained except with a specially designed spring system such as those employed by Behlert, Seecamp and some others. The slide is sawed through just ahead of the scribed lines, after which the cut surface is trued up by filing or milling, flush with the lines. If the original-type barrel bushing is to be retained, then the seat for the bushing locking lug must be milled in the proper location inside the slide muzzle; if a different type, such as Behlert's threaded bushing is to be installed, then the appropriate threading or other machining must be done.

The original bushing is now too long and must be cut off squarely, even with the rear edge of its locking lug, and the edges of the cut lightly chamfered. The barrel and bushing are then installed in the slide, in the locked position, and the barrel is marked flush with the front face of the bushing, then cut off and properly crowned. After the bushing has been fitted, it is necessary to install a new front sight. Any type will do, but it is usually chosen to match whatever new rear sight is being installed.

At this point the recoil-spring plunger is shortened from the rear to match the new slide length. The distance from the face of the slide is measured internally to the shoulder which supports the rear of the plunger, and the plunger is then cut off to that length. It must then enter the underside of the slide barely deep enough to allow the bushing to be rotated for locking and unlocking. The recoil-spring guide is then shortened about ⅜ inch from the front, radiusing the cut end smoothly.

Next, a spacer ring is turned from drill rod of a suitable size. This ring must slip freely over the recoil spring, and also pass smoothly through the lower part of the frame where the recoil spring lies. Its purpose is

If a new bushing is installed, appropriate threading must be done.

to fit over the recoil spring, ahead of the flange on the spring guide and limit rearward slide travel. To accommodate this ring, clearance must be filed or ground on the underside of the barrel, removing the tapered portion which joins the barrel lug to the cylindrical portion of the barrel. No more metal should be removed here than is necessary to provide minimum clearance for the ring as the slide recoils. After all other work has been done and this ring has been fitted and checked for proper functioning, it should be hardened and drawn.

That completes the basic work on the slide and barrel, though individual pistolsmiths offer numerous options in the way of sights, ribs, lightening cuts, ejection-port reshaping, etc., which the buyer may choose.

The recoil-spring seat in the frame must now be modified to provide additional recoil-spring space. Just ahead of the slide-stop pin hole is a vertical abutment against which the flange of the recoil-spring guide seats. This surface must be cut back toward the rear of the frame.

This is usually done in a milling machine, though it can be done in a lathe or drill press with proper fixturing and cutters, the amount varying somewhat among pistolsmiths. Some move the abutment as little as ¹⁄₁₆th inch, others nearly ¼ of an inch, so far that the rear of the recoil-spring guide must be slotted to provide clearance for the barrel link.

What amounts to a great deal of time and effort has been devoted to making room for the longest possible recoil spring; this is absolutely essential for functional reliability. If both steps are not employed, then even specially designed springs cannot load the slide properly into battery nor supply reliable feeding.

Many combat conversions stop at this point, having reduced the gun's length a full inch and its weight by several ounces. However, the butt of most big-bore autos is the principal factor limiting concealment, and it is therefore often shortened. To do this, the frame is completely stripped, and, beginning at the upper edge of the web carrying the lower stock-screw bushing, a section is cut out of the butt frame equal in length to the amount of shortening desired. This may be done with a hacksaw, or on a milling machine. The most common amount of shortening is one-half an inch, this making the butt much more compact and eliminating only one cartridge of the magazine capacity.

After the section has been cut out of the frame, the edges of the cut are properly beveled, and the bottom is moved up and welded back in place, utilizing an old magazine or close-fitting plug to ensure that the cut-off part is properly aligned. After welding, surplus weld-material is removed from the outside of the frame and the inside of the magazine well by filing, grinding or machining. The weld must be perfect, or the frame will not refinish properly. At this time, the opening of the magazine well is generally funneled with files or hand grinder to facilitate rapid insertion of a loaded magazine.

Magazines are then shortened to fit the butt. The follower and spring are removed, the bottom of the body is cut off at the proper point, and either the original floorplate or a new one is silver-soldered in place. The follower spring is usually shortened one coil, and the magazine then reassembled. Usually several magazines are made up for each gun, and at this time they are carefully fitted, polishing and filing both on the well and the magazine body, if necessary, to ensure smooth, easy insertion and positive ejection. The empty magazine must consistently fall clear of its own weight when the catch is disengaged. This is vital to rapid reloading under fire.

Magazines with removable floor plates, such as the Browning and S&W, require more complex shortening inasmuch as after being cut off, new lips must be formed to hold the floor plate. This is usually done with a punch and die set, but can be done satisfactorily by skillful application of a hammer.

The sear spring must now be shortened from the bottom and anchored in the proper position by some method. Some smiths cut a new anchoring slot in the frame, bend a new lip at the bottom of the spring, and anchor it in the original fashion. Others may do the job with a screw or pin. Very careful positioning of the shortened spring is essential for proper sear, trigger and disconnector functioning.

If the function of the grip safety is to be retained (and often it is not) then both it and the mainspring housing must be shortened so that the two parts can be accommodated within the new butt-length. The grip safety must be shortened from the lower end while the housing can be shortened from both ends the mainspring also being shortened a comparable amount. Several smiths have different methods of doing this, and all seem to work rather well. Once the safety and housing have been properly fitted, it may be necessary to shorten the hammer strut, depending upon the treatment given the housing and main spring. Care must be taken throughout these operations to ensure that the hammer blow is not reduced to the point where ignition will suffer.

If the grip-safety function is not to be retained, the inner protrusion of the safety may be cut off and the entire part hollowed by grinding to a thin shell, then shortened and welded to the housing so that together the two parts form a one-piece back strap. In this respect, however, Seecamp makes (at present only for use on his own conversions) a replacement back-strap of either steel or aluminum; it incorporates a modified mainspring-housing and a nicely shaped filler to replace the grip safety. These modifications can be rather ticklish, and if I were doing them I would try to buy the back-strap unit from Seecamp and use it discarding the original parts. That way, the job would be much easier, and would in all probability look nicer. After all this work has been done on the butt frame, either the original grips must be shortened to fit and have new holes drilled to match the relocated lower bushings, or new grips must be made.

At this point, the basic combat-conversion has been completed. The gun has been shortened in both length and height and has also been reduced substantially in weight and bulk. The principal goal of increased handiness and concealment has been achieved.

If trigger guard alteration is desired, the front may be squared by die-forging it out to the desired shape or by cutting it, straightening the two legs, and welding in a short length of steel and filing to shape. If instead the customer desires the hooked-type forefinger rest, it is usually built up by welding and then filed to shape.

The so-called combat-type safety and slide stop may be added. These simply have extended thumb

eces to make them more easily reached and manipu-
ted; they are available as new manufacture, in both
rbon and stainless steel from at least a couple of
urces. Obviously these new parts are merely
stalled and checked for functioning. However, some
istolsmiths modify the original parts. This is done by
ling seats for extensions in the original thumbpieces,
elding or silver-soldering in rough-shaped pieces of
eet steel, then filing the entire assembly to the
sired shape. The job is finished by serrating, checking or stippling the new thumbpieces.

Southpaws will want a left-hand or ambidextrous
fety. This item can be made by hand, but it's a
fficult job. As a result, new-manufacture replace-
ent parts are generally purchased from Swenson or
other source and installed. If a left-hand slide stop
required, the smith will make this, filing a new
ver to shape and cutting a corresponding notch in
e slide, then welding or brazing it to a cross pin and
tting in a new detent spring and plunger on the
ame. The slide stop can be also be shifted to left-
nd operation by making a simple thumb lever and
taching it to the right end of the original stop in
ch a way that it can be removed for disassembly of
e gun. Done this way, the job leaves the original
de stop functioning normally, and simply provides
lever for its manual operation on the right side of
e gun.

Various smiths offer other combat features and
cessories which may be added, some useful and
me not. Seecamp, for example, offers a loaded-
amber indicator pivoted and spring-loaded in a slot
achined in the top of the slide at the rear of the
ection port. Seecamp also offers a unique dual-
ement recoil-spring system which is superior to all
the others we've examined. Austin Behlert offers
s threaded barrel-bushing which copies the unusual
shing/barrel relationship of the S&W M52 target
stol.

The most unusual of these special offerings is the
eviously mentioned double-action conversion of the
lt GM by Seecamp. It consists of machining a
cess in the right side of the frame for a drawbar,
en installing a new pivoted trigger ahead of the
ortened original trigger. An enlarged trigger guard
also installed to provide room for proper operation
the new part. A stud is added to the foot of the
iginal hammer to be engaged by a hook on the
awbar. The recess and new parts are then covered
 a formed sheet-metal side plate held in position by
e grip and grip screws. At this point it is important
note that all of the original functions of the basic
sign remain unimpaired; the entire double-action

system is simply superimposed over the original
setup.

Functioning is simple. With the hammer down,
pulling the new trigger to the rear causes its upper
limb to move the drawbar forward; a hook at the rear
of the drawbar engages the stud on the foot of the
hammer, rotating it toward the full-cock position. As
the hammer approaches full-cock, the new trigger
contacts the stub of the original trigger and presses it
rearward, thus rotating the sear away from the
hammer. After this the drawback hook cams off the
hammer and allows it to be driven forward to strike
the firing pin and fire the cartridge. At this point, the
trigger is released, taking pressure off the original
trigger so that the sear rotates back into position to
catch and hold the hammer at full-cock when it is
driven back by the slide. Complete release of the new
trigger causes it to be thrust forward by its srping, so
that it halts in a rearward single-action position. The
slight rearward movement will force the original trigger to the rear and fire the next shot single-action.
This is simple, neat, thoroughly reliable, and not
terribly expensive, when one looks at all the work that
must be done to install the system.

Those are the steps that must be accomplished to
produce the basic combat conversion of a typical
big-bore autoloader. The foregoing was intended to be
merely descriptive, not a do-it-yourself manual. This
isn't to say the average tool-handy pistolero can't do a
pretty fair job at home. A good many people have
done so, and more will. However, I strongly suggest
reading and studying more detailed references on the
subject. At the risk of being accused of blowing my
own horn I might suggest my book *Pistolsmithing*
published by the Stackpole Company and available
wherever good gun books are sold. It covers the
various operations in considerable detail, particularly
in regard to accomplishing them with the hand tools
that the average gun enthusiast might expect to have
immediately available.

When deciding to order a combat conversion, one
should be a bit cautious. Aside from the fact that
there are good and mediocre pistolsmiths advertising
conversions, one must take note of the fact that the
better smiths run from several months to as much as
a couple of years on delivery time. I think the principal pitfall is in attempting to have the gun made too
light and too short and perhaps overloaded with
features that offer relatively little utility in exchange
for their considerable cost. If you demand an abso-
lute-minimum barrel and slide length, the smith may
not able to guarantee reliable functioning; if you
demand an extraordinarily high degree of accuracy,

the same problem will rear its ugly head.

Neither the smallest nor the most accurate gun in the world will do you one damned bit of good in a fight unless you can be absolutely certain that it will fire every time you want as many times as you need. Be willing to settle for a gun that's somewhat longer than you'd like and maybe an ounce heavier and thus be assured of reliability. Be willing to settle for a gun that will keep its shots in two or three inches at 25 yards, thus not handicapping it as to functioning. After all, the average cops-and-robbers gunfight takes place at a range substantially less than 20 feet. Unless you point the gun deliberately in the wrong direction, even a rusted, shot-out Government Model will hit a man at that range.

I think we can say that the combat conversion idea offers a number of advantages, albeit at considerable cost, to the professional gun carrier. However, it is unfortunate that many of them are so overdone and are so overloaded with questionable features that they become actually less suitable for urban combat than the original gun without alteration. After all, you can buy a Colt LW Commander and then you can spend several hundred more shortening it by ½ inch, reducing its height by a like amount, and trimming almost a couple of ounces off its weight. Afterward, you'll have a beautiful piece of weaponry that makes a great conversation piece, but it's questionable whether you'll be able to tell the difference when carrying it or shooting it.

Chapter Twenty-Two
Sights

arly pistols had no sights worthy of the name. onsidering that their mechanical accuracy capabil-y was nil, this is thoroughly understandable. Rudi-entary sights appeared during the flintlock period, sually consisting of nothing more than a nib on top ' the barrel near the muzzle and a shallow groove ed in the swell of the breech. Even they didn't serve ay tremendously useful purpose, considering that ue barrels were smooth-bored, round balls were ndersized, and ballistic performance was rather different. Worthwhile sights appeared on rifled-arrel target pistols of the late flint and subsequent ercussion periods, but sights didn't really become andard on handguns until the appearance of the ercussion revolver. Even then, they left a good bit to e desired, considering that the most common type as the Colt with a tiny brass cone or bead at the uzzle, and a small V-shaped notch filed in the nose the wobbly hammer.

With cartridge revolvers and their capability of elivering a high degree of accuracy, handgun sights we know them today made their appearance. Two pes developed: the Paine and the Patridge. Both are med for the exhibition shooters who developed them, with the Paine consisting of a round-bead front sight supported on a thin stem or blade, combined with a semi-circular notch at the rear. The Patridge sight consisted of a rectangular-section blade or post up front combined with a rectangular notch in the rear sight. As the two types developed and were used concurrently, it became evident that the Patridge type allowed easier alignment and has since demon-strated other advantages as well. The result was that the Paine type simply fell from favor and by the 1920s and 1930s had disappeared entirely from pro-duction handguns. It is interesting to note, though, that the basic paine design of round bead and semi-circular notch still survives in some rifle sights, though I, for one, wonder why.

Sighting a handgun is no different than with a rifle. Front and rear sighting elements must be affixed to the gun in a particular relationship to the path of the bullet. Once this relationship has been established, one directs the bullet to the target by visually aligning the sight elements upon that target.

Though the same problems exist in sighting all firearms, those of recoil and muzzle lift are exagger-ated in handguns because of their relatively light weight and one-hand configuration. When the typical autoloading pistol is grasped for shooting, whether one or both hands be used, the centerline of the bore and the bulk of the pistol's mass lie above the supporting hand and arm. Consequently, when the gun begins to recoil from a shot, it attempts to move more or less straight rearward in line with the bore, but is restrained from doing so by one's grasp beneath the bore. The result of all this is that the entire gun tends to pivot about the shooting hand, the muzzle moving upward as the entire gun moves to the rear.

The magnitude and speed of this upward muzzle-movement is dependent upon or related to several factors, but mainly the magnitude of the recoil impulse, length of time from primer ignition to the bullet exiting the muzzle (barrel time), gun weight, and the distance the bore lies above the shooting hand.

The Micro Sight is compact and won't be moved by recoil.

If recoil did not begin until the bullet left the muzzle, we wouldn't have much of a problem. But that isn't the case. In accordance with Newton's laws of motion, the recoil impulse begins the instant the bullet starts moving forward out of the cartridge case. Though there may be some delay in overcoming the inertia of the gun, as a practical matter, recoil movement of the gun begins with bullet movement. Recoil impulse and gun movement then build up as the bullet traverses the bore, with the result that muzzle lift also begins at approximately the same time and continues. Consequently, by the time the bullet has exited the muzzle, a substantial portion of recoil movement and muzzle lift has already taken place.

At the instant the bullet exits the muzzle, the gun has already moved rearward and the muzzle has rotated upward. Thus, the barrel is pointed upward at

a substantially greater vertical angle than it was a the instant the hammer fell and the sights wer aligned on target. Pared down to the bare essential this means simply that as the bullet leaves the barre the barrel is no longer pointed at the same spot it w when the trigger was pulled. If the barrel wer pointed precisely at the center of the target at th instant the hammer fell, it would have risen to b pointed *above* the target at the time the bulle departed the muzzle and could not possibly strike th target.

For this reason, handgun sights—at least as far a handgun shooting ranges are concerned—must estab lish the line of sight so that when they are aligned o the target, the bore is actually pointing somewha below the target. Since the amount of muzzle li varies widely according to the factors we've alread listed, the angular amount that the line of sight mu diverge from the bore is not constant for differen guns or different calibers, or for even the same gu (identical in all respects) for more than one particula loading of the cartridge. If bullet weight and veloci are changed, the magnitude of muzzle lift will als change, and it usually isn't possible to predict th amount, or even the direction of change. Doubtless computer could calculate the exact amount and dire tion of change if properly programmed, but th shooter can only guess, and if he's had a lot experience, he can probably guess right most of th time.

There is yet another factor, completely outside th gun and ammunition, which affects the amount muzzle lift. This is the resistance offered to recoil the shooter. The result is that a gun/cartridge comb nation with its sights aligned correctly for one shoot will not necessarily place its bullets at the same poi on target for another. While the amount of differen isn't sufficient to be significant in the typic gunfight, it can certainly be so at the longer ranges competitive shooting and hunting. Even two shoote of approximately the same build and weight may off substantially different resistance to recoil of the gu The effect of this difference on the bullet's point impact may not be much, but it is there. At the oth end of the scale, a 180-pound male shooter stretchi to six feet will find his pistol placing its bulle differently than when it is fired by his slender fiv foot four-inch 110-pound girlfriend.

The problems we've been discussing may not ev be evident when the recoil impulse is quite small a the gun rather heavy. An example of this would be 22 rimfire target auto weighing 40 ounces or so. By t time the tiny recoil impulse of the 22 cartridge h overcome the gun's inertia, the magnitude of muzzle lift will be so small that it won't cause much trouble, even between different shooters. Generally speaking, cartridges and loads using heavy bullets at relatively high velocities require the largest divergence of the line of sight from the bore to compensate for muzzle lift.

Typically, sights on production autoloaders are of the fixed type, with the front element usually brazed or riveted in place and the rear element dovetailed laterally into the top of the slide. Both sights are usually quite low, protruding no more than $\frac{1}{8}$ to $\frac{1}{4}$ inch above the slide. In the smaller pocket-type guns, sights are often machined integrally with the slide, and may even be recessed into a groove in the top of the slide. In the latter case, the sights aren't even visible in profile.

Fixed sights of the type mentioned are generally referred to as "service sights," and at the factory they are installed and regulated to place the bullets of the standard load for the caliber (e.g., in 45 ACP the 230-grain FMC military load) on point of aim at 15 yards. This does not mean that each gun is targeted precisely, but that the sights are dimensioned and installed so that alignment is approximately correct at that range.

Factory sight alignment is usually good enough for ordinary close-range work with standard ammunition. However, precise shooting at the longer ranges and different loadings of the cartridge will usually require some adjustment of the sights unless one is willing to settle for Kentucky windage and Tennessee elevation. Since the medium- and large-sized autos generally have the rear sight dovetailed laterally in the slide, windage corrections may be made without too much difficulty. The rear sight can be moved right or left (in the direction the bullet strike must be moved) by means of a hammer and soft (brass or fiber or aluminum) drift. This is a trial-and-error process, and an index mark should be scribed on both slide and sights so that the amount of movement can be seen. Ideally, the slide should be clamped in a vise or other solid support.

A simpler, easier and more precise method of moving the rear sight is found in a "sight mover," which consists of a U-shaped block of metal which fits over the slide and is provided with a screw which is turned in to bear on the sight and move it. So long as the pitch of the screw thread is known, predetermined amounts of sight movement can be accomplished by counting the turns or fractions of turns.

You may find when you attempt to move the rear sight that it isn't as tight in the dovetail as it should be. If it simply moves fairly easily, no big problem. But, if it's actually loose enough that it doesn't stay in position for firing, then the dovetail needs to be tightened. Peening the edges of the dovetail will help some, but a better job usually results from dimpling the floor of the dovetail with a sharp center punch. The burrs raised by the punch bind tightly on the underside of the sight and keep it tight.

After proper windage adjustment has been obtained by moving the rear sight laterally, the sight should be staked tightly in position. Even though it appears tight in the dovetail, it may shift slightly under the repeated shocks of extensive firing and spoil your zero. Use a sharp center punch to dimple the edge of the dovetail both in front and behind the sight. This will force slide metal tightly against the sight for a secure assembly.

Elevation adjustment of fixed sights is another and more difficult matter. If the gun shoots too low, then the job is easy. Simply file down the top of the front sight; reducing its height raises the point of impact with respect to the line of sight. It's just a question of making a couple of file strokes across the top of the sight, then firing a few shots, and repeating the process until the point of impact has been raised sufficiently.

Unfortunately, you may run out of front sight before the desired result is obtained. Sights are generally quite low, and you can't remove a great deal and still retain a sight that is high enough to be picked up easily and aligned in the rear-sight notch. The alternative when this condition exists is to install a higher rear sight, or have the top built up by welding, then carefully file it to shape. Higher rear sights are available for the Colt GM, but seldom for any other models. When a higher replacement isn't available, you'll be forced to either go the welding and reshaping route or to file a complete, new rear sight out of scrap metal. This isn't a terribly difficult job, but it requires care and attention to detail and is rather time-consuming.

When a new sight is made or the original is built up by welding, we usually guess at the additional height necessary, add a bit more for a safety factor, then file the part down to correct height in the process of zeroing. However, it's a simple enough job to calculate the exact amount needed. First, measure and record the distance that the center of impact must be moved vertically. Then, measure the sight radius in inches, and divide it into the range to the target in inches. This will give you a multiplier factor which is used to translate a specific amount of sight movement into movement on target.

Let's say the factor comes out to 100, the result of a six-inch sight radius and 50-foot range to target. With those values, a .010-inch increase in rear-sight height would move the center of impact one inch. To determine how much higher the rear sight must be made, simply divide the distances (in inches) that the center of impact must be raised by the multiplying factor. The result will be the amount by which the sight height must be increased. It's still a good idea to make the sight just a wee bit higher, and bring it to precise height during zeroing. Naturally, exactly the same method may be used to determine height changes of the front sight or lateral movements of either sight.

If the gun is shooting too high, you have the option of either welding up the front sight to a greater height, replacing it with a higher one, or cutting down the height of the rear sight. The latter is simplest, but here we run into the same problem already mentioned with the front sight. The amount of change necessary may be more than we can cut off the rear sight and still have it remain completely functional.

Once fixed sights have been properly regulated or adjusted for a given cartridge and load, they actually become superior to the adjustable types, assuming they've been given the proper shape. Their principal—and in my opinion only—disadvantage is that they can be adjusted to zero the gun/ammunition combination only by the laborious process just described. Because of this, it is not possible to make quick and easy sight changes to accommodate changes in ammunition and range. Aside from that, fixed sights are actually superior to the adjustable target variety in that they contain no inherent looseness, they are much less likely to be damaged, and no practical joker or mischievous friend can spoil the zero when your back is turned.

If one were choosing a pistol for use under all conditions and with only a single cartridge loading, he would be better served by sturdy fixed sights than the adjustable type, and he'd save a substantial sum of money in the process. In my opinion, many people waste money by insisting upon finely adjustable sights when, as a practical matter, those adjustments will only be used for initial targeting. Beyond that point, adjustable sights can become a costly liability in that they are much more susceptible to damage, often contain internal looseness which reduces accuracy, and are subject to coming out of adjustment either inadvertently or through tampering. On top of all that, adjustable sights are usually much more bulky and obtrusive, and tend to snag on clothing.

Today, adjustable target-type handgun sights incorporate both windage and elevation adjustments in the rear sight. As a practical matter, the front sight is the same as in the fixed variety. Each company that manufactures target autoloaders supplies them fitted with its own peculiar type of adjustable rear sight. However, for those other guns which the maker does not supply so equipped, several independent companies manufacture after-market sights which are often superior in quality to those supplied by the big factories. In addition to that, pistolsmiths and tool-handy shooters often replace the fixed rear sight with one that is supplied on a different model. The most prominent example of this is the wide use of the Smith & Wesson target-revolver sight on big-bore autoloaders. Companies manufacturing after-market sights are Bo-Mar, Elliason, Micro, MMC, and Custom Gun Shop. There may be others of which we are not aware at this time.

Pistolsmiths, naturally, will install any practical sight combination you want as long as you're willing to pay the price. I've seen some pretty odd combinations; all some of them proved was that the owner wanted to be different. Further, there exist excellent adjustable sights which can be installed on virtually any gun if you're willing to expend the appropriate amount of time and money. I've even seen the 25 Colt Pocket Model auto fitted with a rib and target sights!

As in other fields, the gun most-often fitted with target sights is probably the Colt GM. For pure target use, I believe that the Micro and Bo-Mar units are the most popular. Both feature excellent click-adjustments in both windage and elevation, but the Bo-Mar is the heavier and sturdier of the two. Both rear units are much higher than the original. Therefore, it becomes necessary to install a matching front sight in place of the original, and both manufacturers offer the front and rear units as a set. In addition to this, Bo-Mar offers an easily installed rib in which the front and rear sight elements are already properly installed.

Many shooters would prefer to install their own target sights, not only to avoid the substantial cost of having it done by a pistolsmith, but to avoid having the gun out of their hands for an extended period of time. It's unfortunate that only a relatively few localities contain competent pistolsmiths and this makes it necessary quite often to ship a gun away for sight installation. This usually results in the gun being gone for several weeks or months, a conditon that appeals not at all to most of us.

Installing one's own sights is not difficult if the sights themselves are chosen carefully toward that end. In this area, I feel that the Bo-Mar ramp unit stands head and shoulders above all the rest. Though the entire unit costs more than simply buying the two sights, the simple home installation allows you to get by a lot cheaper than employing a pistolsmith to do the more difficult job of installing the separate sights.

We'll run through the procedure for installing the Bo-Mar ramp/sight unit because I feel it is the answer to obtaining top-quality sights without utilizing the services of a pistolsmith.

Remove and completely strip the slide, then drift out the rear sight and file or grind off the front sight. Clamp the slide horizontally and upright in a vise, then carefully position the Bo-Mar unit on top. Take the time to make absolutely certain that alignment is correct; the rib should sit vertically and parallel to the sides of the slide. Once you've got it right, clamp it solidly in place, making certain it doesn't shift in the process. (If you don't have clamps that will work, heavy rubber bands or reinforced tape wrapped tightly around it and the slide will serve the purpose.)

Obtain a punch that is a slip-fit in the screw holes in the rib, and carefully grind a centered point on its end. Use it to very carefully center-punch the slide through the mounting-screw holes in the rib. After punching each hole, recheck the rib's alignment to make certain you haven't knocked it out of place. The punch marks must be centered in each hole with the rib properly aligned. If you do get one of the marks slightly out of position, remove the rib, and by careful hammer-and-punch manipulation, shift the punch mark over so it will be properly centered.

The rest is easy. Simply drill through the roof of the slide at each punch mark ahead of the ejection port, and tap those holes for the mounting screws. Behind the ejection port, drill the holes only about 3/16 inch deep, but under no circumstances allow the drill to break into the firing-pin recess. Tap the rear holes also, then deburr them all, especially inside the slide where the front holes break through. Remove all oil and grease from the top of the slide, the holes, and the underside of the rib, then set the rib in place and turn in the screws. Make certain the rear screws will draw up quite tight without bottoming in the holes; if they won't, shorten them by filing or grinding, but no more than necessary. If the front screws protrude significantly through the slide, shorten them also.

Once you're sure everything will fit correctly, remove the rib and thoroughly degrease the screws and holes. Put a drop of Loc-Tite in each screw hole and a string of it down the top of the slide as well. Set the rib on and turn all the screws in very tightly. After they're tight, set a punch or piece of drill rod in the socket of each head, and give it a healthy rap with the hammer. Usually this will allow the screw to be tightened just a wee bit more. Keep in mind that tremendous G-loads will be placed on those screws as the slide slams back and forth in recoil; they must be tight or they'll work loose or, worse yet, shear off.

Incidentally, take note that Bo-Mar makes this same type of rib/sight unit to fit the S&W M39 and Browning High Power pistols. The GM unit will also fit the bigger Star models, and can be used on the older Llama models without ventilated rib. It can even be installed on the ribbed guns if one files and grinds off the rather small rib.

Individual front and rear sights may also be fitted at home, but the job is a bit more difficult. Some models of rear sights, notably the "High Micro" may simply be drifted into the original dovetail and secured with a clamp screw or by staking. That part is simple enough. Fitting the new front sight is another matter. First, the original blade must be removed, and on the GM, this is done most easily by inverting the slide in a vise, locating the sight rivet where it comes through the slide roof, then punching it out. Then the new front sight is positioned over the original rivet hole, and, if necessary, that hole is enlarged with needle files to accept the stud on the bottom of the new blade. On some replacement sights, this stud is relatively large, thus the hole must be expanded considerably. The hole should be fitted very closely to the stud, after which the underside of the blade and the slide must also be closely fitted. The closer the fit, the stronger the installation will be when completed.

The best method of fitting is to first remove the original finish from the entire joint area, then apply layout blue and spot the two together by scraping and filing. Once a nearly perfect fit is obtained, coat the joint surfaces with fusion or paste-type low-temperature silver solder (available from Brownells and other gunsmithing supply houses) and clamp or wire the new sight tightly in place. Take care to ensure that the sight stands vertical to the slide; this may require some adjustment after clamping and/or wiring.

Next, apply heat to the slide in the vicinity of the sight until the solder liquifies completely. The slide is much more massive than the sight; therefore, heat should be concentrated upon it. If the sight is heated first, it will become hot enough to melt the solder while the slide is still too cold for a proper bond to be formed. By applying the heat to the slide, we depend upon it to melt the solder, and heat the sight to form a perfect joint. If you can do so without disturbing sight alignment, brush or wipe away excess liquid solder. After the joint has cooled sufficiently to permit handling, remove the clamp or wires, and with scrapers or abrasive cloth, get rid of all of the excess solder. This will leave bright metal you'll have to refinish in some manner.

Target sights installed in the foregoing fashion protrude quite high above the slide, and many people would prefer a lower line of sight. This can be obtained with the "Low Micro," which is essentially the same rear sight adapted to a lower position on the slide. It, too, can be installed at home. However, you'll have a lot of filing and hacksaw work to do, and if you don't feel competent to hand-file a precise dovetail and mounting surface, don't attempt it.

Essentially this installation involves sawing out a rectangular section from the upper rear of the slide, then truing up those surfaces with files and filing a lateral dovetail at the front of the surface thus formed. This installation has a good bit to recommend it, but it is best done by a pistolsmith on a milling machine unless you are unusually adept with hacksaw and files. I'm not trying to talk you out of it, just pointing out that it's by no means easy, and if you botch the job, that expensive slide is ruined.

MMC makes its very practical "Combat Sight" for the GM, Browning and some other pistols. This sight is unique in that it incorporates fairly precise windage and elevation adjustments and yet is sufficiently low that it is compatible with the original front sight. In order to accomplish this, it is made quite small; thus the adjustments are accomplished by very small, pyramid-pointed socket-head screws. As such, the adjustments are adequate for zeroing, but not quite up to the standards required for serious target use. Of course, MMC does not espouse this design for target work, but rather as a "low-profile combat sight." It is easily installed by almost any pistolero in only two or three minutes.

First, the original sight must be drifted out, then the upper front edge of the dovetail filed to a slight bevel. Then the MMC sight base is tapped into the dovetail and staked in position, after which the sight leaf is installed. The gun is now ready for zeroing, still with its original front sight.

Probably the most common custom-sight installation on service autoloaders today, particularly on combat conversions, is the fitting of the S&W K-series revolver target sight. This is found most often on the Colt GM, but is applied also to many Brownings and to other makes and models of this general type. This installation is quite popular because it combines precise windage and elevation adjustments with a sight that is very compact, unobtrusive, and lies low and close to the top of the slide. Though it might appear simple to casual observation, this is a difficult and costly installation that is beyond the capability of the home pistolsmith.

While the slot for the spring base and the transverse clearance cut can be filed without too much difficulty, the elevation adjustment mechanism of this sight requires a bastard-sized blind undercut in the frame to accept the elevation-screw nut. There is no way this cut can be made except on a milling machine (or a suitable drill press with milling table), and even then a very fragile special-size milling cutter is required. The basement pistolsmith who has either of those two machines can do the job if he obtains the proper cutters. Fortunately, Trapper Guns has recognized this problem and offers a set of double-ended cutters for the entire job. So, if you really want to do this job yourself and if you have the equipment, you can buy a set of cutters from Trapper and have at it. Frankly, I recommend the job be referred to a competent pistolsmith who has equipped himself for this particular job—and keep in mind that many have not.

One sees and hears a good deal about telescopic sights being used on revolvers and single-shot pistols. A few enthusiasts also install them on autoloaders, and they are no less advantageous there for certain uses than on other types of guns. The principal reason scopes are not often seen on autos is the difficulty of installation and the fact that a scope can very easily interfere with functional reliability. One's first thought is that it would be simple enough to bolt a scope on top of the slide, just as it is mounted on the single-shot barrel or the top strap of a revolver. Unfortunately, that won't work, at least not in most instances. Any autoloading pistol is designed so that the weight and inertial factors of the slide are matched to the recoil impulse of the cartridge. If we hang another pound of scope and mount on top of the slide, we completely destroy the dynamic balance of the design, and if it functions at all, reliability will be marginal at best.

Eliminating the slide doesn't leave any really good places to hang the scope. The most practical mount I have seen for Browning-type autos is the unusual one sold by Whitney Sales. It consists of a plate which fits under the left grip and over the grip-screw bushings. Its upper end curves outward, then inward over the slide, and carries a longitudinal horizontal dovetail which centers over the slide and to which a Bushnell mount base may be clamped. With the scope thus attached to the frame, functioning of the gun is not affected. To the best of my knowledge, this is the only mount of this type available, though I have seen home- and custom-made mounts which attach to the

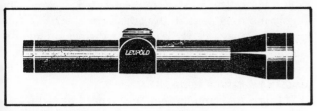

Leupold M8-2.5x scopes fit the Thompson Center single-shot pistol.

frame ahead of the grips. One such mount consisted of a U-shaped yoke through which the slide could recoil freely. The yoke was screwed to both sides of the frame and shaped at the top to accept a standard mount base.

Conventional rifle-type scope-sight designs don't work out well on handguns. Longer eye relief is required, and this is available in several scopes designed specifically for handguns. However, of all the long-eye relief designs available, we have found the Leupold M8-2X (originally designed for rifle use) to be the most durable and reliable. Even though handguns appear to recoil less than heavy-caliber rifles, scopes that hold up well on long guns often will not do so on handguns because of increased recoil-velocity and the multiple loads generated by the reciprocating slide being halted abruptly at both ends of its travel.

Shooting with a scoped autoloader presents one new problem: In order to obtain long eye relief, scopes give up field of view. The field of suitable scopes is thus very narrow, and when this is coupled with the distance of the eyepiece from the shooting eye, it becomes difficult to pick up a target in the scope. This is particularly so in the case of a moving target like a running jack rabbit, and most shooters overcome it by aiming loosely over the top of the scope in shotgun fashion, then dropping down to see the target through the scope. I have even seen rudimentary open sights attached to the top of a handgun scope for this very purpose: One aligns the open sights on the target, then looks through the scope and there it is.

A lesser problem is encountered in that, unless one's line of sight is parallel with the axis of the scope, you see nothing when looking into the eyepiece. Until you've had a bit of experience, you may look into that eyepiece at arm's length, and see nothing; this can be most frustrating. Looking directly at the rear of the scope, it often is not possible to determine the alignment changes necessary to see through it. The same problem exists with ordinary open sights, but there any misalignment can immediately be seen and corrected, so most people don't notice it at all.

One point we've neglected thus far is that today, as in centuries gone by, a good deal of handgun shooting is done without benefit of sights, even though they might be present on the gun. Much of the IPSC-type competition is fired without sights, and more probably could be. The short-range stages of PPC matches are or could be shot well without sights, and in most combat-type situations sights are not used. Further, some of the very small 22 and 25 autoloaders are made without sights, in recognition of the simple fact that their handling and accuracy capabilities are such that sights would be superfluous. Also, they are generally used only in last-ditch situations at table-top distances. In fact, right at this moment there are, hanging on my peg-board walls, several handguns (both autos and revolvers) which carry no sights at all. I've found that for rapid fire at close ranges and on aerial targets, with just a little practice and experience, one can do fully as well without sights as with.

Sights are essential, of course, for pinpoint accuracy at ranges of more than a few feet. While there have been many sight developments in recent years, the typical fully adjustable sight is still a rather fragile device that simply is not suited to rough service. Most are very nicely suited to formal target-shooting where the gun is never holstered or worn, and is protected in a massive wood box except when actually being fired. They are masterpieces of precision that permit shooters to punch a handful of holes in the X-ring at 50 yards, but for carrying guns, they simply aren't practical. The only service-type autoloader factory-fitted with an adjustable rear sight is the S&W M39/59, and it suffers from lack of any elevation adjustment. It's adjustable for windage, and due to sloppy manufacture, it is sometimes found

Smith & Wesson's M39 has a factory-fitted adjustable rear sight.

loosely installed.

Personally, I feel that gun and sight must be designed together to achieve maximum serviceability. Were I designing sights for a service autoloader, I would arrange the slide so that it incorporated up-thrust protective wings at the rear so that a thoroughly reliable, adjustable rear-sight mechanism could be fitted entirely down between them. Providing the slide were designed to serve as the base for the sight, this could be done with no great difficultly. I'd also fit the front sight between protective wings, again, not protruding above them so that no matter how roughly the gun might be treated, it would be highly improbable that any object could strike either sight to damage it. By making the wings of smooth, flowing contour, we'd also eliminate the snagging and holstering problems often encountered with the usual target-type sights.

If there is a common tendency regarding sights, it's to ignore them and their importance. Sights are what enable the shooter to extract and use the inherent accuracy of the gun—without them, you won't hit much, and if they aren't kept in good condition, the situation won't be much better.

Chapter Twenty-Three
Tuning for High-Ammunition Performance

The autoloader has a reputation for reliability less glowing than that of the revolver. As we've pointed out elsewhere in this tome, that reputation has not been truly deserved since the auto's formative days. By the World War I era, the self-loader had become of exemplar reliability when used with proper ammunition.

Unfortunately, the past decade or two has seen some changes in corporate attitudes and social climates which have hurt the auto—and the sixgun as well. Back in the 1950s, the arms plants were still peopled with the "old guard" at both machines and management desks. Production methods, too, were of the pre-jet and pre-nuclear age. Combine those factors, and one could be more than a little bit certain that parts would be made and assembled correctly, and that if on rare occasions they weren't, eagle-eyed and prerogative-jealous inspectors would make damned sure a "bad" gun never left the plant. Alas, but that it were so today.

New holding-company owners demand more profits; new generations of workers lack both pride and skill; costs of production have skyrocketed; replacement-machine, tool, and facility costs have leaped toward the stars; taxes, social security, governmentally demanded administrative and recording costs have multiplied. In short, making guns just ain't like it used to be. For every set of forgings and castings, management demands that a complete gun be invoiced out the door, no matter whether it is "right." Machining and finishing operations are modified or reduced toward that end, and the "ship 'em out" attitude pervades workers and inspectors alike.

Consequently, overall reliability of autos has declined in recent years; designs and materials have improved, but quality of manufacture has deteriorated. And at the same time, prices have gone up, up, up. A first-class used specimen that would bring maybe half of retail in the old days now often sells for virtually full list price, sometimes even more when demand is highest.

To be sure, the manufacturers are sort of between a rock and a hard place. On one hand they are pressured by astronomical cost increases, and on the other by unprecedented demand for their products. On top of that, there is the ever-present fear that government (big brother) will eventually destroy the civilian handgun market. The manufacturers are in an unenviable position.

While I can find some sympathy in my heart for that position, I still can in no way excuse the condition in which far too many new autos leave the factories. A brand-new gun which will not get through a single magazine-full of standard ball ammunition without serious difficulties—and I have seen more than a few—positively never should have been allowed out of the factory. Likewise, a new auto should not come fresh out of its box wearing an extractor which has apparently been broken and welded, then reblued, without even grinding down the weld. If that sounds extreme, perhaps it is, but I bought that particular gun myself. I'll admit that the extractor has not yet failed, but a broken and welded extractor (or any other part, for that matter) has absolutely no business whatever on a brand-new gun.

Among the other problems we've noted in new autos are excessive burrs where they interfere with the feeding of cartridges; horrible trigger pulls; magazines with twisted bodies or incorrectly formed feed lips; stripped stock-screw threads; chambers so rough as to cause extraction failures; burred chamber mouths which actually scrape shavings from incoming cartridges; large blowholes in cast components such as frames; rear sights rattling loosely in their seats, and front sights so improperly attached that recoil of the first few rounds hurls them off to be lost in the grass.

Certainly not all of those conditions—or the others one might encounter these days—can be corrected by the new owner, nor should it be necessary for him to do so. However, it is generally possible for him to correct those defective conditions which prevent the gun from achieving 100 percent functional reliability with the factory-loaded cartridges he wishes to use.

I have found that the first thing that should be done with the gun is to fire it with standard-ball cartridges, even if you have no intention of using this type later on. If the gun will feed ball ammunition reliably and otherwise function correctly, then it can't be too much trouble to tune it up for target and/or high-performance loads. On the other hand, if the gun does not function correctly and consistently with ball ammunition, the problems may be much greater. If problems do show up in the beginning with ball ammunition, the odds are in favor of them disappearing without help during the firing of about 200 rounds. If, after 200 rounds, the gun still doesn't work right, I'd strongly recommend returning it for a replacement or for repair. I'll admit that 200 rounds can be expensive, but in reality, it's a small price to pay if the shooting of it smooths out the gun's problems and enables you to avoid shipping the gun back for repair or replacement.

I will not personally rely upon the new autoloader (or, equally, a new revolver) until it has been fired at least 200 rounds for "break-in." As quality levels change, this break-in firing becomes more and more important. It is entirely possible that a gun fresh out of the box may function perfectly for the first, or perhaps a half-dozen magazines-full of cartridges, and yet show some feeding problems afterwards. It can be fatally embarassing to put 10 or 20 rounds through a new gun without difficulty and then discover a few weeks later that it hangs up in a fight. The only way I have ever discovered of ensuring that the gun may be expected to deliver perfect, functional reliability in the future is to break it in, just like you might do a new automobile. On a new gun (again auto *or* revolver) that functions perfectly or produces only minor malfunctions in the beginning, I continue shooting it with standard-ball ammunition, usually rapid fire, until it functions perfectly for 100 consecutive shots. If it hasn't shown evidence of the ability to do this by the time the first 200 rounds have been fired, then I begin tuning it.

The important thing to remember is that even if the gun begins its new life by functioning perfectly for a handful of rounds, you can only be certain of functional reliability in the future by continued break-in shooting until it demonstrates that it can perform perfectly for 100 consecutive shots. Even 100 perfect shots are probably not an adequate statistical indication, but in my experience, it has worked out well enough.

Another important factor in this break-in firing is the confidence you develop in the gun. Unless you are deplorably naïve, you can't really believe that the gun will function perfectly until its ability to do so has been demonstrated. And, unless you do believe that, you'll be under a psychological disadvantage. This won't be as much of a disadvantage as if the gun had actually demonstrated malfunctioning, but it certainly won't put you in nearly as good a position as will the actual demonstration of perfect functioning for 100 or more rounds.

Assuming that the gun has demonstrated at least reasonable reliability with ball ammunition, it's time to try it out with the high-performance or target loads that you have chosen. If you're lucky, the gun will handle the special loadings just as well as ball. But there's an excellent chance it will not.

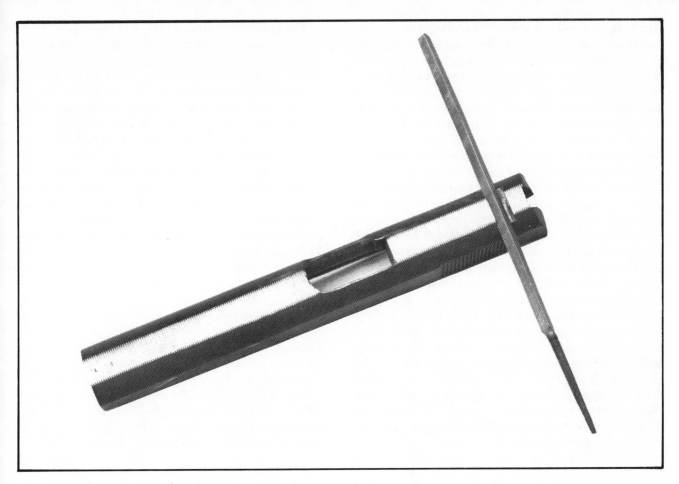

Use a fine triangular file for touching up the sight.

Failures to feed constitute the principal problems and they consist generally of the following, though variations may crop up:

A. Failure of the slide to pick up a fresh round from the magazine;

B. A nose-down jam of the cartridge where the bullet comes to rest wedged into the feed ramp, the base of the cartridge holding the slide open;

C. The cartridge jamming nose-up, with the bullet against the top of the chamber wall or underside of the barrel tang and either the slide against the base of the cartridge, or overriding the cartridge and denting the case somewhat ahead of the rim;

D. A cartridge jammed about halfway into the chamber, the head tipped down slightly, the slide held back by the base of the case;

E. The cartridge almost fully chambered, but the slide lacking 1/16 to 1/8 inch going fully into battery;

F. Condition B, C, D, where the bullet is pushed deeper into the case;

G. After firing, the empty case remaining in the chamber, and the next round jammed bullet-first into it;

H. After the shot, the slide closes and the gun appears normal, but fails to fire, and opening the slide discloses that the fired case is still in the chamber;

I. The fired case caught between the slide-breech face and the barrel;

J. After firing, the gun appears normal, but fails to fire, and opening the slide shows the chamber to be empty (with cartridges remaining in the magazine);

K. After firing one or more shots, the slide remains to the rear, failing to move forward, even though cartridges remain in the magazine;

L. After firing, the slide closes normally, the hammer remains properly cocked, but the trigger does not return forward to re-engage the sear; therefore, a subsequent shot cannot be fired.

The foregoing, as we said, are the malfunctions that will be encountered most often. They often aren't as clearly seen or defined as we've described and may be found in numerous variations and combinations. Some of the following corrective actions will apply to more than one of the common malfunctions, and some of those malfunctions will require more than one of the corrective actions. There isn't any way that we can cover every one of the possibilities that you might encounter, so we'll go through the corrective actions and tuning operations in detail, only generally relating them to the type of malfunction.

Any failure of the slide to pick up the next round from the magazine may be due either to the slide not moving far enough to the rear to allow the cartridge to rise in front of it, or to damage, defects, dirt, or rust which prevents the follower and its spring from raising the cartridges firmly against the underside of the feed lips. If the slide doesn't travel back far enough, excess friction may be slowing it down. This may be due to nicks, dents or burrs on the various sliding surfaces, or excessive dirt and fouling combined with inadequate lubrication. Aside from thorough cleaning and lubrication, remove burrs and polish out roughness on the guide rails in both slide and frame. Polish where the slide rides over the hammer to cock it, and also the top of the disconnector and the portion of the slide that rides over it. A barrel bushing too tight on the barrel can retard the slide and needs freeing.

Another contributing cause, but one which is not normally responsible alone, can be an excessively strong magazine spring which shoves cartridges too tightly against the underside of the slide, creating excessive friction there. This can usually be identified by heavily rubbed streaks on the underside of the slide and also upon the top cartridge in the magazine. Weakening the magazine spring by cutting off a coil or pinching a couple together may serve as a temporary fix, but it's far better to replace it with a new spring. Battered locking lugs or recesses may also slow the slide down, and if lockup is too tight, unlocking can absorb so much of the recoil impulse that there isn't enough left to drive the slide all the way back. These conditions require attention by the factory or a thoroughly competent pistolsmith; they're beyond the capability of the average pistolero.

One other factor seldom considered in this respect is the mainspring. An excessively strong mainspring requires much more of the recoil impulse to cock the hammer, and thus slows the slide down. In addition, dirt, rust, oxidized grease, nicks, burrs, or kinks in the spring can also make cocking much harder and have the same effect. Complete disassembly and thorough cleaning of the mainspring-housing unit will usually solve the problem unless the spring requires replacement. If the spring is too heavy and no replacement is

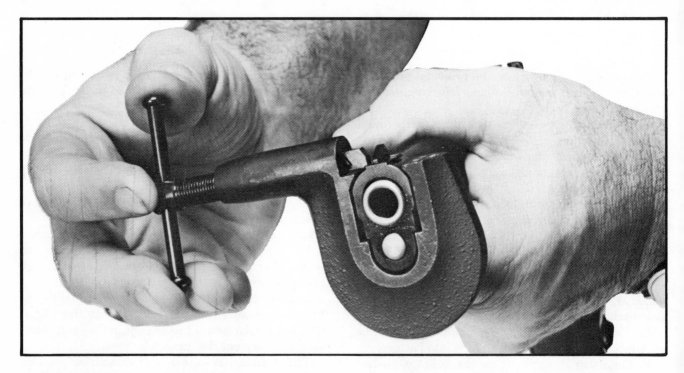

A P-210 showing front-sight pusher in use.

available, clipping off up to two-and-one-half coils constitutes an acceptable temporary repair, but a new spring should be installed as soon as possible.

Magazine feed lips that have been bent, or perhaps just dented inward, may hold the top cartridge too low to be caught by the slide on its counter-recoil stroke. While some people seem to have the knack for straightening and restoring feed lips, most don't, and I must include myself in the latter. Generally, if the feed lips are bad, you'll save time, money, temper and frustration by simply replacing the magazine; if a complete magazine assembly seems too costly, try buying just a new body and installing the original inner parts in it. If it seems unlikely that a new gun would have a damaged magazine, think again: Being dropped once by the packer can mess up any magazine.

Roughness or irregularity on the feed ramp can cause the nose of the bullet—particularly if there is any exposed lead—to jam there, bringing the cartridge and the slide to a screeching halt. One-piece feed ramps such as the Browning and S&W need only light polishing, but the divided type found in the Colt/Browning design, may leave a sharp-edged shelf where the two parts fail to meet in proper alignment. This is pure poison and requires the two parts to be ground or polished into proper alignment. It is also sometimes helpful to break the sharp edges of the joint slightly.

The best tool I've found for polishing feed ramps is a green "Cratex" mounted tip used in a Dremel Moto-Tool or similar hand grinder. This particular tip cuts fast enough to do the job with reasonable dispatch and yet is fine enough to leave a smooth, well-polished surface. Don't make the mistake of using an ordinary coarse grinding wheel or a file of any sort, except the very finest-cut needle type. Aside from removing roughness and any overlap (in the two-piece ramp), don't change the angle or radius of the feed ramp. When polishing the ramp, take particular care not to cut its upper end deeper into the chamber. This area is already a weak spot in most autoloader designs, and increasing its size is sure to result in ruptured cases.

In most guns, the upper edge of the feed ramp breaks into the lower chamber wall leaving a sharp edge. Even if there are no burrs along this edge, its sharpness will often dig into the cartridge case, not only to prevent chambering, but peeling off brass shavings which can eventually foul the action. That same Cratex tip can be used to very lightly break this sharp edge and polish it smooth. A sure sign that the edge is too sharp is a distinct scrape mark on the cartridge case, usually commencing about midway on the body and extending back to the head, often actually outlining the curve of that sharp edge.

Any failure to feed in which the cartridge comes to rest with the head down and not moving properly up under the extractor may be partially caused by roughness on the slide-breech face. In most guns, during early stages of feeding, the case head must move smoothly up over this breech face. If this area is roughly machined or burred, the additional friction and interference may keep the head from moving up smoothly. The rim must also move up under the extractor, and burred or sharp-edged extractor claws seem most common these days. Light stoning, particularly on the lower edge of the hook, will help a great deal. Excessive spring tension on the extractor may cause the same trouble, preventing the case rim from moving up under it.

I have also encountered some new guns in which the entire slide-breech face was not machined-out wide enough to accommodate some of the case rims that are encountered in factory ammunition. Smith & Wesson had quite a rash of this on the M39 several years ago. The machining operation also sometimes leaves burrs at the bottom which are not removed at the factory, and these may also interfere with proper feeding.

In short, anything in the area of the slide-breech face which might impede upward travel of the case head should be cleaned up.

Failure of the slide to go fully into battery after the cartridge has entered the chamber correctly may be due to too-tight lockup (which we've already mentioned) or perhaps shaving of the cartridge case by a sharp chamber mouth. While polishing the feed ramp, it's an excellent idea to radius and polish lightly the entire circumference of the chamber mouth. Of course, this can't be done in the area of the barrel tang found on some models, but all the rest should be given this treatment. It's also possible that the mouth of a case might snag on such a sharp edge, so even if it hasn't given any trouble yet, the mouth should be radiused and polished.

A number of feeding malfunctions—in fact, most of those already mentioned—can be at least partially caused by lack of slide momentum as it runs forward. This can be caused by a weak or kinked recoil spring, or by the slide not moving all the way to the rear on the previous shot.

If the slide stop suddenly engages and holds the action open even though cartridges remain in the magazine, first look at the inward projection which is normally contacted by the magazine follower after the last shot has been fired. I've known this projection to extend too far inward to the point that some shapes of bullets would occasionally nudge it upward as the cartridges were elevated, thus pushing the stop up to engage the slide at the wrong time. If this is the case, file or grind the projection a wee bit shorter.

The slide stop may also bounce up from recoil disturbance and engage the slide if it isn't held securely enough by the detent spring and plunger which usually hold it down. Correction here is obvious. Of course, you might encounter the opposite situation where the slide stop is not pushed up to hold the action open after the last shot is fired. A rough or burred plunger or a plunger spring that is too strong can combine with a weak magazine spring to cause this problem. Polish the plunger and replace the spring(s) and the problem usually disappears. A bent follower can also cause this.

Extraction and ejection failures are more often caused by either inadequate recoil impulse (from the cartridge) or a recoil spring too stiff for the load being used. Generally speaking, all of the high-performance loads produce quite adequate recoil impulses, but when we get into the light target loads, it's another matter entirely. If the model gun involved is one for which a light target-type recoil spring isn't available from the manufacturer (as it is in the case of the Colt GM family), then the spring may be shortened one-half coil at a time until the slide moves back smartly as it should. Just make certain that the mainspring remains sufficiently strong to run the slide fully into battery reliably.

An extraction problem may also be due to a rough chamber (reamer marks, chatter marks, etc.) which causes the case to stick more tightly than normal and thus absorb too much of the recoil impulse in being loosened. Under these conditions, it's possible for the slide to come back, draw the case from the chamber, but stop and start forward again before the case can be struck by the ejector. When this happens, the case will most likely be shoved right back in the chamber. Then, when you open the gun up, it may look as if the slide never opened. In a situation like this, the slide may also move back just far enough for the case to be only lightly touched by the ejector without being hurled clear, then as the slide runs forward, it carries the case with it, jamming it between the slide and barrel breech, perhaps in the classic "smokestack" position.

If you encounter a chamber rough enough to cause this problem in a new gun, the manufacturer owes you a new barrel, though a competent pistolsmith could probably cure the problem by careful polishing, so long as it doesn't enlarge the chamber too much. You may also encounter a gun in which the ejected cases catch on the edge of the ejection port and might occasionally tumble back to be caught as the slide runs forward. If you frequently get a case caught in this fashion and you know the slide is coming all the way back, then look for brass marks around the ejection port where the case may be snagging. Filing a slight relief at that point will usually cure the problem.

Though it happens rarely, you might encounter an improperly located magazine-catch notch which results in the magazine being held just a tiny bit too low for the slide to pick up the top round. Alternatively, I have seen magazine catches which were defective and caused the same problem. In either case, the manufacturer owes you a new part, and there isn't really any practical way you can correct the condition otherwise.

Occasionally a new gun may show up on the market which simply cannot accept all of the different loads currently available. When I obtained my first H&K P9S, I very shortly discovered that while it would handle most other loads well enough, it was chambered so that the Super Vel 112-grain JHP load made heavy contact with the origin of the rifling and would even prevent the slide from going fully into battery. Another possibility was that the bullet would stick there so tightly that opening the action was very difficult. The bearing surface on this bullet extended just a slight amount further forward than the ball bullets for which the gun was chambered. This probably resulted from the fact that at the time the P9S design was finalized and the factory tooled-up for the gun, this particular 9mm Parabellum loading was not available. Obviously, then, the manufacturer couldn't have made certain that the gun would handle it. If you encounter a situation of this sort, don't attempt to correct it yourself, but refer the job to the seller, importer or manufacturer, or, as an alternative, to a first-class pistolsmith.

If we extend maximum reliability to include sustained fire and rapid reloading, you'll want to check to make absolutely certain that all of your magazines will drop freely from the gun when the magazine release is punched after the last shot is fired. Make equally certain that the magazines may be inserted quickly and freely to lock up solidly in a single smooth thrust. If some resistance is encountered, then first try polishing the sides of the magazine, and if that doesn't clear the problem up, deburr the inside of the magazine well very carefully.

If you're not already thoroughly familiar with the

behavior of autoloaders and their limitations in ammunition, perhaps you wonder why high-performance and light target-loads are likely to cause feeding and functioning problems in guns that work well with ball ammunition. Autoloaders are designed to be functioned by a certain amount of recoil energy or recoil impulse produced by the firing of the cartridge. In short, if a given load does not produce recoil energy falling between the minimum and maximum limits designed into the gun, then the mechanism won't function correctly. If the recoil impulse is too light, then there will not be sufficient energy to drive all the moving parts. If the recoil impulse is too heavy, the moving parts will be "over-driven," and the likelihood of excessive wear, battering, and parts breakage increases very quickly.

The ball-cartridge loading around which the design originated represents the middle of this recoil-impulse range. Characteristically, target loads produce substantially less recoil impulse, and a fair number of the high-performance loads on the market produce substantially more. Therefore, the recoil impulse of the target load is generally marginal for a standard-production gun, and any of the interfering factors described in the last few pages can absorb more energy than is available for cycling the moving parts. This makes it especially important that the gun for use with target loads have all springs properly regulated and all friction reduced wherever possible; it also makes proper lubrication quite important.

When we turn over the page and look at high-performance loads, we find that their recoil impulse isn't really high enough to cause any serious functional problems, and if one is concerned about battering or over-driving, installation of a recoil buffer will handle things quite well. The real problem with high-performance loads is that most of them use bullets of substantially less weight than the standard ball type.

Lighter bullets mean shorter bullets; shorter bullets mean shorter overall cartridge length. It might seem that it would be simple enough for the shorter bullets to be seated farther out in the case to obtain standard cartridge length, but it doesn't work out quite that way. Efficient combustion of the powder charges involved requires a fairly stiff bullet pull, and the violent stresses placed upon the cartridge during feeding both require that the bullet be seated rather deeply. The end result is a cartridge substantially shorter than the ball round. Since all elements of the feed system have been designed around the longer ball round, the shorter high-performance round doesn't behave or move in exactly the same manner during its passage from magazine to chamber. So long as there are no outside interferences, these shorter loads will generally feed well enough in the more popular guns. However, this isn't always true for some of the older models such as the Luger/Parabellum. The more recent Walther P38 simply will not feed some of the high-performance loads reliably, no matter how much tuning is done. Generally, this is due to the fact that the cartridge has a greater distance to travel between feed lips and chamber and is not provided with a substantial feed ramp as in other designs.

In addition, high-performance bullets are not of the same profile as the round-nose metal-jacketed ball projectile. A soft point (JHP) can be designed with the same profile as the ball bullet, but in addition to being shorter, it must have at least some soft lead exposed at the nose. This can deform upon impact with the feed ramp, and if the ramp is rough or interrupted, this may result in its jamming there. Of course, the exposed lead can be made harder to resist deformation and jamming, but then the extent and consistency of expansion are both reduced, and a large part of the soft-point effect is lost.

In hollow-point (JHP) bullets, there is simply no way to avoid the bullet having a flat nose in profile while still making the cavity large enough to ensure a reasonable degree of expansion. The result is that all hollow-point bullets either look like a round-nose type with the tip cut off flat or a truncated cone.

Incidentally, in this scribe's well-considered opinion based upon over a decade of experience with high-performance loads, the best feeding shape for the bullet is the truncated cone-nose; the best construction, whether JHP or JSP, consists of the jacket carried fully forward so that no lead is exposed when the bullet is viewed in profile, and, therefore, no soft lead can contact the feed ramp. This bullet form is by no means new, dating back to the turn of the century, but it reached the epitome of its development in calibers of 9mm and above in the now discontinued original Super Vel designs developed by Lee E. Jurras of Shelbyville, Indiana.

In any event, what causes the major feeding problems is the combination of shorter loaded-cartrdge length and different bullet shape.

Because of the fact that the numerous high-performance loads (and to a lesser extent, target loads) do differ in length and profile, you can often eliminate feeding and functioning problems by switching to another make or bullet weight. For instance, a gun that will not feed a round-nose JHP bullet with sufficient reliability may very well handle perfectly a truncated-cone bullet, or an RN design of a different profile. It may also handle one of the semi-RN, JHP loads better. It may be expensive, I know, but often it will be well worth your while to try one or two different loads if the first one causes any trouble. Even if it works out that way, it's still a good idea to tune the gun up so that it works correctly with as wide a variety of ammunition as possible. After all, there'll probably come a time when you won't have immediate access to the one or perhaps two or three load(s) which it will handle perfectly.

Chapter Twenty-Four
Specialty Guns

s much as we like autoloaders, we recognize that hen one gets into the firearms usage field deeply, we nd particular needs that they can't meet. This oesn't reflect on the auto, for there aren't any other andguns of conventional form that will do those jobs ther. Even the average shooter will eventually find at there are particular firearms applications that rdinary guns can't meet—he may also find that some f those applications are actually quite useful, even tally important. The professional gun carrier will nd even more special uses and will discover that nconventional firearms that possess some handgun aaracteristics are needed to fulfill them.

Let's begin with some of the simpler items. The Pen Gun" was once fairly popular, but in recent ears BATF has clamped down on it, even those not tended for firing ball cartridges. (Incidentally, I was ice in London preparing to board a plane for South frica, when the airport security guards stopped my aveling partner, removed the large old-fashioned untain pen from his breast pocket and opened it to ake certain that it wasn't a disguised gun.)

The pen gun has been made in two forms, one actually intended to fire conventional pistol ammunition, the other made only to fire gas or pyrotechnic cartridges. Construction is essentially the same for both types, consisting of a short thin-walled barrel chambered at one end to receive the cartridge, and threaded (usually, though bayonet-type attachments are known) for the attachment of a long cap which contains a spring-backed firing pin and a rudimentary firing mechanism. In its simplest form, the firing mechanism consists simply of firing pin and spring, with a small rod or knob protruding from one side of the pin through a slot in the side of the cap. The mechanism is cocked by pulling back on the knob, compressing the firing-pin spring, then rotating the knob into a notch in the side of the slot. Firing is then accomplished by simply thumbing the knob out of the notch so that the spring drives the firing pin forward.

This design is usually also supplied with a hook-shaped safety notch so that the entire device may be carried in safety when loaded and cocked. This type of pen is loaded—whether with a bulleted cartridge or some other type—by unscrewing the barrel from the cap, finger-seating the cartridge in the chamber, then screwing the two parts back together. The firing mechanism is ordinarily cocked before loading and placed in the safety position for the simple reason that the nose of the firing pin would otherwise be forced against the primer. Not a very good idea.

The pen gun has been made in several forms, with those intended for ball cartridges usually of the type just described, though the firing mechanisms are sometimes more complex. When ball ammunition is intended, the gun must be of relatively sturdy steel construction. Those made only for firing gas or pyrotechnic cartridges can be made much lighter and more compact inasmuch as chamber pressures for such ammunition are very low. One of the most interesting such devices I've seen is a two-barreled unit composed of stamped-steel halves spot-welded together. It was intended only for pyrotechnic or gas cartridges and was supplied in a neat little kit containing several rounds of ammunition.

The use of ball cartridges in a pen gun should be easily understood. Also, the use of cartridges expelling a small cloud of tear gas or other noxious gas, powder, or liquid for defensive purposes makes sense. Unfortunately, many people place far too much faith in the tiny amount of chemical agent contained in a cartridge of reasonable size (usually 38 caliber). The range of the agent is only a very few feet, and it disperses widely and rapidly. As a practical matter, unless such a cartridge is fired directly at an antagonist's face at a range of no more than two or three feet, the effect is minimal. Possession of a pen gun and gas cartridges may be of substantial psychological value, but a reasonably determined antagonist will hardly be more than slightly inconvenienced by the discharge. In short, don't count on a gas cartridge.

The use of pyrotechnic or "flare cartridges" is less well understood. They are not intended for defensive (or even offensive) purposes; however, I'm certain that if one were fired into the face or body of an attacker, it would certainly upset him, probably a good deal more than a gas cartridge. The primary purpose of flare cartridges is signaling or communication. The pyrotechnic element may be projected as much as 200 or more feet vertically from the typical 38 Special cartridge and is designed to produce maximum visibility at the peak of its flight.

Different types have been made, some of which simply burn brilliantly, producing a single point of light, while others are of the "star cluster" type which burst and throw off numerous glowing particles. They are available in a variety of colors, with red, green and white predominating. In the past, they have bee[n] promoted for use as distress signals by outdoorsme[n] (hunters, canoeists, hikers, etc.) and for that applica[tion color doesn't really matter. However, by usin[g] varying combinations of colors and numbers of flare[s] simple and brief prearranged messages can be se[nt] over rather long distances. In reasonably good weath[er], some of the better flares are visible for sever[al] miles, so signaling can be carried out between huntin[g] camps, between remote residences, etc.

While on the subject of flare cartridges, we shoul[d] point out that if one has a real need for this type o[f] signaling or communication, he isn't necessaril[y] limited to the small 38 caliber pen gun. Proper "fla[re] pistols" or "pyrotechnic pistols" are available and a[re] standard equipment on water craft and some aircraf[t]. In literature, one sees frequent reference to a "Ver[y] pistol" and this name is often applied to the enti[re] class, regardless of name or maker. Such pistols a[re] generally large, hinged-frame single-shot guns cham[-] bered for a special flare or pyrotechnic loading of t[he] 12-gauge shotgun shell. Larger calibers will also b[e] encountered, up to 37mm. In 12-bore and larger, t[he] pyrotechnic element has greater range, will bur[n] much more brightly for a longer period of time, an[d] may be of parachute type so that it hangs in the air f[or] a considerable period of time. Illuminating flares a[re] also available, so the big-bore flare pistols becom[e] much more useful. Compared to the true flare pist[ol] and its ammunition, the pen gun and its tiny fla[re] cartridges might seem to have little value. Howeve[r,] they possess the admirable virtue of light weigh[t,] compactness, and low cost. A hiker isn't likely to car[ry] a two-pound 12-bore flare pistol and its heav[y] ammunition, but he can tuck away a 38 pen g[un] without any inconvenience whatever.

A variation on the pen gun theme is a concealab[le] firearm formerly manufactured and sold by MA[C] (Military Armaments Corporation) for law enforc[e]ment and military use and named "Stinger." This [is] really nothing but a short 22 caliber pen gun ma[de] more or less in the shape and size of an egg so that [it] can be handled and controlled more easily.

Machine pistols (submachine guns) and pisto[l] carbines are logical developments of autoloadi[ng] pistols which possess substantial virtues for son[e] applications. Few people in this country associate t[he] machine pistol with a true pistol, but over the pa[st] couple of decades there have been some remarkab[le] compact developments in this field. Most promine[nt] of the type is the MAC Model 11, not current[ly] manufactured, sometimes also referred to as t[he] Ingram M11 after its inventor/designer. The M[AC]

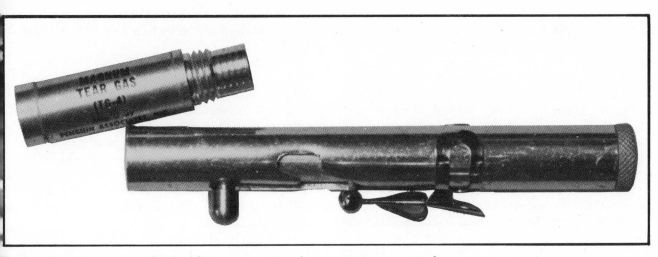

Don't count on the gas cartridge fired from your pen gun: it may not stop your attacker.

SMG is no heavier than the 45 GM pistol, though it is somewhat bulkier. Nevertheless, with its wire shoulder-stock telescoped and without the silencer or suppressor often supplied with it, it can be carried in a conventional belt holster with hardly any more inconvenience than a typical big-bore autoloading pistol and fired as a handgun. This little gem is chambered for the 380 ACP cartridge, firing from a 30-shot magazine at a cyclic rate in the vicinity of 2000 rounds per minute.

A comparable and more recent development is the Heckler & Koch VP-70 machine pistol. This unit is even more compact and upon casual observation appears to be simply an autoloading pistol of conventional size and configuration. It is chambered for the 9mm Parabellum cartridge and is no larger or heavier than the Browning HP pistol. However, it can be fired double-action only (for all shots) when employed as a conventional pistol, and it is of straight blowback operation.

This weapon is supplied with a molded plastic holster unit intended to be attached to a gunbelt in the usual fashion. However, when it is desired to employ the gun in the full-automatic role, the holster is removed from the belt and attached to the upper rear of the pistol receiver. The holster then functions as a short carbine stock, and the gun may be fired from the shoulder for better control and accuracy at longer ranges. Perhaps the VP-70's most unique characteristic is that when the holster/stock is attached, a finger on the stock attachment enters a hole in the frame of the gun and engages a limited-burst full-automatic firing mechanism.

Once this connection has been made—and only when it has been made—the full-auto system is engaged, and pressure on the trigger will cause the gun to fire in machine-gun fashion at a cyclic rate in the vicinity of 2200 rounds per minute. Obviously, free firing at that rate would empty the magazine far too quickly, so a "burst limiter" is incorporated. This is a simple ratchet device that permits only a particular number of shots to be fired with a single pull of the trigger. Press the trigger, the gun will fire three or five shots (depending upon the version) and stop, even though the trigger continues to be held down.

To the best of my knowledge, only the VP-70 possesses these unique characteristics. Used as a pistol, without attaching the stock, it functions conventionally as a double-action-only blowback type and is relatively compact and light of weight. With the stock attached, it not only offers shoulder-weapon accuracy at moderate ranges, but massive volume of fire where circumstances require it. Other pistol-carbines exist, the best known being the old broom-handle Mauser with its wood holster stock, the Parabellum/Luger with its board stock, and the World War II version of the Browning HP with a wood holster stock as employed by Canadian and Chinese military forces. While none of those are currently manufactured and existing specimens fall under the very severe restrictions of GCA'68, Star Bonifacio Echeverria in Spain does still occasionally manufacture a few examples of its big-frame Browning-type auto fitted for a wood holster/stock.

Probably the most unusual device which can be equated with a handgun is the "Tazer," introduced as a non-lethal weapon replacement for conventional firearms a few years back. It was introduced at the peak of the do-gooder's outcry against police use of firearms against criminals. We won't belabor the point here, but it seems utterly ridiculous, even incomprehensible, to me that there should be a large number of supposedly intelligent and adult people in this country who are apparently obsessed with preventing police from even injuring, much less killing criminals. Nevertheless, a great deal of social and political pressure has been exerted during recent years to limit the use or even the possession of firearms by law enforcement officers. At the peak of this gibberish, the Tazer was introduced. Immediately the same people attacked its use as weird.

Essentially, the Tazer consists of a high-voltage power system connected to two barbed, steel darts by hair-thin trailing wires. The darts and the coiled wires are contained in a replaceable cartridge that seats in the front of the device. The Tazer is simply pointed at a victim, the "firing" trigger is pressed, and the darts are expelled at considerable velocity. They pierce the clothing of the individual and enter his flesh, at which point the electrical circuit is closed through the body and a high-voltage electrical shock is administered automatically. This shock is strong enough to instantly immobilize a typical adult human, but yet is sufficiently limited that it will do no permanent injury to a reasonably healthy person. While often touted as a replacement for the handgun, it possesses numerous disadvantages which prevent it from fulfilling that role.

First, the range of the Tazer is only 12 to 15 feet at best under ideal conditions, and often less. Second, the darts are not particularly accurate, and the electrical shock cannot be administered unless both darts at least engage the skin of the target. In addition, the Tazer is bulky, heavy and not nearly so easy and convenient to carry or use as a conventional handgun.

The Tazer can be a very important adjunct to conventional firearms, and it offers tremendous possibilities for certain conditions, but in no way can it replace the firearm.

Incidentally, while the Tazer was not classified as a deadly weapon when first introduced, there was a frantic effort made by anti-gun and anti-violence interests to limit its availability, possession, and use. The result of all this was that a non-lethal weapon designed particularly for personal defense was immediately limited in its availability by administrative classification as a firearm by the BATF. While this is a deplorable situation, it is almost amusing to note that those vocal people who objected most to the Tazer were the same people who object so strenuously to the

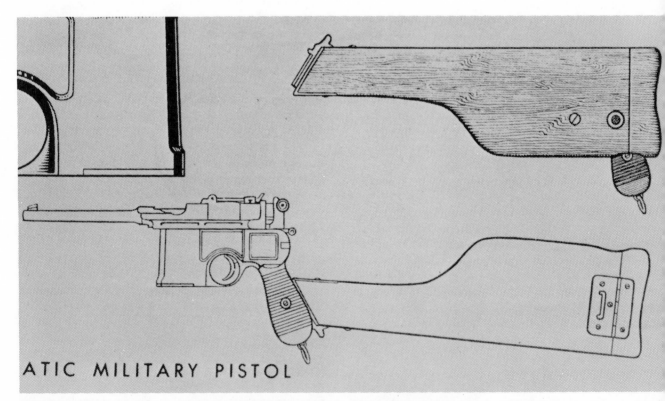

ATIC MILITARY PISTOL

The old broom-handle Mauser (shown here with wooden stock) is the best known of the pistol carbines.

use of firearms by police and are always screaming for non-lethal weapons to be used instead.

There are numerous other unconventional weapons intended to either augment or replace the conventional handgun in unusual situations where a person must be unobtrusively armed. Examples might be (and these do exist): a 22 RF firing device concealed in a cigarette lighter or tobacco pipe; an auto pistol or machine pistol built into an attaché case and fired remotely through a mechanical or electrical trigger concealed in the handle; and a grenade-launching device fitted as an accessory to a pistol. The latter is a cup-shaped gadget clamped to the muzzle of the gun, into which a gas, pyrotechnic or other specialized grenade may be fitted and launched by a special blank cartridge fired in the gun. Much other gun-like gadgetry crops up from time-to-time, but most of it is so highly specialized that it means nothing to the typical pistolero.

Doubtless, we'll see more devices like these as time goes by. Even so, I don't think they'll ever be of more than academic interest to ordinary shooters.

Chapter Twenty-Five
Double Action Versus Single Action

Traditionally, big-bore service-type autoloading pistols have been of single-action persuasion. They have had large, exposed hammers which required manual cocking for firing the first shot (as in a single-action revolver) and the hammer remains at full-cock for subsequent shots, having been cocked by rearward slide travel. Though experimental guns had been made utilizing revolver-type double-action firing methods, none had ever seen quantity production in this country before World War II.

In Europe, Walther developed the P38 pistol which was adopted by the German Army in 1938—a very advanced double-action pistol. About the same time Czechoslovakia adopted a Brno design in which every shot had to be fired double action; there was no cocked-hammer position, and the hammer followed the slide down after each shot. Though the Brno M38 was of only 380 ACP caliber, by governmental adoption, size, and usage, it classified as a service arm. The Brno was never offered for sale here, and did not survive World War II. The P38 was advertised in this country for a short time before the war began, but as a practical matter, it simply wasn't available.

As a result of all this, prior to the early 1940s, an individual was not faced with a choice between single-action and double-action when selecting a service autoloader. During and after the war, thousands of P38s and a few Czech M38s showed up as war trophies, but, aside from their curiosity value, they had little effect, and the single-action auto continued to reign supreme. In the 1950s, Walther resumed manufacture of the P38, albeit in slightly modified form, and it became readily available in this country through Interarms, the importer and exclusive distributor. Further, Smith & Wesson introduced its now-famous M39 double-action auto to the civilian market, having failed to obtain the large military contracts for which the gun had really been designed. Then, in the mid-to-late 1960s, Heckler & Koch introduced its almost-revolutionary double-action P9S pistol, though it was not available in the U.S. in sufficient quantity to provide much more than conversation. Now, nearly a decade later, we find ourselves exposed to another unique double-action, big-bore pistol, the SIG/Sauer P220. There are other double-action designs waiting in the wings, a few of

The Heckler & Koch P9S pistol, which was an exciting addition to the double-action scene in the 1960s.

which will surely see production in the not too distant future, and several more that will probably drop quietly out of sight.

Many thousands of U.S. soldiers were exposed to the P38 pistol during the war, and Lord knows how many civilians encountered this gun on the used market during the late 1940s when like-new examples could be picked up at prices that now seem ridiculously low. A lot of those people got the idea that it sure would be nice to have that double-action feature on other big-bore autos, particularly the 45 GM. Diehard 45 auto buffs didn't think much of the idea, while revolver enthusiasts who envied the auto's advantages but not the necessity of firing that fire shot single-action, eyed the P38s double-action capability because the gun could be drawn and fired just as they were accustomed to doing with DA sixguns. Some shooters developed considerable enthusiasm, and spoke glowingly of the double-action auto as the sidearm of the future. Others laughed, and some stated flatly that it would be impossible to shoot quickly and accurately when the first shot was fired double-action and subsequent shots single-action. As a matter of fact, quite a few people parrot that last story.

As long as the P38 was the only double-action big-bore auto around, and as long as it was available only as a used, war trophy, few serious gun-carrier paid it much mind. However, when in the 1950s i became available as new production from German and was accompanied by the even newer S&W M3 made domestically, people began to pay a bit mor attention.

Two schools of thought grew up, one stating tha the double-action auto was superior as a servic sidearm to the single-action type. The other schoo contended just as strongly that it was not. If yo regularly peruse shooting periodicals, you'll see bot sides of the argument bandied about in print with fai frequency. The question has not yet been resolved t the satisfaction of all parties to the argument, and don't really expect that my comments here will do s Nevertheless, after 40-odd years experience with a manner of autoloading pistols, I have developed som fairly firm views on the subject, I shall set them fort here.

Before doing so, though, we must set forth som ground rules for the discussion. In order to make an valid comparisons between the two types, we have t make the assumption that we have single-action an double-action pistols of the same caliber, essentiall the same configuration and weight, and with at least high degree of similarity in all their other characteris tics. We can't just compare the single-action Colt GM

Smith & Wesson Model 59 9mm Double-Action Automatic Pistol.

Smith & Wesson 39 9mm Double-Action Automatic Pistol.

with the double-action S&W M39—there are too many other differences between those two guns and they cannot help but adversely affect a comparison. We must also assume that both guns represent the current state of the art, are good designs and contain proper materials and workmanship. We must also assume that both guns incorporate the customary safety features that we are familiar with on both types. With all that established, then, we can make an intelligent comparison of single-action and double-action autos.

Differences between the two lie mainly in handling and in safety to the extent that handling affects safety. To be prepared for immediate action, the single-action pistol must be carried in condition one, with a round chambered, the hammer at full-cock, and the manual safety engaged. To be equally ready, the double-action pistol must be carried with a round chambered, the hammer down and the manual safety disengaged.

In that condition, both guns are completely safe when carried in a holster. It is conceivable that if a holster were poorly designed and fitted, relative movement of the SA gun might under some circumstances cause the safety to become disengaged, setting the stage for an inadvertent firing when the gun is drawn or otherwise removed from the holster. However, we can't consider this a disadvantage inasmuch as we must assume that a proper holster will be used. On the other hand, the double-action pistol cannot similarly be made less safe by an ill-fitting holster or carrying method. If the gun is carried simply tucked into the waistband as is often done, there is the possibility (and it has happened to me) that body movement might cause the safety to become disengaged. This cannot happen to the double-action pistol.

At this point, I'd say that the double-action pistol might be very slightly ahead from a theoretical viewpoint, but not as a practical matter.

Carried as described, the two guns present different appearances. We've mentioned earlier that the mere appearance of the cocked single-action hammer incites concern and sometimes even fear in observers. Since the double-action pistol is carried hammer-down, this effect does not occur. This "intimidation factor" (as I choose to call it) of the cocked single-action pistol can be either an advantage or disadvantage, depending upon circumstances and one's viewpoint. It can be an advantage for a police officer in a ticklish spot, or a disadvantage if he's simply on post and surrounded by fearful, law-abiding citizens.

I see no advantage to either gun.

If either gun is dropped, from the holster or from the hand, it should be equally safe from inadvertent discharge. If the single-action pistol falls on its hammer, the manual safety will prevent firing. If the double-action pistol falls similarly, the impact on the hammer cannot be transferred sufficiently to the firing pin to cause firing. If either gun falls and strikes very hard on its muzzle, inadvertent firing may result if there is no automatic firing-pin safety, but neither will if such a safety exists. Again, no advantage either way, since we must assume that the two guns will be similar in this respect.

In drawing from the holster and firing the first shot quickly and accurately, the two guns are handled differently. With the single-action auto, the hand comes down, grasps the butt, and as the gun is pulled from the holster, the thumb curls down over the manual safety, rotating it downward to disengage. As the gun clears the leather, the forefinger goes into the trigger guard against the trigger, ready for slight rearward travel and four to five pounds pressure to fire the gun as it comes to bear on target.

With the double-action pistol, the hand grasps the butt and pulls the gun from the holster, with the forefinger entering the trigger guard to apply perhaps 11 or 12 pounds of pressure and about one-half-inch movement to fire as the gun comes to bear on target.

The only differences between the two are that on the SA one must have his thumb trained to disengage the safety during the draw; on the DA, the trigger finger has to apply more pressure through a greater distance. From past performance, we know that the first shot with either gun can be delivered with equal speed and accuracy, assuming a reasonable amount of training with that particular gun. Many years of experience with revolvers, as well as autos, have shown that there's no difference in the speed or short-range accuracy of the first shot on the draw, regardless of whether it is fired single-action or double-action.

After the first shot has been fired from the draw, both guns remain at full cock, and the second shot must be fired single-action. Here is where some authorities differ; the second and subsequent shots from the SA pistol are fired from the same trigger-finger position as the first and by application of the same amount of pressure. With the DA pistol, after the first shot, the trigger does not return fully forward but comes to rest at a position closely approximating that of the SA pistol. Further, the second and subsequent shots require much lighter pressure on the trigger, on the order of four to five pounds.

Several authorities have contended that this

change in finger position and trigger pressure between the first and second shots will have a deleterious effect on the shooter's ability to continue to fire rapidly and accurately. I can concede that this might be true only if the shooter had substantial experience with the SA pistol and was shooting the DA type for the first time, or without any training whatever. Assuming equal experience and training with both types of guns, this relatively minor shift in position and pressure does not interfere in the least with continuing accurate fire.

There are conditions under which a police officer might find it necessary or desirable to shift the gun to his weak hand in order to keep a suspect covered while performing some other operation with the normal shooting hand. If this is done with the SA pistol in the cocked and locked condition, then it will be difficult, if not impossible, to fire a shot quickly. This is caused by the fact that the manual safety is on the left side of the gun intended for operation by the right thumb. If the gun is in the left hand, the safety can only be disengaged by twisting the gun in the hand and contorting the forefinger to hook it over the safety and pull it down, after which the gun has to be re-gripped, re-pointed, and then fired. A possibly fatal delay can be injected in this fashion. On the other hand, if the double-action pistol is shifted to the weak hand in this fashion, it can be fired instantaneously by simply pulling the trigger: There is no manual safety to be disengaged, and thus no extraneous operations to interfere with getting off a rapid shot.

After firing, the two guns must also be treated differently to make them safe. Obviously, both guns remain at full-cock after firing and must be made safe before being returned to the holster. With the SA gun, the manual safety is simply engaged and the gun holstered. The DA gun requires that the safety first be engaged to drop the hammer properly, then disengaged to make the gun ready for action. I see no advantage on either side in this operation.

In reloading hurriedly under fire, both guns are handled in exactly the same manner. Their differences in lockwork have no effect whatever on ejecting the empty magazine, inserting a full magazine, and closing the action by depressing the slide stop. Again, no advantage either way.

While the two types may be initially loaded in the same fashion, the hammer-dropping/hammer-blocking safety of the DA pistol may and should be employed to make the operation more safe. When the SA pistol is loaded, whether from the open-breech or closed-breech condition, the slide must be allowed to run forcibly forward to chamber the first round and this must be done with the manual safety disengaged.

Experience has shown that occasionally the shock of the slide slamming into battery may jar the sear out of engagement, causing the hammer to fall and be caught by the intercept notch. This can cause slight damage to the sear nose, and occasionally, for no discernible reason (and again, this has happened to me), the hammer may jar off the sear and fall all the way to fire the chambered round. This can be guarded against by holding the hammer back with the thumb as the slide runs forward. In fact, this is what most target shooters do with their finely accurized guns.

With the DA auto, the safety may be engaged before loading. Thus, when the slide slams forward to chamber the first cartridge, the hammer will ride down behind the slide, and at the same time the firing pin is securely blocked so that firing cannot take place. Then, after the round is chambered, the DA safety is disengaged, preparing the gun for instant action. On the other hand, the safety of the SA auto must be engaged, preparing it for holstering. In this particular area, admitting that the hammer follow-down is not common and that firing during loading as described is rare, the double-action auto has a distinct edge in that the problem is completely eliminated.

There may be other minor differences between the single-action and double-action autos which could be explored if we wanted to get into nit-picking, but I don't think it would serve any useful purpose at this time. As we've gone through various operations with the two guns, we've seen relatively minor advantages fall on both sides. When we get to the end of the comparison, I can't really say that there is any overwhelming advantage with either type. In balance, though, it is clear in my mind that the double-action autoloading pistol does possess a modest margin of advantage over the single-action type.

If an individual is properly trained with either type, then he should be fully as effective and as safe with it as a comparable person equally trained with the other type.

What it all boils down to is that even though I prefer the double-action pistol, there are no significant disadvantages or advantages and if an individual takes the time to learn to handle either type properly, then he'll do as well as he would with the other.

Chapter Twenty-Six
Autoloader Functioning

Since the Colt Government Model is the most common locked-breech autoloader in use in this country, and because it is very closely related to other service-type designs, we'll use it as the basis for explanation of locked-breech pistol functioning. Also, aside from the locking system its functioning is similar to that of most blowback guns.

We'll begin with the gun loaded and cocked, a charged magazine in place, and the manual safety engaged.

Grasping the gun in a conventional shooting fashion depresses the grip safety (in the back strap) and moves a stud out of the trigger's path. Rotating the manual safety downward, moves a lug out of the path of the sear so that it is now free to disengage the hammer. The entire trigger assembly slides rearward under finger pressure; there is no rotation of the trigger as in some other types. The rear face of the yoke contacts the foot of the disconnector, which in turn transfers that movement to the foot of the sear and pushes it rearward, rotating the sear nose out of the full-cock notch in the hammer. The hammer is

then free to be driven forward by its strut and mainspring, to strike the head of the firing pin where it protrudes from the firing-pin stop in the rear of the slide. Shortly after striking the firing pin, the hammer is halted by the stop and the firing pin continues forward of its own momentum, compressing its retraction spring and protruding through the slide face to detonate the primer and fire the cartridge. The firing pin is then retracted into the slide.

The cartridge fires and the bullet is driven down the barrel. Recoil begins, with the slide and barrel moving rearward on the frame, locked together by the ribs on top of the barrel seated in recesses in the slide. As the barrel moves rearward, the pivoted link connecting it to the slide-stop pin in the frame rotates back and down. This pulls the rear of the barrel downward until the ribs are fully disengaged from the slide, and the barrel is halted by coming into solid contact with the arresting surface in the frame. The muzzle forms a pivot from which the rear of the barrel moves downward; it is seated rather loosely in a circular bushing to allow this movement.

As the rear of the barrel is pulled downward, it naturally moves the head of the cartridge case downward, wiping it across the slide breech face. This makes it necessary that the firing pin nose be retracted completely inside the slide face before movement begins. If not, the tip of the firing pin will jam in the primer and either prevent downward barrel movement or shear through the primer and case head. During this initial movement of slide and barrel together, the underside of the slide cams the disconnector downward, removing the mechanical connection between the trigger yoke and the bottom of the sear. With the barrel halted, the slide continues rearward, and the extractor hook draws the case out of the chamber by its rim.

As the slide moves rearward, it rotates the hammer down and back, so that the full-cock notch passes over the sear nose; with connection between it and the trigger broken, the sear is forced by its spring to snap into the notch. As the slide nears the rear of its stroke, the head of the fired case comes into contact with the ejector, and the case is hurled from the gun, pivoting about the extractor.

From the beginning of its rearward travel, the slide compresses the recoil spring beneath the barrel against its abutment in the frame; the recoil spring guide prevents kinking as this takes place. Eventually, the rear face of the spring tunnel beneath the front of the slide strikes the flange of the guide which is seated against a corresponding abutment in the frame. This action halts rearward slide movement, after which the recoil spring asserts itself and begins to thrust the slide forward. As the slide breech clears the mouth of the magazine, the magazine spring and follower force the top cartridge up tight against the feed lips.

As the slide moves forward, the lower portion of the breech strikes the top cartridge and drives it forward until the point is reached where the feed lips widen and the cartridge pops free. As the cartridge moves up across the breech face, the rim slips under the extractor hook. It continues to be driven forward by the slide until the bullet strikes the angled feed-ramp and is deflected upward. It then usually strikes the roof of the chamber or the underside of the barrel tang and is deflected downward, straightening the cartridge so it will enter the chamber smoothly. The slide continues forward to strike the barrel tang and begins to carry the barrel forward with it.

At about this point, the rear of the slide clears the hammer face and the hammer is moved forward slightly by the main-spring to be caught and held by the sear. As the slide drives the barrel forward and completes chambering of the cartridge, the barrel link forces the rear of the barrel to rise, seating its locking ribs in the corresponding recesses in the slide roof. As the barrel reaches the fully locked position, the barrel lug comes into contact with the slide stop pin in the receiver. This halts forward barrel and slide movement.

In reality, the pin does not take all of the load, for the force vectors involved around the pin, link, link pin, and locking lugs combine to halt both barrel and slide effectively without overstressing any single component. During the last 3/16 inch or so of slide travel, a cavity in its underside arrives over the top of the disconnector. The sear spring then forces the disconnector upward, again placing the foot of the disconnector in position to contact the sear.

All of the above takes place so rapidly that even if one attempts to beat the system with his trigger finger, the trigger is still fully rearward as the gun locks up in battery. Consequently, the trigger cannot engage the disconnector until it is released and moved forward by its spring. As the spring forces the trigger forward, the rear face of the yoke again makes contact with the front of the disconnector foot and the gun is ready for the next shot. Pulling the trigger at this point will cause all the actions described above to be repeated.

When the last round feeds from the magazine, the follower rises beneath an inward-projecting lug on the slide stop. This forces the stop upward—against the spring action of the detent—so that the shoulder at its upper rear will engage a notch in the slide and hold it to the rear.

While many functions of double-action autos are identical to the above, there are differences worth explaining. The S&W M39/59 is typical, and so makes a good example.

Beginning with the pistol loaded, hammer down, and manual safety disengaged, the operation process is as follows: The trigger is pulled rearward, rotating about its pin moving its upper limb forward; a drawbar attached to the upper limb rides in guide cuts in the frame and, as the trigger is pulled, it moves forward, compressing the spring which actuates it. At the upper rear of the drawbar, there are a couple of shallow, precisely formed shoulders facing forward, to engage corresponding surfaces on the foot of the hammer. The drawbar, under upward spring-pressure, engages and rotates the hammer about its pin as the trigger is pulled. At the proper point in drawbar travel, the "hooks" either slip off the hammer shoulders (a result of their changing angular relationship as the hammer rotates), or the drawbar is cammed downward to produce the same results. At this point, shortly before trigger travel is completed, the hammer falls to fire the cartridge.

The M39 also contains a conventional sear whose purpose is to hold the hammer in the full-cock position after the first and succeeding shots. As the drawbar moves forward, just before it disengages from the hammer, a projection on the bar engages a lug on the sear and rotates it out of the hammer's path. Consequently, the hammer may move through its full travel without danger of its half-cock notch being damaged by striking the sear. After the hammer starts falling and after the cock-notch passes the sear nose, the drawbar cams off of the sear, allowing it to be rotated by its spring back into position so that it will function normally (that is, in the single-action mode) to catch and hold the hammer at full cock as the slide recoils. Then, when the trigger is released after the shot (and the slide is again in battery), the drawbar re-engages the sear, without engaging the hammer, remaining in a forward position. The trigger remains near its rearward position, ready for a short and light single-action pull to fire the next shot.

All other DA auto functions are essentially the same as described for SA autos.

Most other double-action autoloading pistols follow generally the same system and differ only in detail. Some foreign models are considerably more complex and sophisticated, and incorporate such additional features as automatic disengagement of the slide stop, chambered-cartridge indicators, cocking indicators, and cocking and uncocking levers. However, the basic system which provides the double-action function for the first shot and single-action function for succeeding shots is much the same.

The majority of today's double-action autoloading pistols are fitted with what is called a "hammer-dropping, hammer-blocking" manual safety. This is generally mounted on the slide and consists (with a thumb piece for manipulation) of a large-diameter shaft passing laterally through the slide and pierced along the longitudinal axis of the slide to accommodate the firing pin. This safety is further provided with a "trip lever" mounted in the frame (in the case of the M39) or in the slide.

Beginning with the safety in the "fire" or disengaged position and with the hammer cocked, as it would be immediately after chambering a cartridge, it functions as follows: Rotation toward the "safe" position causes a segment of the shaft to move upward and either cover (M39) the head of the firing pin or move into a position so that it extends further rear-

ward than the firing pin to provide a surface which will halt the falling hammer before it can reach the firing pin. This constitutes the "hammer-blocking" portion of the safety, in that it blocks the hammer's path before the firing pin can be reached. The trip lever of this type safety is pivoted so that when pressed downward it brings pressure to bear on the sear (either directly or through some other intervening part) and disengages the sear from the hammer, allowing the hammer to fall.

In the M39 the trip lever is roughly U-shaped and is forced downward by a cam surface on the safety shaft as it is rotated into the "safe" position. This constitutes the "hammer-dropping" of the safety. The timing of the various cams and other working surfaces of this safety system is such that the hammer's path to the firing pin is blocked well before the sear is disengaged to let the hammer fall.

When this safety is engaged, the sear is held out of engagement so that the hammer cannot be cocked; it may be drawn rearward, but it will not be caught by the sear. At the same time, trigger and drawbar movement are made ineffective by the position of the sear. Modern pistols of this type use an inertia-type firing pin so that once the safety has been used to safely drop the hammer, it may be disengaged so that the gun may be drawn and fired double-action without any added operations. As has been pointed out earlier, the hammer may rest safely upon the head of an inertia-type firing pin because even when held forward in that fashion, the pin does not protrude through the slide breech face to touch the primer of a chambered cartridge.

When disengaged, this type of safety functions as follows; initial rotation of the shaft releases pressure upon the trip lever and thus allows the sear to be forced in against the hammer by its spring. Continued rotation uncovers or unblocks the head of the firing pin and allows the hammer to move forward very slightly, forcing the firing pin forward a slight amount and coming to rest on an abutment in the rear of the slide. At the same time, the drawbar and trigger are released to move into their double-action positions, trigger fully forward, and drawbar engaging the hooks or actuating surfaces on the base of the hammer. From this condition, the gun may be fired, without any preparatory action, by simply pulling the trigger through in revolver fashion, or manually cocking and then firing in single-action fashion.

That covers the complete functioning cycle of the basic autoloaders. There are, of course, variations of those types, and there are countless conversions, modifications, or alterations which are produced by some very fine professional pistolsmiths. It would be simply impossible to cover them all in this one chapter, but a study of sectioned views, isometric parts drawings, and the manufacturer's operating or maintenance instructions will usually make the functional differences clear without too much effort.

Manufacturers do not always supply isometric or section drawings, but there are several other sources. You would do well to add them to your library. One source I consider excellent is my own book *Pistolsmithing*, published by the Stackpole Company and available through most booksellers. Another very excellent source of isometric drawings and brief descriptions and historical data is *NRA: Handgun Assembly* available from the National Rifle Association. Probably the largest single collection of isometric drawings is available in *Exploded Firearms Drawings*, published by DBI Books and available almost anywhere shooting books and periodicals are sold. Many other publications contain drawings, photos, and functioning details to lesser degrees. By keeping your eyes open you should be able to obtain references that deal in particular with the guns you own.

Knowing how your gun works may not make you a better marksman, but it will certainly make you more confident with the gun and better able to care for it and to handle problems that arise. That makes it all worthwhile.

Chapter Twenty-Seven
Sub-Caliber Devices and Caliber Conversions

Autoloading pistols are designed to function properly in a given caliber with ammunition loaded within fairly narrow limits of recoil impulse. This means that we do not have the option of varying bullet weight and velocity to any large degree. If we increase bullet weight, we must reduce velocity to maintain the proper recoil impulse. If we reduce bullet weight, we must increase velocity for the same reason. If we reduce velocity much below standard with bullets of ordinary weight, we very quickly run into problems of extraction, ejection, and feeding. If we increase velocity very much with the standard bullet, we overdrive the mechanism and increase the probability of damage or parts breakage. In effect, then, with any autoloader, we are more or less "locked in" to standard factory-loaded ammunition or handloads essentially duplicating its performance.

The revolver suffers no such limitation, being capable of functioning completely and correctly with virtually any load that will firstly fit in the chamber and allow the cylinder to rotate; secondly, at least dribble the bullet out the end of the barrel; and thirdly, not generate such high pressures as to damage the mechanism when fired. Much is made of this revolver advantage to the detriment of the autoloader. In reality, the autoloader possesses advantages over the revolver which, in my opinion, substantially outweigh this, but that is not the point of our discussion.

The autoloader can be given far greater ammunition versatility by either the use of caliber-change conversion kits that are commercially available, or by assembling a basic gun with a different barrel or other parts as are necessary to permit it to function with cartridges or loads for which it was not originally manufactured.

Probably the best known method of doing this in the U.S. is installation of the Colt "22/45 Conversion Unit" upon the standard 45 GM. This unit was designed in the early 1930s by one Marshall Williams, who is credited for the gas system and basic design features of the famous US M1 30 caliber carbine of World War II and numerous smaller wars since. The unit consists of a completely new slide/barrel/recoil spring group and a special 22 LR magazine. Any 45 GM pistol may be converted to 22 LR caliber by simply replacing the original slide group and magazine with the components of this kit. While this conversion unit is not as accurate as a target pistol, it permits practice with the basic gun at a much lower cost and under conditions where the range or other shooting facilities may not be adequate for the powerful 45 cartridge. It is quite valuable for short-range training, with its light recoil and report, as an initial step in introducing new shooters to the big 45.

In addition to the Colt unit, a comparable but not identical unit is manufactured by Day Arms for converting the 45 GM to 22 LR caliber. The Day unit differs greatly, being of much more recent design, and is capable of far greater accuracy. In fact the Day unit possesses the mechanical accuracy of many 22 target pistols. It, too, consists of a complete new

barrel/slide/recoil spring group magazine. Installation is quite simple, with the unit being held in place by the slide-stop pin. Day also supplies sights which are superior to those on the Colt conversion.

A third 22 conversion unit for the 45 GM is available under the name Kart, and while it appears quite similar to the Day device, I've not had an opportunity to compare the two closely enough to determine the differences.

Other 22 conversion units for the same pistol have appeared from time to time in the past, but none seem to have been manufactured in significant quantities, nor did they survive the production interruptions of World War II.

In the past, several continental firms have produced 22 conversion units for different European

The Heckler & Koch HK-4 is loosely based on the prewar gun in this picture, the Mauser HSC.

pistols. None saw wide availability in the States, and they are generally considered collectors items now. Most of them were single-shot conversions, whereas our modern domestic units provide full semi-auto functioning. For a short period of time after World War II, the Walther Company did offer a 22 semi-auto conversion unit for the P38 pistol. This appears to have been discontinued, and instead the P38 is now offered as original manufacture in 22 LR.

In the mid 1960s, the German Heckler and Koch Company introduced its new HK-4, medium-sized auto pistol as a 4-caliber set. The gun could be purchased in 22 LR, 25 ACP, 32 ACP or 380 ACP; however, it was also offered as a cased set with the parts necessary to convert the basic gun to any of those four calibers. The gun—a very much modified

development of the pre-war Mauser HSC—was designed from the beginning to allow these conversions; therefore, the original slide was used in all calibers.

Conversion simply required replacing the barrel/recoil-spring unit and the magazine. When switching between centerfire and rimfire, it was also necessary to turn out a screw in the slide breech face, then rotate a separate firing-pin plate to obtain the correct size case-head recess, and at the same time to position the nose of the firing pin through the proper hole in the plate for the type of cartridge to be used. The screw was then turned back in to secure the plate and the gun was ready to go. One side of the firing-pin plate contained a case-head recess for the 32 and 380 ACP cartridge, while the other was sized for the 22

The HK-4, made in Germany by Heckler & Koch, comes in four calibers, 380, 32, 25 ACP and 22 L.R.

LR and 25 ACP. Two difference firing-pin holes were located in the plate for centerfire and rimfire cartridges, and sufficient vertical freedom was built into the firing pin so that it could be placed in either hole without any other operations.

The HK-4 pistol is currently available, being distributed in this country by Heckler & Koch's U.S. subsidiary. All four calibers are available, however, the 25 and 32 ACP seem superfluous and are not terribly popular. The gun has been well accepted as a two-caliber set in 22 LR and 380 caliber. Set up for the larger cartridge, this pistol is an excellent hideout gun for personal defense or law enforcement use, and it may then be switched over to 22 for low-cost practice and training. In the smaller caliber, it is quite accurate and also makes an excellent plinking or small-game piece.

More recently, the Sig/Sauer P220 has been introduced in the U.S. (manufactured in West Germany) and while conversion kits are not currently sold, it is designed to be easily switched among five different calibers: 22 LR, 7.65mm Parabellum (30 Luger) 9mm Parabellum, 38 Super, and 45 ACP. Brochures furnished by Sig clearly indicate that they anticipate that the parts necessary to convert from any one caliber to any of the others will be made available in the future. Because of the wide spread of calibers, all conversions do not require the same parts.

For example, conversion between 45 and 22 requires replacement of the slide, barrel recoil spring, and magazine. Conversion between 7.65mm and 9mm Parabellum requires changing only the barrel and recoil spring. However, if past experience with converting other pistols between these two calibers is any guide, changing the spring would not really be necessary. Conversion between 9mm Parabellum and 38 Super requires changing of only the barrel and magazine. When parts become available separately, one could very easily assemble a full five-caliber set which could then be cased to make a beautiful outfit available for almost any handgunning project.

Numerous other conversions are possible, though not intended to be so by the manufacture. For example, the Luger/Parabellum pistol (whether of early or post-World War II manufacture) can be converted between 7.65mm and 9mm caliber by simply changing the barrel and barrel extension (upper receiver). Likewise, the Colt GM (or the two Commander variations) can be converted among 9mm Parabellum, 38 Super and 45. This job isn't quite as simple as some others, for a small amount of gunsmithing is required to

permit the ejector to function correctly for all three calibers. Aside from that, the change may be made between 38 Super and 9mm by simply changing the barrel. Switching between either of those calibers and the 45 requires also a new slide, recoil spring, and magazine. Certainly Colt doesn't promote these changes, much preferring to sell complete guns in all three calibers. The Walther P38 is also easily switched between 7.65mm and 9mm Parabellum calibers by merely exchanging barrels.

Other caliber changes or conversions are possible on a great many different guns, however, they generally involve varying degrees of gunsmithing. One example may be found in converting the 45 GM to 38 Super; this can be done by having an old 45 barrel relined and rechambered, slight modifications to the extractor and slide breech, and substitution of the 38 magazine.

Custom pistolsmiths also convert the GM to handle 38 Special wadcutter cartridges, but this is a much more complex and costly job.

Most pistols chambered for the 9mm Parabellum can be converted to 7.65mm Parabellum by simply installing a new or relined barrel in the latter caliber. Pistols chambered for ammunition no longer available or in short supply are often converted to a readily available caliber of reasonably similar characteristics by relining and rechambering the barrel and in some instances a few other minor alterations. Examples of this are: converting the Japanese Nambu service pistol of World War II from 8mm to 9mm or 7.65mm Parabellum; relining and rechambering the French M1935 series of pistols to 32 ACP; conversion of the Astra M400 (9mm Berman Bayard) and Steyr M12 (9mm Steyr) to 9mm Parabellum by either relining the barrel or by simply pressing into the chamber a spacer ring so that the shorter Parabellum case will headspace correctly.

Even more conversions are possible, some at little cost and effort, others being rather complex and costly. We won't attempt to list them here, but if one will take the time to study the problem, compare cartridge characteristics and dimensions, as well as the functioning of the gun, both temporary and permanent conversions will come to mind.

I think the foregoing will make it clear that possession of a good gun in a single caliber doesn't necessarily mean that you'll have to buy a complete gun to be able to shoot another cartridge. Often that goal can be achieved at very little cost by exploring conversion possibilities.

Worthwhile Reference Books

Much can be learned about pistols in general if one assembles a small, specialized reference library and uses it. The following books are recommended, having been quite helpful to the author.

Angier, R.H. *Firearms Blueing and Browning.* 1936. Stackpole.

Bady, Donald B. *Colt Automatic Pistols.* rev. ed. 1973. Borden.

Belford & Dunlap. *Mauser Self-Loading Pistol.* Borden.

Breathed, J.W. Jr. & Schroeder, J.J. Jr. *System Mauser, A Pictorial History of the Model 1896 Self-Loading Pistol.* 1967. Handgun Press.

Brownell, F.R. *Gunsmith Kinks.* 1969. Brownell & Son.

Ezell, Edward C. rev. by. *Small Arms of the World.* 11th ed. 1977. Stackpole.

Hogg, Ian V. & Books, W. *German Pistols and Revolvers 1871-1945.* 1975. Stackpole.

Hogg, Ian V. & Weeks, John. *Military Small Arms of the Twentieth Century.* 3rd ed. 1977. Hippocrene Bks.

Jinks, Roy G. *History of Smith & Wesson.* 1978. Follett.

Jordan, Will H. *No Second Place Winner.* 1962. Jordan.

MacFarland, Harold E. *Gunsmithing Simplified.* A.S. Barnes.

——*Introduction to Modern Gunsmithing.* 1975. B.& N.

Mason, James D. *Combat Handgun Shooting.* 1976. C C Thomas.

Murtz, Harold A. ed. *Gun Digest Book of Exploded Firearms Drawings.* 2nd ed. 1977, DBI.

The NRA Firearms Assembly Guidebook to Handguns. 1973. National Rifle Association.

Neal, Robert J. & Jinks, Roy J. *Smith & Wesson, 1857-1945.* 1975. A.S.Barnes.

Nonte, George C. Jr. *Firearms Encyclopedia.* 1973. Har-Row.

——*Handgun Competition.* 1978. Winchester Pr.

——*Pistolsmithing.* 1974. Stackpole.

——*Pistol & Revolver Guide.* 3rd ed. 1975. Stoeger.

——*Revolver Guide.* 1979. Stoeger.

Nonte, George C., Jr. & Jurras, Lee E. *Handgun Hunting*. 1976. Stoeger.

Pender, Roy G. *Mauser Pocket Pistols, 1910–1946*. 1971. Collectors Press.

Peterson, Harold L. *Encyclopedia of Firearms*. 1964. Dutton.

Petty, Charles E. *High Standard Automatic Pistols 1932–1950*. 1976. American Ordnance Publ.

Rankin, James L. *Walther Models PP and PPK, 1929–1945*. 1974. Rankin.

——*Walther Volume II. Engraved Presentation and Standard Models*. 1977. Rankin.

Stebbins, Henry M. *Pistols: A Modern Encyclopedia*. 1976. Castle Bks.

Steindler, R.A. *Home Gunsmithing Digest*. 2nd ed. 1978. DBI.

Walker, Ralph. *Hobby Gunsmithing*. 1972. DBI.

Whittington, Maj. Robert D. III. *German Pistols and Holsters, 1934–45*. 1976. Gun Room Pr.

Wilson, R.F. & Hogg, Ian V. *Textbook & Automatic Pistols*. 1975. Stackpole.

Case-Forming Data

The more popular and modern auto cartridges are widely distributed and can usually be purchased without too much trouble—local laws permitting, that is. However, there are quite a few dead and obsolete calibers not made for 30 years or more, which have been out-lived by the guns made for them. The guns are still available and serviceable, but the cartridges are either long gone or exceedingly difficult to find. Such guns need not be retired if the owner (or one of his friends) is a handloader. Once cases are at hand, the rest is easy. The following notes tell briefly how to make what you need from what might be at hand. Maybe some of our examples seem extreme, but if done properly, they will work.

7mm Nambu: Turn 32 S&W to rimless head, trim to 0.78″ length, resize.

7.62mm Tokarev (Russian): Resize 30 Mauser.

7.63mm Mauser (30): Trim 223/222 Remington to 0.97″ length, resize, ream neck.

7.65mm French Long: Turn 32 S&W Long head to rimless, trim to 0.78″ length, resize.

7.65mm Parabellum: (a) As for 7.63mm Mauser, (b) Turn 38 Special head to rimless, trim to 0.75″ length, resize, (c) Resize 38 ACP/Super, trim to 0.75″.

7.65mm Mannlicher: Turn 32 S&W Long head to rimless form, trim to 0.84″ length, resize.

32 ACP: Turn 32 S&W Long head to semi-rim form, trim to 0.68″ length, resize.

8mm Nambu: (a) Resize 38 ACP/Super, trim to 0.86″ length.

380 ACP: (a) Turn 38 Special head to rimless, shorten to 0.68″ (9mm Browning Short).

9mm Parabellum: (a) Turn 38 Special head to rimless, shorten to .760″; case will bulge and may split, but functioning is okay. (b) Trim 38 ACP/Super to 0.76″ length, resize. (c) This treatment may also be applied to other longer 9mm cartridges for the same purpose.

9mm Browning Long: (a) Trim 38 ACP/Super to 0.80″ length, and resize. (b) Turn 38 Special head to semi-rim, complete as before. (c) Trim 38 AMU to 0.80″ length and resize.

9mm Mauser: (a) Turn 38 Special head to rimless, trim to 0.980″ length, resize.

9mm Bayard (Largo): (a) Use 38 ACP/Super as is, or reduce rim diameter if necessary. (b) Turn 38 Special to rimless and turn to .900″ length.

9mm Steyr: As for 9mm Bayard.

9mm Glisenti: Use 9mm Parabellum as is.

9mm Ultra: (a) Turn 9mm Parabellum head to 380 ACP (9mm Police) dimensions. (b) Turn 38 ACP/Super or 38 Special head as before, trim to 0.705″ length.

38 ACP/Super: (a) Turn 38 Special head to semi-rim, trim to .900″ length. (b) Trim 223/222 Remington case to .900″ length, ream neck to depth of bullet seat.

38 AMU: Turn 38 Special head to semi-rim 38 ACP dimensions.

45 ACP: (a) Trim 30–06 (308, 270, etc.) to .900 length, ream neck to depth of bullet seat. (b) Turn 45 Colt or 45 Auto Rim to rimless form, trim to .900 length.

455 Webley Scott Auto: Turn 45 Colt or 45 Auto Rim to semi-rim head, trim to 0.93″ length.

Glossary

accelerator: Common to machine guns and other automatic weapons, but only rarely encountered in autoloading pistols. A crescent-shaped device which functions as a lever when acted upon by a recoiling barrel to thrust the slide or breech block rearward at increased velocity.

back strap: That portion of the frame which forms the rear of the grip; not always present, sometimes being deleted to reduce weight, its place then taken by a portion of the stocks.

bar, trigger: The connecting link between trigger and sear or hammer; often known also as "sear bar" or "draw bar."

barrel, fixed: A form of barrel installation wherein the barrel is attached rigidly to the frame and does not move with respect to the frame during functioning.

barrel, mobile: An installation of a barrel in an autoloading pistol wherein the barrel is free to move fore and aft a limited amount as part of normal functioning.

block, accuracy: A device manufactured by Bo-Mar, attached to the top of the slide, and whose purpose is to ensure uniform, vertical positioning of the barrel breech by action as a stop for the barrel tang.

block, breech: Found only in a few pistol designs, a separate part containing the firing pin and extractor and secured inside a hollow slide in place of the traditional solid portion forming the breech face.

block, locking: A separate locking piece found in some designs (Mauser, Walther, Beretta, Lahiti) which acts between the barrel and slide and/or frame to lock all the moving parts together at the instant of discharge. It may take many forms, the most common of which is a pivoted lever.

blowback: A type of pistol design wherein there is no mechanical locking system and the action is held closed against the forces of the discharge only by the inertia of the breech block or slide and by the recoil spring.

blowback, delayed (retarded): A blowback design wherein additional hesitation is provided by cam surfaces, spring-loaded plungers, or friction-producing devices.

bobcat: A descriptive term applied to shortened and

lightened combat conversions of autoloading pistols; used both by Behlert and Sheldon and perhaps others.

buffer, recoil: A device which serves to reduce the impact of the slide striking the frame and being brought to a halt at the end of its rearward travel. May be incorporated in the recoil-spring guide, or be a separate part, and may be a spring, a resilient material or simply a piece of metal.

bushing, barrel: In Colt/Browning and similar designs, a removable tubular part in the muzzle of the slide which provides a smooth bearing for the barrel. In some designs, it may be permanently installed.

bushing, stock-screw: A circular bushing threaded and staked into the sides of the grip frame and threaded internally to accept the stock screws. Its purpose is to provide greater support to the grips than can be offered by a small-diameter screw, and also permit easy replacement if threads are stripped.

cam, locking (unlocking): Cam surfaces formed on the barrel lug and/or inside the barrel seat in the frame to provide the vertical barrel movement needed for locking and unlocking.

cannelure: In ammunition, a peripheral groove rolled into the bullet to provide space for crimping a cartridge case; in a cartridge case, a groove rolled into the case body to either secure the bullet more tightly or to provide a seat against which the bullet rests.

catch, barrel: Usually a spring-loaded plunger which secures a removable barrel to the frame; the barrel is removed for replacement or cleaning by depressing the catch.

catch (release), magazine: The device, usually a spring-loaded plunger or lever, which holds the magazine securely in the gun and in proper position for feeding, and which must be manually actuated before removing the empty magazine.

clip: A word today used interchangeably with magazine, but which refers, originally and more properly, to a sheet-metal device for simply holding a group of cartridges together to facilitate their entry into the magazine proper. The Mauser M96 and Steyr M12 use a *clip* to permit cartridges to be stripped directly into the integral magazine after which the clip is discarded.

counter-recoil: That forward movement of the slide and other recoiling parts which occurs after its rearward travel has been halted. Also, technically, the forward and downward movement of both gun and hand and arm in returning to the position held before the shot was fired.

conversion, combat: A loose term applied to auto-loaders which have been variously modified ar altered to suit urban combat conditions an concealed carrying. Generally involves shortening the slide and barrel and sometimes of the butt.

crimp: In ammunition, a turning-over of the ca mouth into the bullet to provide a more secure assem bly.

disconnector: A device in an autoloading pist which serves to prevent firing at any time excep when the slide is in battery. Generally functions b "disconnecting" the trigger from the sear as soon a slide movement begins and maintains that disconne tion until the slide returns to battery. Sometimes separate part, other times a function of the trigger ba or similar part.

double: An autoloader malfunction where two c more shots are fired with a single pull of the trigge usually due to damage or excessive wear of th sear/hammer relationship.

double action: A term applied to autoloadin pistols in which manual cocking of the hammer is n required, it being possible to raise and drop th hammer for firing by a single relatively long pull c the trigger. Double-action pistols also generall contain provisions for single-action use.

double-action only: An autoloading pistol whic may be fired either by a pivoted hammer or recipro cating striker, and which may not be manuall cocked; every shot must be fired by a single long pu of the trigger which first cocks and then drops th hammer or striker.

double feed: An autoloader malfunction wherein loaded cartridge or fired case remains in the chamb and a second round is picked up from the magazin and jammed against it. Usually produced by a extractor failure.

ejector: That part which is struck by the head of th fired cartridge case as it is extracted and which serve to hurl the empty case clear of the gun; installed o the frame, either rigidly as a separate part, or as portion of the slide stop or other part.

ejector, magazine: Not found on any productio auto, but a spring device beneath the grips which wi hurl the empty magazine clear when the magazin catch is disengaged.

extension, barrel: In pistols such as the Auto-Ma and Parabellum, a separate and generally tubula part threaded to the rear of the barrel and mounted s as to slide the frame. The extension generally houses breech block or bolt and thereby substitutes for th more conventional slide.

extractor: The claw-shaped member installed in th slide which engages the rim of the case as the gun goe into battery and withdraws the fired case from the chamber during recoil.

extractor, internal: A form of extractor apparently originating with John Browning and which is fully enclosed in the slide by being seated in a longitudinal hole.

face, breech: That vertical portion of the slide against which the cartridge case head fits when the gun is in battery, usually containing the extractor and firing pin.

follow-down: A malfunction, usually in highly tuned, target autos where the hammer is jarred or slips off the sear as the slide slams into battery, the hammer then falling to be caught by the intercept notch.

follower: A form of cap over the spring in the magazine, against which the bottom cartridge in the magazine rests; angled to position cartridges correctly in the feed lips.

frame (receiver): That portion of a pistol which forms the grip, contains the lockwork, and to which the barrel and slide are assembled. It is the one part required by federal law to carry the serial number.

front strap: That portion of the frame which forms the front portion of the grip area and also partially encloses the magazine well.

funnel, butt: The beveling or funneling of the edges of the magazine-well mouth to facilitate speed-loading.

guide, recoil spring: A rod or tube passing through the center of the recoil spring, generally to prevent kinking of the spring during compression, though it may also serve other functions. May run the full length of the expanded spring, or only its compressed length; in some guns, the barrel may serve this function.

groove, grasping: The more or less vertical serrations or grooves provided in the sides of the slide to permit a secure grasp when retracting the slide.

headspace: In guns chambered for rimless cartridges, the distance (with the slide in battery) between the breech face and the shoulder in the chamber against which the mouth of the case seats. For rimmed and semi-rimmed cartridges, the distance between the breech face and the mouth of the chamber where the rim seats.

housing, mainspring: In Colt/Browning designs and copies thereof, a separate part into which the captive, semi-compressed mainspring is permanently assembled; removable to aid in disassembly of the rest of the gun.

indicator, chamber: A plunger or lever acted upon by the head of a cartridge so that it protrudes beyond the surface of the slide when a cartridge (or fired case) is in the chamber; this function is sometimes served by the extractor. Usually colored red to catch the eye, but also protruding sufficiently to be felt as well as seen and thus functions as a tactile indicator.

indicator, cocking: A plunger, button or other device which protrudes from the breech area of the pistol to indicate when the gun is cocked; it functions both as a visual and tactile indicator.

inertia firing pin: A form of firing pin apparently introduced by John Browning which is shorter than the recess in which it moves in the slide so that when the hammer is lowered fully upon the firing pin, the pin does not protrude from the breech face to make contact with the primer.

insert: By S&W nomenclature, a removable back strap which covers and provides a seat for the mainspring.

iron, stock: A metal connecting part fitted to the front of an auxiliary stock or holster stock which permits it to be attached securely to the butt of the gun.

jam: A term applied very loosely by the uninformed and inexperienced to virtually any malfunction of an autoloading pistol.

jump (lift): The upward movement of the muzzle brought about by the fact that the resistance to gun recoil is below the centerline of the bore, causing recoil forces to rotate the gun about that point of resistance. Jump begins to occur the instant the bullet starts moving and has progressed substantially by the time the bullet exits the muzzle.

lead (leed, leade): The tapered beginning of the rifling ahead of the chamber, sometimes also called the bullet seat.

lever, cocking: A separate spring-loaded lever, usually situated on the left side of the frame and partially covered by the grip, which permits raising the hammer to the full-cock position by simple downward thumb pressure. Generally applied to hammerless or enclosed-hammer pistols, and apparently first introduced on a substantial basis in the Sauer M38 pocket-sized pistol manufactured extensively in Germany during World War II but not made since.

lever, decocking: A lever provided on the left side of some of the more modern and sophisticated autoloader designs for the purpose of lowering the hammer safely from the full-cock position either after loading or when firing is interrupted. It is used only for this purpose on the SIG P220 design, but in the H&K P9, it serves also as a cocking lever and to actuate the slide stop as well.

lever, dismount (disassembly): A pivoted lever,

usually located on the frame, which is rotated to unlock the barrel from the frame so that the barrel and slide may be removed. Sometimes incorporated into the slide stop.

lever, safety: In an internal automatic safety, the lever which permits the safety to be actuated by the trigger; a term also sometimes applied to an ordinary manual safety.

lever, trip: In the S&W design, a lever pivoted to the frame and acted upon by the safety to disengage the sear and drop the hammer when the safety is engaged.

link, barrel: In Colt/Browning and similar designs, a flat piece of metal pinned to both the barrel and the frame, causing the barrel breech to move vertically for locking and unlocking during recoil and counter-recoil movement.

link, long: An after-market accessory; a replacement barrel link for the Colt GM Auto, made longer (greater distance between the two holes) to seat the barrel more tightly into the roof of the slide and thus increase accuracy.

lips, feed: At the upper end of the magazine, the carefully shaped, over-turned edges of the magazine which position the cartridge correctly for feeding.

lock, roller: A form of locking system applied only recently to autoloading pistols, whereby the slide is locked to the barrel by small hardened-steel rollers entering grooves in both parts. Occurs in two forms, the first with mobile barrel as in the Czechoslovakian M52, and the second with fixed barrel as in the H&K P9.

long-slide: A term generally applied to Colt GM pistols fitted with longer than normal slides prepared by cutting and welding two slides together and fitting a similarly longer barrel.

loop (ring), lanyard: A provision at the butt of a pistol for attachment of a lanyard by means of a spring snap; usually formed from wire or sheet-metal, though sometimes machined directly into a portion of the gun as in the S&W M39.

lug, barrel: In locked-breech autos, a protrusion beneath the chamber area which seats in the frame and which carries the link or cam surfaces to provide locking and unlocking action.

lug, frame: Generally, a raised boss on the pistol frame against which the spring and plunger of a slide stop or other movable part bears. Usually a separate part riveted in place.

lug (rib), locking: A protrusion on the barrel of a locked-breech pistol, usually on the upper surface near the chamber, which engages a corresponding recess in the roof of the slide to lock the two together.

lug, (slot) stock: In older designs (Parabellum and Mauser essentially), a provision on the back strap for attachment of an auxiliary carbine stock or a combination holster/stock to permit the gun to be used as a short, light carbine.

magazine: In modern autoloaders, a metal box containing the gun's cartridge supply and usually inserted removably into the butt or grip. Usually of folded sheet-metal construction and containing the follower and follower spring. Some obsolete designs have the magazine formed integrally with the frame and it is not removable.

magazine, double-column: A pistol magazine containing two, rather than one, vertical columns of cartridges, staggered one-half cartridge diameter so that the two nest together.

mainspring: The spring which drives the hammer; in modern designs, a very strong coil spring which may function in either tension or compression, though leaf-type springs have been used in older models.

mark, proof: A symbol, letter or number (or series thereof) stamped upon the barrel and sometimes other parts of an autoloading pistol to indicate that it has been fired with high-pressure "proof" cartridges to demonstrate its strength.

notch (recess), disconnector: Generally a precisely shaped recess on the underside of the slide which becomes aligned with the upper end of the disconnector only when the slide is fully in battery; the disconnector may then rise into the recess, establishing positive connection between trigger and sear. After the shot is fired, as the slide moves rearward, the leading edge of the notch cams the disconnector downward and disconnects the sear from the trigger to prevent any additional shots being fired until such time as the trigger is released to move forward after the slide is in battery again.

operation, gas: A form of firearms design in which a small portion of the expanding powder gases are trapped to provide the energy necessary for performing all the operations necessary to prepare the gun for the next shot.

operation, recoil: A method of firearms operation, by far the most common in autoloading pistols, whereby recoil forces are harnessed to provide the energy necessary for completing all the actions to prepare the gun for the next shot.

pin, firing: The slender, generally cylindrical pin which moves forward or is driven forward violently to indent the primer and fire the cartridge when the trigger is pulled. Usually housed within the slide.

pin, link: In those Browning designs utilizing a

swinging link, the pin securing that link to the barrel lug.

piston, gas: Not encountered in any modern pistol design currently manufactured, this is simply a metal piston operating inside some kind of cylinder into which a portion of the propellent gases are allowed to expand, driving the piston rearward, and thus providing the energy for functioning the gun.

plate, floor (bottom piece): That part which closes the bottom of the pistol magazine and provides a support for the follower spring. Permanently assembled in older designs, but generally now made to be easily removable for disassembly and cleaning of the magazine.

ramp, feed: A sloped trough-like area leading from the top of the magazine into the chamber; may be in one piece, formed in the barrel lug as on the Browning P35 and S&W M39, or formed partially in the frame and partially in the barrel as in the Colt/Browning Government Model.

recoil: The rearward movement of the gun caused by firing a cartridge; also the rearward travel of the slide and barrel relative to the frame.

rest, finger: Sometimes applied to ledges and ribs on the stocks, but generally a built-up or reshaped trigger-guard forming a seat at the front of the bow for the forefinger of the off hand in two-handed shooting.

safety, combat: The conventional manual safety with its thumbpiece widened and lengthened for quicker and more positive actuation during the draw.

safety, firing-pin: An automatic safety device inside the slide which serves to lock the firing pin rearward so that it cannot reach the primer of a chambered cartridge, even if struck by the hammer or other object, *except* when the trigger is deliberately pulled. May also be designed so that it locks the firing pin rearward at all times except when the slide is fully in battery.

safety, grip: A mechanical safety spring-loaded in the engaged position and designed so that a grasp on the pistol will depress it and disengage it, permitting the gun to be fired. Usually located in the back strap, but occasionally found in the front strap.

safety, hammer block: A manually operated safety which when engaged interposes a solid, steel surface between the hammer and the firing pin. It does not necessarily prevent the hammer from being dropped by trigger movement, but positively prevents the hammer from reaching the firing pin should that occur.

safety, hammer dropping: A manual safety which when engaged acts to disengage the sear and allow the hammer to fall; encountered only in conjunction with and as part of a hammer-blocking safety.

safety, magazine: An automatic safety device actuated by the magazine, which serves to prevent firing when the magazine is totally or partially removed from the gun. Generally functions by either blocking trigger movement or disconnecting the trigger from the sear.

safety, sear block: A form of manual safety which acts only upon the sear when engaged in such a fashion that the sear cannot be disengaged from the hammer by pressure on the trigger.

safety, trigger block: A manual safety which acts only upon the trigger, preventing trigger movement when it is engaged and thus preventing firing.

sear: A pivoted part of the gun lying close to the hammer and connected by some means to the trigger. Its function is to catch and hold the hammer at the full-cock and safety or intercept positions and yet permit firing at will.

shoe, trigger: An after-market accessory which is clamped to the finger piece of the trigger to increase its width and thus facilitate control, but which may also be utilized to increase trigger reach.

short recoil: A term applied to locked-breech pistol mechanisms in which the barrel and slide are locked together for only a very short distance, during which the two separate, the barrel halts and the slide continues to the rear. Also the term applied to a form of malfunction where the slide does not recoil sufficiently far rearward to complete all the actions necessary before the next shot.

sideplate: In S&W nomenclature, a hammer pin containing an unusually large sheet-metal head and lug which keys into the frame so that the pin may be retained by the slide; used on the M39 and M59 autoloaders.

single action: A term applying to those autoloading pistols which must be manually cocked for the first shot and which remain cocked after each subsequent shot.

slide: That major component of the pistol which closes the chamber and reciprocates to provide functioning. In centerfire pistols, the slide usually encloses the barrel (but not always) and generally contains the extractor, firing pin, and other parts necessary to their functioning.

spacer, magazine: A part, usually of sheet metal, inserted in a basic magazine in order to adapt it to functioning with a shorter cartridge; found in the Browning and SIG/Sauer P220 pistol to achieve interchangeability between magazine bodies in 38 ACP and 9mm Parabellum caliber.

speed-load: The act of reloading with a spare magazine as quickly as possible, generally on the "hand-finds-hand" principle while keeping one's eyes on the target.

spring, follower (magazine): The spring, usually of wire, inside the magazine which serves to press cartridges firmly upward against the feed lips.

spring, recoil: The principal spring which holds the slide or breech block forward into battery and which is compressed during recoil movement to then drive the slide forward in counter-recoil.

spring, recoil, captive: A form of recoil spring containing a full-length guide upon which the spring is confined in a semi-compressed condition.

stirrup, trigger: In some Colt/Browning designs, a hollow yoke attached permanently to the trigger and extending rearward to make contact with the sear; the magazine passing through the hollow portion.

stock, holster: Most commonly made of wood, but sometimes of leather and/or metal, a holster shaped like a stock and intended to be attached to the gun to permit its use as a short, light carbine.

stop, slide: Usually (but not always) a member pivoted to the frame which is forced upward by the magazine follower after the last cartridge has been fed to engage the slide and hold it to the rear after the last cartridge has been fired.

stop, trigger: An adjustable device, either a separate part added to the trigger or integral to the trigger construction which limits rearward trigger movement to the amount necessary to disengage the sear; prevents over-travel.

strut, hammer: A precisely shaped rod attached to the hammer and forming the connection with the mainspring; depending upon the gun design, it may serve to keep the mainspring in either tension or compression.

tang (hood), barrel: A projection at the upper rear of the barrel of some Browning-type, locked-breech, pistol designs which serves to align the barrel and to aid in feeding.

throating: A term sometimes applied to cleaning up and polishing the feed ramp and chamber mouth to improve feeding.

tuning: The various operations performed to improve the reliability and accuracy of an auto.

vent (port), barrel: In some 22 RF target autoloaders, a series of vertical holes into the bore from the top of the barrel; vents to be plugged or opened by means of threaded plugs to regulate gas escape to reduce velocity and recoil to the minimum values compatible with reliable functioning.

wraparound: A style of grip or stock wherein·the grip "wraps around" the back of the butt and takes the place of a metal back strap.

Tables

Powder Charges Per Pound
The number of charges to be gotten from one pound of powder.

Charge Grains	Number Per Pound
2	3550
3	2333
4	2750
5	2400
6	1166
7	1000
9	875
10	777
12	700
14	593
16	500
18	437
20	388
25	350
30	280

Lead Bullets
Number of lead bullets that can be cast from one pound of alloy.

Weight (grains)	Bullets per pound	Weight (grains)	Bullets per pound
80	87	160	43
90	77	170	41
100	70	180	38
110	63	200	35
120	58	220	31
130	53	240	29
140	50	260	26
150	46		

Number of bullets rounded off to lowest whole number to allow cushion for waste.

Bullet Velocity/Energy

Here is a table for determining the kinetic energy of any bullet at any practical velocity.

Refer to the left-hand column and locate the velocity; then move to the immediate right and locate the energy value per grain of bullet weight. This is the energy possessed by each grain of weight of any bullet traveling at that velocity. Then multiply the energy value by the bullet's weight in grains to obtain total bullet energy. All you need to know is the bullet's weight and its velocity—finding the energy then takes only a few seconds and should eliminate many of those arguments about which cartridge or load "shoots the hardest."

Velocity in fps	Energy	Velocity in fps	Energy	Velocity in fps	Energy
600	.80	700	1.08	800	1.42
610	.82	710	1.11	810	1.45
620	.85	720	1.15	820	1.49
630	.88	730	1.18	830	1.53
640	.91	740	1.21	840	1.56
650	.94	750	1.24	850	1.60
660	.96	760	1.28	860	1.64
670	.99	770	1.31	870	1.68
680	1.02	780	1.34	880	1.72
690	1.05	790	1.38	890	1.76
900	1.79	1180	3.09	1460	4.73
910	1.83	1190	3.14	1470	4.79
920	1.87	1200	3.19	1480	4.86
930	1.92	1210	3.25	1490	4.93
940	1.96	1220	3.30	1500	5.00
950	2.00	1230	3.36	1510	5.06
960	2.04	1240	3.41	1520	5.13
970	2.08	1250	3.47	1530	5.19
980	2.13	1260	3.52	1540	5.26
990	2.17	1270	3.58	1550	5.33
1000	2.22	1280	3.63	1560	5.40
1010	2.26	1290	3.69	1570	5.47
1020	2.31	1300	3.75	1580	5.54
1030	2.35	1310	3.81	1590	5.61
1040	2.40	1320	3.86	1600	5.68
1050	2.45	1330	3.92	1610	5.75
1060	2.49	1340	3.98	1620	5.82
1070	2.54	1350	4.04	1630	5.90
1080	2.59	1360	4.10	1640	5.97
1090	2.63	1370	4.16	1650	6.04
1100	2.68	1380	4.22	1660	6.12
1110	2.73	1390	4.29	1670	6.19
1120	2.78	1400	4.35	1680	6.26
1130	2.83	1410	4.41	1690	6.34
1140	2.88	1420	4.47	1700	6.41
1150	2.93	1430	4.54		
1160	2.99	1440	4.60		
1170	3.04	1450	4.66		

Autoloading Pistol Domestic & Foreign
Current and Obsolete Centerfire Cartridge

Cartridge	Case type	Bullet diameter	Mouth diameter	Shoulder diameter	Base diameter	Rim diameter	Case length	Loaded length
2.7mm Kolibri (1)	D	.107	.139	—	.140	.140	0.37	0.43
3mm Kolibri (1)	D	.120	.150	—	.150	.150	0.32	0.43
4.25mm Liliput (1)	D	.167	.198	—	.198	.198	0.41	0.56
5mm Clement (1)	D	.202	.223	.277	.281	.281	0.71	1.01
5mm Bergmann (1)	D	.203	.230	—	.273	.274	0.59	0.96
25 ACP (3)	D	.251	.276	—	.277	.298	0.62	0.91
6.5mm Bergmann (1)	C	.264	.289	.325	.367	.370	0.87	1.23
7mm Nambu (1)	C	.280	.296	.337	.351	.359	0.78	1.06
7.62 Takarev	C	.307	.330	.370	.380	.390	0.97	1.35
7.63mm Mauser	C	.308	.332	.370	.381	.390	0.99	1.36
30 Borchardt (1) (3)	C	.307	.331	.370	.385	.390	0.99	1.34
7.63mm (7.65) Mannlicher (1)	D	.308	.331	—	.332	.334	0.84	1.12
7.65mm (30) Luger	C	.308	.322	.374	.388	.391	0.75	1.15
7.65mm MAS (French)	D	.309	.336	—	.337	.337	0.78	1.19
7.65mm Roth-Sauer (1)	D	.301	.332	—	.335	.335	0.51	0.84
32 ACP (3)	H	.309	.336	—	.336	.354	0.68	1.03
32 S&W Long (2)	B	.312	.335	—	.335	.375	0.93	1.27
35 S&W Auto (1) (3)	D	.309	.345	—	.346	.348	0.67	0.97
8mm Nambu (1)	G	.320	.338	.388	.408	.413	0.86	1.25
8mm Roth-Steyr (1)	D	.329	.353	—	.355	.356	0.74	1.14
9mm Glisenti (1)	D	.355	.380	—	.392	.393	0.75	1.15
9mm Luger	D	.355	.380	—	.392	.393	.076	1.16
9mm Bayard	D	.355	.375	—	.390	.392	0.91	1.32
9mm Steyr (1)	D	.355	.380	—	.380	.381	0.90	1.30
9mm Browning Long	D	.355	.376	—	.384	.404	0.80	1.10
9mm Makarov	D	.363	.384	—	.389	.396	0.71	0.97
38 Special (2) (3)	B	.357	.379	—	.379	.440	1.16	1.55
38 Colt ACP & Super Auto (3)	H	.358	.382	—	.383	.405	0.90	1.28
380 ACP (9mm Browning Short) (3)	D	.356	.373	—	.373	.374	0.68	0.98
45 Colt ACP (3)	D	.452	.476	—	.476	.476	0.898	1.17

Notes on handgun primers: Handgun pistol cartridges are usually loaded with special Magnum primers and the 22 Remington Jet and 256 Winchester are sometimes loaded with small rifle primers. During World War I, Frankford Arsenal made 45 ACP cases with special #70 primer of .204″ diameter instead of the standard .210″.

A—Rim, bottleneck

B—Rim, straight

C—Rimless, bottleneck

D—Rimless, straight

G—Semi-rimmed, bottleneck

H—Semi-rimmed, straight

Unless otherwise noted, all dimensions are in inches.

(1) Obsolete

(2) Original revolver cartridge for which modern target autos have been made.

(3) U.S. origin.

Trade Directory

Domestic Revolvers

Charter Arms Corporation, 430 Sniffens Lane, Stratford, Connecticut 06497

Colt, 150 Huyshope Avenue, Hartford, Connecticut 06102

Interarms, 10 Prince Street, Alexandria, Virginia 22313

Iver Johnson Arms and Cycle Works, Fitchburg, Massachusetts 01420

EMF Company, Inc., 2911 West Olive Avenue, Burbank, California 91505

Harrington and Richardson, Industrial Rowe, Gardner, Massachusetts 01440

High Standard Sporting Firearms, 31 Prestige Park Circle, East Hartford, Connecticut 06108

Ruger (see Sturm, Ruger and Company)

Smith & Wesson, Inc., 2100 Roosevelt Avenue, Springfield, Massachusetts 01101

Sturm, Ruger and Company, Southport, Connecticut 06490

Dan Wesson Arms, 293 South Main Street, Monson, Massachusetts 01057

Foreign Revolvers

American Import Company, 1167 Mission Street, San Francisco, California 94103

Armoury Inc., Route 202, New Preston, Connecticut 06777

Beretta Arms Company, P.O. 697, Ridgefield, Connecticut 06877

Browning, Route 4, Box 624-B, Arnold, Missouri 63010

Centennial Arms Corporation, 3318 West Devon, Chicago, (Lincolnwood) Illinois 60645

Century Arms Company 3-5 Federal Street, St. Albans, Vermont 05478

Connecticut Valley Arms Company (CVA), Saybrook Rd., Haddam, Connecticut 06438

Walter Craig, Inc., Box 927-A Selma, Alabama 36701

Dixie Gun Works, Inc., Highway 51, South, Union City, Tennessee 38261

Euroarms, Via Solferino 13/A, 25100 Brescia, Italy

Firearms Imp. & Exp. Company (FIE), 2470 N.W. 21st Street, Miami, Florida 33142

J.L. Galef & Son, Inc., 85 Chambers Street, New York, New York 10007

Hawes National Corporation, 15424 Cabrito Road, Van Nuys, California 91406

Healthways, Box 45055, Los Angeles, California 90061

Gil Hebard Guns, Box 1, Knoxville, Illinois 61448 (Hammerli)

Herter's, Waseca, Minnesota 56093

Interarms Ltd., 10 Prince Street, Alexandria, Virginia 22313 (Mauser, Astra, Star, Rossi, Bernardelli pistols, Walther, Virginian)

International Distributors, Inc., 7290 S.W. 42nd Street, Miami, Florida 33155 (Taurus)

Italguns, Via Leonardo Da Vinci 169, 20090 Trezzano (Milano) Italy

Kimel Industries, P.O. Box 335, Matthews, North Carolina 28105

Kleinguenther's, P.O. Box 1261, Seguin, Texas 78155

L.A. Distributors, 4 Centre Market Place, New York, New York 10013

L.E.S., 3640 Dempster, Skokie, Illinois 60076 (Steyr, Mannlicher-Schoenauer)

Liberty Arms Organization, Box 306, Montrose, California 91020

Mandall Shooting Supplies, 7150 East 4th Street, Scottsdale, Arizona 85252

Mars Equipment Corporation, 3318 West Devon, Chicago, Illinois 60645

Navy Arms Company, 689 Bergen Boulevard, Ridgefield, New Jersey 07657

Pachmayr Gun Works, 1220 South Grand Avenue, Los Angeles, California 90015

RG Industries, Inc., 2485 N.W. 20th Street, Miami, Florida 33142 (Erma)

Security Arms Company, % Heckler & Koch, Suite 218, 933 North Kenmore Street, Arlington, Virginia 22209

Service Armament, 689 Bergen Boulevard, Ridgefield, New Jersey 07657

Steyr-Daimler-Puch of America, Inc., 3560-64 Roger B. Chaffee Boulevard Grand Rapids, Michigan 49508

Stoeger Arms Company, 55 Ruta Court, South Hackensack, New Jersey 07606

Universal Sporting Goods, Inc., 3740 East 10th Court, Hialeah, Florida 33103

Valor Import Corporation, 5555 N.W. 36th Avenue, Miami, Florida 33142

Dan Wesson Arms, 293 South Main, Monson, Massachusetts 01057

Holsters & Leather Goods

American Sales & Managers Company, P.O. Box 677, Laredo, Texas 78040

Andy Anderson, P.O. Box 225, North Hollywood, California 91603 (Gunfighter Custom Holsters)

Bianchi Holster Company, 100 Calle Cortez, Temecula, California, 92390

Boyt Company, Division of Welch Sporting Goods, Box 1107, Iowa Falls, Iowa 51026

Brauer Brothers Manufacturing, 817 North 17th Street, Louis, Missouri 63106

Browning, Route 4, Box 624-B, Arnold, Missouri 62010

J.M. Bucheimer Company, Airport Road, Frederick, Maryland 21701

Cathey Enterprises, Inc., 9516 Neils Thompson Drive, Austin, Texas 78758

Colt, 150 Huyshope Avenue, Hartford, Connecticut 06102

Daisy Manufacturing Company, Rogers, Arkansas 72756

Eugene DeMayo & Sons, Inc., 2795 Third Avenue, Bronx, New York 10455

El Dorado Leather Company, 1045 Vernon Way, El Cajon, California 92020

Ellwood Epps (Orilla) Ltd., Highway 11 North, Orilla, Ontario, Canada

The Eutaw Company, P.O. Box 398, Highway 33 West, Cameron, South Carolina 29030

Georg Enterprises, 6543-140th Place, N.E., Redmond, Washington 98052

Gunfighter (See Anderson)

Hoyt Holster Company, P.O. Box 1783, Costa Mesa, California 92626

Don Hume, Box 351, Miami, Oklahoma 74354

The Hunter Company, 3300 W. 71st Avenue, Westminster, Colorado 80030

Jackass Leather Company, 920 Waukegan Road, Glenview, Illinois 60025

Jumbo Sports Products, P.O. Box 280 Airport Road, Frederick, Maryland 21701

George Lawrence Company, 306 S.W. First Avenue, Portland, Oregon 97204

Leathercrafters, 710 South Washington, Alexandria, Virginia, 22314

S.D. Myres Saddle Company, 5530 East Paisano, El Paso, Texas 79905

Pancake Holsters, Roy Baker, Box 245, Magnolia, Arkansas 71753

Pony Express Sport Shop Inc., 17460 Ventura Boulevard, Encino, California 91316

Red Head Brand Company, 4100 Platinum Way, Dallas, Texas 75237

Rickenbacker's, P.O. Box 532, State Avenue, Holly Hill, South Carolina 29059

Roy's Custom Leather Goods, P.O. Box 852, Magnolia, Arkansas 71753

Safariland Leather Products, 1941 Walker Avenue, Monrovia, California 91016

Safety Speed Holster, Inc., 910 South Vail, Montebello, California 90640

Buddy Schoelkopf Products Inc., 4949 Joseph Hardin Drive, Dallas, Texas 75236

Seventrees, Ltd., 315 West 39th Street, New York, New York 10018

Sile Distributors, 7 Centre Market Place, New York, New York 10013

Smith & Wesson Leather Company, 83 Stevens Street, Springfield, Massachusetts 01104

Tandy Leather Co., 1051 Foch, Fort Worth, Texas 76107

Torel, Inc., 1053 North South Street, Yoakurn, Texas 77995 (gun slings)

Triple-K Manufacturing Company, 568 Sixth Avenue, San Diego, California 92101

Whitco, Box 1712, Brownsville, Texas 87520 (Hide-A-Way)

Miscellaneous

Accurizing Service, Herbert G. Troester, 2292 West 100 North, Vernal, Utah 84078

Arms Restoration, J.J. Jenkins, 375 Pine Avenue, Number 25, Goleta, California 93017

Bedding Kit, Bisonite Company, P.O. Box 84, Kenmore Station, Buffalo, New York 14217

Bedding Kit, Fenwal, Inc., Resin Systems Division, 400 Main Street, Ashland, Massachusetts 01721

Bore Lamp, Spacetron, Inc., Box 84 Broadview, Illinois 60155 (Teenie-Genie)

Case Gauge, Plum City Ballistics Range, Route 1, Box 29A, Plum City, Wisconsin 54761

Chrome Barrel Lining, Marker Machine Company, Box 426, Charleston, Illinois 61920

Ear-Valv, Sigma Engineering Company, 11320 Burbank Blvd., North Hollywood, California 91601 (Lee-Sonic)

Firearms Consultant, Shelley Braverman, Four Mile Point, Athens, New York 12015

Flares, Colt Industries, Huyshope Avenue, Hartford, Connecticut 06102

Flares, Smith & Wesson Chemical Company, 2399 Forman Road, Rock Creek, Ohio 44084

Gas Pistol, Penguin Industries, Inc., Box 97, Parkesburg, Pennsylvania 19365

Gun Jewelry, Sid Bell Originals, R.D.2, Tully, New York 13159

Gun Jewelry, Al Popper, 614 Turnpike Street, Stoughton, Massachussetts 02072

Gun Lock, E&C Enterprises, 9582 Bickley Drive, Huntington Beach, California 92646

Gun Record Book, B.J. Company, Bridge Street, Bluffton, South Carolina 29910

Hollow Pointer, Georg Enterprises, 6543-140th Plaza Northeast, Redmond, Washington 98052

Locks, Gun, Bor-Lok Products, 105 5th Street Arbuckle, California 95912

Locks, Gun, Master Lock Company, 2600 North 32nd Street, Milwaukee, Wisconsin 53245

Military Museum, Lt. Col. E.H. Hoffman, 768 South Main Street, Woodstock, Virginia 22664

Miniature Guns, Charles H. Stoppler, 5 Minerva Place, New York, New York 10468

Muzzle Top, Allen Associates, 7502 Limekiln Pike, Philadelphia, Pennsylvania 19150 (plastic gun muzzle cap)

Powder Storage Magazine, C&M Gunworks, 2603 41st Street, Moline, Illinois 61265

Pressure Testing Machine, M. York, 19381 Keymar Way, Gaithersburg, Maryland 20760

Ranson Handgun Rests, C'Arco, P.O. Box 308, Highland, California 92346

RIG, NRA Scoring Plug, Rig Products Company, Box 279, Oregon, Illinois 60161

Sharpening Stones, Russell's Arkansas Oilstones, 1705 Highway 71, North Springdale, Arkansas 73764

Shooting Coats, 10-X Manufacturing Company, 6185 Arapahoe, Boulder, Colorado 80303

Shooting Glases, Wilson Safety Products Division, P.O. Box 622, Reading, Pennsylvania 19603

Shooting Ranges, Kory Shooting Equipment, 233 South Wacker, Sears Tower, Suite 7130, Chicago, Illinois 60606

Springs W. Wolff Company, Box 232, Ardmore, Pennsylvania 19003

Tear Gas Pistol, Casady Engineering Associates, 560 Alaska Avenue, Torrance, California 90503

World Hunting Information, Jack Atcheson & Sons, Inc., 3210 Ottawa Street, Butte, Montana 59701

World Hunting Information, Jack Jonas Safaris, Inc., 8000 East Dorado, Denver, Colorado 80123

World Hunting Information, Wayne Preston, Inc., 3444 Northhaven Road, Dallas, Texas, 75229

Parts, U.S. and Foreign

Federal Ordnance, Inc., 9634 Alpaca Street, South El Monte, California 91733

Fenwick's Gun Annex, P.O. Box 38, Weisberg Road, Whitehall, Maryland 21161

Hunter's Haven, Zero Prince Street, Alexandria, Virginia 22314

Numrich Arms Company, West Hurley, New York 12491

Pacific International Merchandise Corporation, 2215 J Street, Sacramento, California 95816 (Vega 45 Colt Mag.)

Potomac Arms Corporation, (See Hunter's Haven)

Martin B. Retting, Inc., 11029 Washington, Culver City, California 90230

Sarco, Inc., 323 Union Street, Stirling, New Jersey 07980

Sherwood Distributor, Inc., 18714 Parthenia Street, Northridge, California 91324

N.F. Strebe Gunworks, 4926 Marlboro Pike, S.E., Washington, D.C. 20027

Triple-K Manufacturing Company, 568-6th Avenue, San Diego, California 92101

Pistolsmiths

Allen Associates, 7502 Limekiln Pike, Philadelphia, Pennsylvania 19150 (speed-cock lever for 45 ACP)

Bain and Davis Sporting Goods, 559 West Las Tunas Drive, San Gabriel, California 91776

Bar-Sto Precision Machine, 633 South Victory Boulevard, Burbank, California 91502 (S.S. bbls. for 45 ACP)

Behlert & Freed, Inc., 725 Lehigh Avenue, Union, New Jersey 07083 (short action)

Centaur Firearms, Inc., U.S. Highway No. 46, Lodi, New Jersey 07644

F. Bob Chow, Gun Shop, 3185 Mission, San Francisco, California 94110

J.E. Clark, Route 2, Box 22A, Keithville, Louisiana 71047

Day Arms Corporation, 2412 S.W. Loop 410, San Antonio, Texas 78227

Dominic DiStefano, 4303 Friar Lane, Colorado Springs, Colorado 80907 (accurizing)

Dan Dwyer, 915 West Washington, San Diego, California, 92103

Ehresman Tool Company, Inc., 5424 Planeview Drive, Ft. Wayne, Indiana 46805 (custom)

Giles' 45 Shop, Route 2, Box 847, Odessa, Florida 33556

H.H. Harris, 1237 South State, Chicago, Illinois 60605

Gil Hebard Guns, Box 1, Knoxville, Illinois 61448

Lee E. Jurras & Associates, Inc., P.O. Drawer F, Hagerman, New Mexico 88232

Kart Sporting Arms Corp., RD 2, Box 929-Broad Avenue, Riverhead, New York 11901 (handgun conversions)

Lenz Firearms Company, 1480 Elkay Drive, Eugene, Oregon 97404

Rudolf Marent, 9711 Tiltree, Houston, Texas, 77075 (Hammerli)

Maryland Gun Exchange, Inc., Route 40 West, RD 5, Frederick, Maryland 21701

Match Arms Company, 831 Mary Street, Springdale, Pennsylvania 15144

Nu-Line Guns, 3727 Jennings Road, Saint Louis, Missouri 63121

Pachmayr Gun Works, 1220 South Grand Avenue, Los Angeles, California 90015

L.W. Seacamp Company Inc., Box 255, New Haven, Connecticut 06502 (DA Colt Auto conversions)

R.L. Shockey Guns, Inc., 1614 South Choctaw, East Reno, Oklahoma 73036

Silver Dollar Guns, P.O. Box 475, 10 Frances Street, Franklin, New Hampshire 03235 (45 ACP)

Sportsmens Equipment Company, 915 West Washington, San Diego, California 92103

Irving O. Stone, Jr., 633 Victory Boulevard, Burbank, California 91502

Victor W. Strawbridge, 6 Pineview Drive, Dover Point, Dover, New Hampshire 03820

A.D. Swenson's 45 Shop, P.O. Box 606, Fallbrook, California 92028

Dennis A. Ulrich, 2511 South 57th Avenue, Cicero, Illinois 60650

Tom Wilson Company, 1406 South Oak Cliff Boulevard, Dallas, Texas 75208

Dave Woodruff, Box 5, Bear, Delaware 19701

Reboring and Rerifling

P.O. Ackley, 2235 Arbor Lane, Salt Lake City, UT 84117

Atkinson Gun Company, P.O. 512, Prescott, Arizona 86301

Bain & Davis Sporting Goods, 559 West Las Tunas Drive, San Gabriel, California 91776

Fuller Gun Shop, Cooper Landing, Alaska 99572

John Kaufield Small Arms Engineering Company, 7698 Garden Prairie Road, Garden Prairie, Illinois 61038

Ward Koozer, Box 18, Walterville, Oregon 97489

Les' Gun Shop, (Les Bauska), Box 511, Kalispell, Montana 59901

Morgan's Custom Reboring, 707 Union Avenue, Grants Pass, Oregon 97526

Nu-Line Guns, 3727 Jennings Road, St. Louis, Missouri 63121 (handguns)

Al Peterson, Box 8, Riverhurst, Saskatchewan,

Canada SOH 3PO

Schuetzen Gun Works, Route 2, Olympia, Washington 98503

Siegrist Gun Shop, 2689 McLean Road, Whittemore, Michigan 48770

Snapp's Gunshop, 6911 East Washington Road, Clare, Michigan 48617

R. Southgate, Route 2, Franklin, Tennessee 37064 (Muzzleloaders)

J.W. Van Patten, Box 145, Foster Hill, Milford, Pennsylvania 18337

Robert G. West, 27211 Huey Avenue, Eugene, Oregon 97402

Sights

Bo-Mar Tool & Manufacturing Company, Box 168, Carthage, Texas 75633

Firearms Development Laboratory, 360 Mount Ida Road, Oroville, California 95965 (F.D.L. Wondersight)

Lyman Gun Sight Products, Route 147, Middlefield, Connecticut 06455

Marble Arms Corporation, 420 Industrial Park, Gladstone, Michigan 49837

Micro Sight Company, 242 Harbor Boulevard, Belmont, California 94002

Miniature Machine Company, 212 East Spruce, Deming, New Mexico 88030

Poly Choke Company, Inc., P.O. Box 296, Hartford, Connecticut 06101

Williams Gun Sight Company, 7389 Lapeer Road, Davison, Michigan 48432

Accessories

A.R. Sales Company, P.O. Box 3192, South El Monte, California 91733

Baramie Corporation, 6250 East 7 Mile Road, Detroit, Michigan 48234 (Hip-Grip)

Bar-Sto Precision Machine, 633 South Victory Boulevard, Burbank, California 91502

B.L. Broadway, Route 1, Box 381, Alpine, California 92001 (machine rest)

C'Arco, P.O. Box 308, Highland, California 92346 (Ransom Rest)

Case Master, 4675 East 10 Avenue, Miami, Florida 33013

Central Specialties Company, 6030 Northwest Highway, Chicago, Illinois 60631

D&E Magazines Manufacturing, P.O. Box 4579, Downey, California 90242 (Clips)

John Dangelzer, 3056 Frontier Avenue, Northeast

Albuquerque, New Mexico 73102 (flasks)

Bill Dyer, 503 Midwest Building, Oklahoma City, Oklahoma 73102 (grip caps)

Essex Arms, Box 345 Phaerring Street, Island Pond, Vermont 05846 (45 auto frames)

R.S. Frielich, 396 Broome Street, New York, New York 10013 (cases)

JAC Associates, 1750 Berkeley Street, Santa Monica, California 90404 (stainless steel 45 Auto parts)

R.G. Jensen, 16153½ Parthenia, Sepulveda, California 91343 (auxilary chambers)

Laka Tool Company, 62 Kinkel Street, Westbury, Long Island, New York 11590 (stainless steel 45 Auto parts)

Lee Custom Engineering, Inc.,46 East Jackson, Hartford, Wisconsin 53027 (pistol rest holders)

Los Gatos Grip & Speciality Company, P.O. Box 1850, Los Gatos, California 95030 (custom made)

Matich Loader, 10439 Rush Street, South El Monte, California 91733 (Quick Load)

W.A. Miller Company, Inc., Mingo Loop, Oguossoc, Maine 04964 (cases)

So-Sho Manufacturing Company, 10727 Glenfield Court, Houston, Texas 77096

Pachmayr, 1220 South Grand, Los Angeles, California, 90015 (cases)

Pacific International Merchandising Corp., 2215 "J" Street, Sacramento, California 95817 (Vega 45 Colt combination magazine)

Pelson Inc., 1391 Equitable Road, Cerritos, California 90701 (cases)

Pistolsafe, Dr. L. ,Chili, New York 14514 (handgun safe)

Platt Luggage, Inc., 2301 South Prairie, Chicago, Illinois 60616 (cases)

Sportsman's Equipment Company, 415 West Washington, San Diego, California 92103

M. Tyler, 1326 West Britton, Oklahoma City, Oklahoma, 73114 (grip adapter)

Dave Woodruff, 116 Stahl Avenue, Wilmington Manor, New Castle, Delaware 19720 (relining and conversions)

Commercial Ammunition

Alcan Shells (See: Smith & Wesson Ammunition Co.)

Cascade Cartridge, Inc., (See Omark)

DWM (See RWS)

Eastern Sports International, Inc., Savage Road, Milford, New Hampshire 03055

Federal Cartridge Company, 2700 Foshay Tower, Minneapolis, Minnesota 55402

Frontier Cartridge Company, Inc., Box 1848 Grand

Island, Nebraska 68801

H&H Cartridge Corporation, Greensburg, Indiana 47240 (Super Vel)

Omark-CCI, Inc., Box 856, Lewiston, Idaho 83501

RWS (See Eastern Sports)

Remington Arms Company, 939 Barnum Avenue, Bridgeport, Connecticut 06602

Service Armament, 689 Bergen Boulevard, Ridgefield, New Jersey 07657

Smith & Wesson Ammunition Company, 2399 Forman Road, Rock Creek, Ohio 44084

Super Vel (See H&H Cartridge Corp.)

Weatherby's, 2781 E. Firestone Boulevard, South Gate, California 90280

Winchester-Western, 275 Winchester Avenue, New Haven, Connecticut 06504

Custom Ammunition

Ballistek, Box 459, Laconia, New Hampshire 03246

Beal's Bullets, 170 West Marshall Road, Lansdowne, Pennsylvania 19050 (Auto Mag Specialists)

Russell Campbell, 219 Leisure Drive, San Antonio, Texas 78201

Crown City Arms, P.O. Box 1126, Cortland, New York 13045

Ellwood Epps (Orillia) Ltd., Highway 11, North, Orillia, Ontario, Canada

Gussert Bullet & Cartridge Company, 1868 Lenwood Avenue, Green Bay, Wisconsin 54303

Jensen's Custom Ammunition, 5146 East Pima, Tucson, Arizona 85716

KTW Inc., 710 Foster Park Road, Lorain, Ohio 44053 (bullets)

Lomont Precision Bullets, 4421 South Wayne Avenue, Fort Wayne, Indiana 46807 (Custom bullets)

Robert Pomeroy, Morison Avenue, Corinth, Maine 04427 (Custom Shells)

Precision Ammunition & Reloading, 122 Hildenboro Square, Agincourt, Ontario, M1W 1Y3, Canada

Anthony F. Sailer-Ammunition, P.O. Box L, Owen, Wisconsin 54460

George Spence, P.O. Box 222, Steele, Missouri 63877 (Box-primed cartridges)

The 3-D Company, Box 142, Doniphan, Nebraska 68832 (reloaded police ammo)

Foreign Ammunition

Canadian Industry, Ltd. (C.I.L.) Ammo Div., Howard House, Brownsburg, Quebec, JOV 1AO, Canada

Colonial Ammunition Company, Box 8511, Auckland, New Zealand

Eastern Sports International Inc., Savage Road, Milford, New Hampshire 03055 (RWS: Geco)

Gevelot of Canada, Box 1593, Saskatoon, Saskatchewan, Canada

Hirtenberger Patronen-Zundhutchen & Metallwarenfabrik, A.G. Leobersdorfer Str. 33, A2552 Hirtenberg, Austria

Hy-Score Arms Company, 200 Tillary, Brooklyn, New York 11201

Paul Jaeger Inc., 211 Leemom Street, Jenkintown, Pennsylvania 19046

S.E. Laszlo, 200 Tillary, Brooklyn, New York 11201

NORMA-Precision, Lansing, New York 14882

The Outrider Inc., 3288 LaVenture Drive, Chamblee, Georgia 30341

RWS (Rheinische-Westfallische Sprengstoff) See: Eastern Sports

Grips

Beckelhmyer's, Hidalgo & San Bernardo, Laredo, Texas 78040

Crest Carving Company, 8091 Bolsa Avenue, Midway City, California 92655

Fitz, Box 49697, Los Angeles, California 90049

Herrett's, Box 741, Twin Falls, Idaho 83301

Hogue Custom Combat Grips, % Gateway Shooter's Supply, Inc., 10145-103rd Street, Jacksonville, Florida 32210

Mershon Company, Inc., 1230 South Grand Avenue, Los Angeles, California 90015

Mustang Custom Pistol Grips, 28030 Del Rio Road, Temecula, California 92390

Robert H. Newell, 55 Coyote, Los Alamos, New Mexico 87544 (custom)

Safety Grip Corp., Box 456 Riverside Street, Miami, Florida 33135

Sanderson Custom Pistol Stocks, 17695 Fenton, Detroit, Michigan 48219

Sile Distributor, 7 Centre Market Place, New York, New York 10013

Sports Inc., P.O. Box 683, Park Ridge, Illinois 60068 (Franzite)

Reloading Tools and Accessories

Bonanza Sports, Inc., Rt. 4, Faribault, Minnesota 55021 (scale)

C-H Die Co., Box 431, Gardena, California 90247

Division Lead Co., 7742 W. 61st Pl., Summit, Illinois 60502

Flambeau Plastics, 801 Lynn, Baraboo, Wisconsin

53913

Forster-Appelt Mfg. Co., Inc., 82 E. Lanark Ave., Lanark, Illinois 61046

H & H Sealants, Box 448, Saugerties, New York 12477 (Loctite)

Hensley & Gibbs, Box 10, Murphy, Oregon 97533

Herter's, Inc., RR1, Waseca, Minnesota 56093

Lyman Gun Sight Corp., Middlefield, Connecticut 06455

Micro-Precision, Box 1422, Omaha, Nebraska 68101

RCBS, Inc., Box 729, Oroville, California 95965

Redco, Box 15523, Salt Lake City, Utah 84115

Redding-Hunter, Inc., 114 Starr Rd., Cortland, New York 13045 (leadwire)

Rotex Mfg. Co., 8305 Sovereign Row, Dallas, Texas 75222

Savage Arms Co., Westfield, Massachusetts 01085

Index